AP*
EDITION

Countries and Concepts

AP* EDITION

Countries and Concepts

Michael G. Roskin
Lycoming College

PEARSON

Prentice Hall

UPPER SADDLE RIVER, NEW JERSEY 07458

Library of Congress Cataloging-in-Publication Data

Roskin, Michael
   Countries and concepts/Michael G. Roskin.—AP ed.
     p. cm.
   Includes bibliographical references and index.
   ISBN 0-13-194751-6
   1. Comparative government—Textbooks. I. Title.
   JF51.R542   2006
   320.3—dc22

                          2005019263

Editorial Director: Charlyce Jones Owen
Editorial Supervisor/Assistant: Maureen Diana
Editorial Assistant: Suzanne Remore
Marketing Assistant: Jennifer Lang
Managing Editor: Lisa Iarkowski
Project Liaison: Jean Lapidus
Prepress and Manufacturing Buyer: Sherry Lewis
Interior Design: John P. Mazzola
Cover Art Director: Jayne Conte
Cover Design: Kiwi Design
Cover Photos: Cover photos in top and middle rows and cover photo in center of bottom row © copyright 1999–2002
   Getty Images, Inc. All rights reserved. Bottom left cover photo from World Bank Photo Library. Bottom right cover
   photo from Iranian Embassy.
Composition/Full-Service Project Management: Kari Callaghan Mazzola and John P. Mazzola
Printer/Binder: Courier Companies, Inc.
Cover Printer: Phoenix Color Corp.

This book was set in 10/11.5 Goudy.

Pearson Education LTD.
Pearson Education Singapore, Pte. Ltd
Pearson Education, Canada, Ltd
Pearson Education–Japan
Pearson Education Australia PTY, Limited

Pearson Education North Asia Ltd
Pearson Educación de Mexico, S.A. de C.V.
Pearson Education Malaysia, Pte. Ltd
Pearson Education, Upper Saddle River, NJ

10 9 8 7 6 5 4 3 2
ISBN 0-13-194751-6

Contents

CHAPTER 11   WHAT RUSSIANS QUARREL ABOUT   168

PART III   THE THIRD WORLD   184

CHAPTER 12   CHINA   188

CHAPTER 13   MEXICO   223

CHAPTER 14   NIGERIA   259

Feature Boxes

CHAPTER 7

CHAPTER 8

CHAPTER 9

CHAPTER 10

CHAPTER 11

PART III

CHAPTER 12

CHAPTER 13

CHAPTER 14

CHAPTER 15

A Note to AP* Teachers

This Advanced Placement edition of *Countries and Concepts* has been designed to correspond to the curriculum and selection of countries that have become standard for the Advanced Placement (AP) Comparative Government and Politics examination—Britain, Russia, China, Mexico, Nigeria, and Iran. The basic approach, developed over eight editions of *Countries and Concepts,* remains. We consider two European systems, Britain and Russia, at some length, and give briefer treatment to each of four emerging systems—China, Mexico, Nigeria, and Iran. We strive to use each country to illustrate several general and abstract concepts. Britain, for example, illustrates the Westminster model of prime ministerial government. China illustrates the effects of a sweeping revolution. Mexico illustrates how a dominant party, for a time, can stabilize a turbulent country.

Many teachers reported favorably on the inclusion of geographical material in previous editions of *Countries and Concepts,* so it is retained here. They agree that ignorance of geography is widespread. *Countries and Concepts* combines political with geographical material. For example, the discussion of Russia lends itself to a box on federalism.

This AP* edition includes the "Comparison," "Democracy," "Geography," "Key Concepts," "Personalities," and "Political Culture" feature boxes of earlier editions. Teachers have found these to be useful. Also preserved are the chapter-opening "Questions to Consider" to prime students for the main points, as well as the running glossaries at the base of pages—labeled "Key Terms"—to help students build their vocabularies as they read. The definitions in the "Key Terms" sections and in the end-of-book Glossary are those of a political scientist. In other contexts one might find different definitions.

Countries and Concepts does not attempt to create young scholars out of beginners. It sees, rather, comparative politics as an important but usually neglected grounding in citizenship that we should be making available to our young people. The late Morris Janowitz stated (in his 1983 *The Reconstruction of Patriotism: Education for Civic Consciousness*) that civic education has declined in the United States and that this poses dangers for democracy. Our students are often ill-prepared in the historical, political, economic, geographical, and moral aspects of democracy. To expose them to professional-level abstractions in political science ignores their civic education and offers material that is largely meaningless to them.

Accordingly, *Countries and Concepts* includes a good deal of fundamental vocabulary and concepts, buttressed by many examples. It is readable. Many students will find the assigned readings in *Countries and Concepts* clear and understandable.

Some reviewers have noted that *Countries and Concepts* contains values and criticisms. This is part of my purpose. The two go together; if you have no values, you have no basis from which to criticize. Value-free instruction is probably impossible. If successful, it would produce value-free students, and that, I think, should not be the aim of the educational enterprise. If one knows something with the head but not with the heart, one really doesn't know it at all.

Is *Countries and Concepts* too critical? It treats politics as a series of ongoing quarrels for which no very good solutions can be found. It casts a skeptical eye on all political systems and all solutions proposed for political problems. As such, the book is not "out to get" any one country; it merely treats all with equal candor. *Countries and Concepts* tries to act as a counter-point to analyses that depict political systems as well-oiled machines or gigantic computers that never break down or make mistakes. Put it this way: If we are critical of the workings of our own country's politics—and many, perhaps most, of us are—why should we abandon the critical spirit in looking at other lands?

The AP* edition continues the theoretical approach of the previous editions with the simple observation that politics, on the surface at least, is composed of a number of human conflicts or quarrels. These quarrels, if observed over time, usually form patterns of some durability beyond the specific issues involved. What I call "patterns of interaction" are the relationships among politically relevant groups and individuals, what they call in Russian *kto-kovo*, who does what to whom? There are two general types of such patterns of interaction: (1) between elites and masses, and (2) among and within elites.

Before we can appreciate these patterns, however, we must first study the political culture of a particular country, which leads us to its political institutions and ultimately to its political history. Thus we have a five-fold division in the study of each country. We could start with a country's contemporary political quarrels and work backward, but it is probably better to begin with the underlying factors as a foundation from which to understand their impact on modern social conflict. This book goes from history to institutions to political culture to patterns of interaction to quarrels. This arrangement need not supplant other approaches. Teachers have had no trouble utilizing this book in connection with their preferred theoretical insights.

Covering the Third World in a first comparative course is problematic. The Third World is so complex and differentiated that many (myself included) suspect that the concept should be discarded. But if students are going to take only one comparative course—all too often the case nowadays—they should get some exposure to five-sixths of humankind. We include, therefore, briefer treatment of four non-European systems: China, Mexico, Nigeria, and Iran. They are not "representative" systems—what Third-World countries are?—but are interesting in their four different relationships to democracy: (1) democracy in China blocked by a Communist elite, (2) democracy growing in Mexico after a long period of one-party dominance, (3) the overcoming of a colonial heritage to found a stable democracy in Nigeria, and (4) democracy thwarted by an Islamic revolution in Iran.

SUPPLEMENTS

Study and Preparation Guide for the Comparative Government AP* Exam

This guide is designed to help students prepare for the examination by connecting review material for the text content to the Advanced Placement examination.

Teacher's Manual and Test Item File

The teacher's manual provides suggestions and outside resources in addition to a test item file of multiple-choice, true/false, and essay questions. The multiple-choice questions have five distractors to conform to the AP* exam format.

Prentice Hall Test Generator

This commercial-quality computerized test management program, available for Windows and Macintosh environments, allows teachers to select from testing material in the printed test item file and design their own exams as well as edit and add questions.

Companion Website™

www.prenhall.com/roskinap   This Web site brings an online study guide to students. When students log on, they find a wealth of study and research sources. Chapter outline and summary information, true/false tests, fill-in-the-blank tests, and multiple-choice tests, all with immediate feedback and chapter page numbers, give students ample opportunity to review the text material. The site also includes an archive of the maps found in the text, as well as links to sites pertaining to the countries covered in the text.

ACKNOWLEDGMENTS

I welcome your suggestions on any area of the book and its supplementary materials. Many have generously offered their comments, corrections, and criticism. Especially valuable have been the comments of Edward Dew, Fairfield University; John Peeler, Bucknell University; Stephen Chilton, University of Minnesota-Duluth; Christian Soe, California State University at Long Beach; Shlomo Bachrach of the East Africa Forum (on Nigeria); Cheryl L. Brown, University of North Carolina at Charlotte; Karl W. Ryavec, University of Massachusetts at Amherst; Frank Myers, State University of New York at Stony Brook; Ronald F. Bunn, University of Missouri-Columbia; Said A. Arjomand, State University of New York at Stony Brook; Larry Elowitz, Georgia College; Arend Lijphart, University of California at San Diego; Thomas P. Wolf, Indiana University, Southeast; Susan Matarese, University of Louisville; Carol Nechemias, Penn State, Harrisburg; Yury Polsky, West Chester University; and Marcia Weigle, Bowdoin College (all on Russia); Dan O'Connell, Palm Beach Community College (on China); Jim Coyle and Lycoming colleagues Mehrdad Madresehee and Bahram Golshan (on Iran); and Richard Morris of Lycoming (on Mexico). And to a student in China—who must remain nameless—who reviewed my China chapter I say thanks and *Minzhu!* All errors, of course, are my own. Teachers may send comments and corrections to me at Lycoming College, Williamsport, PA 17701, or e-mail roskin@lycoming.edu. I am grateful for suggestions for subsequent editions.

Michael G. Roskin

AP*
EDITION

Countries and Concepts

1

The Concept of Country

What are we chiefly studying? **Nations**? The Latin root of nation means *birth*, but instead of blood ties, nation now means people with a sense of identity and often the same language, culture, or religion. This process is not always easy or natural. To build modern France, kings united several regions first by the sword and then by language and culture. The United States is a bizarre mix of peoples, processed over time into a set of common values.

Should we call these entities **states**? Obviously we are not using *state* in the sense of the fifty U.S. states, which lack **sovereignty** because ultimately Washington's laws prevail. State means governmental institutions and laws. Historically, states preceded and often formed nations. Over the centuries the French government, by decreeing use of a certain dialect and spelling and enforcing nationwide educational standards, molded a French consciousness. The French state invented the French nation. All states are to a certain degree **constructed**, so they are somewhat artificial.

We might settle on *country*, which originally meant a rural area where people shared the same dialect and traditions but broadened in meaning until most use it as synonymous with nation or state. Some use *nation-state* to

KEY TERMS

nation Cultural element of country; people psychologically bound to one another.

state Institutional or governmental element of country.

sovereignty Last word in law in given territory; boss on your own turf.

constructed Deliberately created but widely accepted as natural.

Questions to Consider

1. What is the difference between nation and state?
2. Why are standard definitions of nation-state inadequate?
3. What factors produced the modern state?
4. Where did nationalism originate?
5. What does the author mean by "quarrels"?
6. How do we define Europe's regions?
7. Does stable democracy need a certain level of economic development?
8. What is a political institution?
9. What is political culture?
10. How are generalizations and theories related?
11. Should we study the European Union rather than separate countries of Europe?
12. What is "redistribution" and why is it never settled?

1

GEOGRAPHY

BOUNDING

An old technique for teaching geography has been forgotten; we are going to revive it. It requires the student to cite, from forced recall, the boundaries of a given country in the following form:

Germany is bounded on the north by the Atlantic, Denmark, and the Baltic Sea;

on the east by Poland and the Czech Republic;

on the south by Austria and Switzerland;

and on the west by France, Luxembourg, Belgium, and the Netherlands.

Bounding is a more effective learning tool than labeling a blank map, as a map gives several clues. **Bounding** forces students to reconstruct the map in their minds without clues. Once you can bound each of our six countries, you will be able to label much of all the continents except Africa, which is extremely fragmented and complex. We also include other countries in our bounding exercises.

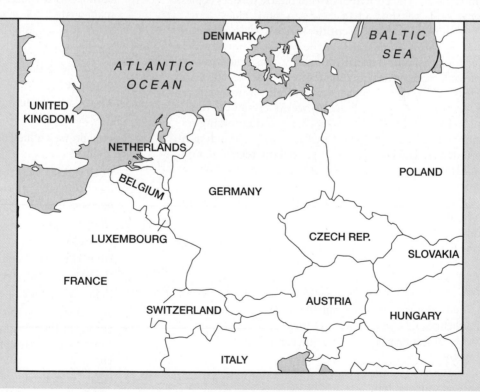

KEY TERM

bound   To name bordering countries.

combine the psychological and structural elements, but the term did not catch on. Nation-states were often defined as having territory, population, independence, government, and other attributes, but none of them are clear-cut.

Territory would seem to be basic, but what about those who have a strong sense of peoplehood but lack real estate? For example, the Jews turned their sense of peoplehood into Israel, and the Palestinians now define themselves as a nation that is ready for statehood. This brings up the next problem: What happens when territorial claims overlap? Which claim is just? History is a poor guide, as typically many tribes and invaders have washed over the land over the centuries. France's Alsatians, on the west bank of the Rhine River, speak German and have Germanic family names. But they also speak French and think of themselves as French. Should Alsace belong to France or Germany? Wars are fought over such questions.

Population is obviously essential. But many countries are **multinational**, with populations divided by language or **ethnicity**. Sometimes the nationalities are angry and wish to break away. Like the ex-Soviet Union, ex-Yugoslavia was composed of several quarrelsome nationalities, most of whom (Slovenes, Croats, Macedonians, Bosnian Muslims) left the Yugoslav state, which, they believed, was unfairly dominated by the largest nationality, the Serbs. Yugoslavia is an example of a recent (1918) and artificial construct that did not jell as a nation-state. All countries, to be sure, are more or less artificial, but over time some, such as France, have psychologically inculcated a sense of common nationness that overrides earlier regional or ethnic loyalties. Germany has done this more recently, and Spain is still working on it. In Afghanistan and Iraq the process has barely begun.

Independence means that the state governs itself as a sovereign entity. Colonies, such as Algeria under the French, become nation-states when the imperial power departs, as the French did in 1962. **Diplomatic recognition** by other countries, especially by the major powers, confirms and deepens a country's independence. Without such recognition, South Africa's four nominally independent black homelands were fake little countries that were dissolved in 1994. Some countries, however, are more sovereign and independent than others. East European lands during the Cold War were Soviet satellites, less than sovereign since the last word ultimately came from Moscow. Are Central American "banana republics" and Iraq, under U.S. supervision, truly sovereign and independent? Sovereign independence may be a convenient legal fiction.

Government is probably the crux of being a state. No government means anarchy, with the high probability that the country will fall apart or be conquered. Some call countries like Afghanistan **failed states**. Sometimes government can precede states. The Continental Congress preceded and founded the United States. A government can be in exile, as was de Gaulle's Free French government during World War II. The mere existence of a government does not automatically mean that it effectively governs the whole country. In much of the Third World, the government's writ falls off as one travels from the capital. In Brazil's vast Amazon region, cattle ranchers, gold prospectors, and rubber tappers fight Wild West style while the Brazilian government tries to bring the chaos under legal control.

KEY TERMS

multinational   Country composed of several peoples with distinct national feelings.

ethnicity   Cultural characteristics differentiating one group from another.

diplomatic recognition   State announcing official contact with other state.

failed state   One incapable of exercising even minimal governing power.

GEOGRAPHY

CORE AREAS

Most countries have an identifiable **core** area, a region where, in most cases, the state originated. Some countries contain more than one core area, and this may produce regional tension. Typically the country's capital is in its core area. Farther out are the peripheral areas, often more recent additions where people may speak a different language and resent rule by the core area. At times the resentment can turn deadly, as when provinces such as Serbia's Kosovo, Turkey's Kurdish area, and China's Taiwan attempt to break away. Part of the tragedy of Kosovo is that it was the medieval Serbian core, but after Turkish conquest in 1389 Serbs were displaced northward, and Kosovo slowly became a majority Albanian. Looking to their history, Serbs refused to give up their ancient heartland.

France is an almost perfect example of a core area, centered on Paris, spreading its rule, language, and culture with an eye toward perfecting national integration. This has been a slow process and one still not complete. In the nineteenth century, regions of France spoke unique dialects. By deliberate educational policy, corps of schoolteachers directed by Paris spread across France to turn "peasants into Frenchmen," in the words of historian Eugen Weber. Some peripheral areas still harbor resentments against Paris. Brittany, Corsica, and Languedoc try to keep alive local dialects and regional culture. Extremists in Corsica practice occasional violence.

England is the core area of the United Kingdom, and the Valley of Mexico is Mexico's core, established and reinforced by Toltecs, Aztecs, and Spaniards. A German core area is much less clear. The many German ministates of the Middle Ages kept their sovereignty and dialects for an unusually long time. Prussia led German unification in the nineteenth century, and Berlin indeed became the nation's capital. But many regions accorded Prussia little respect; Catholic lands such as Bavaria and the Rhineland disliked Prussia's authoritarianism and Protestantism. Germany remained riven by **particularism**, a factor that contributed to present-day federalism. Nazism was in part a contrived effort to bring all German regions under central control by means of lunatic nationalism. Nigeria faces a parallel problem as it lacks a clear core, and its several tribal regions dislike being ruled by any other.

The Soviet Union represented a huge gap between its Slavic core area and its non-Slavic peripheral areas. Russia's numerous nationalities are still distinct and discontent. Lacking the kind of cohesion of other nation-states, the Soviet Union was a type of colonial empire. The Slavic core of Russia, Belarus, and Ukraine gradually beat back Tatars, Turks, and Swedes until it straddled the vast belt where Europe meets Asia. Then the tsars sent expeditions eastward to claim Siberia to the Pacific. In the mid-nineteenth century Russia acquired most of the Muslim-Turkic peoples of Central Asia. **Russification** proved impossible and fostered nationalist hatred against Moscow. The breakaway of republics from the Soviet Union may be seen as decolonization. The remaining Russian Federation still contains lands like Chechnya that would like to break away.

China's core area was the Yangtze Valley, but by the time of Christ, China had consolidated a major kingdom. So numerous and united—despite occasional civil wars—were the **Han** Chinese that the addition to the kingdom of a few outer barbarians (Mongols, Tibetans, Turkic Muslims, and others) bothered the Han little. Recently, however, Central Asian dissidents have set off bombs to protest rule by Beijing. Iran has non–Persian-speaking peripheral areas that resent rule by Tehran. The U.S. core area began with the thirteen colonies along the Atlantic seaboard, especially the northern ones, which are still somewhat resented by the rest of the union.

   In sum, nation-states are not as clear-cut as supposed; their realities are messy but interesting. This is one reason for using the admittedly vague term *country:* It avoids **reification**, a constant temptation in the social sciences, but one we must guard against.

THE MODERN STATE

Whatever we call it—country, state, or nation-state—we must recognize that its current form is relatively recent. To be sure, we find states at the dawn of written history. (Ancient kingdoms, in fact, invented writing in order to tax and control.) But the modern state is only about half-a-millennium old and traces back to the replacement of old European feudal monarchies by what were called "new monarchies" and subsequently the "strong state." There are many factors in this shift; it is impossible to pinpoint which were the causes and which the consequences. **Causality** is difficult to demonstrate in the social sciences, but the box on page 6 discusses changes that ushered in the modern state. Notice how they happened about the same time and how each reinforced the others in a package of change.

   By the end of the Thirty Years' War in 1648, the feudal system had been displaced by the modern or strong state. **Feudalism** balanced power between monarch and nobles; it was loose and sloppy and did not tolerate strong national government. It was not oriented to change or expansion. The new monarchies were **absolutist**, concentrating all power in themselves, disdaining the old medieval constitution in which their powers balanced with nobles, and using new economic, administrative, and military tools to increase their power. Royalist philosophers extolled the strong monarch, and coined the term *sovereignty.* In consolidating their powers, monarchs had the nation celebrated, giving rise to the concept of nationality, of belonging to a nation rather than merely being the subject of a ruler.

THE RISE OF NATIONALISM

The French Revolution unleashed modern nationalism. As the armies of German princes closed in on the Revolution in 1792, the French people rallied *en masse* to repel the foe, believing they were defending both the Revolution and the *patrie* (fatherland), and the two concepts merged. France, argued the revolutionaries, was destined to liberate and reform the rest of Europe. The concept of a nation embodying everything *good* was thus born and spread throughout Europe by Napoleon's enthusiastic legions.

KEY TERMS

core   Region where the state originated (on page 4).

particularism   Region's sense of its difference (on page 4).

Russification   Making non-Russian nationalities learn Russian (on page 4).

Han   Original and main people of China (on page 4).

reification   Taking a theory as reality.

causality   Proving that one thing causes another.

feudalism   Political system of power dispersed and balanced between king and nobles.

absolutism   Royal dictatorship that bypasses nobles.

GEOGRAPHY

WHAT MADE THE MODERN STATE?

Europe began to stir in the eleventh century (late Middle Ages), but the Renaissance, starting in the fourteenth century, accelerated growth in art, philosophy, science, commerce, and population across Europe. The political system changed from feudalism to absolutism as monarchs increased and centralized their power over the nobles. By the middle of the fifteenth century, Europe was set for a revolution:

1453   The Turks use cannons to crack open the walls of Constantinople. European monarchs quickly acquired the new weapon to subdue nobles and consolidate their kingdoms.

1454   Gutenburg prints with moveable type. Printing increased the rate of diffusion of information, speeding up all other processes and displacing Latin with local tongues. Printed materials helped the national capital govern outlying provinces.

1488   Portuguese round Africa, soon followed by:

1492   The New World opens. Countries with access to the sea (Spain, Portugal, England, France, the Netherlands) rushed to Asia, Africa, and the Americas for trade and colonies.

1494   Italian monk Luca Pacioli invents accounting, making it possible to control large businesses and thus encouraging growth.

1517   Luther nails his ninety-five theses to the church door and founds Protestantism. Soon Protestant kings split from Rome and set up national churches, as in England and Sweden.

1545   This led to the wars of religion, first the Schmalkaldic War of 1545–1555 and then the devastating Thirty Years' War of 1618–1648. These conflicts increased state power and curtailed the church's temporal power, leading to **secularization**.

1618–1648   During the Thirty Years' War, state administration greatly improves. Warring monarchs, desperate for money, needed reliable tax bases and tax collectors. France's Richelieu and Sweden's Oxenstierna founded modern, rational administration to control and tax an entire country. The state got its own budget, separate from the royal household budget.

By its very nature, nationalism could not stay confined to the French soldiers, who soon turned into brutal and arrogant occupiers. All over Europe, local patriots rose up against them with the same kind of nationalistic feelings the French had brought with them. The spillover of French nationalism thus gave rise to Spanish, German, and Russian nationalism. By the late nineteenth century, with German and Italian unification, most Europeans had either formed nationalistic states or desired to (for example, Poland). Thinkers such as Germany's Hegel and Italy's Mazzini extolled the nation as the highest level of human (or possibly divine) development.

KEY TERM

secularization   Diminishing role of religion in government and society.

The modern state and its nationalism did not stay in West Europe. Driven to expand, the Europeans conquered Latin America, Asia, and Africa. Only Japan and Turkey kept the Europeans out; Meiji Japan carried out a brilliant "defensive modernization." The European imperialists introduced nationalism to their subject peoples. By their very integration and administration of previously fragmented territories, the British in India, the French in Indochina, and the Dutch in Indonesia taught "the natives" to think of themselves as a nation that, of right, deserved to be independent. Now virtually the entire globe is populated by national states, each jealous of their sovereign independence and many of them fired by nationalism.

LOOKING FOR QUARRELS

One way to begin the study of a political system is to ask what its people fight about. There is no country without political **quarrels**. They range from calm discussions over whether to include dental care in nationalized health insurance to angry conflicts over language rights to murderous civil wars over who should rule the country.

You can get a fair idea of a country's quarrels by talking with its people, interviewing officials, following the local media, and attending election rallies. This is how journalists work. Political scientists, however, go further. They want to know the whys and wherefores of these controversies, whether they are long-standing issues or short-term problems. Our next step, then, is to observe the quarrels over time. If the basic quarrel lasts a long time, we are onto an important topic. To explain the quarrel, we must dig into the country's past, its institutions, and its culture.

In this book, we look at six countries, considering each in five sections, each focusing on a subject area. We start with the underlying causes of current quarrels:

- The Impact of the Past
- The Key Institutions
- The Political Culture

We study the past, including the country's geography, in order to understand the present. We do not seek the fascinating details of history but the major patterns that have set up present institutions and culture. We study institutions to see how **power** is structured, for that is what institutions are: structures of power. We study culture to see how people look at their social and political system, how deeply they support it, and how political views differ among groups.

Moving from underlying factors to current politics brings us to the next two areas:

- Patterns of Interaction
- What People Quarrel About

KEY TERMS

quarrels   As used here, important, long-term political issues.
power   Ability of A to get B to do what A wants.

Here we get more specific and more current. The previous sections are, respectively, about the traditions, rules, and spirit of the game; the patterns of interaction are how the game is actually played. We look here for recurring behavior. The last section, the specific quarrels, represents the stuff of politics, the kind of things you see in a country's newspaper.

THE IMPACT OF THE PAST

We look first at a country's geography. *Physical geography* concerns the natural features of the earth, whereas **political geography** studies what is largely human-made. There is, of course, a connection between the two, as physical limits set by nature influence the formation, consolidation, and governing mentality of political systems.

Next, moving on to history, was the country unified early or late? For the most part, countries are artificial—not natural—entities, created when one group or tribe conquered its neighbors and unified them by the sword. The founding of nations is usually a bloody business, and the longer ago it took place, the better. We look at Sweden and say, "What a nice, peaceful country." We look at Afghanistan and say, "What a mess of warlords battling each other." Long ago, however, Sweden resembled Afghanistan.

The unification and consolidation of a country leaves behind regional memories of incredible staying power. People whose ancestors were conquered centuries ago still act out their resentments in political ways, in the voting booth, or in civil violence. This is one way history has an impact on the present.

Becoming "modern" is a wrenching experience. Industrialization, urbanization, and the growth of education and communications uproot people from their traditional villages and lifestyles and send them to work in factories in cities. In the process, previously passive people become aware of their condition and want to change it. Mobilized by new parties, they start to participate in politics and demand economic improvement. This is a delicate time in the life of nations. If traditional **elites** do not devise some way to take account of newly awakened **mass** demands, the system may be heading toward revolution.

No country has industrialized in a nice way; it is always a process marked by low wages, bad working conditions, and, usually, political repression. The longer in the past this stage has happened, the more peaceful and stable a country is likely to be. We must look for a country's stage of development. A country just undergoing industrialization can expect domestic tensions of the sort that existed earlier in Europe.

Religion is a crucial historical question. Does the country have its church-state relationship settled? If not, it is a lingering political sore. Protestant countries had an easier time secularizing; their churches cut their ties to Rome, the state became stronger than the church early on, and the church stayed out of politics. In Roman Catholic countries, where the church had power in its own right, there was a long church-state struggle called the "clerical-anticlerical split," which is still alive today in France and Mexico: Conservatives are more religious and liberals and leftists are indifferent or hostile to religion. Iran now has the Muslim equivalent of a clerical-anticlerical split.

KEY TERMS

political geography   How territory and politics influence each other.
elites   Those few persons with great influence.
mass   Most people, those without influence.

GEOGRAPHY

EUROPE'S REGIONS

There are no binding definitions of Europe's regions, but the end of the Cold War made the old division into eastern and western obsolete. There is still, to be sure, a West Europe that may be defined as those states that touch the Atlantic, plus Italy and Switzerland. The ex-Communist countries in what used to be called East Europe, though, should be separated into Central Europe (a pre–World War II term now revived) and the Balkans.

Central Europe is the region between West Europe and Russia that used to be, in whole or in part, the Habsburgs' Austro-Hungarian Empire. It includes Austria, Hungary, the Czech Republic, Slovakia, Slovenia (do not confuse the two), Croatia, and Poland (southern Poland was Austrian-ruled before World War I, as was part of northern Italy). These countries are predominantly Catholic and (with the exception of Austria, which was never Communist) poorer than West Europe. Freed from Communist rule, most turned quickly to democracy and market economies.

The Balkans (Turkish for mountain), for centuries part of the Ottoman Turkish Empire, are largely Eastern Orthodox and a more backward area that includes Romania, Bulgaria, Albania, Greece (which was never Communist), and half of Yugoslavia. These countries lag behind Central Europe in setting up democracies and market economies. Yugoslavia was a special problem, because half of it (Slovenia and Croatia) was under the Habsburgs while the other half (Serbia, Bosnia, and Macedonia) was under the Turks. And it is precisely on this fault line that Yugoslavia violently split apart in the early 1990s, with half Central European in character and the other half Balkan. Russia, because it reaches clear to the Pacific is, along with other ex-Soviet republics, sometimes called "Eurasia."

At a certain point in their development, countries become ready for **democracy**. Very few poor countries can sustain democracy, which seems to require a good-sized middle class to work right. Attempts to implant democracy in countries with **per capita GDPs** below $5,000 generally fail, but democracy usually takes root in countries that have per capita GDPs above $6,000. Notice in the table on page 10 that several of our countries are in this borderline area. This is one way economics influences politics.

As we learned in Iraq, democracy implanted by foreigners may not always work. Countries have to be ready for it. Trying to start democracy too early often fails amidst rigged elections, powerful warlords, and civil unrest. Democracy can also come too late. If the traditional elite waits too long, the masses may mobilize, turn radical, and fall into the hands

KEY TERMS

democracy   Political system of mass participation, competitive elections, and human and civil rights.

per capita   GDP divided by population, giving approximate level of well-being.

GDP   Gross Domestic Product, sum total of goods and services produced in country in one year.

COMPARING SOME BASIC FIGURES

	Population		Per Capita GDP		Workforce	Infant Mortality
	in Millions 2004	Annual Growth Rate	ppp* 2004	Growth 2004	in Agriculture	per 1,000 Live Births
Britain	60	0.29%	$27,700	2.2%	1%	5
Russia	144	−0.45	8,900	7.3	12	17
China	1,300	0.57	5,000	9.1	50	25
Mexico	105	1.18	9,000	1.3	18	22
Nigeria	137	2.45	900	7.1	70	70
Iran	69	1.07	7,000	6.1	30	43
United States	293	0.92	37,800	3.1	2	7

*Purchasing Power Parity, explained in Chapter 12.

Source: *CIA World Factbook.* Regard all such tables with skepticism. Figures from developing countries are estimates that often change wildly from year to year. Statistical quirks throw off economic growth figures. For example Nigeria, with a low base, enjoyed a jump in oil revenues in 2004 that registers as a big percent increase and makes Nigeria look like a fast-growing economy. Population growth includes immigration, important for the U.S. figure. Averages deceive: Mexican figures, for instance, do not show the major gaps between rich and poor in income, population growth, and infant mortality. Even the U.S. labor force in agriculture can vary, depending on whether illegal or temporary Mexican workers are counted.

of revolutionary demagogues. What happened in Russia in 1917 happened again in Iran in 1979. The gradual expansion of the **electoral franchise**, as in Britain, is probably best.

The widening of the franchise means the rise of political parties. On what was a party first based? Urban middle class, farmers, workers, or a denomination? When was it founded? What were its initial aims, and how has it changed over the years? Was the party strongly ideological? Left-wing parties argued that government should provide jobs, welfare, and education. Other parties, on the political center or right, either reject the welfarist ideas, compromise with them, or steal them. Gradually, the country becomes a welfare state with a heavy tax burden.

Finally, history establishes political **symbols** that can awaken powerful feelings. Flags, monarchs, religion, and national holidays and anthems often help cement a country together, giving citizens the feeling they are part of a common enterprise. To fully know a country, one must know its symbols, their historical origins, and their current connotation.

THE KEY INSTITUTIONS

A political **institution** is a web of relationships lasting over time, an established structure of power. An institution may or may not be housed in an impressive building. With institutions we look for durable sets of human relationships, not architecture.

KEY TERMS

electoral franchise   Right to vote.
symbol   Political artifact that stirs mass emotions.
institution   Established rules and relationships of power.

DEMOCRACY

WAVES OF DEMOCRACY

Harvard political scientist Samuel P. Huntington saw democracy as spreading in three waves. The first wave, a long one, lasted from the American and French Revolutions through World War I. It gradually and unevenly spread democracy through most of West Europe. But between the two world wars, a *reverse wave* of communist and fascist **authoritarian** regimes pushed back democracy in Russia, Italy, Germany, Spain, Portugal, and Japan.

The second wave, a short one, lasted from the end of World War II until the mid-1960s. It brought democracy to most of West Europe plus the many Asian and African colonies that got their independence. Most of Asia, Africa, and Latin America, however, quickly turned authoritarian.

Huntington's third wave began in the mid-1970s with the return of democracy to Portugal, Spain, and Greece and thence to Latin America and East Asia. In 1989, as communist regimes collapsed, democracy took over much of East Europe and, with the Soviet collapse of 1991, Russia. Even Mexico's long-dominant party relaxed its grip so that an opposition party could win the 2000 presidential election. At least on paper, most of the world's 194 countries are at least approximately democratic. But, warned Huntington, get ready for another reverse wave as some shaky democratic regimes revert to authoritarianism. Russia did precisely that.

A good way to chart institutions is to ask, "Who has the power?" When A commands, do B and C follow? Or do they ignore or counterbalance A? A nation's **constitution**—itself an institution—may give us some clues, but it does not always pinpoint real power centers. Britain's monarch and Iran's president are more for decoration than governing. Real power lies elsewhere.

Is the system presidential or parliamentary? (See box on page 47.) Both systems have **parliaments**, but a presidential system has a **president** who is elected and serves separately from the legislature; the legislature cannot vote out the president. The United States and Mexico are presidential systems. In parliamentary systems, such as Britain, action focuses on the **prime minister**, who is a member of parliament delegated by it to form a government (another word for cabinet). The prime minister and his or her cabinet can be ousted by a vote of no-confidence in parliament. Americans used to assume presidential systems were

KEY TERMS

authoritarian Nondemocratic or dictatorial politics.

constitution Written organization of a country's institutions.

parliament National assembly that considers and enacts laws.

president Elected head of state.

prime minister Chief of government in parliamentary systems.

better and more stable than parliamentary systems. Recent problems might make Americans aware of the advantages of a parliamentary system, which can easily oust a chief executive. Besides, parliamentary systems can be quite stable.

How powerful is the legislature? In most cases it is less powerful than the executive, and its power is generally declining. Parliaments still pass laws, but most of them originate with the civil servants and cabinet and are passed according to party wishes. In most legislatures (but not in the U.S. Congress), party discipline is so strong that a member of parliament simply votes the way party whips instruct. Parliaments can be important in nonlegislative ways: They represent citizens, educate the public, structure interests, and, most important, oversee and criticize executive-branch activities.

Does the parliament have two chambers (bicameral) or one (unicameral)? Two chambers are necessary in federal systems to represent the territorial divisions, but they are often extra baggage in unitary systems. Most of the countries studied in this book have bicameral legislatures.

How many parties are there? Are we looking at a one-party system, such as China, a dominant-party system, such as Mexico, two-party systems, such as Britain and the United States, or multiparty systems, such as France and Germany? Party system is partly determined by a country's electoral system, of which there are basically two types, majoritarian and proportional. A majoritarian system, as in the United States and Britain, enables one party to have a majority in parliament. This encourages two-party systems. Proportional systems, where parliamentarians are elected according to the percentage of the vote their party won, as in Germany and Israel, rarely give one party control of parliament, so **coalitions** are necessary. Proportional representation encourages multiparty systems, which in turn may contribute to cabinet instability as coalition members quarrel.

How powerful is the country's permanent civil service—its bureaucracy? The bureaucracy today has eclipsed both cabinet and parliament in expertise, information, outside contacts, and sheer numbers. Some lobbyists no longer bother with the legislature; they go where the action is, to the important decision makers in the bureaucracy.

POLITICAL CULTURE

After World War II, political scientists shifted their emphasis from institutions to attitudes. The institutional approach had become suspect. On paper, Germany's Weimar constitution was a magnificent achievement after World War I, but it did not work in practice because too few Germans supported democracy. By the late 1950s a new **political culture** approach to comparative politics became prominent, one that sought to explain systems in terms of peoples' attitudes. This is a two-way street, however, because attitudes determine government, and government determines attitudes. Americans became much more **cynical** in the wake of Vietnam and Watergate, while Germans became more committed democrats as their country achieved economic success and political stability.

KEY TERMS

coalition   Multiparty alliance to form government.

political culture   Values and attitudes of citizens on politics and society.

cynical   Untrusting; belief that political system is wrong and corrupt.

POLITICAL CULTURE

THE CIVIC CULTURE STUDY

In a massive 1959 study, political scientists Gabriel Almond and Sidney Verba led teams that asked approximately one thousand people in each of five countries—the United States, Britain, West Germany, Italy, and Mexico—identical questions on their political values and attitudes. The Civic Culture study, which was a benchmark in cross-national research, discerned three types of political culture:

1. *Participant*, in which people know a lot about politics and feel they should participate in politics.
2. *Subject*, in which people are aware of politics but cautious about participating; they are more conditioned to obeying.
3. *Parochial*, meaning narrow or focused only on their immediate concerns, is one in which people are not even much aware of politics and do not participate.

Almond and Verba emphasized that each country is a mixture of these types, with perhaps one type dominating: participant in America, subject in West Germany and Italy, parochial in Mexico. A good mixture, which they found in America and Britain, produces what they called "the civic culture." Question: If Americans are so participant, why do they vote so little?

Legitimacy is basic to political culture. It originally meant that the rightful king was on the throne, not a usurper. Now it means a mass attitude that people think the government's rule is valid and that it should generally be obeyed. Governments are not automatically legitimate; they have to earn the respect of their citizens. Legitimacy can be created over a long time as a government endures and governs well. Legitimacy can also erode as unstable and corrupt regimes come and go, never winning the people's respect. One quick test of legitimacy is how many police officers a country has. With high legitimacy, it needs few police because people obey the law voluntarily. With low legitimacy, a country needs many police. Regimes attempt to shore up their legitimacy by manipulating symbols.

One symbol frequently manipulated is **ideology**. An ideology is a grand plan to save or improve the country (see box on page 14). Typically, leaders at the top of a system take their ideology with a grain of salt. But for mass consumption, the Soviets and Chinese cranked out reams of ideological propaganda (which, in fact, many people ignored.) Now Iran is highly ideological—Islamic fundamentalism—but many Iranians wish it was not.

KEY TERMS

legitimacy   Mass perception that regime's rule is rightful.

ideology   Belief system to improve society.

KEY CONCEPTS

WHAT IS "IDEOLOGY"?

Political ideologies can be an important part of political culture. They are belief systems—usually ending in *-ism*—that claim to aim at improving society. Believers in an ideology say: "If we move in this direction, things will be much better. People will be happier, catastrophe will be avoided, society will become perfected." An ideology usually contains four elements:

1. The *perception* that things are going wrong, that society is headed down the wrong path. Fanatic ideologies insist that catastrophe is just around the corner.
2. An *evaluation* or analysis of why things are going wrong. This means a criticism of all or part of the existing system.
3. A *prescription* or cure for the problem. Moderate ideologies advocate reforms; extremist ideologies urge revolution and overthrow of the present system.
4. An effort to form a *movement* to carry out the cure. Without a party or movement, the above points are just talk without serious intent.

Marxism-Leninism is a perfect example of ideology. First, we have Marx's perception that capitalism is unjust and doomed. Second we have his analysis that capitalism contains internal contradictions that bring economic depressions. Third, we have a Marxist prescription: Abolish capitalism in favor of collective ownership of the means of production—socialism. And fourth, especially with Lenin, we have the determined movement to form a strong Communist party—the "organizational weapon"—to put the cure into effect by overthrowing the capitalist system. (How well does environmentalism fit this fourfold pattern?)

Ideologies are usually based on a serious thinker, often an important philosopher. Communism traces back to Hegel, classic liberalism to John Locke. But the philosopher's original ideas become popularized, vulgarized, and often distorted at the hands of ideologists who are trying to mass-market them. Deep thoughts are turned into cheap slogans. It often ends up that the original philosopher would reject what is being done in his name. Toward the end of his life, Marx worried about the distortions of his ideas by younger thinkers and sadly commented, "One thing is for sure, I am not a Marxist."

An important point about ideologies is that they are always defective; that is, they never deliver what they promise: perfect societies and happy humans. Classic liberalism produced an underclass, Marxism-Leninism produced brutal dictatorships, and Iran's Islamic fundamentalism produced rule by rigid and corrupt clerics.

Most political systems are not so ideologically explicit, but all espouse various ideologies to greater or lesser degrees: British Labourites are committed to a moderate welfare state and Chinese Communists to "socialism with Chinese characteristics." Does every system have some sort of ideology? Probably. A system run on purely **pragmatic** grounds—if it works, use it—would be unideological, but such systems are rare. Even Americans, who pride themselves on being pragmatic, are usually convinced of the effectiveness of the free market (Republicans) or moderate government intervention (Democrats). Thus, one of our questions: How ideological or pragmatic is a particular system and its political parties?

Another contributor to political culture is a country's educational system. Nearly everywhere, education is the main path to elite status. Who gets educated and in what way helps structure who gets political power and what they do with it. No country has totally equal educational opportunity. Even where schooling is legally open to all, social-, economic-, and even political-screening devices work against some sectors of the population. Most countries have elite universities that produce a big share of their political leadership, at times a near monopoly. The elite views formed in such schools are a major determinant of a country's politics.

PATTERNS OF INTERACTION

Here we come to what is conventionally called *politics:* Who does what to whom? We look for the interactions of parties, interest groups, and bureaucracies. Elites play a major role in these interactions. Even democratic politics is usually the work of a few. Most people, most of the time, do not participate in politics. But there are various kinds of elites, some more democratic and dedicated to the common good than others. How much of these interactions are an elite game with little or no mass participation?

Do groups come together to compete or strike deals? How do political parties persuade the public to support them? We look not for one-time events but for things that occur with some regularity. Finding such patterns is the beginning of making **generalizations**, and generalizing is the beginning of **theory**.

Once we have found a pattern, we ask why. The answer will be found partly from what we have learned about each country in preceding chapters and partly from the nature of political life where struggle and competition are normal and universal.

Some interactions are open and public; others are closed and secretive. The interactions of parties and citizenry are mostly open. Every party tries to convince the public that their party is the one fit to govern. This holds equally true for democratic and authoritarian systems. Do they succeed? Whom do the parties aim for, and how do they win them over? By ideology? Promises? Common interests? Or by convincing people the other party is worse?

The parties interact with each other, sometimes cooperatively but more often competitively. How do they denounce and discredit each other? Under what circumstances do they make deals? Is their competition murderous or moderate?

KEY TERMS

pragmatic   Without ideological considerations, based on practicality.

generalization   Finding repeated examples and patterns.

theory   Firm generalization supported by evidence.

KEY CONCEPTS

THE POLITICS OF SOCIAL CLEAVAGES

Most societies are split along one or more lines. Often these splits, or *cleavages,* become the society's fault lines along which political views form. Here are some of the more politically relevant social cleavages.

Social Class   Karl Marx thought social class determined everything, that it was the only important social cleavage. Whether one was bourgeois or proletarian determined most political orientations. Marx held that middle- and upper-class people were conservative; working-class people, progressive or radical. This oversimplifies, as some poor people are extremely conservative, and some middle-class intellectuals are radical.

   Still, social class does matter in structuring attitudes. The working class does tend toward the left, but never 100 percent, and it tends to be the moderate left of social democracy rather than the radical left of communism. Such is the case of the British Labour party. Social class by itself seldom explains all political orientations. Other factors—such as religion and region—are usually present. The question, as Joseph LaPalombara put it, is, "Class plus what?"

Geographic Region   Most countries have regional differences, often politically important. Once a region gets set in its politics it can stay that way for generations. Often the region remembers past conquests and injustices. Scotland still resents England. The Muslim north and Christian south of Nigeria dislike each other. We must study the regions of a nation, what their politics are, and how they got to be that way.

Religion   Religious struggles played major roles in most nations' histories and in some countries are still important. You can predict with fair accuracy how a French person will vote by knowing how often he or she attends Mass. In Iran, religion dominates politics. Notice the close connection in recent U.S. elections between religiosity and voting: the more religious, the more Republican. Religion accounts for the formation of more political parties than does social class.

Urban-Rural   Urban dwellers tend to be more aware of politics, more participatory, and more liberal or leftist. This is especially true in the Third World, where the countryside remains backward while the cities modernize. China, for example, has a major urban-rural split in terms of living conditions, education, and political orientation. Recent U.S. elections graphically illustrated our urban-rural split.

   There are other politically relevant social cleavages. In some countries gender matters, as in the United States where women vote more Democrat than men. Occupation, as distinct from social class, can also influence political attitudes. A miner and a farmer may have the same income, but the miner will likely be leftist and the farmer conservative. Age can be a political factor. Young people are usually more open to new ideas and more likely to embrace radical and even violent causes than older citizens. China's Red Guards and Iran's *hezbollahi* were young.

   Almost any social cleavage or category can become politically relevant. Ask yourself, from where did you get your political views? Is it your age? Did you get them from your family? And why does your family hold these views? Is it their religion? Their ethnic group? Their regional tradition?

DEMOCRACY

CRISIS OF DEMOCRACY?

Worldwide, social scientists worry that the attitudes in firmly established democracies are becoming more cynical about government. If the trend deepens, it could undermine the basis of democracy. Observers focus on two trends: (1) A falloff of roughly 10 percent in voting turnout from the 1950s to the 1990s. (2) Public-opinion polls that show Americans, Europeans, and Japanese all trust government and politicians less. Is democracy threatened?

Be careful of doomsters; their predictions are usually wrong. The voting falloff may be due in part to the lowering of the voting age in the early 1970s, nearly everywhere, from twenty-one to eighteen. Young people vote less. Cynical opinions may be due to increased expectations that government must provide jobs, health, and happiness—hyped by politicians—that government cannot possibly deliver. Viewed in this light, democracy may have been too successful.

Democracy may be entering a new phase in which better-educated citizens know more and criticize more: "critical citizens." Citizen efforts to fight corruption, curb the influence of powerful interest groups, and reform defective institutions are widespread. And how will the Internet affect democracy?

Parties also interact with the government. In China, the Party nearly is the government. In more politically open countries, parties try to capture and retain governmental power. How do parties form coalitions? Who gets the top cabinet jobs? Once in power, is the party able to act, or is it immobilized by contrary political forces?

Politics within the parties is important, as most parties have factions. In Japan, the factions of the leading party are more important than most of the other separate parties. Does the party have left and right wings? How do its leaders hold it together? Do they pay off factions with ministerial positions? Do factional quarrels paralyze the party? Could it split?

Parties also interact with **interest groups**. Some groups enjoy "structured access" to like-minded parties. In Europe, labor unions are often linked formally to labor parties. Here we need to know: Does the party co-opt the interest group, or vice versa? How powerful are interest-group views in determining party policy?

Interest groups often decide it is not worth working on the electoral-legislative side and instead focus their attention on bureaucracies. One of the key areas of politics is where bureaucracies and businesses interface. Are interest groups controlled by government, or vice versa? What kind of relationships do businessmen and bureaucrats establish? Which groups are the most influential? These important interactions are generally out of the public sight and often corrupt. Does money change hands?

KEY TERM

interest group   Association aimed at getting favorable policies.

GEOGRAPHY

WHAT IS THE EUROPEAN UNION?

A big nation? No, not nearly. A trade bloc? More than that. A confederation? Stronger than that. A federation? Well, working on becoming one. There is no good name for this emerging entity. Instead of "nation-state," some suggest "market-state." At what point should we treat the EU as sovereign? Perhaps when it demonstrates that the powers of the EU headquarters in Brussels override the sovereignty of member states. In the United States, this began only with the Civil War.

Europe has a way to go to reach the U.S. level of federation, but with the debut of the **euro** currency took a big step in that direction. Some observers of the European scene argue that it makes less sense to consider the nations of West Europe separately, because increasingly it is the **European Union** that determines the laws and economy of West Europe. They have a point. In standardizing currency, taxes, and regulations, increasingly the EU calls the tune.

But the EU is not yet a union in the way the United States is. EU members may opt out of provisions they dislike. Of the EU's twenty-five members, only twelve use the euro. Sovereignty still resides in London, Paris, Berlin, and other national capitals rather than in Brussels. Institutionally, the EU structure is still rather corrupt and undemocratic. The EU's inability to do anything about Bosnia illustrates the EU's lack of concerted foreign and security policies. European unity was put on hold by the French and Dutch rejection of a new EU constitution in 2005.

Grouping EU members into six groups of three plus one group of five and one of two helps you remember them. (Yes, they will be on the exam.)

The Big Three: Britain, France, Germany

The "Benelux" Countries: Belgium, Netherlands, Luxembourg

Latin Europe: Portugal, Spain, Italy

The Nordics: Denmark, Sweden, Finland

The Periphery: Ireland, Austria, Greece

Ten joined in 2004:

The *Baltics*: Lithuania, Latvia, Estonia (former Soviet republics)

The *Central Europeans*: Czech Republic, Hungary, Poland, Slovakia, Slovenia (first four were Soviet satellites; Slovenia was part of Yugoslavia)

The Mediterraneans: Cyprus (just the Greek part) and Malta

Notice that Norway and Switzerland are not members.

KEY TERMS

euro   (symbol: €) Currency of most of West Europe (but not Britain) since 2002; now worth about $1.30.

European Union (EU)   Quasi-federation of most European states; began in 1957 as Common Market.

COMPARISON

THE IMPORTANCE OF BEING COMPARATIVE

"You cannot be scientific if you are not comparing," UCLA's late, great James Coleman used to tell his students. Countries are not unique; they are comparable with other countries. When we say, for example, the parliament of country X has become a rubber stamp for the executive, this is not a meaningful statement until we note it is also the tendency in countries Y and Z.

The *uniqueness trap* often catches commentators of the American scene off-guard. We hear statements such as: "The U.S. political system is breaking down." Compared to what? To France in 1958? To Russia in 1991? Or to the United States itself in 1861? Compared to these other cases, the United States today is in great shape. We hear statements like: "Taxes in this country are outrageous." But what percentage of GDP do Americans pay in taxes compared to Britons, French, and Germans? Our thinking on politics will be greatly clarified if we put ourselves into a comparative mood by frequently asking, "Compared to what?"

WHAT PEOPLE QUARREL ABOUT

Here we move to current issues, the political struggles of the day. We start with economics, the universal and permanent quarrel over who gets what. Politics and economics are closely connected; one can make or break the other. (Political scientists should have a grounding in economics; take an economics course.)

First, we inquire if the economy of the country is growing. Rapidly or slowly? Why? Are workers lazy or energetic? Are managers inept or clever? How much of the economy is supervised and planned by government? Is government interference a hindrance to the economy? If the economy is declining, will it lead to political upheaval (as in the Soviet Union)? Why are some countries economic success stories and others not? How big a role does politics play in economic growth?

Other issues: Have unions and management reached durable understandings, or are strikes frequent? Have unions won laws on wages, benefits, and layoffs? Has this led to "labor-force rigidities" that slow growth? Does government try to influence wage increases? Do workers have any say in running their companies? How much imported labor is there? How much unemployment?

Once we have a realistic picture of the economic pie, we inquire who gets what slice. How equal—or unequal—is the distribution of income and wealth? Does the government redistribute incomes to make people more equal or does it let inequality grow? Does unequal distribution lead to social and political resentment? **Redistribution** is another name for a

KEY TERM

redistribution   Taxing better off to help worse off.

welfare system, and all advanced democracies are to some extent welfare states. How high and how progressive are taxes? How many and how generous are welfare benefits? Do people want more welfare and higher taxes or less welfare and lower taxes? Which people? If stuck with an overgenerous welfare system, can the government trim it?

There are, to be sure, noneconomic quarrels as well. Regionalism is persistent and growing. Britain and Russia have breakaway regional movements. Mexico's regions vote differently from one another. What are a country's regions? Which of them are discontent? Over what? How do they show discontent? Is there violence? Is there movement to decentralize or devolve power to the regions? One quarrel getting nastier throughout West Europe is what to do with the millions of immigrants, usually from Third World lands: Let in more or keep them out? Integrate them or send them home?

KEY WEB SITES

Elections around the world
electionworld.org

European Union
europa.eu.int

National leaders through history
rulers.org

Economist country briefings
economist.com/countries

KEY TERMS

absolutism (p. 5)	European Union (p. 18)
authoritarian (p. 11)	failed state (p. 3)
bound (p. 2)	feudalism (p. 5)
causality (p. 5)	GDP (p. 9)
coalition (p. 12)	generalization (p. 15)
constitution (p. 11)	Han (p. 5)
constructed (p. 1)	ideology (p. 13)
core (p. 5)	institution (p. 10)
cynical (p. 12)	interest group (p. 17)
democracy (p. 9)	legitimacy (p. 13)
diplomatic recognition (p. 3)	mass (p. 8)
electoral franchise (p. 10)	multinational (p. 3)
elites (p. 8)	nation (p. 1)
ethnicity (p. 3)	parliament (p. 11)
euro (p. 18)	particularism (p. 5)

per capita (p. 9)

political culture (p. 12)

political geography (p. 8)

power (p. 7)

pragmatic (p. 15)

president (p. 11)

prime minister (p. 11)

quarrels (p. 7)

redistribution (p. 19)

reification (p. 5)

Russification (p. 5)

secularization (p. 6)

sovereignty (p. 1)

state (p. 1)

symbol (p. 10)

theory (p. 15)

FURTHER REFERENCE

Dalton, Russell J. *Citizen Politics: Public Opinion and Political Parties in Advanced Industrial Democracies*, 3rd ed. New York: Chatham House, 2002.

Kryzanek, Michael. *Comparative Politics: A Policy Approach*. Boulder, CO: Westview, 2003.

Lane, Ruth. *The Art of Comparative Politics*. Needham Heights, MA: Allyn & Bacon, 1997.

Lijphart, Arend. *Electoral Systems and Party Systems: A Study of Twenty-Seven Democracies, 1945–1990*. New York: Oxford University Press, 1994.

Lim, Timothy. *Doing Comparative Politics: An Introduction to Approaches and Issues*. Boulder, CO: L. Rienner, 2005.

Norris, Pippa, ed. *Critical Citizens: Global Support for Democratic Governance*. New York: Oxford University Press, 1999.

Perry, Robert L., and John D. Robertson. *Comparative Analysis of Nations: Quantitative Approaches*. Boulder, CO: Westview, 2001.

Peters, B. Guy. *Comparative Politics: Theory and Method*. New York: New York University Press, 1998.

Rokkan, Stein. *State Formation, Nation-Building, and Mass Politics in Europe*. New York: Oxford University Press, 1995.

Slomp, Hans. *European Politics into the Twenty-First Century: Integration and Division*. Westport, CT: Praeger, 2000.

Stepan, Alfred. *Arguing Comparative Politics*. New York: Oxford University Press, 2001.

Sullivan, Michael J. *Comparing State Polities: A Framework for Analyzing 100 Governments*. Westport, CT: Greenwood, 1996.

Wiarda, Howard J., ed. *New Directions in Comparative Politics*, 3rd ed. Boulder, CO: Westview, 2002.

PART I
GREAT BRITAIN

KEY WEB SITES

British Broadcasting Corporation
bbc.co.uk

Prime Minister's Office
number-10.gov.uk

British Monarchy
royal.gov.uk

British Newspapers
times.co.uk
guardian.co.uk
telegraph.co.uk

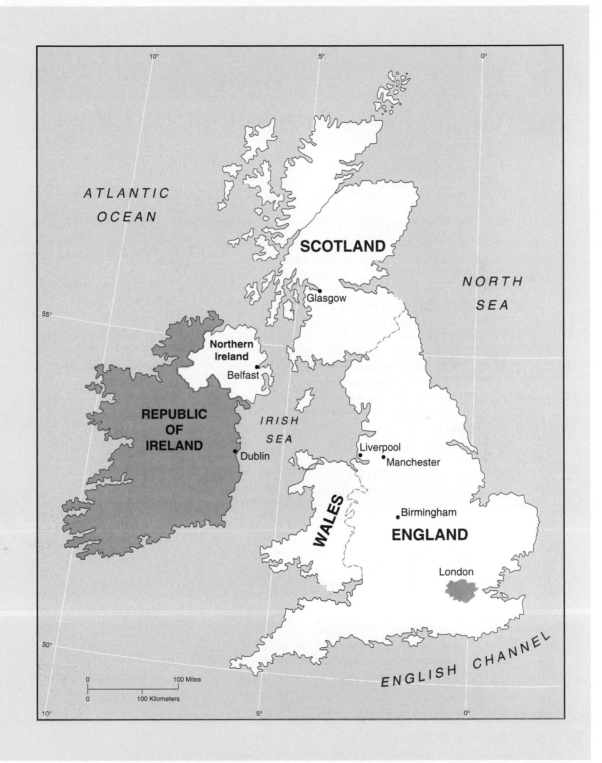

2

Britain:
The Impact of the Past

A Polish student I once knew at UCLA had to write a paper for her English class on what she most wished for her native land. She took the question as a geographical one and wrote: "I wish Poland be island like England." She would like to fix Poland's problem, its location on a plain between large, hostile neighbors (Germany and Russia) that has given it a sad history of invasion and partition.

England long ago was invaded many times. For a millennium and a half, waves of **Celts**, Romans, Angles and Saxons, Danes, and finally **Normans** washed upon Britain. One tribe of Celts, the Britons, gave their name to the entire island. Britishers, like most peoples, are not of one stock but of many.

The fierce Germanic tribesmen who rowed across the North Sea during the third to fifth centuries A.D. brought over Anglisch, what we call Old English, the language of the Angles, close to the Frisian of the Netherlands and German coast. "England" was simply the land of the Angles. The Angles and Saxons slowly moved across England, destroying towns and massacring inhabitants. The Celts were pushed back to present-day Wales and Scotland, which became a "Celtic fringe" to England. Some Celts fled to France and gave their name to Brittany. Preserving their distinct identity and languages (Cymric in Wales, Gaelic in Scotland), Britain's Celts never quite forgot what the newer arrivals did to them.

Other invaders followed. In the ninth century, Danish Vikings held much of eastern England (the Danelaw), but they were eventually absorbed. Another group of

Questions to Consider

1. How has geography influenced British development?
2. What does the Union Jack stand for?
3. What did the Magna Carta preserve?
4. What is the Common Law?
5. When did Parliament eclipse the monarch?
6. How did Puritanism influence democracy?
7. How did democracy come to Britain?
8. What was the difference between Hobbes and Locke?
9. How are Britain and Sweden so comparable?

KEY TERMS

Celts   Pre-Roman inhabitants of Europe.

Normans   Vikings who settled in and gave their name to Normandy, France.

24

GEOGRAPHY

INVADABILITY

Britain is hard to invade. The last successful invasion of England (by the Normans) was in 1066. The barrier posed by the English Channel has kept Spaniards, French, and Germans from conquering Britain. Politically, this has meant that England could develop its own institutions without foreign interference, a luxury not enjoyed by most **Continental** lands.

Militarily, it has meant that England rarely needed or had a large army, a point of great importance in the seventeenth century when British kings were unable to tame Parliament precisely because the monarch had few soldiers.

Vikings had meanwhile settled in France; these Norsemen (Normans) gave their name to Normandy. In 1066, with the English throne in dispute, William of Normandy put forward his own dubious claim to it and invaded with a force gathered from all over France. He defeated the English King Harold at the famous battle of Hastings, and England changed dramatically.

William the Conqueror replaced the entire Saxon ruling class with Norman nobles, who earned their **fiefdoms** by military service. At first the Norman conquerors spoke only French, so vast numbers of French words soon enriched the English language. Backed by military power, administration was better and tighter. William ordered a complete inventory of all lands and population in his new domain; the resulting Domesday Book provided a detailed tool for governance. The **Exchequer**—the name derived from the French word for a checkered counting table—became the king's powerful treasury minister, a title and office that still exists. Furthermore, since William and his descendants ruled both England and parts of France, England was tied for centuries to the affairs of the Continent.

MAGNA CARTA

The Normans brought to England a political system that had first emerged on the Continent—*feudalism*. The feudal system was a contractual agreement between lords and vassals in which the lords would grant the vassals land and protection while the vassal would support

KEY TERMS

the Continent British term for mainland Europe, implying they are not part of it.

fiefdom Land granted by a king to a noble in exchange for support.

Exchequer Britain's treasury ministry.

GEOGRAPHY

THE UNITED KINGDOM

The full and official name of Britain is the United Kingdom of Great Britain and Northern Ireland. "Great Britain" refers to the whole island, which includes Wales and Scotland as well as England.

The British flag, the "Union Jack," stands for three saints representing different parts of the United Kingdom. The larger red cross is the Cross of St. George of England, the diagonal white cross is that of St. Andrew of Scotland, and the thinner, diagonal red cross is that of St. Patrick of Ireland. (Note this cross is off-center.) Now some English nationalists display just the English flag (red cross on a white field). In Edinburgh, capital of Scotland, most of the flags are now Scottish (diagonal white cross on a blue field), an indication that the United Kingdom has grown less united. Symbols matter.

the lord with military service. Feudalism appears when central authority breaks down and a money economy disappears, for then land and fighting ability take on tremendous importance. In Europe, the collapse of the Roman Empire meant kings could survive and thrive only if they had enough lords and knights to fight for them. The lords and knights in turn got land. Power here was a two-way street: The king needed the nobles and vice versa.

The **mixed monarchy** of the Middle Ages was a balance between king and nobles. The nobles of Aragon (in the northeast of Spain) expressed it bluntly in their oath to a new monarch: "We who are as good as you swear to you, who are no better than we, to accept you as our king and sovereign lord provided you observe all our statutes and laws; and if not, no."

KEY TERM

mixed monarchy   King balanced by nobles.

Centuries of English history were dominated by the struggle to make sure the king did not exceed his feudal bounds and become an absolute monarch, which happened in most of Europe. This English struggle laid the foundation for limited, representative government, democracy, and civil rights, even though the participants at the time had no such intent.

The Great Charter the barons forced upon King John at Runnymede in 1215 is nothing so far-reaching or idealistic; it never mentions liberty or democracy. The barons and top churchmen simply wanted to stop the king from encroaching on feudal customs, rights, and laws by which they held sway in their localities. In this sense the **Magna Carta**, one of the great documents of democracy, was feudal and reactionary. Far more important than its content, however, was its effect of limiting the monarch's powers and making sure he stayed within the law.

The Magna Carta meant the king stayed in balance with the nobles, thus preventing either despotism or anarchy, the twin ills of the Continent, where countries either went to *absolutism*, as in France, or broke up into small principalities, as in Germany. British, and by extension, American democracy owes a lot to the stubborn English barons who stood up for their feudal rights.

THE RISE OF PARLIAMENT

During the same century as the Magna Carta, English kings started calling to London, by now the capital, two to four knights from each shire (roughly a county) and a similar number of **burghers** from the towns to consult with the king on matters of the realm. These kings were not latent democrats but needed to raise taxes and get the support of those who had local power. The French holdings of English kings meant that they had to fight wars in France. These were expensive, and the only way to raise revenues to pay for them was by inviting local notables to participate, at least symbolically, in the affairs of state. Little did the kings know they were founding an institution in the thirteenth century that would overshadow the monarchy by the seventeenth century.

Parliament began as an extension of the king's court, but over the centuries took on a life of its own. Knights and burghers formed what we call a lower house, the House of **Commons**. Those of noble rank, along with the top churchmen, formed what we call an upper house, the House of **Lords**. In time, a leading member of the Commons, its Speaker, became its representative to the king. In order to conduct business unhampered, parliamentary privileges developed to prevent the arrest of members.

The House of Commons at this stage was not "representative," at least not in our sense. It represented only a few males who were locally wealthy or powerful. But more important than fair representation (which came in the nineteenth century), Parliament continued the

KEY TERMS

Magna Carta   1215 agreement to preserve rights of English nobles.

burghers   Originally, town dwellers; by extension, the middle class; French *bourgeoisie*.

Parliament   When capitalized, Britain's legislature, now usually meaning the House of Commons.

Commons   Lower house of Parliament; the elected, important chamber.

Lords   Upper house of Parliament; less important than *Commons*.

COMPARISON

COMMON LAW

One of England's contributions to civilization is the **Common Law**, the legal system now also practiced in the United States, Canada, Australia, and other countries once administered by Britain (but not South Africa). Common Law grew out of the customary usage of the Germanic tribal laws of the Angles and Saxons, which stressed the rights of free men. It developed on the basis of **precedent** set by earlier decisions and thus has been called "judge-made law." After the Normans conquered England, they found the purely local nature of this law was too fragmented, so they set up central courts to systematize the local laws and produce a "common" law for all parts of England—hence the name.

Common Law is heavily case law and differs from code law, which is used by most of the Continent (and Scotland) and much of the world, that emphasizes fixed legal codes rather than precedent and case-study. Code law is essentially Roman Law that was kept alive in the Canon Law of the Catholic Church, revived by modernizing Continental monarchs, and updated in 1804 into the *Code Napoléon*. Compared to code law, Common Law is flexible and adapts gradually with new cases.

blocking mechanism of the Magna Carta: It diffused power and prevented the king from getting too much. Parliament thus unknowingly laid one of the foundations of democracy.

HENRY VIII

Parliament got a major boost during the reign of Henry VIII (1509–1547), when Henry declared a partnership with Parliament in his struggle against Rome. In addition to growing tensions between the **Vatican** and London—the universal Church on the one hand and new religious ideas on the other—Henry needed the pope to grant him a divorce. His marriage to Catherine of Aragon had failed to produce the male heir Henry felt he needed to ensure stability after him. (Ironically, it was his daughter Elizabeth who went down in history as one of England's greatest monarchs.)

The pope refused—Catherine's Spanish relatives at that time controlled the papacy—so Henry summoned a parliament in 1529 and kept it busy for seven years, passing law after law to get England out of the Catholic church and the Catholic church out of England. The new **Anglican** church was at first identical to the Roman Catholic church (it

KEY TERMS

Common Law   System of judge-made law developed in England.
precedent   Legal reasoning based on previous cases.
Vatican   Headquarters of the Roman Catholic church.
Anglican   Church of England, Episcopalian in America.

GEOGRAPHY

SEACOAST

A country with outlet to the sea has a major economic advantage over **landlocked** countries. Sea transport is cheap and does not require crossing neighboring countries. Usable natural harbors also help. Peter the Great battled for years to obtain Russian outlets on the Baltic and Black Seas. Atlantic Europe had an incredible advantage from the start. England's Atlantic orientation contributed to its empire, early industrialization, and prosperity.

turned Protestant later), but at its head was an Englishman, not the pontiff of Rome. The new church granted Henry his divorce in 1533. Henry married a total of six wives (and had two of them beheaded) but was not lusting for new brides; he was desperate for a male heir.

The impact of Henry's break with Rome was major. England was cut free from Catholic guidance and direction. Countries that stayed Catholic, such as France, Spain, and Italy, experienced wrenching splits for centuries between prochurch and **anticlerical** forces. England (and Sweden) avoided this nasty division because the state early on was stronger than the church and controlled it. This meant that in England it was far easier to *secularize* society and politics than in Roman Catholic countries, where the church was still an independent power.

Parliament became more important, as Henry needed it for his break with Rome. In 1543 Henry praised Parliament as an indispensable part of his government: "We be informed by our judges that we at no time stand so highly in our estate royal as in the time of parliament, wherein we as head and you as members are conjoined and knit together into one body politic." Without knowing it, Henry started an institutional shift from monarch to parliament. A century later Parliament beheaded an English king.

PARLIAMENT VERSUS KING

In the late fifteenth century several European monarchs expanded their powers and undermined the old feudal *mixed monarchy*. The weakened power of Rome in the sixteenth century gave kings more independence and introduced the notion that kings ruled by divine right, that is, that they received their authority directly from God without the pope as intermediary. Political theorists searched for the seat of *sovereignty* and concluded it must

KEY TERMS

landlocked   Country with no seacoast.
anticlerical   Favoring getting the Roman Catholic church out of politics.

lie in one person, the monarch. This gave rise to absolutism. By 1660 absolute monarchs governed most lands of Europe—but not England.

The seventeenth century brought uninterrupted turmoil to England: Religious splits, civil war, a royal beheading, and a military dictatorship. The net winner, when the dust had settled, was Parliament.

Trouble started when James I brought the Stuart dynasty from Scotland to take over the English throne after the death of Elizabeth I, the last Tudor, in 1603. James united the crowns of Scotland and England, but they remained separate countries until the 1707 Act of Union. James I carried the absolutist notions then common throughout Europe; he did not like to share power and thought that existing institutions should simply support the king. This brought him into conflict with Puritanism, an extreme Protestant movement that aimed to reform the "popish" elements out of the Anglican church. James preferred the Anglican church to stay just the way it was, for it was one of the pillars of his regime. With James's harassment, some Puritans ran away to Massachusetts.

By now Parliament had grown to feel equal with the king and, in the area of raising revenues, superior. Hard up for cash, James tried to impose taxes without consent of Parliament, which grew angry over the move. James's son, Charles I, took over in 1625, and fared even worse. He took England into wars with Spain and France; both were unsuccessful and increased the king's desperation for money. Charles tried to play the role of a Continental absolute monarch, but the English people and Parliament would not let him.

When the **Royalists** fought the **Parliamentarians** in the English Civil War (1642–1648), the latter proved stronger, for the Parliamentarian cause was aided by Puritans and the growing merchant class. The Parliamentarians created a "New Model Army," which trounced the Royalists. (The king, as was mentioned, had no standing army at his disposal.) Charles was captured, tried by Parliament, and beheaded in 1649.

CROMWELL'S COMMONWEALTH

From 1649 to 1660 England had no king. Who, then, was to rule? The only organized force left was the army, led by Oliver Cromwell. Briefly, England became a **republic** called the **Commonwealth**, led by Cromwell. Discord grew. To restore order, Cromwell in 1653 was designated Lord Protector, a sort of uncrowned king, and imposed a military dictatorship on England. When Cromwell died in 1658, most Englishmen had had enough of turbulent republicanism and longed for stability and order. In 1660, Parliament invited Charles II, son of the beheaded king, to return from Dutch exile and reclaim the throne. The English monarchy was restored, but now Parliament was much stronger and demanded respect.

KEY TERMS

Royalists   Supporters of the king in English Civil War.

Parliamentarians   Supporters of Parliament.

republic   Country not headed by a monarch.

commonwealth   A republic.

DEMOCRACY

"ONE MAN, ONE VOTE"

Among the antiroyalists were **republicans**, called **Levellers**, who sought political equality. Soldiers in the New Model Army argued that people like themselves—tradesmen, artisans, and farmers—should have the vote. They were influenced in their thinking by Puritanism, which taught that all men were equal before God and needed no spiritual or temporal superiors to guide them. (This Puritan influence also powerfully impacted American democracy.)

One group of Levellers, meeting in Putney in 1647, even went so far as to advocate "one man, one vote." This radical idea was a good two centuries ahead of its time, and the more conservative forces of England, including Cromwell himself, rejected it out of hand. Still, the Putney meeting had introduced the idea of the universal franchise—that is, giving everybody the right to vote.

THE "GLORIOUS REVOLUTION"

Charles II knew he could not be an absolute monarch; instead, he tried to manipulate Parliament discreetly, but religion tripped him up. Charles was pro-Catholic and secretly ready to proclaim allegiance to Rome. In 1673 he issued the Declaration of Indulgence, lifting laws against Catholics and non-Anglican Protestants. Parliament saw this act of tolerance toward minority religions as an illegal return to Catholicism and blocked it. Anti-Catholic hysteria swept England with fabricated stories of popish plots to take over the country.

When Charles II died in 1685, his openly Catholic brother, James, took the throne as James II. Again, a Declaration of Indulgence was issued, and again Parliament took it as a return to both Catholicism and absolutism. Parliament dumped James II (but let him escape) and invited his Protestant daughter, Mary, and her Dutch husband, William, to be England's queen and king. This was the "Glorious Revolution" of 1688: A major shift of regime took place with scarcely a shot fired. (In 1690, William beat James in Ireland, but that was after the Revolution.) In 1689 a *Bill of Rights*—unlike its U.S. namesake—spelled out Parliament's relationship to the Crown: no laws or taxes without Parliament's assent.

The majority of Englishmen approved. If it was not clear before, it was now: Parliament was supreme and could invite and dismiss monarchs. In 1714 Parliament invited George I from Hanover in Germany to become king; the present royal family is descended from him. Since that time, the British monarch has been increasingly a figurehead, one who reigns but does not rule.

KEY TERMS

republican In its original sense, favoring getting rid of monarchy.
Levellers Radicals during English Civil War who argued for equality and "one man, one vote."

DEMOCRACY

"POWER CORRUPTS"

Nineteenth-century British historian and philosopher Lord Acton distilled the lessons of centuries of English political development in his famous remark: "Power tends to corrupt; absolute power corrupts absolutely." Acton feared the human tendency to abuse power. His insight is absolutely accurate—check today's news—and underlays democratic thinking.

THE RISE OF THE PRIME MINISTER

One of the consequences of bringing George I to England was that he could not govern even if he wanted to. He spoke no English and preferred Hanover to London. So he turned to an institutional device that had been slowly developing and gave it executive power—the cabinet, composed of ministers and presided over by a first or prime minister. Headed by Sir Robert Walpole from 1721 to 1742, the cabinet developed nearly into its present form, but lacked two important present-day features: The prime minister could not pick his **ministers** (that was reserved for the king), and the cabinet was not responsible—meaning, in its original sense, *answerable*—to Parliament.

Absolutism had one last, temporary gasp. George III packed Commons with his supporters and governed with the obedient Lord North as prime minister. One unforeseen result: the U.S. Declaration of Independence, which sought to regain the traditional rights of Englishmen against a too-powerful king. Following this British defeat, William Pitt the Younger restored the cabinet and prime minister to power and made them responsible only to Commons, not to the king. This began the tradition (it has never been written into law) that the *government* consists of the leader of the largest party in the House of Commons plus other people he or she picks. As party chief, top member of Parliament, and head of government combined, the prime minister became the focus of political power in Britain.

THE DEMOCRATIZATION OF PARLIAMENT

Parliament was supreme by the late eighteenth century, but it was not democratic or representative. In the country, the right to vote was limited to landowners. In the towns, often only a dozen or so men were eligible to vote, although in the cities the franchise was much wider.

KEY TERM

minister   Head of a major department (ministry) of government.

In the eighteenth century, parties began to form. The labels **Whig** and **Tory** first appeared under Charles II, connoting his opposition and his supporters, respectively. Both were derisive names: The original Whigs were Scottish bandits, and the original Tories were Irish bandits. At first these proto-parties were simply parliamentary caucuses, Tories representing the landed aristocracy, Whigs the merchants and manufacturers. Only in the next century did they take root in the electorate.

During the nineteenth century, a two-party system emerged. The Whigs grew into the Liberal party and the Tories into the Conservative party (still nicknamed Tories). Whatever their party label, parliamentarians were not ordinary people. The House of Lords was limited to hereditary peers. The House of Commons, despite its name, was the home of gentry, landowners, and better-off people. Elections were often won by bribing the few voters. This pattern, called **Whig democracy**, is typically the way democracy begins in most countries; it starts with the few and later expands to include the many. Do not expect a new democracy to be very democratic; it takes time.

By the time of the American and French revolutions in the late eighteenth century, however, Parliament noticed winds stirring in favor of expanding the electorate. People talked about democracy and the right to vote. Under the impact of the industrial revolution and economic growth, two powerful new social classes arose—the middle class and the working class. Whigs and Tories, both elite in their makeup, at first viewed demands for the mass vote with disdain and even horror; it reminded them of how democracy ran amok during the French Revolution.

Gradually, though, it dawned on the Whigs that the way to head off revolution was to incorporate some ordinary Britons into politics and give them a stake in the system. Furthermore, they realized that the party that supported broadening the franchise would most likely win the new voters. After much resistance by Tories in Commons and by the entire House of Lords, Parliament passed the **Reform Act** of 1832, which allowed more of the middle class to vote but still only expanded the electorate by about half, to about 7 percent of adults. The Reform Act established the principle, though, that the Commons ought to be representative of, and responsive to, the broad mass of citizens, not just the notables. In 1867, it was the Conservatives' turn. Under Prime Minister Benjamin Disraeli, the Second Reform Act doubled the size of the electorate, giving about 16 percent of adult Britons the vote. In 1884, the Third Reform Act added farm workers to the electorate and thus achieved nearly complete male suffrage. Women finally got the vote in 1918.

The interesting point about the British electorate is that its growth was slow. New elements were added to the voting rolls only gradually, giving Parliament time to assimilate the forces of mass politics without going through an upheaval. The gradual tempo also meant citizens got the vote when they were ready for it. In some countries where the universal franchise—one person, one vote—was instituted early, the result was fake democracy, as crafty officials rigged the voting of people who did not understand electoral politics. Spain, for example, got universal suffrage in the 1870s, but election results were

Key Terms

Whigs Faction of Parliament that became Liberal party.

Tories Faction of Parliament that became Conservative party.

Whig democracy Democracy for the few.

Reform Acts Series of laws expanding the British electoral franchise.

PERSONALITIES

HOBBES, LOCKE, BURKE

Thomas Hobbes lived through the upheavals of the English Civil War in the seventeenth century and opposed them for making people insecure and frightened. Hobbes imagined that life in the **state of nature**, before **civil society** was founded, must have been terrible. Every man would have been the enemy of every other man, a "war of each against all." Humans would live in savage squalor with "no arts; no letters; no society; and which is worst of all, continual fear, and danger of violent death; and the life of man, solitary, poor, nasty, brutish, and short." To escape this horror, people would—out of self-interest—rationally join together to form civil society. Society thus arises naturally out of fear. People would also gladly submit to a king, even a bad one, in order to prevent anarchy.

John Locke saw the same upheavals but came to less harsh conclusions. Locke theorized that the original state of nature was not so bad; people lived in equality and tolerance with one another. But they could not secure their property: There was no money, title deeds, or courts of law, so their property was uncertain. To remedy this, they contractually formed civil society and thus secured "life, liberty, and property." Locke is to property rights as Hobbes is to fear of violent death. Americans are the children of Locke; notice the American emphasis on "the natural right to property."

Edmund Burke, a Whig member of Parliament, was horrified at the French Revolution, warning it would end up a military dictatorship (it did). The French revolutionists had broken the historical continuity, institutions, and symbols that restrain people from bestial behavior, argued Burke. Old institutions, such as the monarchy and church, must be pretty good because they have evolved over centuries. If you scrap them, society breaks down and leads to tyranny. Burke understood that **conservatism** means constant, but never radical, change. Wrote Burke: "A state without the means of some change is without the means of its conservation." Progress comes not from chucking out the old but from gradually modifying the parts that need changing while preserving the overall structure, keeping the form but reforming the contents.

set in advance. By the time the British working class got the vote, they were ready to use it intelligently.

With the expansion of the voting franchise, political parties turned from parliamentary clubs into modern parties. They had to win elections involving thousands of voters. This meant organization, programs, promises, and continuity. The growth of the electorate forced parties to become vehicles for democracy.

KEY TERMS

state of nature   Humans before civilization.

civil society   Humans after becoming civilized. Modern usage: associations between family and government.

conservatism   Ideology aimed at preserving existing institutions and usages.

COMPARISON

THE ORIGINS OF TWO WELFARE STATES

Both Britain and Sweden are welfare states, Sweden more so than Britain. How did this come to be? In comparing their histories, we get some clues.

- Swedish King Gustav Vasa broke with Rome in the 1520s, a few years earlier than Henry VIII. In setting up churches that were dependent on their respective states—Lutheran in Sweden, Anglican in England—the two countries eliminated religion as a source of opposition to government.
- Because of this, politics in both lands avoided getting stuck in a clerical-anticlerical dispute over the role of the church, as happened in France, Italy, and Spain. In Britain and Sweden, the main political split was along class lines, working class versus middle class.
- Britain and Sweden both developed efficient and uncorrupt civil services, an absolute essential for the effective functioning of welfare programs.
- Workers in both countries organized strong—but not Marxist—labor unions, the TUC in Britain and LO in Sweden.
- These two labor movements gave rise to moderate, worker-oriented parties, Labour in Britain and the Social Democrats in Sweden, which demanded, and over time got, numerous welfare measures passed. One big difference is that the Social Democrats have been in power in Sweden for all but a few years since 1932 and have implemented a more thorough—and more expensive—welfare state.

THE RISE OF THE WELFARE STATE

By the beginning of the twentieth century, with working men having the right to vote, British parties had to pay attention to demands for welfare measures—public education, housing, jobs, and medical care—that the upper-crust gentlemen of the Liberal and Conservative parties had earlier minimized. Expansion of the electoral franchise led to the growth of the **welfare state**.

One force pushing for welfare measures was the new Labour party, founded in 1900. At first, Labour worked with the Liberals—the "Lib-Lab" coalition—but by the end of World War I, Labour pushed the Liberals into the weak third-party status they have languished in to this day. Unlike most Continental socialists, few British Labourites were

KEY TERM

welfare state Political system that redistributes wealth from rich to poor, standard in West Europe.

Marxists. Instead, they combined militant trade unionism with intellectual social democracy to produce a pragmatic, gradualist ideology that sought to level class differences in Britain. As one observer put it, the British Labour party "owed more to Methodism than to Marx."

The British labor movement of the late nineteenth century was tough, a quality it long retained. Resentful of being treated like dirt, many working men went into politics with a militancy that still characterizes some of their heirs. In the 1926 General Strike, the trade unions attempted to bring the entire British economy to a halt to gain their wage demands. They failed.

Briefly and weakly in power under Ramsay MacDonald in the 1920s, Labour won resoundingly in 1945 and implemented an ambitious welfare program plus state takeover of utilities, railroads, coal mines, and much heavy manufacturing. Since then, the chief quarrel in British politics has been between people who like the welfare state and state ownership and people who do not.

KEY TERMS

Anglican (p. 28)
anticlerical (p. 29)
burghers (p. 27)
Celts (p. 24)
civil society (p. 34)
Common Law (p. 28)
Commons (p. 27)
commonwealth (p. 30)
conservatism (p. 34)
Continent, the (p. 25)
Exchequer (p. 25)
fiefdom (p. 25)
landlocked (p. 29)
Levellers (p. 31)
Lords (p. 27)
Magna Carta (p. 27)

minister (p. 32)
mixed monarchy (p. 26)
Normans (p. 24)
Parliament (p. 27)
Parliamentarians (p. 30)
precedent (p. 28)
Reform Acts (p. 33)
republic (p. 30)
republican (p. 31)
Royalists (p. 30)
state of nature (p. 34)
Tories (p. 33)
Vatican (p. 28)
welfare state (p. 35)
Whig (p. 33)
Whig democracy (p. 33)

FURTHER REFERENCE

Beloff, Max. *Wars and Welfare: Britain 1914–1945*. London: Edward Arnold, 1984.

Callaghan, John. *Socialism in Britain since 1884*. Cambridge, MA: Basil Blackwell, 1990.

Chrimes, S. B. *English Constitutional History*. London: Oxford University Press, 1967.

Clarke, Peter. *Hope and Glory: Britain 1900–1990*. New York: Penguin, 1996.

Colley, Linda. *Britons: Forging the Nation, 1707–1837*. New Haven, CT: Yale University Press, 1992.

Davies, Norman. *The Isles: A History*. New York: Oxford University Press, 1999.

Greenleaf, W. H. *The British Political Tradition*, 3 vols. London: Methuen, 1987.

Hibbert, Christopher. *Cavaliers & Roundheads: The English Civil War, 1642–1649*. New York: Scribner's, 1993.

Kishlansky, Mark. *A Monarchy Transformed: Britain, 1603–1714*. New York: Allen Lane/Penguin Press, 1997.

McKibben, Ross. *Classes and Cultures: England 1918–1951*. New York: Oxford University Press, 1998.

Thorpe, Andrew. *A History of the British Labour Party*. New York: St. Martin's, 1997.

Williams, Glyn, and John Ramsden. *Ruling Britannia: A Political History of Britain, 1688–1988*, 2nd ed. New York: Longman, 1990.

3

Britain:
The Key Institutions

It is commonly said that Britain has no written constitution, but parts of the British constitution are written. It does not consist of a single document but is rather a centuries-old collection of Common Law, historic charters, **statutes** passed by Parliament, and, most important, established custom.

This **eclectic** quality gives the British constitution flexibility. With no single, written document to refer to, nothing can be declared "unconstitutional." Parliament—specifically the House of Commons—can pass any law it likes, letting the British political system change over time without a systemic crisis. The U.S. Supreme Court sometimes blocks changes as unconstitutional, rarely a problem in Britain.

The negative side to this was that Britain had little to guarantee human rights. In 1991, six men convicted as IRA bombers in 1975 were freed with the shameful admission that confessions had been beaten out of them and the police had rigged evidence. The European Court of Human Rights, located in Strasbourg, France, ruled against British justice in several such cases, a considerable embarrassment for Britain. In 2000, Britain adopted the European Convention on Human Rights as domestic law, finally giving Britons the equivalent of a U.S. Bill of Rights.

The British people often speak of the **Crown**, an all-encompassing term meaning the powers of government in

Questions to Consider

1. What did Bagehot mean by "dignified" as opposed to "efficient" offices? Examples?
2. How may Britain be described as "prime ministerial government"?
3. Does Britain have checks and balances?
4. Describe Blair's political positions.
5. When does Britain hold general elections?
6. What are the differences between presidential and parliamentary systems?
7. What did Blair do with Lords?
8. Describe the British electoral system.
9. What are Britain's main parties?

KEY TERMS

statute   Ordinary law, usually for specific problem.
eclectic   Drawn from a variety of sources.
Crown   The powers of the British government.

general. Originally, the Crown meant the king, but over the centuries it has broadened to include everyone helping the king or queen, such as Parliament, the cabinet, and civil servants. Let us consider some of these.

THE MONARCH

In Britain there is a clear distinction between "head of state" and "chief of government." In America this distinction is ignored because the two are merged into one in the presidency. In most of the rest of the world, however, there is a top figure without much power who symbolizes the nation, receives foreign ambassadors, and gives speeches on patriotic occasions. This person—often a figurehead—can be either a hereditary monarch or an elected president, although not a U.S.-style president. Britain, Sweden, Norway, Denmark, the Netherlands, Belgium, and Spain are monarchies. This does not mean they are undemocratic; it just means the head of state is a carry-over from the old days.

A hereditary head of state can be useful. Above politics, a monarch can serve as psychological cement to hold a country together because he or she has no important role in government. Because the top position in the land—what royalist philosophers used to call the sovereign—is already occupied, there are no political battles over it. The nastiest struggles in the world are precisely over who is to be sovereign; in Britain, the issue has long been settled.

The great commentator on the British constitution, Sir Walter Bagehot, divided it into **dignified** and **efficient** parts. The monarch, as head of state, is a dignified office with much symbolic but no real political power. He or she "reigns but does not rule." The king or queen nominally appoints a cabinet of His or Her Majesty's servants (see box on page 42), but otherwise a monarch is more like an official greeter.

The "efficient" office in Britain is the chief of government, the prime minister—a working politician who fights elections, leads his or her party, and makes political deals. Despite the prestige of a prime minister, it does not have nearly the "dignity" that the monarch has. There is an advantage in the way Britain and other countries split the two positions. If the chief of government does something foolish or illegal, he or she will catch the public's ire, but the blame will fall on the individual prime minister, and respect will not diminish for the head of state, the "dignified" office. The system retains its legitimacy. Where the two offices are combined, as in the United States, and the president is involved in something crooked, the public gets disgusted at both the working politician and the nation's symbolic leader. "The British do not need to love their prime minister," said one diplomat. "They love their queen."

The 1997 death of Princess Di, ex-wife of Prince Charles, jolted Britain, including the royal family. Di was the only royal with the common touch; her charity work and love life upstaged the cold and remote House of Windsor. Amidst the outpouring of grief for Di came mutterings that the royal family really did not much care. Some even thought it

KEY TERMS

dignified   In Bagehot's terms, symbolic or decorative offices.

efficient   In Bagehot's terms, working, political offices.

Prince Charles, Britain's future king and head of the state, in happier days with his then-wife, the late Princess Diana, and their children, Prince William, also a future king, and Prince Henry. The divorce of Charles and Diana in 1996 did not affect Charles's succession to the throne. (Central Office of Information, London)

might be time to dump the monarchy. But old dynasties know how to survive, and the Queen and Prince Charles quickly became more public and outgoing.

Although few would exchange the monarchy for a republic, some (including Queen Elizabeth herself) suggest reforms that would cut government funds for the royal house and make female heirs to the throne the equal of males. Look for a major decision point when Queen Elizabeth dies. Will Charles automatically accede to the throne, even with his 2005 remarriage to a commoner (herself divorced)? The last time this happened, in 1936, King Edward VIII abdicated, but a replay is unlikely; times have changed. Britain will likely retain a monarchy, but it may be a monarch with reduced financial support and political roles.

THE CABINET

The British cabinet also differs from the U.S. cabinet. The former consists of members of Parliament (most in Commons, a few in Lords) who are high up in their parties and important political figures. Most have lots of experience, first as ordinary **MPs** (members of Parliament), then as **junior ministers**, and finally as cabinet ministers. The American cabinet, which now seldom meets and counts for little, usually consists of experts from businesses, law offices, and universities, mostly without political experience, who serve as

KEY TERMS

MP   Member of Parliament
junior minister   MP with executive responsibilities below cabinet rank.

DEMOCRACY

THE LAST POLITICAL MONARCH

Unlike other European monarchs, King Juan Carlos of Spain retains some crucial political functions. Juan Carlos took over as head of state after Franco's death in 1975 and initiated and backstopped a process that turned Spain from dictatorship to democracy. He named a prime minister who dismantled the Franco structure, carried out Spain's first free elections in forty-one years, and drafted a new constitution—all with the open approval of the king.

Juan Carlos's real test as defender of democracy came in 1981 when some disgruntled officers attempted a coup; they held the entire **Cortes** at gunpoint. In military uniform, the king addressed the nation on television and ordered the troops back to their barracks. They complied, and democratic Spaniards of all parties thanked God for the king. Democracy and monarchy are not **antithetical**; one can support the other. *¡Viva el rey!*

administrators, not policy innovators. British cabinet government has been declining since World War I, which required speedy, centralized decisions. Now Prime Minister Blair develops policy with a small personal staff and then informs the cabinet of it. British commentators fear the rise of a "command premiership" in this development.

Originally, the British cabinet consisted of ministers to the king. Starting in the seventeenth century, the cabinet became more and more responsible to Parliament and less and less to the king. A British minister is not necessarily an expert in his or her **portfolio** but is carefully picked by the prime minister for political qualifications. Both major British parties contain several viewpoints and power centers, and prime ministers usually take care to see they are represented in the cabinet. When Prime Minister Thatcher ignored this principle by picking as ministers only Tories loyal to her and her philosophy, she was criticized as dictatorial and ultimately lost her job. Balancing party factions in the cabinet helps keep the party together in Parliament and in power.

Notice the British cabinet straddles the gap between *executive* and *legislative*. The elaborate American separation of powers (adopted by the Founding Fathers from an earlier misperception of British government by Montesquieu) does not hold in Britain or in most of the world. The United Kingdom has a combining or **fusion of powers**. The British

KEY TERMS

Cortes   Spain's parliament.

antithetical   Ideas opposed to one another.

portfolio   Minister's assigned ministry.

fusion of powers   Connection of executive and legislative branches in parliamentary systems; opposite of U.S. separation of powers.

DEMOCRACY

THE QUEEN CHOOSES A NEW PRIME MINISTER

In May 1997 an old ritual was repeated. Ostensibly Queen Elizabeth II chose a new prime minister, but of course she really had no choice at all. Events unrolled according to the fiction that the prime minister is still chief advisor to the monarch.

Britain's governing Conservative party saw their voter support erode due to some unpopular policies of Prime Minister Margaret Thatcher and the weak leadership of her successor, John Major, who had narrowly won the 1992 elections. The House of Commons can go up to five years between elections, so in 1997 Major had to call them. His Conservatives lost massively to a resurgent Labour party.

No longer leader of the party with a majority of the Commons seats, Major could not remain prime minister, so the day after elections he called on the Queen to formally resign as first minister to Her Majesty. (He continued as a member of parliament but was dumped as Tory leader.) That same day the Queen called Tony Blair, as leader of what was now the largest party in the Commons, to Buckingham Palace and "asked" him to form a new government. He accepted.

cabinet practices "collective responsibility," meaning they all stick together and, in public at least, support the prime minister. Occasionally, a minister resigns in protest over a major controversy.

In recent years, the cabinet has consisted of some twenty ministers, although this number and portfolio titles change. Commons routinely approves the prime minister's requests to add, drop, or combine ministries. Most countries function that way (not, of course, the United States). In the early 2000s, Prime Minister Blair's cabinet consisted of the following "secretaries of state," or ministers:

Chancellor of the Exchequer (treasury)
Lord Chancellor (member of Lords, heads judiciary)
Foreign and Commonwealth Affairs
Home Development (internal governance, including police)
Environment, Food, and Rural Affairs
International Development
Work and Pensions
Transport, Local Government, and the Regions
Health
Northern Ireland
Wales
Scotland
Defense

KEY CONCEPTS

PRIME MINISTERS INTO PRESIDENTS

Political scientists have for some time suggested that prime ministers are becoming more and more presidential. With Tony Blair, this theory gained credence, for Blair indeed concentrated and centralized power in his immediate office at the expense of the cabinet and Commons.

Blair no longer pretended to be "first among equals" in his cabinet, which met less often and decided issues less frequently. Like the U.S. cabinet secretaries, British ministers became more like top administrators. Instead, Blair tripled the size of the staff at 10 Downing Street, headed them with trusted advisors, and used them to make decisions, rather like the White House.

Continuing a trend, Blair spent less time in Commons. Prime Minister Churchill voted in 55 percent of Commons divisions in 1951. Prime Minister Wilson voted 43 percent of the time in 1974. Tony Blair voted 5 percent of the time in Commons in 1997.

Some called Blair a "control freak" who broke with British tradition in order to amass personal power. Maybe, but personality alone does not explain the long-term trend for prime ministers everywhere to become presidential. One key factor changing political systems worldwide: television, which centralizes election campaigns, emphasizes the top candidates, creates massive need for fundraising, bypasses parties and parliaments, and enables leaders to reach people directly. Blair was good on television. There are other factors, too, such as the decline of legislatures, the growth of interest groups, and the tendency of voters to concentrate in the center of the political spectrum.

Things have changed for parliamentary systems; they cannot operate as before. Systems as different as Britain, France, Germany, and Japan have tended to "presidentialize" themselves as prime ministers gain power and start acting as if they have been directly elected. Everywhere, even in parliamentary systems, parties in elections showcase their leading personality as if he or she was a presidential candidate. Parliamentary systems will not turn completely into U.S.-type systems; all will retain distinctive characteristics. But neither will any of them return to the pure parliamentary model, which was never completely realistic. Even in parliamentary systems, power long ago began shifting to prime ministers, and this has continued. A strong prime minister begins to resemble a U.S.-type president.

Trade and Industry
Education and Skills
Culture, Media, and Sport

In addition, the leaders of both Commons and Lords are in the cabinet, along with a chief secretary for the cabinet as a whole.

Below cabinet rank are more than thirty noncabinet "departmental ministers" and a similar number of "junior ministers" assigned to help cabinet and departmental ministers. All totaled, at any given time about a hundred MPs are also serving in the executive branch. The hope of being named to one of these positions ensures the loyalty and obedience of most younger MPs.

For all intents and purposes, in Britain (and in most parliamentary systems) cabinet equals **government**; the two terms are used interchangeably. One speaks of the "Blair government." (Only the United States uses the word "administration.") When the "government falls" it simply means the cabinet has resigned. Britain is often referred to as "cabinet government," although some call it "prime ministerial government."

THE PRIME MINISTER

The prime minister, PM for short (not to be confused with MP, which he or she also is), is the linchpin of the British system. In theory, the PM's powers could be dictatorial. Because the prime minister picks and controls the cabinet and heads the largest party in Parliament, he or she should be able to get nearly any measure passed. British parliamentarians are well-disciplined; party **whips** make sure their MPs turn out for **divisions** and vote the straight party line. Yet even with the reins of power held by one person, prime ministers do not turn into dictators, chiefly because general elections are never more than five years away.

Prime ministers are usually cautious about introducing measures that might provoke public ire. When John Major saw his popularity slipping, he knew he would lose if he "went to the country" with new elections, so he tried to stall, hoping his party's fortunes would rise before the five years were up. Typically, prime ministers introduce moderate, piecemeal measures to avoid offending key blocks of voters. The fear of losing the next election keeps most prime ministers (but not Thatcher) cautious.

Furthermore, a prime minister has to be careful of the major currents of opinion within party ranks. As in the United States, the two large British parties contain left, right, and center wings, as well as regional viewpoints, and a prime minister usually constructs the cabinet with top MPs representing several views within the majority party. In cabinet meetings the PM tries to fashion a consensus from the several stands.

Then the cabinet has to sell the policy to their MPs back in Commons. Party discipline is good but rarely total. The prime minister, through the chief whip, has a hold on the MPs. One who does not "take the whip" (follow the party line on a vote) risks losing his or her nomination for reelection—in effect, getting fired from Parliament. But this is a two-way street. If a party policy really bothers an MP, the member can threaten to quit and make a stink. Every few years an MP "crosses the aisle" and joins the other party in protest (as did the young Winston Churchill). In 1995 one moderate Conservative MP was so upset by what he saw as right-wing domination of his party that he quit the Tories and ran (successfully) as a Labourite, the ultimate slap at party leadership. If a PM fails badly, he or she can even be dumped by MPs. Several times in the past two decades, both Labour and Conservative cabinets have had to withdraw or water down their legislative proposals for fear of backbenchers' revolt within the ranks of their own party. A backbenchers' revolt helped oust Thatcher in 1990.

KEY TERMS

government   A particular cabinet, what Americans call the administration.

whip   Parliamentary party leader who makes sure members obey party in voting.

division   Vote in the House of Commons.

PERSONALITIES

TONY BLAIR: A NEW MODEL PRIME MINISTER

Tony Blair, first elected prime minister in 1997 at age forty-three (Britain's youngest prime minister since 1812) continued a trend that some observers contend has been underway since the 1960s: prime ministers acting more like presidents. Blair indeed centralized and concentrated power in his immediate office at the expense of the cabinet and Commons (see box on page 43).

Blair did several things that made him look like his friend, President Bill Clinton. (Blair was also close to President Bush.) First, he recast the Labour party—which he called "New Labour"—into a reformist but not radical centrist party. Blair jettisoned uncritical support for unions, higher taxes, and the welfare state in favor of Clinton-type ideas on economic growth and getting people off welfare. With an upbeat personality, he trounced the Conservatives and John Major, who had trouble leading a divided party, in the 1997 general elections to form the first Labour government since 1979.

Some called Blair's ideology—a "Third Way" between capitalism and socialism—vague. Like Clinton, Blair had stolen much of the right's economic agenda but put a smiling face on it. Within two years, leaders across Europe wanted to be like Tony Blair, the man with a vision of a humane but flexible market-based system who refused to get stuck in yesterday's thinking.

Blair supported market economics but concentrated on modernizing Britain's sometimes creaky institutions. He brought a shaky peace to Northern Ireland, devolved some powers to Scotland and Wales, reformed the House of Lords, gave Britain the equivalent of a U.S. Bill of Rights, and managed the economy well. He even considered changing Britain's electoral system in favor of proportional representation. He also cut a swath on the world stage with visits to other chiefs and use of British forces in chaotic areas such as Iraq. By tackling problems that his predecessors ignored, Blair proved himself a new type of prime minister: a fresh-thinking optimist who won re-election in 2001 over the pessimistic Tories.

By 2003, however, Blair was in trouble over British participation in the Iraq war, which some 80 percent of Britons, like other Europeans, opposed. Blair faced a revolt within Labour's ranks that included backbenchers and his own cabinet ministers, some of whom resigned in protest. They felt that he followed President Bush too uncritically. The Labour party and Blair won the 2005 elections, but with a reduced majority. (Blair's already-named replacement: Chancellor of the Exchequer Gordon Brown, whose eagerness to succeed Blair led to open friction.)

Tony Blair. (British Information Services)

Who Was When: Britain's Postwar Prime Ministers

Clement Attlee	Labour	1945–1951
Winston Churchill	Conservative	1951–1955
Anthony Eden	Conservative	1955–1957
Harold Macmillan	Conservative	1957–1963
Alec Douglas-Home	Conservative	1963–1964
Harold Wilson	Labour	1964–1970
Edward Heath	Conservative	1970–1974
Harold Wilson	Labour	1974–1976
James Callaghan	Labour	1976–1979
Margaret Thatcher	Conservative	1979–1990
John Major	Conservative	1990–1997
Tony Blair	Labour	1997–

The PM does, however, have a potent political weapon: the power to call new elections whenever he or she wishes. By law, the Commons can go up to five years without a general election. **By-elections** when an MP dies or retires can come any time; they are closely watched as political barometers. A crafty prime minister calls for new general elections when he or she thinks the party will do best. A good economy and sunny weather tend to produce a happy electorate, one that will increase the seats of the incumbent party. In 1974 Britain held two general elections because Prime Minister Harold Wilson thought he could boost Labour's strength in the Commons (he did). In 2001 and 2005 Tony Blair called elections a year early to take advantage of good economic news and disarray in the Conservative party; he won handily. Public-opinion polls and by-elections help the prime minister decide when to ask the queen to dissolve Parliament and hold new elections.

Since 1735 British prime ministers have resided in an ordinary brick row house, No. 10 Downing Street. Except for a couple of London bobbies on guard outside, it looks like a private home. This is deceptive; behind the walls, Downing Street is actually the nerve center of **Whitehall**. Upstairs at No. 10, the prime minister has his or her apartment. On the ground floor, in the back, the cabinet meets in a long white room. No. 10 connects to No. 12 Downing Street, the residence of the chief whip, the prime minister's parliamentary enforcer. They can visit without being seen from the street. Also connecting out of sight is No. 11 Downing Street, residence of the important Chancellor of the Exchequer, head of the powerful Treasury Ministry. Next door is the Foreign Office. At the corner of Downing Street, also with a connecting door to No. 10, is the cabinet secretariat, responsible for communication and coordination among the departments.

Key Terms

by-election   Special election for vacant seat in Parliament.
Whitehall   Main British government offices.

DEMOCRACY

PARLIAMENTARY VERSUS PRESIDENTIAL SYSTEMS

In a parliamentary system, like Britain, voters choose only a parliament, which in turn chooses (and can oust) the executive branch, headed by a prime minister. The executive is a committee of the legislature. In a presidential system, such as the United States, voters choose both a legislature and a chief executive, and the two are expected to check and balance each other. In a parliamentary system, they are not.

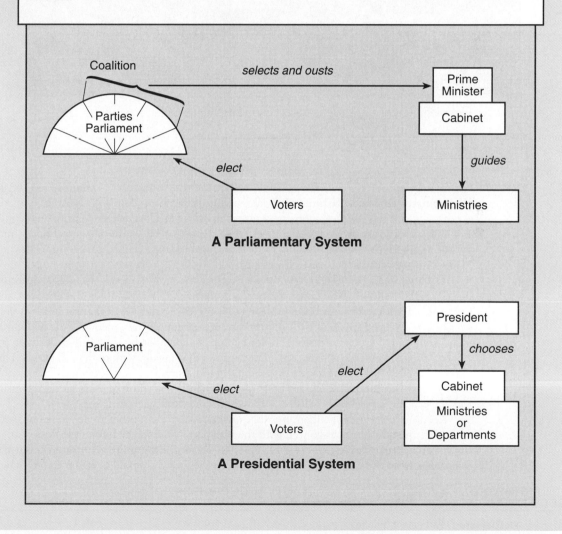

A Parliamentary System

A Presidential System

House of Commons in session. Notice how small it is. (British Information Service)

COMMONS

One can look at the cabinet as a committee of the House of Commons sent from **Westminster** to nearby Whitehall to keep administration under parliamentary control. Another way is to view Commons as an electoral college that stays in operation even after it has chosen the executive (the cabinet). In Lockean theory, legislative power has primacy, but in practice Commons has rarely been free and independent and is becoming less so. Prime ministers lead and control Commons.

The two main parties in Commons—Conservative and Labour—face each other on long, parallel benches. The largest party is automatically Her Majesty's Government and the other Her Majesty's Loyal **Opposition**. The size of Commons explains a lot: It is very small, only 45 by 68 feet (14 by 21 meters) and was originally designed for only about 400 members. How then can it possibly hold the current membership of 646? (Seats have increased over the years as Britain's population grows in some areas more than in others. Parliament in 2005 cut thirteen seats by combining some smaller constituencies.) It does not, at least not comfortably. Members have no individual desks, unlike most modern legislators. For an important vote, MPs pack in like sardines and sit in the aisles.

Keeping Commons small ensures that members face each other in debate a few yards apart. The parallel benches go well with the two-party system; the half-circle floor plan of most Continental legislatures facilitates pielike division into multiparty systems. But the main reason for the chamber's small size is that it was always small, ever since 1547 when

KEY TERMS

Westminster   Parliament building.

opposition   Parties in parliament that are not in cabinet.

Henry VIII first gave Commons the use of the St. Stephen's royal chapel. During World War II when Commons was damaged by German bombs, Prime Minister Winston Churchill ordered it rebuilt exactly the way it had been.

Each side of the oblong chamber has five rows of benches. The front row on either side is reserved for the leading team of each major party, the cabinet of the government party, and the *shadow cabinet* of the opposition. Behind them sit the **backbenchers**, the MP rank and file. A neutral Speaker, elected for life from the MPs, sits in a thronelike chair at one end. The Speaker, who never votes or takes sides, manages the floor debate and preserves order. In 1992, Commons elected its first woman Speaker, Labourite Betty Boothroyd.

A table in the center, between the party benches, is where legislation is placed (the origin of the verb "to table" a proposal). The Speaker calls the house to order at 11:30 A.M. and sessions can go on until 7:30 P.M. Unless "the whip is on"—meaning an MP had better be there because an important vote is expected—many MPs are busy elsewhere.

How Commons Works

Each year Parliament opens in November with a Speech from the Throne by the queen, another tradition. The MPs are ritually summoned by Black Rod, the queen's messenger, from Commons and file into the nearby House of Lords. (Neither monarchs nor lords may enter Commons.) From a gold-paneled dais in Lords, Her Majesty reads a statement outlining the policies "my government" will pursue. The speech has been written by the prime minister with the queen serving as announcer. A conservative king, George VI, read a Labour speech in 1945 promising extensive nationalization of industry.

Just as the queen takes her cues from the prime minister, so does Commons. Practically all legislation is introduced by the government (that is, the cabinet) and stands a high chance of passing nearly intact because of the party discipline discussed previously. What the PM wants, the PM usually gets. When a Labour government introduces bills into Commons, Labour MPs—unlike their American counterparts in Congress—rarely question them. Their job is to support the party, and individual conscience seldom gets in the way.

The task of challenging proposals falls to the opposition, seated on the Speaker's left. From the opposition benches come questions, denunciations, warnings of dire consequences, anything that might make the government look bad. A spirit of bipartisanship seldom gets in the way. Government MPs, particularly the cabinet and subcabinet ministers on the front bench, are duty-bound to defend the bills. In situations like these, the famous rhetorical ability of MPs produces debates matched by few other legislatures.

Although the rhetoric is brilliant and witty, the homework is weak. Because they are expected simply to obey their party, few MPs bother specializing. Traditionally, British parliamentary committees were also unspecialized; they went over the precise wording of bills but called no witnesses and gathered no data. The structure of legislative committees is key to their power, and gradually some MPs saw the need for a more American type of committee system. In 1979, fourteen **select committees** were set up to scrutinize the workings of each

KEY TERMS

backbencher   Ordinary MP with no executive responsibility.
select committee   Specialized committee of Commons focusing on one ministry.

COMPARISON

HOW MUCH ARE PARLIAMENTARIANS PAID?

Compared to other advanced democracies, British MPs are paid little and do not enjoy substantial allowances. And this is after a pay raise for MPs in 1996.

Member of	Salary	Allowances
British House of Commons	$67,000	$72,000
French National Assembly	94,400	14,600
German Bundestag	89,000	110,700
Russian Duma	7,000	—
Japanese Diet	146,200	108,900
U.S. House of Representatives	133,600	887,000

Many MPs work at other jobs, some as "consultants" for interest groups. This gives some a reputation for "sleaze" that they detest. Many MPs would like to stop or limit outside pay, but the cost of living in London is high, and MPs' salaries are totally inadequate. The huge allowances for U.S. Representatives (Senators can get almost $2 million) illustrate the strong constituency orientation of U.S. legislators: They need large, specialized staffs both to help the folks back home and to study current issues, functions that are not as highly developed in other parliaments.

ministry; they have the power to take written and oral evidence. The select committees, with stable membership, resemble to some extent U.S. Congressional committees.

Neither Tory nor Labour governments have been enthusiastic about specialized committees that can monitor and criticize executive functions. That may be part of the U.S. system of separation of powers, some say, but it has no place in the U.K. system of fusion of powers. In general, the British cabinet would like to use Commons to rubber-stamp its decisions. Fortunately, such rubber-stamping is not always the case, as we shall see later.

PEERLESS LORDS

In 1999, Parliament drastically reformed the House of Lords by kicking out most of its hereditary peers, thus turning it over to **life peers**. Since 1958, distinguished Britons in science, literature, politics, military service, business, and the arts have been named as Lords

KEY TERM

life peers   Distinguished Britons named lords for their lifetimes (does not pass on to children).

DEMOCRACY

THE DECLINE OF LEGISLATURES

Commons is less important than it used to be. As in most of the world, legislatures, the great avenues of democracy, are declining in power. Fewer people—especially young people—bother voting and fewer follow debates in Commons, which get less media attention. The debates matter little; thanks to Britain's (over)disciplined parties, the prime minister almost always gets his or her way. The only way to jump-start Commons back into life would be to let MPs ignore the whip and vote as they wish. A deliberate weakening of Britain's parties might make Commons exciting, unpredictable, and messy, like the U.S. Congress. A word of caution here: Capitol Hill has also been losing power to the White House. This may be an unstoppable world trend. Even so, legislatures are invaluable for scrutinizing executive power, holding it accountable, and occasionally ousting it. If they do this, they are still bulwarks of democracy.

or Ladies of the Realm, but for their life only. The change did nothing to enhance Lords' weak powers. Lords now has over five hundred life peers (a number that changes with deaths and new appointments) plus ninety-two hereditary peers and twenty-six top churchmen.

The British Parliament is nominally bicameral, but Commons has limited Lords' powers over the centuries, so that now when one says "Parliament," one really means Commons. Early on, Commons established supremacy in the key area of money: raising revenues and spending them. (An echo of this is the U.S. provision that money bills originate in the lower chamber, the House of Representatives.) Britain's seventeenth-century battles centered on the power of Commons, and it emerged the winner; Lords gradually took a back seat. By 1867 Bagehot considered Lords a "dignified" part of the constitution.

Since Britain's unwritten constitution does not specify or make permanent the powers of the two chambers, it was legally possible for Commons to change Lords. Its powers now are severely limited. The 1911 Parliament Act allows Lords to delay legislation not more than thirty days on financial bills and two years (since 1949, one year) on other bills. Lords can amend legislation and send it back to Commons, which in turn can (and usually does) delete the changes by a simple majority. Every few years, however, Lords jolts the government by forcing Commons to take another look at bills passed without sufficient scrutiny. Lords, then, is somewhat more important than a debating club. It is the only British institution in a position to check the powers of a prime minister who has a large and disciplined majority in Commons. It is thus a weak analog to the U.S. Supreme Court, a "conscience of the nation." Lords is also able to debate questions too hot for elected officials—for example, laws concerning abortion and homosexuality.

Usually, fewer than three hundred lords turn up in the House of Lords; a quorum is three. A few lords are named to the cabinet or to other high political or diplomatic positions.

The chamber is also home to several **law lords**, life peers who are the top judges in the British court system to whom cases may be appealed. Now that Britain has a Human Rights Act (see page 90), a sort of embryonic constitution, the law lords can declare something "unconstitutional." The law lords may thus turn into a U.S.-style Supreme Court.

Most Britons agree that Lords is an **anachronism** ripe for reform but cannot agree on what to do with it. Blair's 1999 step depriving most hereditary peers of their seats made Lords meritocratic but not democratic. Blair has considered a more sweeping proposal: a 600-member House of Lords with 120 elected lords and the rest named by political parties and the government. Criticism from all parties and the media shot down the proposal. Many feared prime ministers would stack the new chamber with loyal supporters, giving the prime minister control of both houses and depriving Lords of its independence to criticize. Many Britons want to make Lords fully elected, like the U.S. Senate, but some fear that would dilute the legislative supremacy of Commons and turn Lords over to vote-seeking party politicians. Changing constitutions is tricky: When you change one thing, you change everything.

THE PARTIES

Commons works as it does because of the British party system. This is a fairly recent development; only since the time of the French Revolution (1789) has it been possible to speak of coherent parties in Britain. Parties are now the cornerstone of British government. If a party elects a majority of the MPs, that party controls Commons and forms the government.

British parties are more cohesive, centralized, and ideological than U.S. parties. (There are as many differences within the two big U.S. parties as between them.) Now, however, like their U.S. counterparts, the two large British parties tend to converge to the center. Earlier, British Labourites, who sometimes called themselves Socialists, favored nationalization of industry, more welfare measures, and higher taxes. Conservatives urged less government involvement in society and the economy and lower taxes. Internal party differences arose from the degree to which party members supported these general points of view. Now, as we shall explore subsequently, differences between the two parties are muted.

In 1981, the moderate wing of the Labour party split off to form a centrist Social Democratic party. They argued that Labour had fallen under the control of leftist radicals. The Social Democrats faced the problem that besets Britain's third party, the struggling Liberals, namely, that single-member plurality districts severely penalize smaller parties. The Liberal party illustrates this. In the last century the Liberals were one of the two big parties, but by the 1920s they had been pushed into a weak third place by Labour. Now, although the Liberal Democrats often win nearly 20 percent of the vote, they rarely get more than a few dozen Commons seats because their vote is territorially dispersed, so in few constituencies does it top Tories or Labourites.

In 1983 and 1987, the Liberals and Social Democrats ran jointly as the "Alliance," and in 1988 they merged into the Liberal Democratic party. Because they are spread rather evenly, the "Lib Dems" still get shortchanged on parliamentary seats (see box on page 53). The Liberal Democrats would like to move away from the majoritarian system and toward

KEY TERMS

law lords   Britain's top judges, members of Lords.
anachronism   Something from the past that does not fit present times.

KEY CONCEPTS

BRITAIN'S TWO-PARTY SYSTEM

Britain is usually described as a two-party system, but some third parties are important. Britain, like many democracies, is more accurately a **"two-plus" party system**. In 1979, for example, the withdrawal of support by the eleven Scottish Nationalists in Commons brought down the Callaghan government in a rare **vote of no-confidence**. The Liberal Democrats may get one vote in five, forcing the Labour and Conservative parties to move to more centrist positions.

Britain's electoral system keeps two parties big and penalizes smaller parties. Britain, like the United States and Canada, uses **single-member districts** as the basis for elections. This old English system is simple: Each electoral district or constituency sends one person to the legislature, the candidate that gets the most votes even if less than a majority, sometimes called "first past the post" **(FPTP)**. In 1992, for example, a Lib Dem in Scotland won with just 26 percent of the vote. This system of single-member districts with **plurality** victors tends to produce two large political parties. The reason: There is a big premium to combine small parties into big ones in order to edge out competitors. If one of the two large parties splits, which sometimes happens, the election is thrown to the other party, the one that hangs together. In countries with proportional representation there is not such a great premium on forming two large parties, and that contributes to multiparty systems.

The countries that inherited the British **majoritarian** system tend toward two large parties, one left, the other right, such as the U.S. Democrats and Republicans. Canada is an exception to this pattern, because its third parties are territorially concentrated, especially the separatist Bloc Québécois. New Zealand used the Anglo-American system, and it too yielded two large parties. It also left many New Zealanders discontent, because other viewpoints got ignored, so its parliament in 1993 adopted a new electoral law, modeled on Germany's hybrid system of half single-member districts and half PR. New Zealand soon developed a more complex party system.

proportional representation (PR), something Blair pledged to hold a referendum on. The leading proposal is to keep FPTP but "top off" seats to more accurately reflect nationwide party strengths. (The German system, by contrast, starts with PR but adds FPTP.)

KEY TERMS

"two-plus" party system   Two big parties and several small ones.

vote of no-confidence   Parliamentary vote to oust cabinet.

single-member district   Sends one representative to parliament.

FPTP   "First past the post," short way of saying "single-member districts with plurality win."

plurality   Largest quantity, even if less than a majority.

majoritarian   Electoral system that encourages dominance of one party in parliament, as in Britain and the United States.

proportional representation   Electoral system of multimember districts with seats awarded by percentage parties win.

Scottish and Welsh nationalist parties have had spurts of growth and decline. Their territorial concentration enables them to obtain a few seats in Westminster and many seats in the Scottish and Welsh assemblies instituted in 1999. A new party opposes British membership in the European Union, the UK Independence party (UKIP). We will explore patterns of interaction among the parties and the voters in Chapter 5.

KEY TERMS

anachronism (p. 52)

antithetical (p. 41)

backbencher (p. 49)

by-election (p. 46)

Cortes (p. 41)

Crown (p. 38)

dignified (p. 39)

division (p. 44)

eclectic (p. 38)

efficient (p. 39)

FPTP (p. 53)

fusion of powers (p. 41)

government (p. 44)

junior minister (p. 40)

law lords (p. 52)

life peers (p. 50)

majoritarian (p. 53)

MP (p. 40)

opposition (p. 48)

plurality (p. 53)

portfolio (p. 41)

proportional representation (p. 53)

select committee (p. 49)

single-member district (p. 53)

statute (p. 38)

"two-plus" party system (p. 53)

vote of no-confidence (p. 53)

Westminster (p. 48)

whip (p. 44)

Whitehall (p. 46)

FURTHER REFERENCE

Birch, Anthony H. *The British System of Government*, 10th ed. New York: Routledge, 1998.

Blackburn, Robert. *The Electoral System in Britain*. New York: St. Martin's, 1995.

Carmichael, Paul, and Brice Dickson, eds. *The House of Lords: Its Parliamentary and Judicial Roles*. Portland, OR: Hart, 1999.

Foley, Michael. *The Politics of the British Constitution*. New York: St. Martin's, 1999.

———. *The British Presidency: Tony Blair and the Politics of Public Leadership*. New York: St. Martin's, 2000.

Hennessey, Peter. *The Prime Minister: The Office and Its Holders since 1945*. New York: Palgrave, 2001.

Lipsey, David. *The Secret Treasury*. New York: Viking, 2000.

Norton, Philip. *The British Polity*, 4th ed. White Plains, NY: Longman, 2000.

Rentoul, John. *Tony Blair: Prime Minister*. London: Time Warner, 2002.

Rhodes, R. A. W., and Patrick Dunleavy, eds. *Prime Minister, Cabinet and Core Executive*. New York: St. Martin's, 1995.

Riddell, Peter. *Parliament under Blair*. London: Politico, 2000.

Rose, Richard. *The Prime Minister in a Shrinking World*. Oxford: Polity Press, 2001.

Selden, Anthony. *Blair*. New York: Free Press, 2004.

Wright, Anthony. *British Politics: A Very Short Introduction*. New York: Oxford, 2002.

4

British Political Culture

"England is a snob country," one longtime American resident in London told me. She added: "And I'm a snob, so I like it here." Her candor touched one of the facets of British political life: the large and often invidious distinctions made between and by social classes.

Social class can be analyzed in two ways, objectively and subjectively. The objective approach uses data such as income and neighborhood to put people into categories. The subjective approach asks people to put themselves into categories. There are often discrepancies between the two, as when a self-made businessman, thinking of his humble origins, describes himself as **working class**, or when a poorly paid schoolteacher, thinking of her university degrees, describes herself as **middle class**. In Britain and in most industrialized democracies, the main politically relevant distinction is between working class and middle class.

Objectively, class differences in Britain are no greater than in the rest of West Europe. The time has passed since Disraeli could write that Britain was not one nation but two, the rich and the poor. Since then, the British working class has grown richer, the middle class bigger, and the small upper class poorer. But **subjectively** or psychologically, class

Questions to Consider

1. How does a wage differ from a salary? In class terms?
2. What is the difference between objective and subjective?
3. What is a British "public" school?
4. How does an "Oxbridge" education form an elite?
5. What is "class voting" and has it declined?
6. What story does a map of the 2005 elections tell?
7. What sort of center-periphery tension does Britain have?
8. Have British parties always been pragmatic?
9. What do polls tell politicians about voters' ideology?
10. How did Northern Ireland become such a problem?

KEY TERMS

social class   Layer or section of population of similar income and status.

working class   Those paid an hourly wage, typically less affluent and educated.

middle class   Professionals or those paid salaries, typically more affluent and educated.

objective   Judged by observable criteria.

subjective   Judged by feeling or intuition.

differences remain. Working-class people live, dress, speak, and enjoy themselves differently than the middle class. Britons seem to like these differences and try to preserve them.

German sociologist Ralf Dahrendorf felt the key word in Britain is not class but **solidarity**. While there has been a leveling of objective class differences, Dahrendorf held, the idea of individual competition and improvement has not caught on in Britain as in other industrial countries. Rather than struggling to improve themselves individually, many Britons relish the feeling of solidarity they get by sticking with their old jobs, neighborhoods, and pubs. "Britain is a society in which the values of solidarity are held in higher esteem than those of individual success at the expense of others," Dahrendorf wrote.

Whether one calls it class or solidarity, these divisions influence British politics. They contribute to the way Britons vote, color the attitudes of labor unions and of the Labour party, and—very importantly—give birth to Britain's elites through the education system.

"PUBLIC" SCHOOLS

Although many claim that since World War II Britain has become a **meritocracy**, having the right parents still makes a big difference. No society, including the United States, is purely merit-based. One way the British upper and upper-middle classes pass on their advantages is the **"public" school**—actually private and expensive—so-called after their original purpose of training boys for public life in the military, civil service, or politics. Eton, Harrow, Rugby, St. Paul's, Winchester, and other famous academies have for generations molded the sons of better-off Britons into a ruling elite.

What a small minority of young Britons (now about 7 percent) learns from ages thirteen to eighteen is more than their demanding curriculum. It is the personal style inculcated in public schools: self-confident to the point of arrogance, self-disciplined, bred to rule. Spy novelist John Le Carré recalled with distaste how his public schoolmates during World War II felt nothing but contempt for lower-class "oiks." In terms of class relations, added Le Carré decades later, "nothing, but absolutely nothing, has changed" since the 1940s.

The British private-school system generates an **old boy** network that assists graduates later in life. The years of floggings, vile food, and bullying by upper-classmen forge bonds among old schoolmates, and they often help each other get positions in industry and government. Much of Britain's elite have gone to private boarding schools, including a majority of Conservative MPs (but few Labour MPs).

KEY TERMS

solidarity   Feeling of cohesion within a social class.

meritocracy   Promotion by brains and ability rather than heredity.

public school   In Britain, a private, boarding school, equivalent to a U.S. prep school.

old boy   Someone you knew at public school.

DEMOCRACY

WHAT TO DO WITH "PUBLIC" SCHOOLS?

The British Labour party long sought to do away with the country's private boarding schools. Few British parents can afford them at up to £20,000 ($38,000) a year. Labourites regarded them as undemocratic, part of a class system that benefits a privileged few. Conservatives want to maintain the schools, arguing that they train the best people and imbue them with a sense of public service.

In actual practice, Labour governments essentially let the private boarding schools alone while they try to upgrade the quality of publicly supported comprehensive schools. Blair's emphasis on education, for example, leaves the public schools untouched. The problem may be solving itself: Boarding-school enrollment has slumped while day-school popularity has climbed. Changing lifestyles have convinced many British parents that sending their children away is cruel and unloving.

Until the 1970s, most young Britons took a frightening exam at age eleven (the "11-plus") that selected the best into state-funded *grammar* schools but left most in *secondary modern* schools. In all but Northern Ireland, Labor governments phased out this selective system in favor of *comprehensive* schools for all, like U.S. high schools. This did not solve the twin problems of educational quality and equality. Now better-off children get excellent boarding schools, middle-class children get good private day schools, while working-class children get state-funded comprehensive and technical schools that lead to the workplace. Until after World War II, there was no free high-school system in Britain. Only 65 percent of British seventeen-year-olds are still in school (including technical training), the lowest level of any industrial land. (Comparative figures: Germany, 97 percent; United States, 88 percent; Japan, 83 percent.) In spite of the efforts of the Labour party since World War II, British education still lags behind other countries and is still divided by class.

"OXBRIDGE"

The real path to position and power in Britain is through the elite universities of Oxford or Cambridge. Nearly half of Conservative MPs are Oxford or Cambridge graduates (usually after attending a public school, such as Eton), while a quarter of Labour MPs are **Oxbridge** products. In the cabinet, these percentages are higher. And prime ministers are almost always graduates of either Oxford or Cambridge; Thatcher and Blair were

KEY TERM

Oxbridge   Informal, Oxford and Cambridge universities.

Oxonians. In recent years, only Labour Prime Minister James Callaghan (1976–1979) and Conservative John Major (1990–1997) never went to college. In few other industrialized countries are the political elite drawn so heavily from just two universities.

British university education used to be elitist, enrolling the products of private schools. Since World War II, however, education opened to the working and lower-middle classes by direct-grant secondary schools and scholarships for deserving youths. Oxford and Cambridge became less class-biased in their admissions, and many lesser institutions were founded or expanded. (They are now euphemistically called "mainstream" universities.) The percentage of British secondary (high-school) graduates going to some type of higher education shot up from 14 in 1985 to nearly 40 today, approaching U.S. levels.

Only a small percentage of Oxbridge students go into politics, but those who do start with advantages. An Oxford or Cambridge degree—which takes three years to earn—commands respect. The Oxbridge experience hones political skills. One popular major for aspiring politicians is "PPE"—philosophy, politics, and economics—in effect, how to run a country. Debating in the Oxford or Cambridge Unions trains students to think on their feet and confound their opponents with rhetorical cleverness, a style that carries over into the House of Commons. Perhaps the main advantage of an Oxbridge education, however, is the "sense of effortless superiority" graduates carry all their lives. One U.S. president (Clinton), two Supreme Court justices, and several cabinet secretaries attended Oxford on **Rhodes scholarships**.

Class and Voting

Britain used to be a good example of **class voting**—a situation in which most of the working class votes for the left party (in this case, Labour) while most of the middle class votes for the right (in this case, Conservative). Actually, class voting in Sweden is higher than in Britain, but nowhere is it 100 percent because some working-class people vote Conservative, and some middle-class people vote Labour. Class differences may be part of Britain's political culture, but they do not translate into class voting on a one-to-one basis.

What dilutes class voting? Some working-class people are simply convinced that Conservatives do a better job of governing than Labourites. Some workers have a sentimental attachment to the country's oldest party. Some issues have little to do with class. The Tories win a large part of the working class on the issues of economic growth, keeping taxes down, and keeping out immigrants.

Going the other way, many middle-class and educated people are intellectually convinced that the Labour party is the answer to what they see as an establishment-ruled, snobbish class system. Such intellectuals provide important leadership in the Labour party. The leader of the Labour left for a long time was an aristocrat, Anthony Wedgewood Benn, or, as he liked to be known, Tony Benn. Furthermore, some middle-class people grew up in working-class families and vote like their parents.

Key Terms

Rhodes scholarship   Founded by South African millionaire, sends top foreign students to Oxford.

class voting   Tendency of classes to vote for parties that represent them.

GEOGRAPHY

ELECTIONS AND MAPS

Virtually all elections when charted on maps show geographical voting patterns. There are almost always durable regional variations in party strength. The map of Britain showing where parties scored above average seldom needs to be changed: Labour always does well in Scotland, Wales, and the big cities of England. Once rooted, regional voting patterns can persist for decades. Here are some of the patterns.

1. *Cities vote liberal or left.* Cities are places of education and critical thinking. Many intellectuals live in cities, and they tend to criticize the existing state of affairs and to call for change and reform. Workers tend to live in cities, and they are often discontent over wages and the cost of living. The countryside tends to be calmer and more conservative, often influenced by old traditions. Rural people often resent urban intellectuals for having more experimental notions than common sense. England outside of the big cities votes Conservative; central London votes Labour. Catholic Bavaria votes Christian Social, but swinging Munich votes Social Democrat. The 2000 and 2004 U.S. elections showed an urban-rural split.

2. *Every country has regional voting.* Regions vote their resentments. Typically, the periphery votes against the core area; if the core votes for party X, the periphery votes for party Y. A conquered region long remembers it, as has the U.S. South. Scotland and Wales show their resentments at England by voting Labour, but England stays Tory. France south of the Loire River and Spain south of the Tagus River show a greater tendency to go Socialist than the country as a whole. In this way, they act out their resentments of, respectively, Paris and Madrid.

3. *Voting follows religion.* Religious attitudes tend to be distributed regionally. Indeed, the religion factor is one explanation for above points 1 and 2. Big cities tend to be less religious than small towns, and this inclines the former to vote liberal or left. Some regions have different religious affiliations than the core area. Scottish Presbyterians show their difference with Anglicans by not voting Tory. German Protestants are still a bit inclined to see the Christian Democratic Union as a Catholic party and to vote against it.

Class voting changes over time. The British generation that came of age during and after World War II, especially the working class, was quite loyal to the Labour party, which it swept to power in 1945. Since then, class voting has declined in Britain and other advanced, industrialized democracies, including the United States. Class is not what it used to be in any country's voting patterns.

It is, however, still a factor. Typically, political scientists find voting behavior is influenced by social class plus one or more other factors, such as region, ethnic group, religion, and urban-rural differences. The 2005 British general election partially bears this out (see box above). Tories were strongest in England, especially the south of England, and in small towns and rural areas. They were weaker in Scotland and Wales and in the big industrial cities, places with a long-term Labour identification and concern over unemployment. Class by itself explains only part of British voting patterns. Class plus region explains more.

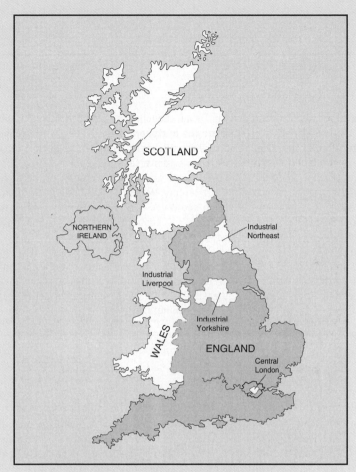

SHADED: WHERE TORIES WON ABOVE AVERAGE IN 2005

THE DEFERENTIAL BRITISH?

One old image of the British was that they were **deferential**, that is, the average Briton deferred to the political judgment of the Oxbridge-educated **Establishment** and let it lead. The deferential model was oversold and is now obsolete. Perhaps in earlier decades, when class differences were enormous, the working class deferred to its social betters, but they also built up resentment. As noted in Chapter 2, the labor movement came into British

KEY TERMS

deferential Accepting leadership of social superiors.

the Establishment Half in jest, supposed monopoly of clubby social elite in British politics.

Geography

Centers and Peripheries

A country's capital is often called its "center," even though it may not be in the precise center of the land. Closer to the boundaries of the state are the **peripheral** areas. Often these are more recent additions to the territory of the state. Some of them still speak a different language and resent rule by the capital. This **center-periphery tension** is nearly universal.

Over the centuries, England added Wales, Scotland, and Ireland. Resentment was so high in Ireland that Britain granted it independence in the last century. Now Britain retains only Northern Ireland, long a source of resentment and violence. Scotland and Wales also harbor grudges against rule by London and demand more home rule. As we shall consider in Chapter 6, Tony Blair's Labour government tried to calm these feelings by granting Scotland and Wales their own legislatures.

The U.S. Civil War was an effort by the southern periphery to cast off rule by Washington. In terms of attitudes and economics, the North and South really were two different countries, a gap that has been partly closed since then. The center of U.S. population, politics, economics, communications, education, and culture long remained in the northeast. This still fosters slight center-periphery tension; some western politicians express irritation at rule by Washington.

politics in the nineteenth century with a snarl. Some British working-class members still show resentment in militant socialism within the Labour party and in indifferent work attitudes and a readiness to strike. The deferential model cannot explain such behavior.

The "working-class Tory" has been explained as a working-class person who defers to the Conservatives and votes for them. But such voting may have little to do with deference. Many such voters think the Conservatives have the right policies, the Labour party had swung too far left, and there are too many nonwhite immigrants. Furthermore, the 1997, 2001, and 2005 elections saw a return of the "middle-class Labour voter," a shift that has nothing to do with social deference.

British Civility

In Britain, **civility** is based on a sense of limits: Do not let anything go too far; do not let the system come unstuck. Thus, while Labourites and Conservatives have serious arguments, they keep them verbal. The British political game is not one of total annihilation,

Key Terms

periphery   Nation's outlying regions.
center-periphery tension   Resentment of outlying areas at rule by nation's capital.
civility   Good manners in politics.

POLITICAL CULTURE

FOOTBALL HOOLIGANISM

Underscoring the decline in British civility was the rise of football **hooliganism**, the gleeful rioting of some British soccer fans. Some drunken fans charge onto the field in the middle of a game. In 1985, Liverpool fans killed thirty-eight Italian spectators by causing their bleachers to collapse. All over Europe, the English fanatics were feared and sometimes barred from games.

What causes the violence? Some blame unemployment; the games offer the jobless one of their few diversions. But most hooligans are employed and some earn good livings. Others see hooliganism as the erosion of civilization itself. "The truth is," said one self-confessed Manchester hooligan, "we just like scrappin'."

as it has sometimes been in France, Germany, and Russia. Accordingly, British politicians are fairly decent toward each other.

But British civility allows **heckling**. In Parliament a cabinet minister presenting a difficult case sometimes faces cries of "Shame!" or "Treason!" from the opposition benches. Margaret Thatcher faced Labourites chanting "Ditch the bitch." Insults and heckling are a normal part of British debates and are not viewed as out of bounds but rather as tests of a debater's poise and verbal skills.

Civility is usually the case in public also—but not always. Amateur orators at the famous Speakers' Corner of Hyde Park in London can have their say on any subject they like, although they too face heckling. British politics turned uncivil on the question of race, which we will discuss later, and there have been demonstrations and riots that led to deaths. Murder rather than civility became the norm for Northern Ireland. British civility has been overstated; Swedes are more civil.

PRAGMATISM

As noted in Chapter 1, *pragmatic* has the same root as *practical* and means using what works without paying much attention to theory or ideology. British attitudes, like American or Swedish ones, are generally pragmatic. The Conservatives used to pride themselves on being the most pragmatic of all British parties. They were willing to adopt the policies of another party if they won votes. In the nineteenth century, Disraeli crowed he

KEY TERMS

hooliganism Violent and destructive behavior.
heckling Interrupting a speaker.

POLITICAL CULTURE

THE SHAPE OF THE BRITISH ELECTORATE

Virtually all modern democracies show a strong clustering in the ideological center, with a tapering off toward the extremes: bell-shaped curves. Such a **center-peaked** distribution is probably necessary to sustain democracy, for it encourages **center-seeking** politics. A U-shaped distribution indicates extreme division, possibly heading toward civil war (example: Spain, 1936). Pollsters and political consultants constantly remind their clients of the distribution of ideological opinion and warn them not to position themselves too far left or right. It took the Labour party several electoral defeats to get the message. Tony Blair finally pushed Labour into about the 5 position (exact center) with vague but upbeat party positions.

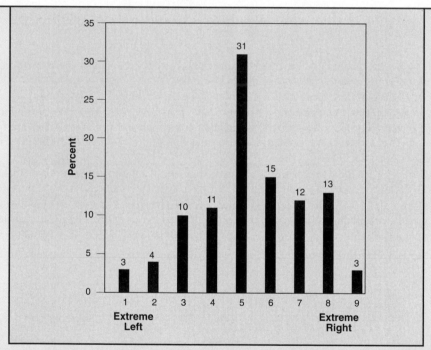

THE SELF-PLACEMENT OF BRITISH VOTERS ON A LEFT/RIGHT IDEOLOGICAL SCALE

KEY TERMS

center-peaked   Distribution with most people in the middle, a bell-shaped curve.

center-seeking   Tendency of political parties toward moderate politics calculated to win the center.

had "dished the Whigs" by stealing their drive to expand the voting franchise. In the 1950s, the returning Conservative government did not throw out Labour's welfare state; instead they boasted that Tories ran it more efficiently. This changed with the laissez-faire economic program of Prime Minister Thatcher in 1979. The fixity of her goals contributed to ideological debates within and between the two large and usually pragmatic parties. Pragmatism returned to the Tories after Thatcher.

The British Labour party historically offered little ideology beyond the hopeful image of a welfare state. With the Callaghan government in the 1970s, however, ideological controversy engulfed Labour. Callaghan was a very moderate, pragmatic Labourite, hard to distinguish from moderate Conservatives. Many Labour personalities, including some union heads, resented Callaghan's centrism and rammed through a socialist party platform despite him. The moderate wing of the Labour party split off in 1981 to form a centrist party, the Social Democrats. As we shall consider in Chapter 5, a series of Labour party leaders pushed the party back to the nonideological center, leading to its 1997, 2001, and 2005 electoral victories.

There is and always has been a certain amount of ideology in British politics, but it has usually been balanced with a shrewd practical appreciation that ideology neither wins elections nor effectively governs a country. The ideological flare-up of the 1980s in Britain made it perhaps the most polarized land of West Europe. Ironically, at this same time, French parties, long said to be far more ideological than British parties, moved to the center, where British parties used to cluster.

One aspect of British pragmatism is their "muddling-through" style of problem solving. The British tend not to thoroughly analyze a problem and come up with detailed options or "game plans." They try to "muddle through somehow," improvising as they go. This often works with small problems, but with a big problem, such as the situation in Northern Ireland, it amounts to a nonsolution.

TRADITIONS AND SYMBOLS

As noted earlier, British politics keeps traditions. Political usages often follow well-worn paths, observed even by left-wing Labourites, who, whether they recognize it or not, subscribe to Burke's idea of keeping the forms but changing the contents. As Burke saw, traditions and symbols contribute to society's stability and continuity; people feel disoriented without them.

The typical British man or woman likes traditions and symbols. Although some Britons wince at the tabloid lifestyle of the younger generation of "royals," only a minority would abolish the monarchy in favor of a republic with a president. Parades with golden coaches and horsemen in red tunics are not just for tourists—although they help Britain's economy—they also serve to deepen British feelings about the rightness of the system.

Traditions can also tame political radicals. Once they win seats in Commons, radicals find themselves playing according to the established parliamentary usages. "Well, it simply is not done, old boy," is the standard lesson taught to newcomers in Parliament. The radicals may still have radical views, but they voice them within traditional bounds.

LEGITIMACY AND AUTHORITY

Legitimacy is a feeling of rightness about the political system. As we noted in Chapter 1, it originally meant the right king was on the throne, not a usurper. As used by political scientists, it refers to public attitudes that the government's rule is rightful. Legitimacy is a feeling among the people; it is not the same as "legal." When a political system enjoys high legitimacy, people generally obey it. They will even do things they do not want to, such as paying their income taxes.

Legitimacy is closely related to **authority**, obeying duly constituted officials. British legitimacy and authority were famous, but they were exaggerated and oversold. British policemen did not carry guns and had good relations with the people on their beat. Political scientists used to cite such points to illustrate Britain's nonviolent qualities. During the 1970s, however, Britain turned more violent. The **Irish Republican Army** (IRA) spread their murderous tactics from Ulster, planting bombs that killed dozens. In 1984, one bomb blew up near Prime Minister Thatcher. Criminals started using handguns. In Britain's inner cities, relations between police and youths, especially black youths, grew hateful and contributed to urban riots (which, nonetheless, cost very few lives). A few British policemen now carry guns and riot gear, a symbol of the erosion of legitimacy and authority in Britain.

THE ULSTER ULCER

While we can say Britons on the whole still have attitudes of civility, pragmatism, legitimacy, respect for authority, and nonviolence, we must also note Northern Ireland (sometimes called Ulster) as a massive exception. Northern Ireland illustrates how a system that works amid widespread legitimacy fails when it is lacking. Unlike the rest of Britain, Ulster is a split society, more like those of Latin Europe—France, Spain, and Italy—where part of the population sees the government as illegitimate.

The Ulster problem has its roots in the eight centuries England ruled Ireland, at times treating the Irish as subhuman, seizing their land, deporting them, even outlawing the Catholic faith. In the 1846–1854 Potato Famine a million Irish starved to death while the English, with plentiful food stocks, watched. (An example of what happens when you make too many babies, admonished English **Malthusians**.) At that time about a million and a half Irish emigrated, most to the United States. The Irish problem was the great issue of nineteenth-century British politics, "the damnable question" of whether to keep it firmly under British control or grant it **home rule**.

KEY TERMS

authority   Political leaders' ability to be obeyed.

Irish Republican Army   Anti-British terrorists who seek unification of all Ireland.

Malthusian   View that population growth outstrips food.

home rule   Giving region some autonomy to govern itself.

POLITICAL CULTURE

THE IRA: BALLOTS AND BULLETS

The Irish Republican Army (IRA) is illegal in both Eire and Northern Ireland, but its political arm, Sinn Fein (pronounced *shin fain,* meaning "We Ourselves") is not. Many Northern Irish Catholics vote for Sinn Fein candidates—five were elected to Parliament in 2005—but these candidates do not actually take their Westminster seats (because then they would have to take an oath to the British queen). Sinn Fein leader Gerry Adams denies belonging to the IRA but did not condemn its violence. He now urges peace and can "envisage a future without the IRA," but still calls Queen Elizabeth "Mrs. Windsor."

In 1981 Ulster's Catholics elected Bobby Sands, an imprisoned IRA gunman, who starved himself to death in a hunger strike. The fact that so many men and women of Ulster are willing to vote for an extremist party indicates the depth of hatred and the difficulty of compromise.

In the spring of 1916, while the English were hard-pressed in World War I, the "Irish Volunteers" used guerrilla warfare in the Easter Rising in an attempt to win freedom for Ireland. (In 1919, they renamed themselves the IRA.) By 1922, after brutally crushing the uprising, the British had had enough; Ireland became a *free state* of the British Commonwealth. In 1949, the bulk of Ireland ended this free-state status and became sovereign **Eire**.

But this sovereignty did not solve the Ulster problem; a majority of the 1.5 million people in these six northern counties are fiercely Protestant (descended from seventeenth-century Scottish immigrants), and they are determined to remain part of Britain. For years these **Orangemen** treated the Irish Catholics as a different race, discriminated against them, and feared that they had "popish" plots to bring Northern Ireland into the Catholic-dominated Irish Republic to the south. In control of Ulster's local government, Protestants shortchanged the Irish Catholic minority in jobs, housing, and political power. For many years, most Irish Catholics did not even have the right to vote for the Ulster legislature.

KEY TERMS

Eire   Republic of Ireland.

Orangemen   After King William of Orange (symbol of Netherlands royal house), Northern Irish Protestants.

In 1968 the Irish Catholic protests started, and they were initially modeled on the peaceful U.S. civil-rights marches. Eventually, however, Catholic *nationalists* or *republicans*, who sought to join the Republic of Ireland, began to battle with Protestant *loyalists* or *unionists*, who insisted that Northern Ireland should stay a part of Britain. A *provisional* wing of the IRA enrolled Catholic gunmen, and Protestant counterparts reciprocated. Murder became nearly random. Over 3,600 were killed—including MPs, Earl Mountbatten, and British soldiers, but mostly innocent civilians—and for some years the United Kingdom was the most violent nation in West Europe. Most Ulstermen welcomed a 1998 power-sharing agreement. Violence largely ended, but mistrust remains (see Chapter 6).

A CHANGING POLITICAL CULTURE

We are attempting here to put British political culture into perspective. Britons are neither angels nor devils. Political scientists used to present Britain as a model of stability, moderation, calm, justice, niceness, and civility. In contrast, France was often presented as a model of instability and immoderate political attitudes. The contrast was overdrawn; neither the British nor the French are as good or as bad as they are sometimes portrayed.

Observations of a country's political culture can err in two ways. First, if you are favorably disposed toward a country—and Americans are great **anglophiles** (while many are **francophobes**)—you may tend to overlook some of the nasty things lurking under the surface or dismiss them as aberrations. For years American textbooks on British politics ignored or played down the violence in Northern Ireland. Such "incivility" seemed too un-British to mention. Riots in impoverished parts of British inner cities caught many observers by surprise.

Second, studies of political culture are carried out during particular times, and things change. The data for Almond and Verba's *Civic Culture* (see box on page 13) were collected in 1959 and 1960. Their composite portrait of Britain as a "deferential civic culture" has not been valid for decades. Since World War II, Britain has undergone trying times, especially in the area of economics. These times did not erase British culture wholesale; they simply made manifest what had been latent. Political attitudes change; they can get nastier or better.

KEY TERMS

anglophile   Someone who loves England and the English.
francophobe   Someone who dislikes France and the French.

Key Terms

anglophile (p. 68)
authority (p. 66)
center-peaked (p. 64)
center-periphery tension (p. 62)
center-seeking (p. 64)
civility (p. 62)
class voting (p. 59)
deferential (p. 61)
Eire (p. 67)
Establishment, the (p. 61)
francophobe (p. 68)
heckling (p. 63)
home rule (p. 66)
hooliganism (p. 63)
Irish Republican Army (p. 66)

Malthusian (p. 66)
meritocracy (p. 57)
middle class (p. 56)
objective (p. 56)
old boy (p. 57)
Orangemen (p. 67)
Oxbridge (p. 58)
periphery (p. 62)
public school (p. 57)
Rhodes scholarship (p. 59)
social class (p. 56)
solidarity (p. 57)
subjective (p. 56)
working class (p. 56)

Further Reference

Adams, Ian. *Ideology and Politics in Britain Today*. New York: St. Martin's, 1998.

Adonis, Andrew, and Stephen Pollard. *A Class Act: The Myth of Britain's Classless Society*. London: Hamish Hamilton, 1997.

Curtice, John, Katarina Thomson, Lindsey Jarvis, Catharine Bromley, and Nina Stratford. *British Social Attitudes: Public Policy, Social Ties*. Thousand Oaks, CA: Sage, 2002.

Dahrendorf, Ralf. *On Britain*. Chicago, IL: University of Chicago Press, 1982.

Field, William H. *Regional Dynamics: The Basis of Electoral Support in Britain*. Portland, OR: F. Cass, 1997.

Madgwick, Peter, and Richard Rose, eds. *The Territorial Dimension in United Kingdom Politics*. Atlantic Highlands, NJ: Humanities Press, 1982.

Miller, William, L., Annis May Timpson, and Michael Lessnoff. *Political Culture in Contemporary Britain: People and Politicians, Principles and Practice*. New York: Oxford University Press, 1996.

Mitchell, Paul, and Rick Wilford, eds. *Politics in Northern Ireland*. Boulder, CO: Westview, 1999.

Parry, Geraint, George Moyser, and Neil Day. *Political Participation and Democracy in Britain*. New York: Cambridge University Press, 1991.

Rose, Richard, and Ian McAllister. *The Loyalties of Voters: A Lifetime Learning Model*. Newbury Park, CA: Sage, 1990.

Ruane, Joseph, and Jennifer Todd. *The Dynamics of Conflict in Northern Ireland.* New York: Cambridge University Press, 1996.

Townshend, Charles. *Making the Peace: Public Order and Public Security.* New York: Oxford University Press, 1993.

Wald, Kenneth D. *Crosses on the Ballot: Patterns of British Voter Alignment since 1885.* Princeton, NJ: Princeton University Press, 1983.

5

Britain:
Patterns of Interaction

In Britain, as in most democratic countries, the relationship between people and political parties is complex, a two-way street in which each influences the other. The parties project something called **party image**, what people think of the party's policies, leaders, and ideology. Most voters, on the other hand, carry in their heads a **party identification**, a long-term tendency to think of themselves as "Tory" or "Democrat" or whatever. The strategy of intelligent party leadership is to project a party image that wins the loyalty of large numbers of voters and gets them to identify permanently with that party. If they can do this, the party prospers and wins many elections.

Both party image and party identification are reasonably clear in Britain: Most Britons recognize what the main parties stand for in general terms, and most identify with a party. The situation is never static, however, for the parties constantly change the images they project, and some voters lose their party identification and shift their votes.

In every country, parents contribute heavily to their children's party identification. In Britain, if both parents are of the same party, most of their children first identify with that party, although this may later erode as young people develop their own perspectives. By the same token, party images are rather clear, and most Britons are able to see differences between their two largest parties: Labour aiming at helping people through social and educational reforms, and Conservatives aiming at economic growth through hard work with little state intervention.

Questions to Consider

1. What is party image? Party identification?

2. What is a "safe seat" and how do you get one?

3. Who names British candidates?

4. What did Tony Blair call his party? What did it mean?

5. Why do the Liberal Democrats have such an uphill struggle?

6. How did Thatcher differ from a traditional Tory?

7. What is the big British labor confederation? How big?

8. Where and what is the Question Hour?

9. How democratic is Britain? As much as the United States?

KEY TERMS

party image Electorate's perception of a given party.

party identification Psychological attachment of voter to political party.

For confirmed Labour or Conservative voters—those whose party identification closely matches the image of their preferred party—there is little doubt about whom to vote for. Until recently, most British voters were reliably Labour or Conservative. The **swing** vote are those who move their votes among parties, either because their party identification is not strong, or their perceptions of the parties' images shifts, or both. A swing of a few percentage points can determine who will form the next government, for if each constituency shifts a little one way, say, toward Labour, the Labour candidate will win in many constituencies. Single-member districts often exaggerate percentage trends and turn them into large majorities of **seats**.

The game of British electoral politics consists of the parties trying to mobilize all of their party identifiers—that is, making sure their people bother to vote—plus winning over the uncommitted swing vote. In 1970 the Labour government of Harold Wilson suffered a surprise defeat by the Conservatives under Edward Heath. Labour identifiers had not suddenly switched parties; rather, some were unhappy with Wilson's policies and did not vote.

National and Local Party

Political scientists used to describe the British national party—Conservative or Labour—as nearly all-powerful, able to dictate to local party organizations whom to nominate for Parliament. As usual, though, when you look more closely you find that things are more complicated.

The name of the game for parliamentary candidates is the **safe seat** and getting adopted by the local **constituency** organization to run for it. Party leaders are normally assigned very safe seats, for it is highly embarrassing if one of them loses his or her seat in the Commons. About 450 (of 646) seats are usually considered safe. There is a bargaining relationship between the parties' London headquarters and the local constituency party. The local party often requests lists of possible candidates from headquarters, settles on one, and then gets it approved by the central headquarters. Unlike the U.S. system, there is both national and local input into British candidate selection with a veto on both sides.

Some constituency organizations insist that a candidate actually live in the district. Americans expect all candidates to be from the district they represent; those who are not are called **carpetbaggers** and have an uphill battle. Most countries, however, including Britain, impose no such requirements, although being a local person can help. Some British constituencies like their people to establish a residence there once they have won. But many constituencies do not insist that their MP actually live there; after all, the MP's job is mainly in London, and periodic visits are sufficient for him or her to hear complaints and maintain ties with electors. Besides, in Britain, party is more important than personality.

Key Terms

swing Voters who change party from one election to next.

seat Membership in a legislature.

safe seat Constituency where voting has long favored a given party.

constituency The district or population that elects a legislator.

carpetbagger In U.S. usage, candidate from outside the constituency.

DEMOCRACY

2005: LABOUR SQUEAKS THROUGH

In the May 2005 **general election**, after eight years in office, Britain's Labour party won a third term, the first time Labour had done that. Its vote dropped from 41 percent in 2001 to 35 percent, but Labour still won a majority of Commons' 646 seats. Remember, Britain's electoral system overrepresents the winning party, just as in the United States. As usual for Britain, 2005 gave Labour only a plurality of the votes cast; since 1935 no British party has scored an actual majority. Turnout was a weak 61.3 percent (but higher than 59.4 percent in 2001).

The Conservatives gained a little in the popular vote and moved up from 25 percent of the seats to 30 percent. The Liberal Democrats gained, too, but were still underrepresented because their voters are territorially dispersed. The rest of the vote, 10.5 percent, was scattered among small, mostly regional parties. Scottish, Welsh, and Northern Irish parties won a few seats each.

Labour won again because the British economy was excellent. Many Labour supporters, however, detested Blair ("Bush's poodle") for supporting President Bush in the Iraq War and voted Lib Dem. The Tories could not use this issue because they also supported U.S. policy on Iraq. The third Tory chief in four years, Michael Howard, made anti-immigration the Conservatives' big issue, but it never caught fire. Howard resigned after the 2005 elections, and the Conservatives remained divided and unfocused.

	% Votes		Seats	
	2005	*2001*	*2005*	*2001*
Labour	35.2	40.7	356 (55%)	413 (63%)
Conservative	32.3	31.7	197 (30%)	166 (25%)
Liberal Democrat	22.0	18.3	62 (10%)	52 (8%)

In any given House of Commons, probably a minority of MPs are natives of the constituency they represent.

What about the unsafe seats, those where the other party usually wins? These are the testing grounds for energetic newcomers to politics. The Conservative or Labour **central offices** in London may send a promising beginner to a constituency organization that knows it cannot win. Again, the local unit must approve the candidate. Even if the candidate loses, his or her energy and ability are carefully watched—by measuring how much better the candidate did than the previous one—and promising comers are marked. For the next election, the London headquarters may offer the candidate a safer constituency, one where he or she stands a better chance. Finally, the candidate either wins an election in a contested constituency, is adopted by a safe constituency, or bows out of politics. Many of Britain's top politicians, including several prime ministers (Blair among them), lost their first races and were transferred to other constituencies. There is no stigma attached; it is normal, part of the training and testing of a British politician.

POLITICS WITHIN THE PARTIES

British political parties, like British cabinets, are balancing acts. A party leader must neither pay too much attention to his or her party's factions nor totally ignore them. In constructing their policies, leaders usually try to give various factions a say but keep the whole thing under moderate control with an eye to winning the next election.

Party leaders must balance between sometimes extremist party militants and a generally moderate voting public. If a party takes too firm an ideological stand—too left in the case of Labour or too right in the Conservative case—it costs the party votes. Thus party leaders tend to hedge and moderate their positions, trying to please both the true believers within their party and the general electorate. If they slip in this balancing act, they can lose either party members or voters or both. When Labour veered left in the 1980s and the Conservatives followed their hard-right Thatcher course, the centrist Liberal Democratic Alliance (later turned into a party) won a quarter of the 1983 vote, a warning to both major parties.

Although long described as ideologically moderate, both the British Labour and Conservative parties have important ideological viewpoints within their ranks. The Labour party is divided into "left" and "right" wings. The Labour left, springing from a tradition of militant trade unionism and intellectual radicalism, wants nationalization of industry, the dismantling of "public" schools, higher taxes on the rich, and leaving the European Union. Most Labourites opposed their own leader, Blair, on Iraq. The Labour right, on the other hand, is moderate and centrist. It favors some of the welfarist approach of Continental social-democratic parties, such as the German SPD, but now wants no government takeovers of industry or higher taxes. It is pro-Europe and pro-American, although skeptical about the war in Iraq. With Tony Blair, the Labour right won, and in the 1997 election Blair called his party **New Labour**, friendly to business, growth, and political reform. Such a victory is never permanent, though, and the Labour party could dump Blair over Iraq.

As an amorphous party proud of its pragmatism, Conservatives were long thought immune to ideological controversy or factional viewpoints. This is not completely true, for the Tories comprise two broad streams of thought, which we might label as traditional and Thatcherite tendencies. The former is not a U.S.-style conservative, advocating a totally free economy with no government intervention. Instead, the **traditional Tory** wants a

KEY TERMS

New Labour   Tony Blair's name for his very moderate Labour party.
traditional Tory   Moderate or centrist Conservative, not Thatcherite.

DEMOCRACY

THE STRUGGLE OF THE LIBERAL DEMOCRATS

Public-opinion polls at times suggest that the new Liberal Democratic party could become Britain's second-largest party. But what Britons tell pollsters and how they vote are two different things; they speak more radically than they vote. Still, widespread disillusionment with the two large parties could give the Liberal Democrats a chance for major-party status.

The Liberal Democrats were born of the 1988 merger of the old Liberal party and the small, new Social Democratic party that in 1981 had broken away from Labour. The two strands did not see eye-to-eye. On many questions—especially on the economy and defense matters—the Social Democrats were more conservative than the Liberals. The Liberals tended to be ultra-liberal on questions of gay rights and open immigration. They wanted Britain out of NATO and free of nuclear weapons. True to their origins in the right wing of the Labour party, the Social Democrats were not unilateral disarmers and felt that lifestyle questions cost the party votes. The new party is a parallel to the many and incoherent viewpoints of the U.S. Democratic party.

The British electoral system—single-member districts with plurality win—is brutal on third parties (just as it is in the United States), especially those like the Liberal Democrats that are territorially dispersed. This discourages potential voters, who do not want to waste their votes on a party they fear will never be in power. The Liberal Democrats' great hope is to bring to Britain some elements of a proportional-representation election system.

party that takes everybody's interests into account, plus traditional ways of doing things, and under the guidance of people born and bred to lead. This has been called a "one-nation" Tory.

The **Thatcherite** wing (which traces back to nineteenth-century liberalism and is called **neoliberalism** in Europe) is like American conservativism: They want to roll back government and free the economy. After World War II this view crept into the Conservative party and, with the 1975 elevation of Margaret Thatcher to party chief, moved to the forefront. Under Thatcher, the traditional Tories were dubbed **wets**, the militant Thatcherites **dries**. (The terms were taken from boarding-school slang. "Wets" are frightened little boys who wet their pants; "dries" are strong and brave lads who do not.)

KEY TERMS

Thatcherite   Free-market, anti-welfarist ideology of former British Prime Minister Margaret Thatcher.

neoliberalism   Revival of free-market economics, exemplified by Margaret Thatcher.

wets   In Thatcher's usage, Tories too timid to apply her militant neoliberalism.

dries   In Thatcher's usage, Tories who shared her neoliberal vision.

DEMOCRACY

SAVING LABOUR FROM THE UNIONS

From its 1983 electoral disaster, the Labour party struggled to recover. Part of its problem was a too-left party image. Another part was its doddering and ineffective leader, Michael Foot. At its annual conference that fall, the Labour party tried to repair both areas by overwhelmingly choosing as its new leader Neil Kinnock, a silver-tongued Welshman as charming as Margaret Thatcher was aloof. At forty-one, Kinnock, son of a coal miner, was the youngest Labour leader ever. Kinnock first had to curb Labour extremists; he got the Trotskyist Militant Tendency faction expelled (it formed a miniparty). Kinnock did well, lifting Labour from 27.6 percent of the popular vote in 1983 to 35.2 percent in 1992. But he came across as too slick and was still hurt by the Tory charge that Labour was dominated by the unions. Labour indeed was founded by and heavily based on trade unions, some led by militant socialists who would rather lose elections than lose their principles.

Following Labour's fourth defeat in a row in 1992, Kinnock resigned, making way for John Smith, a fifty-three-year-old Scottish lawyer even more pragmatic than Kinnock. Smith, a wooden speaker with little **charisma**, set out to reorient Labour more to the middle than to the working class. Higher taxes and public ownership were out; discipline in education was in. But Smith had to break the union hold on the Labour party. Many union leaders resisted; they liked being able to control—through the proxy votes of millions of union members—90 percent of the vote at Labour's annual conferences. This union domination, often with a strong leftist slant, rendered Labour unacceptable to most British voters. In 1993, Smith got a change in Labour's rules to return the candidate selection process back to local party organizations; unions now control less than half the conference votes. In 1994 Smith died of a heart attack.

Tony Blair then took on the unions and got the party to drop its Clause Four, part of its constitution since 1918, that called for the "common ownership of the means of production," in other words, socialism. With Blair's very moderate 1996 manifesto, Labour—now called "New Labour"—started looking a lot like the U.S. Democrats. Although union and leftist militants dislike Blair, Labour's membership and electoral support climbed until it won three elections in a row, 1997, 2001, and 2005. It was not just Blair's doing, though; the process of pushing Labour back to the center had been underway since Kinnock began it in 1983.

The trouble here is that some old-style British Conservatives find total capitalism almost as threatening as socialism. As industries went bankrupt in record number, Thatcher faced a revolt of Tory "wets" against her "dry" policies. After Major took over, Thatcherite MPs sought to dump him. Attitudes toward European unity still split the Tories. Thatcher favored the Common Market but opposed turning it into a European Union

KEY TERM

charisma   (pronounced "kar-isma"; Greek for gift) political drawing power.

that infringed on British sovereignty. She and followers were dubbed **Eurosceptics**. Major and his followers were enthusiastically pro-Europe—**Euroenthusiasts**—including the 1992 Maastricht Treaty, which took European unity a big step forward. Tory chief Michael Howard, a Eurosceptic, had trouble leading a party split between forward-looking "modernizers" and backward-looking "traditionalists," and he could be dumped, as several of his predecessors were. As Labour did in the 1980s and 1990s, now the Tories must shed their image as the "nasty party" in favor of a centrist one with new ideas.

PARTIES AND INTEREST GROUPS

What politicians say and what they deliver are two different things. Politicians speak to different audiences. To party rank and file they affirm party gospel (championing either the welfare state or free enterprise, as the case may be). To the electorate as a whole they usually tone down their ideological statements and offer vague slogans, such as "Stability and prosperity," or "Time for a change." But quietly, usually behind the scenes, politicians are also striking important deals with influential interest groups representing industry, commerce, professions, and labor. About half of the British electorate belong to at least one interest group.

Some 25 percent of the British work force is unionized, down from 55 percent when Thatcher took office but still a much higher percentage than in the United States or France (but only half that of Sweden). Labor unions are constituent members of the Labour party and, until recently, controlled a majority of votes at Labour's annual conference, contributed the most to the party's budgets and campaign funds, and provided grass-roots manpower and organization. Especially important are the views of the head of the **Trades Union Congress** (TUC). No Labour party leader can totally ignore the wishes of Britain's union leaders.

This opened up Labour to charges that it is run by and for the unions, which earned a reputation as too far left, too powerful, and too ready to strike. To counteract this, both Labour party and union leaders deny union dominance. Indeed, one Labour party campaign tactic is to claim that only the Labour party can control the unions, rather than the other way around. Tony Blair forcefully pointed out to union chiefs the folly of losing one election after another. Ironically, Blair's Thatcherite economic policies pushed some British unions back into militancy. Blair partially broke the close association of labor federation to social-democratic party that had been the norm for the industrialized countries of Northern Europe and is still the case in Germany.

Dozens of union members sit as Labour MPs in Parliament; dozens more MPs are beholden to local unions for their election. This union bloc inside the Labour party can force a Labour government to moderate measures that might harm unions. At times, however, Labour party chiefs have made union leaders back down, explaining to them that if the

KEY TERMS

Eurosceptic   Does not wish to strengthen EU at expense of national sovereignty.

Euroenthusiast   Likes EU and wishes to strengthen it.

Trades Union Congress   British labor federation, equivalent to the U.S. AFL-CIO.

unions get too much, the Labour party will lose elections. To reiterate, to be a party leader means performing a balancing act among several forces.

MPs known to directly represent special interests—an **interested member**—are not limited to the Labour side. Numerous Tory MPs are interested members for various industries and do not try to hide it. When the connection is concealed or when money changes hands, an MP pushing for favors to a group becomes known as sleazy. The **sleaze factor** hurt the Tories under Major, but several Labourites under Blair got caught accepting money from questionable sources; some resigned. Politicians taking money on the side are found everywhere, in all parties.

The Conservative counterpart of the TUC is the influential **Confederation of British Industry** (CBI), formed by an amalgamation of three smaller groups in 1965. The CBI speaks for most British employers but has no formal links to the Conservative party, even though their views are often parallel. The CBI was delighted at Thatcher's antinationalization policies, although British industrialists gulped when they found this meant withdrawal of **subsidies** to their own industries. Thatcher could not totally ignore them, for CBI members and money support the Tories, and dozens of CBI-affiliated company directors occupy Conservative seats in Commons.

THE PARTIES FACE EACH OTHER

There are two ways of looking at British elections. The first is to see them as three- to four-week campaigns coming once every few years, each a model of brevity and efficiency, especially compared to the long, expensive U.S. campaigns. Another way, however, is to see them as nearly permanent campaigns that begin the day a new Parliament reconvenes after the latest balloting. The formal campaign may be only a few weeks, but long before then the opposition party is planning how to oust the current government.

The chief arena for this is the House of Commons. Unlike the U.S. Congress, British parliamentarians are seldom animated by a spirit of bipartisanship. The duty of the opposition is to oppose, and this they do by accusing the government of everything from incompetence and corruption to sexual **scandal**. The great weapon here is embarrassment, making a cabinet minister look like a fool. The time for this is the **Question Hour**, held Monday through Thursday when Commons opens. By tradition, this hour is reserved for MPs to aim written questions at cabinet ministers, who are on the front bench on a rotating basis. Most Thursdays might be the turn of the education secretary, for example. The PM is usually there once a week, along with most of the cabinet. Each written question can be followed up by supplementary oral questions. The opposition tries to push a minister into

POLITICAL CULTURE

THE PROFUMO SCANDAL

In Commons' game of embarrassment, a classic play came with the 1963 Profumo affair. The Labour opposition got wind that Tory War Minister (at the departmental, not the cabinet, level) John Profumo was dating a party girl who at the same time was dating the Soviet naval attaché, a known spy. Questioned by Labour in the Commons, Profumo swore there had been no impropriety in his relationship with Christine Keeler and threatened to sue anyone who said otherwise. Being a gentleman of impeccable credentials—Harrow, Oxford, army brigadier—Profumo was believed by the Macmillan government. But the scandal refused to die down; it began to appear that security had been breached and that Profumo had been set up for blackmail.

Sensational news stories charged the Conservative government with laxity on national security, covering up for one of its "old boys," and debauchery at the highest levels of the Establishment. There was some truth to the charges, and Profumo resigned in shame. It was not, however, the shame of a married man, forty-eight, caught with a twenty-one-year-old call girl. That was forgivable. What was unforgivable in British political culture was that a gentleman had lied to Parliament. The Tory government mishandled the incident; Conservative MPs lost confidence in Prime Minister Macmillan, and voters lost confidence in the Conservative party, which was voted out the following year.

---

an awkward position where he or she has to tell a lie, fluff an answer, or break into anger. Then the opposition, in effect, smirks, "You see, they are not fit to govern."

THE CABINET AND THE CIVIL SERVANTS

As we discussed earlier, British cabinet ministers are generalists, not specialists, and are chosen more for political reasons than for any special ability to run their departments. Who then does run them? The nominal head of each British department is the minister; he or she represents that ministry in cabinet discussions and defends it in Commons. But the minister does not run the department; civil servants do.

Ministers come and go every few years; the highest civil servants, known as **permanent secretaries** are there much longer. The permanent secretary often has an edge on his or her minister in social and economic terms as well. Most permanent secretaries are knighted later in life while few ministers are. Although **knighthood** is now purely honorific in Britain, it still conveys social superiority. Permanent secretaries earn more than ministers, in some

KEY TERMS

permanent secretary   Highest civil servant who runs a ministry, nominally under a minister.

knighthood   Lowest rank of nobility, carries title "Sir."

cases nearly twice as much. Ministers find it nearly impossible to fire or transfer permanent secretaries, who have a say in determining who will replace them when they retire or
leave for lush positions in private industry; they tend to be a self-selecting elite. Permanent
secretaries always play the role of humble, obedient servants, but some ministers come to
wonder just who the boss really is.

The permanent secretary is assisted by several deputy secretaries who in turn are supported by undersecretaries and assistant secretaries. These names look like those of an
American department, but there is a major catch: In most U.S. departments, all or most
of these people are political appointees, serving at the pleasure of the president and re-
signing when a new president takes office. In Britain, only the ministers assisted by some
junior ministers—about a hundred persons in all—change with a new government. What
in America are temporary political appointees are permanent officials in Britain.

This gives them power. They are not amateurs but know their ministry—its personnel,
problems, interests, and budget. Knowledge is power, and over time top civil servants come
to quietly exercise a lot of it. While permanent secretaries or their assistants never—well,
hardly ever—go public with their viewpoints, they reveal them through the kinds of ideas,
programs, bills, and budgets they submit to the minister, their nominal boss. The minister
theoretically commands them, but in practice he or she simply does not know enough about
the workings of the ministry. Instead, the minister relies on them. Accordingly, while most
bills and budget proposals pass through the cabinet, they do not originate there. The permanent civil servants do the jobs that are the stuff of governance.

The real power among the many British ministries is the **Treasury**. Sometimes called
the "department of departments," Treasury not only supervises the main lines of economic policy but has the last word on who gets what among the ministries. Anyone with a
bright idea in British government—a new minister or an innovative civil servant—soon
comes up against the stone wall of Treasury, the ministry that says "no."

Britain's treasury minister goes by the old name of Chancellor of the Exchequer—originally the king's checker of taxes—and is now the second most powerful figure in the cabinet, the first being the prime minister. Some Chancellors of the Exchequer later become
prime ministers, likely to be the case with the popular and effective Gordon Brown.

Under the Chancellor are the usual secretaries and civil servants, but they are a breed
unto themselves, smarter and more powerful than other bureaucrats. Operating on a team-
spirit basis, Treasury chaps trust only other Treasury chaps, for only Treasury can see the
whole picture of the British government and economy and how the many parts interre-
late. The other departments see only their corner, hence they should not be heeded. This
attitude gives Treasury and its people an image of cold, callous remoteness, "government
by mandarins"—but no one has tried to replace them.

THE CIVIL SERVICE AND INTEREST GROUPS

We mentioned earlier the relationship between interest groups and political parties. But this
is only one way interest groups make their voices heard and is often not the most important way. Much interest-group impact is in their quiet, behind-the-scenes contact with the

DEMOCRACY

HOW DEMOCRATIC IS BRITAIN?

The power of bureaucrats brings us to a fine irony. In centuries of British political evolution, we have seen how Britons marched toward democracy by first limiting the power of the monarch and then expanding participation. If we look closely, though, we notice that much important decision making is only partly democratically controlled. Civil servants make much policy with no democratic input.

Does this mean there is no real democracy in Britain? No, it means we must understand that no country exercises perfect control over its bureaucracy and that parties and elections are only attempts to do so.

Indeed, most of the interactions we have talked about are not under any form of popular control. Ideological infighting, the influence of interest groups on parties and the bureaucracy, the relationship of top civil servants with ministers, the granting of titles—these and other interactions are removed from democratic control. The people do not even choose whom they get to vote for; that is a matter for party influentials. All the people get to do is vote every few years, and the choice is limited.

Again, does this mean there is no democracy in Britain? No, not at all. Some people have an exaggerated vision of democracy as a system in which everyone gets to decide on everything. Such a system never existed at the national level, nor could it. The most we can ask of a democracy is that the leading team—in Britain, the prime minister and cabinet—are held accountable periodically in elections. This keeps them on their toes and anxious to pay attention to the public good, holds down special favors and corruption, and makes sure the bureaucracy functions. It is in the fear of electoral punishment that Britain, or any other country, qualifies as a democracy. What the great Carl J. Friedrich called the **rule of anticipated reactions** keeps the governors attentive. We will learn not to expect much more of political systems.

bureaucracy. Indeed, with Parliament's role curtailed as a result of powerful prime ministers and party discipline, and cabinet ministers themselves dependent on permanent civil servants, many interest groups ask themselves, "Why bother with Parliament? Why not go straight to where the action is, the bureaucracy?"

This approach is especially true of business and industry; the major effort of the unions is still focused on the Labour party. The reason for this is partly in the nature of what trade unions want as opposed to what business groups want. Unions want general policies on employment, wages, welfare, and so on, that apply to tens of millions of

KEY TERM

rule of anticipated reactions   Friedrich's theory that politicians plan their moves so as not to anger the public.

POLITICAL CULTURE

THE UTILITY OF DIGNITY

Another quaint British holdover from the past is the monarch's bestowal of an honor such as knight-hood. But more than quaint, it is a payoff system that serves a number of purposes. The granting of titles is a reward and an encouragement to retire, opening positions to fresh, energetic, younger people. A person looking forward to a knighthood (Sir) or a **peerage** (Lord) is more likely to go quietly. These honors also civilize recipients; even militant union leaders and rapacious businessmen start talking philosophically about the common good once they have impressive titles in front of their names.

The queen awards some 3,000 of these and other distinctions annually on the advice of the prime minister, who has a small staff that watches for meritorious civil servants, business people, union-ists, soldiers, politicians, scholars, artists, and writers, and recommends who should get what. In ad-dition to becoming knights and peers, distinguished Britons may be named to the Order of the British Empire, Order of the Garter, Order of Merit, Order of the Bath, the Royal Victorian Order, and many others. The granting of honors is part of British political culture and bolsters loyalty to and cooper-ation with the system.

people. Industry usually wants specific, narrow rulings on taxes, subsidies, regulations, and the like that apply to a few firms. Thus unions tend to battle in the more open environment of party policy while business groups often prefer to quietly take a government official to lunch.

In working closely with a branch of Britain's economic life, a given ministry comes to see itself not as an impartial administrator but as a concerned and attentive helper. After all, if that industry falters, it reflects on the government agency assigned to supervise it. In this manner civil servants come to see leaders of economic interest groups as their "clients" and to reflect their clients' views. When this happens—and it happens in every country—the industry is said to have "captured" or "colonized" the executive department.

Reinforcing this pattern is the interchange between civil service and private industry. A permanent secretary can make much more money in business than in Whitehall; every now and then one of them leaves government service for greener pastures. (We also find this pattern in France and Japan.) By the same token, business executives are sometimes brought into high administrative positions on the dubious theory that if they can run a company well, they can do the same for government. The point is that cozy relationships develop between civil servants and private business.

KEY TERM

peerage   A Lord or Lady, higher than knighthood.

KEY TERMS

carpetbagger (p. 72)

central office (p. 73)

charisma (p. 76)

Confederation of British Industry (p. 78)

constituency (p. 72)

dries (p. 75)

Euroenthusiast (p. 77)

Eurosceptic (p. 77)

general election (p. 73)

interested member (p. 78)

knighthood (p. 79)

neoliberalism (p. 75)

New Labor (p. 74)

party identification (p. 71)

party image (p. 71)

peerage (p. 82)

permanent secretary (p. 79)

Question Hour (p. 78)

rule of anticipated reactions (p. 81)

safe seat (p. 72)

scandal (p. 78)

seat (p. 72)

sleaze factor (p. 78)

subsidy (p. 78)

swing (p. 72)

Thatcherite (p. 75)

Trades Union Congress (p. 77)

traditional Tory (p. 74)

Treasury (p. 80)

wets (p. 75)

FURTHER REFERENCE

Barberis, Peter. *The Elite of the Elite: Permanent Secretaries in the British Higher Civil Service*. Brookfield, VT: Ashgate, 1996.

Bartle, John, and Anthony King, eds. *Britain at the Polls, 2005*. Washington, D.C.: CQ Press, 2005.

Bevir, Mark, and R. A. W. Rhodes. *Interpreting British Governance*. New York: Routledge, 2003.

Brivati, Brian, and Richard Heffernan, eds. *The Labour Party: A Centenary History*. New York: St. Martin's, 2000.

Butler, David, and Dennis Kavanagh. *The British General Election of 2001*. New York: Palgrave, 2002.

Dunleavy, Patrick, Andrew Gamble, Richard Heffernan, and Ian Holliday. *Developments in British Politics 6*. New York: Palgrave, 2002.

Geddes, Andrew, and Jonathan Tonge, eds. *Labour's Second Landslide: The British General Election 2001*. New York: Palgrave, 2002.

Kelly, Richard, ed. *Changing Party Policy in Britain: An Introduction*. Malden, MA: Blackwell, 1999.

McKinstry, Leo. *Fit to Govern*. London: Bantam Press, 1996.

McLean, Iain. *Rational Choice and British Politics: An Analysis of Rhetoric and Manipulation from Peel to Blair*. New York: Oxford, 2001.

Reitan, Earl A. *Tory Radicalism: Margaret Thatcher, John Major, and the Transformation of Modern Britain, 1979–1997*. Lanham, MD: Rowman & Littlefield, 1997.

Seyd, Patrick, and Paul Whiteley. *New Labour's Grassroots: The Transformation of the Labour Party Membership*. New York: Palgrave, 2002.

6

What Britons Quarrel About

Britain was in economic decline for decades. At first it was only **relative decline** as the economies of West Europe and Japan grew more rapidly than the British economy. By the 1970s, however, Britain was in **absolute decline** that left people with lower living standards as inflation outstripped wage increases. The first industrial nation was embarrassed to see Italy overtake it in per capita GDP in the 1980s. Likewise, Britain's former colonies of Hong Kong and Singapore have higher per caps than does Britain. In Britain, **deindustrialization** seemed to be taking place; in some years the British GDP shrank. They called it the "British disease," and some Americans feared it was contagious.

THE "BRITISH DISEASE"

Why did Britain decline? There are two basic approaches to such a complex problem. One begins with what happens in people's attitudes—a psycho-cultural approach. The other begins with what happens in the physical world—a politico-economic approach. The two are not mutually exclusive but have a chicken-egg relationship to each other: One feeds into the other.

KEY TERMS

relative decline   Failing to keep up economically with other nations.

absolute decline   Growing weaker economically compared to one's own past.

deindustrialization   Decline of heavy industry.

Questions to Consider

1. What is the difference between relative and absolute decline?
2. What was the Thatcher cure for Britain's economy? Did it work?
3. What is the Beer thesis on Britain's decline?
4. What is productivity and why is it so important?
5. In what areas could Britain undergo constitutional reform?
6. Did Britain's National Health Service work? Compared to U.S.?
7. What is devolution? Does it indicate quasi-federalism?
8. Did Northern Ireland return to peace? Why or why not?
9. What is Britain's stance on the European Union? On the euro?

Some emphasize British nonwork attitudes as the root of the problem. The old aristocracy, which disdained work as tawdry moneymaking, was never thoroughly displaced in Britain. Rather, the rising entrepreneurs aped the old elite and became gentlemen of leisure and culture. In public schools and Oxbridge, young Britons learn to despise commercial and technical skills in favor of the humanities. The emphasis was on having wealth rather than creating it. Accordingly, Britain tended to lack daring and innovative capitalists. Many Britons prefer more leisure time to more money.

The British class system makes matters worse. British managers—mostly middle class—are snobbish toward workers; they do not mix with them and provide inadequate guidance and incentives. British workers react by showing solidarity with their "mates" and more loyalty to their union than to their company. If the psycho-cultural approach is correct, the only way to save Britain is to change British culture, but deep-seated attitudes resist change.

The other approach, the politico-economic, argues that the bad attitudes reflect faulty government policy. Change the policy to create a new context, and attitudes will change. Thatcherites propounded this view, blaming the growth of the welfare state that Labour introduced in 1945. This let many **consume** without **producing** and subsidized inefficient industries. Unions, given free rein by previous governments, raised wages and lowered **productivity**. The growing costs of the welfare state drained away funds that should have gone for investment. Insufficient investment meant insufficient production, which meant stagnating living standards. Cut both welfare benefits and industry subsidies and you will force—with some pain—a change in attitudes, argued Thatcherites.

THE THATCHER CURE

The Thatcher cure for Britain's economic problems is still debated in Britain. Thatcherites argue that her policies were not implemented thoroughly. Anti-Thatcherites in all the parties argue that the policies were brutal and ineffective. The way Thatcherites see it, the permissive policies of both Labour and previous Conservative governments had expanded welfare programs beyond the country's ability to pay for them. Unions won wage increases out of line with productivity. Nationalized and subsidized industries lost money. The result: **inflation** and falling productivity that were making Britain the sick man of Europe. The cure, in part, came from the **monetarist** theory of American economist (and Nobel Prize winner) Milton Friedman, which posits too-rapid growth of the money supply as the cause of inflation. Thatcher cut bureaucracy, the growth of welfare, and subsidies to industry in an effort to control Britain's money supply and restore economic health.

KEY TERMS

consumption   Buying things.

production   Making things.

productivity   Efficiency with which things are made.

inflation   Increase in most prices.

monetarism   Friedman's theory that rate of growth of money supply governs much economic development.

KEY CONCEPTS

"PLURALISTIC STAGNATION"

Harvard political scientist Samuel Beer advanced a provocative thesis on the cause of Britain's decline: too many interest groups making too many demands on parties who are too willing to promise everyone everything. The result was **pluralistic stagnation** as British groups scrambled for welfare benefits, pay hikes, and subsidies for industry. The two main parties bid against each other with promises of more benefits to more groups. In the late 1960s, a strong **counterculture** emerged in Britain, which repudiated traditional civility and deference and made groups' demands more strident. With every group demanding and getting more, no one saw any reason for self-restraint that would leave them behind. Government benefits fed union wage demands, which fed inflation, which fed government benefits . . .

The interesting point about the Beer thesis is that it blamed precisely what political scientists long celebrated as the foundation of freedom and democracy: **pluralism**. Beer demonstrated, though, that it can run amok; groups block each other and government, leading to what Beer called the "paralysis of public choice." Any comparison with your system?

Some Britons wondered if the cure was worse than the disease. Unemployment at one point reached 14 percent of the work force, thousands of firms went bankrupt, and Britain's GDP growth was still anemic. Even moderate Conservatives pleaded for her to relent, but Thatcher was not called the Iron Lady for nothing. "The lady's not for turning," she intoned. She saw the economic difficulties as a purge Britain needed to get well. One of her economists said: "I don't shed tears when I see inefficient factories shut down. I rejoice." Thatcher and her supporters repeated endlessly, "You cannot consume until you produce."

Gradually the argument began to take hold. Many Britons had to admit they had been consuming more than they were producing, that subsidized factories and mines were a drain on the economy, and that bitter medicine was necessary to correct matters. It was almost as if Britons had become guilty about their free rides and knew they now had to pay up. In the 1980s, more working-class Britons voted Tory than voted Labour.

But did Thatchernomics work? By the new millennium the picture was generally positive. Britain became the fourth largest economy in the world. Inflation and unemployment were down and economic growth was better than most of West Europe. State-owned industries that had been nationalized since the war to prevent unemployment were sold

KEY TERMS

pluralistic stagnation   Theory that out-of-control interest groups produce policy logjams.

counterculture   Rejection of conventional values, as in 1960s.

pluralism   Autonomous interaction of social groups on themselves and on government.

A Privatization too Far? Scotland's beautiful Isle of Skye used to be reached by a short ferry ride, but the new, private bridge costs $10 each way. Many Britons protest the new bridge as an example of privatization run amok, turning over a public service to private greed. (Michael Roskin)

off, a process called **privatization**. Competition was increased through **deregulation**. Renters of public housing got the chance to buy their homes at low cost, a move that made some of them Conservatives. Unions eased their wage and other demands, and union membership dropped sharply. Many weak firms went under, but thousands of new small and middle-sized firms sprang up. Capital and labor were channeled away from losing industries and into winners, exactly what a good economic system should do. A California-like computer industry produced a "silicon glen" in Scotland and a "software valley" around Cambridge University.

Part of the impact of Thatchernomics came from jolting workers out of their trade-union complacency ("I'm all right, Jack"). When the government's National Coal Board closed hundreds of unprofitable pits and eliminated twenty thousand jobs, miners staged a long and violent strike in 1984, which was supported by some other unionists. Thatcher would not back down; after a year, the miners did. (At about the same time, President Reagan faced down striking air-traffic controllers.) New legislation limited union chiefs' abilities to call strikes, and the number and length of strikes in Britain dropped drastically.

Just as in the United States under Reagan, income inequality grew in Britain. The number of Britons in families with less than half the average income increased under

KEY TERMS

privatization　Selling state-owned industry to private interests.
deregulation　Cutting governmental rules on industry.

Comparison

The Cost of the Welfare State

The other side of the welfare state is how expensive it is. In the early 2000s, all types of taxes at all levels of government took the following percentages of GDP:

Sweden	53
France	46
Italy	42
Germany	41
Britain	38
Canada	36
Spain	35
Australia	31
United States	29
Japan	28

Source: OECD.

Thatcher and Major from 5 million in 1979 to 14 million in 1993. High youth unemployment led to urban riots. Major regional disparities appeared between a rich, resurgent South of England, with new high-tech industries, and a decaying, abandoned North, where unemployment hit hardest. Thatcher never did get a handle on government spending, much of which, like U.S. **entitlements**, must by law be paid. British welfare benefits actually climbed sharply during the Thatcher and Major years despite their best efforts to trim them. Cutting the welfare state is tempting but rarely successful; too many people have come to depend on its benefits. Furthermore, in the late 1980s, a credit and spending boom kicked inflation back up to over 10 percent, and the economy slumped into **recession**. Competitively, British productivity was low and its wages high, so Britain continued to lose manufacturing jobs to other countries.

Thatcher's main legacy is the changed terms of Britain's political debate. In 1945, Labour had shifted the debate to the welfare state, and Tories had to compete with them

Key Terms

entitlement   Spending programs citizens are automatically entitled to, such as Social Security.
recession   A shrinking economy, indicated by falling GDP.

COMPARISON

THE PRODUCTIVITY RACE

No production, no goodies. Production is what gets turned out. Productivity is how efficiently it gets turned out. You can have a lot of production with low productivity, the Soviet problem that brought down the Communist regime. Among the major economies, Britain's productivity was weak. In 2000, GDP per worker in the United States was 42 percent higher than in Britain, in France 13 percent higher, in Germany 7 percent higher, and in Japan 2 percent higher.

The growth of productivity—the additional amount a worker cranks out per hour from one year to the next—is the measure of future prosperity. Rapid growth in productivity means quickly rising standards of living; low growth means stagnation or even decline. The percent average annual growth in manufacturing productivity from 1995 to 2000:

South Korea	11.5
United States	4.5
France	4.1
Japan	3.9
Germany	2.5
Britain	2.3

Source: U.S. Bureau of Labor Statistics

South Korea's rapid productivity growth was similar to Japan's in earlier decades. Newly industrializing countries, because they are starting from a low level, show the biggest percentage gains. After a while, all the easy gains have been made, and a country becomes more "normal," like Japan. Earlier, U.S. productivity growth had been among the weakest of the industrialized countries. Its surge in the late 1990s reflected major investments in efficiency and information technology.

Productivity does not tell the whole story of an economy, because it focuses on manufacturing. Advanced economies employ most people not in factories but in the service sector, where productivity gains are harder to make and to measure.

on their own terms, never seriously challenging the underlying premise that redistribution is good. Thatcher changed this all around and made the debate one about productivity and economic growth; now Labour had to compete on *her* terms. It was a historic shift, and one that influenced the political debate in other lands, including the United States. Labour Prime Minister Blair did not repudiate Thatcher's free-market economic policies; he stole them and got excellent economic results.

DEMOCRACY

WHICH BLAIR PROJECT?

Blair's chief project was not Britain's economy but its institutions. His bold constitutional reforms modernized Britain's political institutions, many of which had been little changed in centuries. Some of his projects have already been passed into law while others are still debated. Blair will go down in history as Britain's modernizer.

1. *A written constitution.* With no fixed limits, power can be abused in Britain. Written rules could make Britons freer, especially with the addition of . . .
2. *A bill of rights,* U.S.-style. Blair accomplished this by having Parliament adopt the European Convention on Human Rights as domestic law, bringing Britain into line with the rest of the EU, starting in 2000. For the first time Britons got legal guarantees of media freedom and protection from heavy-handed police methods.
3. *Judicial review.* Any bill Parliament passes is automatically constitutional in Britain. As in most of the world, British courts cannot check executive excesses. The Law Lords, part of the House of Lords, were not the equivalent of the U.S. Supreme Court, which many Britons admired. Blair sought to turn the Law Lords into a British Supreme Court.
4. *Freedom of information.* Until recently, Britain had an Official Secrets Act that was close to censorship. All manner of government wrongdoing was concealed. At the start of 2005 Britain's Freedom of Information Act, modeled on a similar New Zealand law, lets anyone

THE TROUBLE WITH NATIONAL HEALTH

The centerpiece of Britain's extensive welfare state is the National Health Service (NHS), which went into operation in 1948 as part of Labour's longstanding commitment to helping working Britons. Before World War II, British medical care was spotty, and many Britons were too scrawny and unhealthy for military service during the war. Conservatives and the British Medical Association fought the NHS, but the tide was against them.

Did the NHS work? The answer is both yes and no. The British population is much healthier than it used to be. Infant mortality, one key measure of overall health standards, dropped from 64 out of 1,000 live births in 1931 to 7 now. The British working class has especially benefited. In 2003 Britons spent only 7.7 percent of their GDP on health care but were as healthy as the Americans, who spent 15 percent.

But NHS has been unable to keep up with skyrocketing costs. Britons have become more elderly, and old people consume many times as much medical care as younger people. Technical advances in medicine are terribly expensive, and the system requires many request data from an independent *information commissioner,* who vowed to err on the side of the public's right to know.

5. *A meaningful upper house.* As we discussed in Chapter 3, in 1999 Blair modernized Lords by kicking out most hereditary peers and leaving it largely in the hands of life peers. This still left it with little power. A next step would be to give it some powers to check Commons and the cabinet.

6. *Devolution,* which Blair carried out smartly in granting extensive home rule and elected assemblies to Northern Ireland, Scotland, and Wales. (See the subsequent discussions.)

7. *A new electoral system.* As we considered in Chapter 3, the traditional FPTP system overrewards the two big parties and penalizes third parties. Adding some PR ("topping off"), as was done in the 1999 elections for the new Scottish and Welsh parliaments, would be much fairer, especially to the Lib Dems.

8. *Public services* are hurting in Britain. Railways and the National Health Service lagged behind those of the Continent. New management and money were needed to improve them, but who should pay? Users or taxpayers?

9. *Universities* are public and cheap ($2,000 a year) but overcrowded and decaying. Many top scholars leave for U.S. teaching positions. (America spends 2.7 percent of its GDP on higher education, Britain and France 1.1 percent, Germany 1 percent.) With students and the Labour left howling, Blair narrowly got Parliament to boost fees to $6,000 in 2006.

10. *Fox hunting,* scheduled to be banned in 2006, is a hot issue. Some call it the symbol of an overall "crisis in the countryside." Rural-dwellers protest declining farm incomes, outsiders driving up home prices, and mishandling of a big hoof-and-mouth outbreak in 2001. Now they're taking away our old tradition and right of "riding to hounds," they complain. Most Britons see it as elitist and barbaric.

bureaucrats. With a staff of 1 million, the NHS is the largest employer in West Europe, but personnel and facilities have not kept pace with demand. The money simply is not there. If surgery is not for an emergency, patients may wait a year or more. The debate in Britain is over whether to keep funding the NHS by general tax revenues, which Labour favors, or to adopt European funding models, which include mandatory employee and employer contributions and a bigger role for private health care.

IS NORTHERN IRELAND SETTLED?

After thirty years of violence, peace glimmered in Northern Ireland. In 1998, on Good Friday, the two sides reached a power-sharing agreement, even though extremists on both sides try to undermine it. A breakaway group, the Real IRA, set off a bomb on a crowded street in Omagh, killing twenty-eight (most of them Catholic). This horrified everyone and solidified the agreement. Even Gerry Adams, the Sinn Fein chief who once advocated violence, said violence "must be for all of us now a thing of the past, over, done with and gone." Most agreed, but peace was still fragile.

Prime Minister Tony Blair took some of the credit for the **Good Friday agreement**; his Conservative predecessors would not negotiate with Sinn Fein. The agreement reopened the Northern Ireland Assembly at Stormont, which had been closed since 1974. Previously dominated by Protestants, it was one of the reasons for Catholic protest. Now it is freely and fairly elected, using the type of proportional representation used in the Republic of Ireland. Ministries are awarded on a balanced basis; most of the nine parties in Stormont get at least one. First minister, for example, is leader of the (Protestant) Ulster Unionist party, but his deputy is leader of the (Catholic) Social Democratic and Labour party. Political scientists call such an arrangement **consociation**, useful for holding together badly fractured societies.

Stormont's powers and budget are not trivial. It runs Northern Ireland's education, medical, social, housing, and agricultural services. In addition, a "north-south council" of officials from Northern Ireland and the Republic of Ireland supervises cross-border policies. The whole package aims to give peace a chance by involving both sides in governance, but they so mistrusted each other that London had to suspend Stormont's powers several times and resume direct rule.

BRITISH RACISM

British society, like U.S. society, is split along racial lines. Whites have little to do with nonwhites, and there is animosity between the two groups. Starting in 1958, race riots flare in Britain every few years. Nonwhites, most born in Britain, are now about 7 percent (4 percent Asian, mostly Pakistanis, and 2 percent black) of Britain's population, many ghettoized in the declining industrial cities in the north of England.

The race problem in Britain is a legacy of empire. Britain in 1948 legally made the natives of its many colonies British **subjects**, entitled to live and work in the United Kingdom. Although the colonies were granted independence from the late 1940s through the 1960s, as members of the British **Commonwealth** their people were still entitled to immigrate to Britain. In the 1950s, West Indians arrived from the Caribbean, then Indians and Pakistanis, taking lowly jobs that Britons did not want, then sending for relatives. Two forces keep Muslims segregated: discrimination by whites and wanting to preserve their original faith and culture. Caught between two cultures, some alienated Muslim youths turn to crime or Islamism (see page 303). (The leader of the gang that murdered U.S. newsman Daniel Pearl in Pakistan in 2002 was born and raised in England.)

KEY TERMS

Good Friday agreement   1998 pact to share power in Northern Ireland.

consociation   Sharing of political power at the executive level, giving all major parties cabinet positions.

subject   Originally, a subject of the Crown; now means British citizen.

Commonwealth   Organization of countries that were once British colonies.

A black Labour candidate campaigns in London. Several black MPs have won Labour seats in Parliament. (British Information Services)

White resentment built, especially among the working class in areas of industrial decline and high unemployment. In 1967 an openly racist National Front formed, advocating the expulsion of all "coloureds" back to their native lands. Skinheads, supporting the Front or its successor British National party (BNP), like "Paki bashing." With slogans such as "Rights for Whites," the anti-immigrant vote grew but never won a seat. (The BNP took 0.2 percent in 2001, but in a few tense areas topped 10 percent.) The BNP was much weaker than its Continental counterparts such as the French National Front.

Margaret Thatcher won Tory votes with her call for a "clear end to immigration" before it "swamped" British culture, but both parties have successively tightened immigration to Britain since 1962, and it is now very restrictive. Demographers say the immigrants will not swamp anything. France and Germany face the identical problem: Historically countries of **emigration**, they do not handle **immigration** very well. The United States handles it much better, precisely because we are all immigrants or their descendants.

Key Terms

emigration (one m) Moving out of your native country.
immigration (two ms) Resettling into a new country.

GEOGRAPHY

DEVOLUTION FOR SCOTLAND AND WALES

Britain, a highly centralized **unitary system**, has become a bit federal. Northern Ireland, Scotland, and Wales show the center-periphery tensions that afflict many countries. In general, the farther from the nation's capital, the more regional resentment. Britain has the long Celtic memories of conquered Scots and Welsh. Wales has been a part of England since the Middle Ages; the thrones of England and Scotland were united only in 1603, and in 1707 both countries agreed to a single Parliament in London. But old resentments never died; they lingered as feelings of regional distinctiveness. Wales and Scotland, always poorer than England, left Welsh and Scots feeling economically exploited.

In the twentieth century the political beneficiary of these feelings was the Labour party, which still holds sway in Wales and Scotland. Voting Labour in Scotland and Wales became a form of regional nationalism, a way of repudiating rule by England, which goes Conservative. Center-periphery tensions almost always reveal themselves in voting patterns. In the 1960s the small Plaid Cymru (pronounced plyde kum-REE, meaning "Party of Wales") and the Scottish Nationalist party began to grow; both win a few seats in Parliament.

Regional nationalism increased in many countries during the 1970s—Corsican and Breton in France, Quebecker in Canada, Basque and Catalan in Spain. In the 1990s, the Soviet Union and Yugoslavia fell apart. There are several causes for local separatism. Economics plays a role; local nationalists claim their regions are shortchanged by central governments. Nationalists emphasize their regions' distinct languages and cultures and demand that they be taught in schools. Some of the impulse behind local nationalism is the largeness and remoteness of the modern state, the feeling that important decisions are out of local control, made by far-away bureaucrats. And often smoldering under the surface are historical resentments of a region that once was conquered, occupied, and deprived of its own identity. Whatever the mixture, local nationalism sometimes turns its adherents into fanatics who are willing to wreck the entire country to get their way. Happily, this did not happen in Britain. The Scots and Welsh never became as extreme as Basques in Spain or Corsicans in France.

In Scotland, the economic factor played a large part in its rising nationalism. When oil was discovered in the North Sea off Scotland in the 1960s, some Scots did not want to share the petroleum revenues with the United Kingdom as a whole: "It's Scotland's oil!" Oil offered Scotland the possibility of economic independence and self-government, of becoming something more than a poor, northerly part of Britain.

The leading issue for Welsh nationalists has been language, the ancient Celtic tongue of Cymric (pronounced *kim-rick*). Fewer than one Welsh person in five speaks Cymric, and most are elderly. In recent years, however, there has been an upsurge of people learning Welsh, and the language is now officially coequal with English within Wales. There is even a Welsh TV channel.

KEY TERMS

unitary system   Country that centralizes power in capital with little autonomy for component areas (opposite: federal system).

regional nationalism   *Particularist* and separatist movements in some peripheral areas.

The strategy of the Labour party has been to offer home rule or autonomy to Scotland and Wales. This was called **devolution**, the granting of certain governing powers by the center to the periphery. A 1977 devolution bill to set up Scottish and Welsh assemblies failed in **referendums**.

After the 1997 election, in which Scotland and Wales stayed overwhelmingly Labour, Tony Blair again offered Scotland and Wales their own parliaments, and this time the referendums passed. In 1999, at about the same time Ulster got home rule, Scots and Welsh elected regional parliaments with a new voting system that could be what Blair has in mind for Britain as a whole. The German-style system gave each voter two votes, the first for FPTP single-member districts and the second for parties in multimember districts. The results of the second vote were used to "top off" the number of seats for each party until they were roughly proportional to its share of the votes. Labour took the most seats in both Scotland and Wales but not a majority, forcing them to form coalitions. This too could be a harbinger for things to come in Britain. The new assemblies have some powers in education, economic planning, and taxation. Some Scots dismiss their assembly as "a wee pretendy parliament."

Britons do not use the word, but these moves amount to **quasi-federalism** or *regionalism*. France and Spain, beset by similar regional resentments, have also decentralized somewhat. Will it solve Britain's problem or just whet appetites for more? The Scot Nats and about half the people of Scotland still say they want full independence. In addition, the Blair government set up eight Regional Development Agencies for England, whose task was economic growth. Some took these agencies as the beginnings of regionalism within England.

How do you say "post office" in Gaelic? Although few Scots speak it, in the Highlands many public signs are now in Gaelic as well as English, an example of regional nationalism. (Michael Roskin)

KEY TERMS

devolution   Central government turns some powers over to regions.

referendum   Vote on an issue rather than for an office.

quasi-federal   Halfway federal.

COMPARISON

HOW TO IMPROVE BRITISH EDUCATION

One limit to British economic growth has been poor educational levels, something Tony Blair worked to correct. Britain's **human capital** did not compare favorably with other countries. Many leave school early with weak math and verbal skills, forming a U.S.-style **underclass**.

As in the United States, the British debate how to raise educational standards. Many Tories want to return to the system of testing to send the best to elite high schools. Northern Ireland kept the selective system and shows better overall school performance. Labour, still seeking equality, generally prefers comprehensive schools but with improved funding, standards, and discipline.

By 2000, British 15-year-olds tested better than most of the Continent and much better than U.S. scores. Surprising: the drop in German scores to U.S. levels. Unsurprising: high Japanese math scores. The message: America, get serious about schooling.

BRITAIN AND EUROPE

Until recent decades, Britons did not see themselves as Europeans; most looked down on anyone from across the English Channel. Rather than working toward a united Europe after World War II, as the Continental countries did, Britain emphasized its Commonwealth ties and its "special relationship" to the United States. As the rest of Europe kept distant from the U.S. war in Iraq, Tony Blair supported it, even as most Britons turned against it.

Britain stayed out of the 1957 Treaty of Rome, which set up the European Community (EC, since 1993 the EU, for European Union), but in 1960 built a much looser grouping, the European Free Trade Association (EFTA). While the EC Six (France, West Germany, Italy, Belgium, the Netherlands, Luxembourg) economies surged ahead, the EFTA Outer Seven (Britain, Austria, Denmark, Finland, Iceland, Norway, Portugal, Sweden, and Switzerland) were slowly cut off from the main European market. In 1963, Britain applied to join the EC, but French President Charles de Gaulle vetoed British entry, charging that Britain was still too tied to the Commonwealth and the United States to be a good European. He was right.

By the time de Gaulle resigned in 1969, Britain was ready to join the EC, but not all Britons liked the idea. For traditional Tories, it meant giving up some British sovereignty to the EC headquarters in Brussels and even treating Europeans as equals. For everyone it meant higher food prices. For manufacturers it meant British products had to compete with often better and cheaper Continental imports that now come in tariff-free. For fishermen it meant

KEY TERMS

human capital   Education, skills, and enthusiasm of nation's work force.
underclass   Permanently disadvantaged people.

British fishing areas were open to all EC fishermen. For workers it meant loss of some jobs. Many Britons want to stay firmly British.

The arguments in favor of the EU stress that Britain needs change and competition, the very forces that had invigorated European industries. Furthermore, geographically, strategically, economically, even spiritually, Britain really is part of Europe and should start acting like it. The Euro-debate cuts across party lines, sometimes producing a strange coalition of right-wing Tories and left-wing Labourites, each opposing Europe for their own reasons. In 1971, under a Tory government, the Commons voted 356 to 244 to join; 69 Labour MPs defied their party whip to vote in favor while 39 Conservatives, freed from party discipline, voted "no" along with Labour, demonstrating that British party discipline is not perfect. On January 1, 1973, Britain, along with Denmark and Ireland, made the Common Market Six, the Nine.

When Labour returned to power, Prime Minister Harold Wilson offered the British public a first—a referendum, something common in France. But Britain, with its tradition of parliamentary supremacy, had never held one before. The 1975 referendum found that most Britons wanted to stay in Europe, but one-third voted no. If put to a referendum, the EU constitution would have been rejected by British voters.

Thatcher, a British nationalist and Eurosceptic (as is current Tory leadership) took a tough line on the EU. A common market was fine, she argued, but not a supranational entity that infringes on Britain's sovereignty and imposes tons of bureaucratic rules. Many Britons reject joining the European Monetary Union (EMU) and its euro currency. Their slogan: "Europe yes, euro no." The EMU indeed takes away an important part of sovereignty, the ability of each country to control its currency, and gives it to the European Central Bank (ECB) in Frankfurt. Many Britons (and some other Europeans) feared that Europe's strongest economy—Germany—would dominate the ECB and set its policies on money supply and interest rates. Britain (along with Denmark and Sweden) stood aside as the euro was introduced. Blair, a cautious Euroenthusiast, waited to see how the euro worked. He also proposed a 2006 referendum to ratify the European Union's new constitution, but that became meaningless after the French and Dutch rejected it in 2005. Some Britons would like to drop out of the EU. Perhaps Britain really is an Atlantic country and not a European one. Britain's natural community may be the English-speaking lands across the oceans.

GREAT BRITAIN OR LITTLE ENGLAND?

This sums up the dilemma of modern Britain: the problem of scaling down its vision of itself. Britain, in the course of a century, has clearly declined, both internationally and domestically. When Britain was a mighty empire and the most industrialized country in the world in the second half of the nineteenth century, it had power, wealth, and a sense of mission. This in turn fostered order, discipline, and deference among the British people. Losing its empire and slipping behind the economies of West Europe caused decay, violence, and resentment.

Britain's trajectory refutes the idea that progress is **unilinear**. In the case of Britain we see that what goes up can eventually come down. But this process is never static. Now that Britain

KEY TERM

unilinear   Progressing evenly and always upward.

is adjusting to its new reality—as one European country among many—regeneration has already begun.

KEY TERMS

absolute decline (p. 84)

Commonwealth (p. 92)

consociation (p. 92)

consumption (p. 85)

counterculture (p. 86)

deindustrialization (p. 84)

deregulation (p. 87)

devolution (p. 95)

emigration (p. 93)

entitlement (p. 88)

Good Friday agreement (p. 92)

human capital (p. 96)

immigration (p. 93)

inflation (p. 85)

monetarism (p. 85)

pluralism (p. 86)

pluralistic stagnation (p. 86)

privatization (p. 87)

production (p. 85)

productivity (p. 85)

quasi-federal (p. 95)

recession (p. 88)

referendum (p. 95)

regional nationalism (p. 94)

relative decline (p. 84)

subject (p. 92)

underclass (p. 96)

unilinear (p. 97)

unitary system (p. 94)

FURTHER REFERENCE

Burgess, Michael. *The British Tradition of Federalism*. Rutherford, NJ: Farleigh Dickinson, 1995.

De Bréadún, Deaglán. *The Far Side of Revenge: Making Peace in Northern Ireland*. Wilton, Ireland: Collins, 2001.

Denver, David. *Scotland Decides: The Devolution Issue and the 1997 Referendum*. Portland, OR: F. Cass, 2000.

Freedman, Leonard. *Politics and Policy in Britain*. New York: Longman, 1996.

Hansen, Randall. *Citizenship and Immigration in Post-War Britain: The Institutional Origins of a Multicultural Nation*. New York: Oxford University Press, 2000.

Hearn, Jonathan. *Claiming Scotland: National Identity and Liberal Culture*. New York: Columbia University Press, 2001.

Mac Ginty, Roger, and John Darby. *Guns and Government: The Management of the Northern Ireland Peace Process*. New York: Palgrave, 2002.

Owen, Geoffrey. *From Empire to Europe*. New York: HarperCollins, 1999.

Paul, Kathleen. *Whitewashing Britain: Race and Citizenship in the Postwar Era*. Ithaca, NY: Cornell University Press, 1997.

Pierson, Paul. *Dismantling the Welfare State?: Reagan, Thatcher, and the Politics of Retrench-ment.* New York: Cambridge University Press, 1994.

Redwood, John. *The Death of Britain?: The UK's Constitutional Crisis.* New York: St. Mar-tin's: 1999.

Robins, Lynton, and Bill Jones, eds. *Debates in British Politics Today.* New York: Palgrave, 2001.

Seldon, Anthony, ed. *The Blair Effect.* Boston: Little, Brown, 2001.

PART II

RUSSIA

KEY WEB SITES

Country Study
lcweb21.loc.gov/frd/cs/rutoc.html

Historical and Ethnic Photos
loc.gov/exhibits/empire

Scholarly Reviews
www2.h-net.msu.edu/~russia

Russian Embassy in Washington
russianembassy.org

Institute for the Economy in Transition
iet.ru/index_e.htm

Democracy in Russia (Yablko Party)
eng.yabloko.ru

Radio Free Europe/Radio Liberty
rferl.org

News Sources
europeaninternet.com/russia
russiatoday.com
moscowtimes.ru
russiajournal.com
valley.net/~transnat
wps.ru:8101/chitlaks/politruk/en

7

Russia:
The Impact of the Past

Russia is immense, stretching eleven time zones across the northern half of Asia to the Pacific. Looking at a map of Russia, you notice that only a small part of it is in Europe. (Look at a globe and you notice that Europe itself is only a small peninsula of Asia.) Perhaps a country as big and ethnically diverse as the Soviet Union was not meant to be. Just holding it together meant its rulers needed strong central control backed by force. Even now, the very size of Russia may incline it to **tyranny**.

With few natural boundaries, Russia is easy to invade from east or west, although its size and harsh winters doomed the invasions of Charles XII of Sweden, Napoleon, and Hitler. Winters give Russia a short growing season. Russian agriculture is a chancy business, with crops failing on an average of one year in three. Geography is not as kind to Russia as it is to the United States. The vast territory that **Siberia** adds to Russia's size is problematic; its weather is hostile to settlement, and its mineral and forest wealth is hard to extract. Most of the Russian population continues to live in the European part, that is, west of the Ural Mountains. Plans to settle in and develop Siberia, some of them going back to tsarist days, fall short of expectations.

Another geographic problem is the difficulty of reaching the open sea. The first Russian states were totally landlocked; only under Peter the Great at the beginning of the eighteenth century did Russians overcome the Swedes to reach the Baltic and the Turks to reach the Black Sea. The

Questions to Consider

1. Does Russia's size make it inherently difficult to govern?
2. What geographic disadvantages has Russia faced over its history?
3. Why does Russia always seem to require modernization from above? Why can it not come from below?
4. How much practice has Russia had with democracy?
5. How does the clash of Westernizers and Slavophiles echo to this day?
6. Why did Marxism catch on in Russia, where it was not supposed to?
7. How did Lenin alter Marxism?
8. Could the Provisional Government have stayed in power? How?
9. Was Stalin an accident?

KEY TERMS

tyranny Coercive rule, usually by one person.
Siberia From Russian for "north"; that part of Russia east of the Ural Mountains.

North Russian ports ice over in winter, and the Black Sea is controlled by the Turkish Straits, still leaving European Russia without year-round, secure ports. One of the great dreams of tsarists and Communists alike was for warm-water ports under exclusive Russian control.

THE SLAVIC PEOPLE

Occupying most of East Europe, the Slavic peoples are the most numerous in Europe. Russians, Ukrainians, Poles, Czechs, Slovaks, Serbs, Croats, Bulgarians, and others speak languages closer to each other than are the Romance languages (Italian, Spanish, French) of West Europe. It is said a Slovak peasant can converse with any other Slavic peasant—so similar are their vocabularies and syntax.

But the way the Slavic languages are written differentiates them. The Western Slavs (Poles, Czechs, and others) were Christianized from Rome; hence their alphabet is Latin. The Eastern Slavs (Russians, Ukrainians, Serbs, and others) were converted by Eastern Orthodox monks from **Constantinople**, and their languages are written in a variation of the Greek alphabet called **Cyrillic**, after St. Cyril, one of the monks who first converted Slavs.

Their Orthodox Christianity (as opposed to Roman Catholicism) and Cyrillic writing contributed to the Russians' isolation from the rest of Europe. In addition to being at the geographical fringe of Europe, Russia was beyond its cultural fringe for centuries. The important ideas that helped modernize Catholic and Protestant Europe penetrated Russia only much later. Rome was a lively fountainhead of thought in West Europe, but Constantinople, the headquarters of the Orthodox faith under the Turks, ceased to provide intellectual guidance for its followers. At the same time that West Europe was experiencing the invigoration of the Renaissance, which rippled outward from Catholic Italy, Russia stayed isolated and asleep. It missed most of the **Enlightenment**.

A more important factor explaining Russia's isolation and backwardness was its conquest in the thirteenth century by the Mongols, later known as the **Tatars**. The Mongols crushed the first Russian state, centered at Kiev in present-day Ukraine, and enslaved much of the population. For two centuries, while West Europe moved ahead, Russian culture under the barbaric Mongols declined. Some historians believe that even after the Tatar yoke was lifted, it still took five centuries for Russia to catch up with the West.

RUSSIAN AUTOCRACY

Under the Tatars, the duchy of Moscow became the most powerful of the Russian states, first as a tax collector for the Tatars, then as their triumphant enemy. Moscovy's Ivan the Terrible (1530–1584) had himself crowned **tsar**. Under Ivan, Russian territory expanded

KEY TERMS

Constantinople   Capital of Byzantium, conquered by Turks in 1453.

Cyrillic   Greek-based alphabet of Eastern Slavic languages.

Enlightenment   Eighteenth-century philosophical movement advocating reason and tolerance.

Tatar   Mongol-origin tribes who ruled Russia for centuries. (*Not* Tartar.)

tsar   From "caesar"; Russia's emperor. Sometimes spelled old Polish style, czar.

GEOGRAPHY

BOUNDARIES: LINES ON A MAP

Precisely where one state leaves off and another begins is often unsettled. Looking at maps, you get the feeling that boundary lines are real, perhaps decreed by nature, or at least hallowed by time to demarcate each people's allotted territory. Would that it were so. In point of fact, there are practically no natural boundaries in the world. Almost all boundaries are artificial, some more artificial than others.

The boundaries of Germany, Poland, and Russia consolidated, expanded, and contracted with great fluidity, almost like accordions. Which are their "correct" boundaries? It is impossible to apply historical, moral, or even demographic standards to determine them with certainty. One might attempt, as Hitler did, to draw Germany's borders so as to include all Germans. But the peoples of Europe—as in most of the world—are not neatly arrayed in demographic ranks, with, say, Germans on one side of a river and Poles on the other. Instead, they are often *interdigitized,* with some German villages in Polish territory and Poles living in some German cities. Whatever border you draw will leave some Germans in Poland and some Poles in Germany.

Poland's boundaries are a perplexing example of border questions. As the empires that had partitioned Poland since the 1790s—German, Austrian, and Russian—collapsed in World War I, Polish patriots under Pilsudski reestablished Poland, but it included many Lithuanians, Belorussians, and Ukrainians. Stalin never liked that boundary and during World War II pushed Soviet borders westward. In compensation, Poland got former German territories, so that now its western border is formed by the Oder and Neisse Rivers. Millions of Germans were expelled. In effect, Poland was picked up and moved over 100 miles westward!

Only boundaries that have been set up and observed over the centuries are without controversy. To be legal, a border must be agreed upon in a boundary treaty and demarcated with physical indicators, such as concrete pylons. Few borders in the world are like that.

Control of borders is a chief attribute of sovereignty, and nations go to great lengths to demonstrate that they alone are in charge of who and what goes in and goes out across their borders. One of the first points of violence in Lithuania and Slovenia were their passport and customs houses. In forcibly taking over these border checkpoints, Soviet and Yugoslav federal forces respectively attempted to show that they, rather than the breakaway republics, were in charge of the entire national territory.

Boundary questions abound, such as India's border with Pakistan (especially over Kashmir), China's borders with India and with Russia, Venezuela with Guyana, Argentina with Chile (over Tierra del Fuego)

greatly, down the Volga to the Caspian Sea and into Siberia. Ivan was both murderous and successful; his brutal use of force set a standard for later rulers. To this day, many Russians think only a strong and ruthless leader can achieve national greatness.

Whenever the Russian nobles (*boyars*) came into conflict with Ivan, his secret police, the *Oprichnina,* exiled or executed them. From that time onward, the Russian nobility never played an autonomous role in political life. It was as if the absolutism of France was applied early and completely to a culturally backward country. The result was

and with Britain (over the Falklands), Syria with Lebanon (over the Bekaa Valley), Morocco with Algeria (over the former Spanish Sahara), and Iraq with Iran (over the Shatt al-Arab waterway). Such questions cause wars.

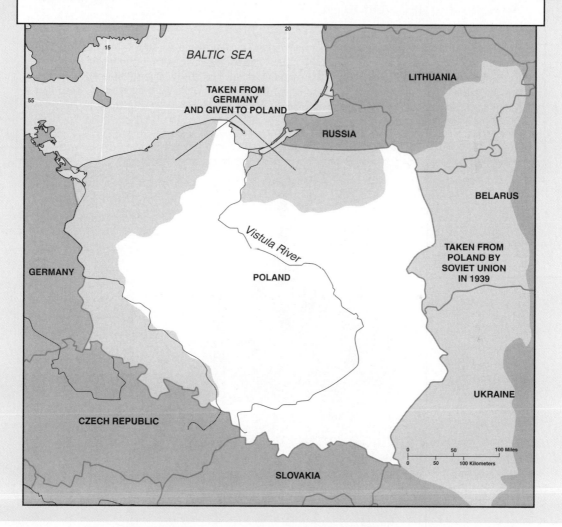

autocracy under the tsar. Unlike the countries of West Europe, Russia never experienced the mixed monarchy of autonomous nobles, church, commoners, and king. Accordingly, Russians had no experience with limited government, checks and balances, or pluralism.

KEY TERM

autocracy   Absolute rule of one person in centralized state.

POLITICAL CULTURE

"MOSCOW IS THE THIRD ROME"

The monk Philotheus of Pskov uttered these words after Constantinople fell to the Turks in 1453, indicating that Russia was the last and only center of true Christianity. Rome and Constantinople had failed; now Moscow would guard the faith. Over the centuries, many Russians repeated Philotheus's dictum: "Moscow is the third Rome; a fourth is not to be." After the Bolshevik Revolution, Russia's new rulers felt the same way about world communism, namely, Moscow was its capital and there could be no other. Even today, some Russians still feel that Russia has a holy mission.

St. Basil's cathedral recalls Moscow's former role as a center of Christianity. Russia's tsars were not merely heads of state but also heads of the Russian Orthodox Church. (Michael Roskin)

GEOGRAPHY

BOUND RUSSIA

Russia is bounded on the north by the Arctic Ocean;

on the east by the Bering Sea and Sea of Okhotsk;

on the south by North Korea (tiny), China, Mongolia, Kazakhstan, Azerbaijan, Georgia, and the Black Sea;

and on the west by Ukraine, Belarus, Lithuania, Latvia, Estonia, Finland, and Norway.

The four directions need be only approximate. The Russian **exclave** of Kaliningrad Oblast (region), formerly Königsberg of old East Prussia, is wedged between Poland and Lithuania.

As Ivan grew older he became madder. Able to trust no one, he murdered those around him—even his own son—at the least suspicion. By the time he died he had carved out the modern Russian state.

ABSOLUTISM OR ANARCHY?

One of the reasons Russians put up with autocracy—and sometimes admired it—was because they felt that without a firm hand at the top the system would degenerate into anarchy. This happened in the early seventeenth century, the "Time of Troubles." Lacking a strong tsar, unrest, banditry, civil war, and a Polish invasion plagued the land. Russians also accepted the idea that they had to serve a powerful state. The Russian Orthodox church, which the tsar also headed, became a pillar of autocracy, teaching the faithful to worship the tsar as the "little father" who protected all Russians. The tsar integrated the offices of head of state and head of church, a pattern called **caesaropapism**. Russia has been called a "service state" in which all walks of life, from nobles to peasants to priests, served the autocrat. Western concepts such as liberty and individual rights were absent.

KEY TERMS

exclave   Part of country separated from main territory.

caesaropapism   Combining top civil ruler (caesar) with top spiritual ruler (pope), as in Russia's tsars.

During the fifteenth and sixteenth centuries, Russia actually moved backwards in one crucial area. Previously free peasants became serfs, tied to the land to labor for aristocrats as almost subhuman beasts. While West Europe ended serfdom centuries earlier, Russia found itself with the vast majority of its population poor and ignorant farm laborers.

From time to time these wretched people revolted. Some ran off and joined the Cossacks, bands of mounted freebooters in the border regions between the tsarist and Turkish empires. One Cossack leader, Stenka Razin, immortalized in ballad, led a peasant revolt that seized much of **Ukraine**. In time, the Cossacks turned into semimilitary federations, which the tsars enrolled as effective and ruthless cavalry.

FORCED MODERNIZATION

By the time Peter I became tsar in 1682, Russia lagged behind the rest of Europe. Peter, who stood six feet nine inches (206 cm.), forced Russia to modernize and become a major power. Peter personally handled Russia's legislation, diplomacy, war, and technical innovation and was the first tsar to travel in West Europe. Admiring its industries, he ordered them duplicated in Russia. Nearly continually at war, Peter pushed the Swedes back to give Russia an outlet on the Baltic. There he ordered built a magnificent new capital, St. Petersburg (later Leningrad), modeled after Amsterdam, to serve as Russia's window to the West.

Copying the tight Swedish administrative system, Peter divided Russia into provinces, counties, and districts, each supervised by bureaucrats drawn from the nobility. All male nobles had to serve the tsar from age fifteen until death, either as bureaucrats or military officers. Even the bureaucrats were organized on military lines, complete with ranks and uniforms. With Peter, the Russian government apparatus penetrated deep into society. A census determined the number of males available for military conscription, and each community had a quota. Draftees served for life. Taxation squeezed everybody as Peter ordered his officials to "collect money, as much as possible, for money is the artery of war."

When Peter died in 1725, Russia was more modern and Westernized but still behind West Europe. Peter the Great contributed a pattern of forced modernization from the top, pushing a poor, gigantic country forward despite itself. Russia paid dearly. The mass of peasants, heavily taxed, were worse off than ever. The Westernized nobility—forced, for instance, to shave for the first time—was cut off from the hopes and feelings of the peasantry. The pattern continued for a long time.

WESTERNIZERS AND SLAVOPHILES

Napoleon's invasion of Russia and capture of Moscow in 1812 made Russian intellectuals painfully aware of the backwardness of their land. Many sought to bring in Western politics and institutions, including a constitutional monarchy that would limit the autocratic powers of the tsar. These were called **Westernizers**. Others disliked the West; they saw it

KEY TERMS

Ukraine From Slavic for "borderland"; region south of Russia, now independent.
Westernizers Nineteenth-century Russians who wished to copy the West.

as spiritually shallow and materialistic. The answer to Russia's problems, they argued, was to cultivate their own Slavic roots and develop institutions and styles different from and superior to the West's. "Russia will teach the world," was their view. These **Slavophiles** (literally, "lovers of the Slavs"), who stressed the spiritual depth and warm humanity of Russian peasants, were romantic nationalists who disdained West European culture. In our day this pattern continues in parts of the Third World that reject Western materialism in favor of traditional spiritual values. And in Russia today the old debate still echoes: Liberal reformers are still pro-West while conservatives are anti-West nationalists.

FROM FRUSTRATION TO REVOLUTION

Despite calls for far-reaching changes in Russia, reform during the nineteenth century made little progress. All tsars rejected becoming a **constitutional monarchy**. Even Alexander II, the "tsar-liberator," carried out only limited reforms. In 1861 he issued his famous Edict of Emancipation, freeing serfs from legal bondage. Most of them remained in economic bondage, however. He set up district and provincial assemblies called **zemstvos** but gave them only marginal local power.

The reforms were meant both to modernize Russia and to improve the living conditions of the masses. Under certain conditions, however, reforms may actually make **revolution** more likely rather than less. Alexander's reforms, which he saw as extensive and generous, were regarded by an increasingly critical *intelligentsia* (the educated class) as not nearly enough. Whatever he granted, they wanted more. The reforms merely whetted the critics' appetites. Many intellectuals became bitter and frustrated.

Some tried action at the grass-roots level. In the 1870s thousands of idealistic students put on peasant clothes and tried "going to the people" in the villages to incite radical action. These **Narodniki** made absolutely no progress; the suspicious peasants either ignored them or turned them over to the police. Others tried assassination, believing that killing the right official constituted "propaganda of the deed," a way to arouse the inert masses. One group of committed terrorists, *Narodnaya Volya* (People's Will), after seven attempts killed the tsar with a bomb thrown into his carriage in 1881.

Actually, Russia did make considerable progress in the nineteenth century. Archaic usages were swept away, industry started (with an infusion of British, French, and German capital), railroads were built, and intellectual life flourished. But in the crucial area of political reform—parliaments, parties, elections, and the sharing of power—Russia essentially stood still. Political reforms do not make themselves, and in many ways they are more basic to

KEY TERMS

Slavophiles   Nineteenth-century Russians who wished to develop Russia along native, non-Western lines. Also known as "Russophiles."

constitutional monarchy   King with limited powers.

zemtsvo   Local parliaments in old Russia.

revolution   Sudden and complete overthrow of regime.

Narodniki   From Russian for "people," *narod;* radical populist agitators of late nineteenth-century Russia.

the peaceful evolution of society than social, cultural, or economic reforms. A ruler who modernizes his economy but not his political system is asking for trouble.

MARXISM COMES TO RUSSIA

According to Marx's theory, backward Russia was far from ready for proletarian revolution. There simply was not much of a **proletariat** in the still overwhelmingly agricultural land, where industrialization was just beginning in the late nineteenth century. Marx believed revolution would come first in the most industrially advanced countries, such as Britain and Germany. Curiously, though, Marxism caught on more strongly in Russia than anywhere else. Marx's works were eagerly seized upon by frustrated Russian intellectuals who badly wanted change but did not have a theoretical framework for it. Here at last, they believed, they had found a reason and a means to carry out a revolution.

There were several schools of Marxism in Russia. The *Legal Marxists*, noting Russia's economic underdevelopment, thought the country would first have to go through capitalism before it could start on socialism. Marx had a very deterministic view of history and saw it developing in economic stages, first capitalism, then socialism. Loyal to Marx's historical analysis, the Legal Marxists believed they would have a long wait for revolution and must first work to promote capitalism.

Another school of Russian Marxism was called *Economism*. Stressing better wages and working conditions through labor unions, the Economists thought the immediate economic improvement of the working class was the essence of Marxism. In this they resembled West European social democrats, whose Marxism mellowed into welfarism.

Opposing these two gradualist schools were impassioned intellectuals who wanted first and foremost to make a revolution. They argued they could "give history a shove" by starting a revolution with only a small proletariat, gaining power, and then using the state to move directly into socialism. Lenin made some theoretical changes in Marxism so it fit Russian conditions (see box on page 111). Since then, the doctrine of Russian **communism** has been known as Marxism-Leninism.

In 1898, after several small groups had discussed Marxist approaches to Russia, the Russian Social Democratic Labor party was formed. Immediately penetrated and harassed by the *Okhrana*, the tsarist secret police, many of its leaders went into exile in West Europe. Its newspaper, *Iskra* (the Spark), was published in Zurich and smuggled into Russia. One of its editors was Lenin.

In 1903 the small party split over a crucial question: organization. Some of its leaders wanted a normal party along the lines of the German Social Democrats, with open but committed membership that tried to enroll the Russian working class. Lenin scoffed at this kind of organization, arguing tsarist secret police would make mincemeat out of an open party. Instead, he urged a small, tightly knit underground party of professional revolutionaries, more a conspiracy than a conventional party.

KEY TERMS

proletariat   According to Marx, class of industrial workers.

communism   Economic theories of Marx combined with organization of Lenin.

imperialism   Powerful, rich countries spreading their influence around the globe (see page 111).

PERSONALITIES

LENIN, THE GREAT REVOLUTIONARY

Some claim that Lenin was out for revenge against the tsarist system for hanging his older brother, Alexander, in 1887 for his part in a bomb plot against the tsar. It is clear Lenin was dominated by a cold, contained fury aimed at one goal: revolutionary socialism in Russia.

Born in 1870 as Vladimir Ilyich Ulyanov, son of a provincial education official, Lenin was from the intellectual middle class rather than the proletariat in whose name he struggled—a pattern typical of revolutionary socialist leaders. Quickly expelled from university for alleged subversive activity, Lenin was sent into rural exile. Equipped with incredible self-discipline, Lenin taught himself and breezed through law exams with top marks.

In the early 1890s Lenin, like many Russian intellectuals, discovered Marx and wrote Marxist analyses of the rapidly growing Russian economy. Recognized as a leading Marxist thinker, Lenin quickly rose to prominence in underground revolutionary circles.

In December 1895, while editing an illegal socialist newspaper, Lenin was arrested and sent to prison for a year followed by three years' exile on the Lena River in Siberia. There he took the name Lenin, the man from the Lena. The solitary hours gave him time to read, learn foreign languages, and write. Released in 1900, Lenin made his way to Zurich, Switzerland, where he spent most of the next seventeen years. Until taking power in Russia in 1917, Lenin never held a job.

In Swiss exile, Lenin at times worried there would never be a revolution in Russia. The working class was concentrating on higher wages rather than revolution. The Russian Social Democratic Labor party was small, with only a few thousand members in Russia and in exile.

Lenin was determined to transform this small party into an effective underground force. Size was not important; organization was everything. In his 1902 pamphlet *What Is to Be Done?* Lenin demanded a tightly disciplined party of professional revolutionaries, not a conventional social-democratic party open to everybody. Under Lenin the early Communists forged the "organizational weapon": the Party.

But how could a proletarian revolution happen in preindustrial Russia? In solving this problem, Lenin greatly changed Marxism. Marx theorized that revolution will come in the most advanced countries, where the proletariat was biggest. Lenin said not necessarily: Revolution could come where capitalism is weakest, where it is just starting. **Imperialism** had changed capitalism, Lenin argued, giving it a new lease on life. By exploiting weaker countries, the big imperialist powers were able to bribe their own working class with higher wages and thus keep them quiet. Where capitalism was beginning—as in Russia with heavy foreign investment—was where it could be overthrown. The newly developing countries, such as Russia and Spain, were "capitalism's weakest link," said Lenin.

Lenin also disagreed with Marx's insistence that peasants could not be revolutionary. Marx dismissed country life as "rural idiocy," but Lenin believed that with certain conditions and leadership they could turn revolutionary and, joining the small working class, form a massive revolutionary army. (Three decades later, Mao Zedong elaborated on these themes to argue that China, a victim of imperialism, could have a socialist revolution based entirely on the peasantry. Mao completed the train of thought Lenin started.)

Lenin was not a great theoretician but a brilliant opportunist, switching doctrine to take advantage of situations, like all successful revolutionaries. He was less concerned with pure Marxism than with using it to overthrow the system he hated. Once in power, he practiced the same bloody ruthlessness later associated with Stalin's rule. It is not clear that had Lenin lived he would have been any better than Stalin.

Lenin got his way. At the 1903 party congress in Brussels, Belgium (it could not be held in Russia), he controlled thirty-three of the fifty-one votes. Although probably unrepresentative of total party membership, Lenin proclaimed his faction **Bolshevik** (majority), and the name stuck. The *menshevik* (minority) faction at the congress continued to exist, advocating a more moderate line.

CURTAIN RAISER: THE 1905 REVOLUTION

At the beginning of the twentieth century two expanding powers, Russia and Japan, collided. The Russians were pushing eastward, consolidating their position on the Pacific by building the Trans-Siberian Railway, the last leg of which ran through Manchuria. Japan was meanwhile pushing up from Korea to Manchuria, which was nominally a part of China. The tsar's cabinet, certain they could defeat any Asian army and hoping to deflect domestic unrest, thought war with Japan might be a good idea. Said the interior minister: "We need a little victorious war to stem the tide of revolution." Instead, the Japanese fleet launched a surprise attack against the Russians at Port Arthur, then beat the Russians on both land and sea.

The Russo-Japanese War revealed the tsarist military as unprepared, inept, and stupid. Weak regimes should not count on a "little victorious war" to paper over domestic unrest; wars make troubles worse. In Russia, rioting and then revolution broke out. Some naval units mutinied. (See Eisenstein's film classic *Battleship Potemkin*.) Workers briefly seized factories at St. Petersburg. It looked like revolution was breaking out.

Tsar Nicholas II gave way and decreed potentially important reforms: freedom of speech, press, and assembly and the democratic election of a **Duma**. Briefly, his 1905 October Manifesto looked as if it would turn autocracy into constitutional monarchy. The tsar and his reactionary advisors backed down on their promises, however. Nicholas, none too bright, refused to yield any of his autocratic powers. Four Dumas were subsequently elected; each was dissolved when it grew too critical. Finally the Duma was turned into an undemocratic debating society without power. The Duma was Russia's last hope for a peaceful transition to democracy. People in modern times need to feel they participate at least in a small way in the affairs of government. Parties, elections, and parliaments may be imperfect means of participation, but they are better than violent revolution. Since the failed Decembrist revolt of 1825, Russian intellectuals had been trying to tell this to the tsar, but he refused to listen.

WORLD WAR I AND COLLAPSE

Communists liked to speak of the Russian Revolution as inevitable, the playing out of historical forces that had to lead to the collapse of imperialism and capitalism. There was nothing inevitable about the October Revolution. Indeed, without World War I, there

KEY TERMS

Bolshevik   "Majority" in Russian; early name for Soviet Communist party.
Duma   Russia's national parliament.

PERSONALITIES

KERENSKY: NICE GUYS LOSE

In the late 1950s at UCLA I had an eerie experience: seeing and hearing Alexander Kerensky speak. History lives. Still fit and articulate in his seventies, Kerensky recalled his brief stint (July to November 1917) as head of Russia's Provisional Government. One man in the audience, a Russian emigré, asked angrily why Kerensky didn't use his power to have Lenin killed. Kerensky reflected a moment and said, "Sometimes when you have power it's hard to use it."

That was Kerensky's problem. A decent man, he wouldn't have a political opponent murdered. The Western Allies begged him to keep Russia in the war, and he didn't have the heart to betray them. What Kerensky lacked in political ruthlessness he may have gained in longevity. Living in New York City, he spent his years justifying his brief rule and denouncing both the Bolsheviks and Russian rightists who tried to bring him down. He died in 1970 at age eighty-nine.

would have been no revolution in Russia at all, let alone a Bolshevik revolution. Lenin himself, in early 1917, doubted he would live to see a revolution in Russia.

Things were not so terrible in Russia before the war. The Duma struggled to erode tsarist autocracy and in time might have succeeded. Industry grew rapidly. Peasants, freed from old restrictions on land ownership, turned into prosperous and productive small farmers. The war changed everything. Repeating their overconfidence of 1904, the tsarist military marched happily to war against Germany in 1914, and this doomed the system. It was a large army, but badly equipped and poorly led. Major offensives ground to a halt before the more effective German forces. The Russian economy fell apart. Troop morale disintegrated, and many deserted. Peasants seized their landlord's grounds. The government was paralyzed, but the tsar refused to change anything.

By 1917 the situation was desperate. In March of that year a group of democratic moderates seized power and deposed the tsar. Resembling Western liberals, the people of the Provisional Government hoped to modernize and democratize Russia. The Western powers, including the United States, welcomed them, thinking they would rally Russians to continue the war. The Provisional Government, which by July was headed by Alexander Kerensky, tried to stay in the war, and that was its undoing. If Kerensky had betrayed the Western Allies and made a separate peace with Germany, the moderates might have been able to retain power.

Meanwhile, the German General Staff, looking for a way to knock Russia out of the war, thought it would be clever to send the agitator Lenin into Russia to create havoc. In April 1917 Lenin and his colleagues traveled in a famous "sealed train"—so the Bolshevik bacillus would not infect Germany, where revolutionary discontent was also growing—across Germany, Sweden, and Finland to Petrograd, the World War I name for St. Petersburg (which sounded too German). Without German help and funds, Lenin might never have made it back to Russia.

GEOGRAPHY

WHY THE OCTOBER REVOLUTION WAS IN NOVEMBER

Every November 7, Russia used to celebrate the anniversary of the Great October Revolution. If this sounds curious, it is because Russia, following its Orthodox church, in 1917 was still using the ancient Julian calendar, which (because it counted too many leap years) ran thirteen days behind the more-accurate Gregorian calendar, in use in Catholic countries since 1582. Protestant countries, fearing a popish plot, also delayed adopting the Gregorian calendar. The Bolsheviks finally switched Russia to the Gregorian calendar but then had to recalculate the October Revolution into November.

At Petrograd's Finland Station, Lenin issued his stirring slogan, "Bread, Land, Peace," speaking respectively to workers, peasants, and soldiers. Lenin immediately saw that a "dual authority" was trying to rule Russia. The Provisional Government controlled the army and foreign policy. But in the most important city, Petrograd, a council (*soviet* in Russian) of workers, soldiers, sailors, and revolutionaries ran things. Soon these councils appeared in many Russian cities. The composition of these soviets was mixed, with the Bolsheviks a small minority. Lenin pursued a double strategy: Make the soviets the only effective governing power and make the Bolsheviks the dominant power in the soviets. Lenin's slogan for this: "All Power to the Soviets."

THE REVOLUTION AND CIVIL WAR

The actual seizure of power in October (see box above) was amazingly easy. In a scene exaggerated by Soviet historians, soldiers and sailors loyal to the Petrograd soviet charged across a big square into the Winter Palace to oust the Provisional Government. But control of Petrograd and Moscow was one thing, control of all gigantic Russia was something else.

The tight organization and discipline of Lenin's Bolsheviks paid off. In a situation of almost total chaos, the best organized win. By a series of shrewd moves, the Bolsheviks were able to dominate the soviets and win many converts from deserting soldiers and sailors. Lenin headed the new government and immediately took Russia out of the war, accepting a punitive peace treaty from the Germans at Brest-Litovsk in March 1918. It was a dictated treaty (*Diktat* in German) that enabled the Germans to seize large areas of Russia and redeploy nearly a million troops to the western front.

Feeling betrayed and concerned that allied military supplies would fall into German hands, the Western Allies sent small expeditionary forces into Russia. American troops actually fought the Bolsheviks in North Russia and Siberia in 1918–1919. This started the Soviet propaganda that the capitalist powers tried to strangle the infant Bolshevik regime in its cradle.

From 1918 to 1920 civil war raged. The White Army, led by reactionary Russian generals and admirals and supplied by the Western Allies, tried to crush the Communists' Red Army. Both sides displayed incredible ruthlessness in a life-or-death struggle. Millions of Russians perished from starvation. Expecting their revolution to spread, the Red Army invaded Poland in 1920, hoping to trigger a Europe-wide socialist upheaval. Instead, the Poles threw back the Red Army and seized parts of Ukraine and Belarus. Lenin and his colleagues saw there would be no world revolution and settled for building the world's first socialist country.

War Communism and NEP

During the civil war, the Bolsheviks tried to plunge directly into their utopian system by running the ruined economy by executive fiat. This **war communism**, as it was euphemistically called, was due as much to the demands of a desperate civil war as to visionary schemes. To motivate workers, Lenin ordered: "He who does not work, neither shall he eat" (from 2 Thessalonians 3:10). War communism led immediately to starvation, and only the charity of American grain shipments (supervised by Herbert Hoover) held the number of deaths to a few million.

Lenin saw Russia was far from ready for pure socialism, so he conducted a planned retreat of state control to the "commanding heights" of heavy industry and let most of the rest of the economy revert to private hands. This period of Lenin's **New Economic Policy** (NEP) brought relative prosperity; farmers worked their own land, "nepmen" behaved like small private entrepreneurs, and life in general relaxed. There was one catch: The NEP was not moving the Soviet Union, as it was now called, any closer to socialism, and industry grew only slowly. It is likely Lenin meant the NEP only as a temporary rest before moving on to socialist construction.

That changed when Stalin took full power in the late 1920s. In 1928 he began the first of the government-enforced **Five-Year Plans** that accelerated collectivization and industrialization (see box on pages 116–117). Peasants resisted giving up their fields, farm production dropped, and millions (especially Ukrainians) were deliberately starved to death. In new factories, workers toiled with primitive tools to boost production of **capital goods**. Setting a pattern for all communist countries, **consumer goods** were deliberately neglected, and the standard of living declined. While many admit the forced industrialization of the 1930s was brutal, some argue it gave the Soviet Union the industrial base to arm against the German invasion in 1941.

As it was, the German invasion caused some twenty-seven million Soviet deaths. The Nazis cared nothing for Slavic lives; starvation was their standard treatment for Russian

Key Terms

war communism   Temporary strict socialism in Russia 1918–1921.

New Economic Policy   Lenin's New Economic Policy that allowed considerable private activity, 1921–1928.

Five-Year Plans   Stalin's forced industrialization of Soviet Union starting in 1928.

capital goods   Implements used to make other things.

consumer goods   Things people use, such as food, clothing, and housing.

PERSONALITIES

STALIN: "ONE DEATH IS A TRAGEDY; A MILLION IS A STATISTIC"

The Soviet system was not so much Lenin's as Stalin's. Lenin was fifty-four when he died in 1924, before giving definitive form to the system. Exactly who is to blame for the horrors that developed—Lenin or Stalin—is a matter of controversy both within and outside Russia. Some still argue that if Lenin had lived, his intelligence and sophistication would have set the country on the path to "true socialism." Others say the structure Lenin created—concentrating power first in the party, then in the Central Committee, and finally in his own person—made the abuse of power inevitable.

Stalin aptly illustrates Acton's dictum, "power corrupts." Stalin lived in order to amass political power and was very good at it. Born Yosif Vissarionovich Djugashvili in 1879, son of a poor shoemaker, Stalin lacked Lenin's intellectual family background and education. Some of Stalin's behavior can be traced to his homeland of Georgia, part of the Caucasus, a mountainous land with a warm climate and fiery people given to personal hatred and blood-feuds. In Georgia, "Soso" (his Georgian nickname) is still praised as a local boy who made good.

The young Djugashvili started to study for the Orthodox priesthood but soon turned to revolution. Expelled from the seminary, he joined the Georgian Marxist underground as an agitator and strike organizer. Repeatedly arrested, jailed, and exiled to Siberia, he always managed to escape. (There is some evidence that he was a double agent for the tsarist police.) Going underground, he took the name Stalin, Russian for "man of steel."

Never a great theoretician, Stalin attracted Lenin's attention as a non-Russian who could write the Bolsheviks' position on the nationalities question. Playing only a moderate role in the October Revolution, Stalin was named commissar for nationalities in 1918 and then, in Lenin's worst mistake, chosen as the party's first general secretary in 1922. People thought the new office would be a clerical job with little power. Lenin and Stalin were never close—although Stalin's historians tried to make it look that way—and toward the end of his life Lenin had an inkling of what Stalin was like. In one of his last messages Lenin urged the party to reject Stalin as "too rude."

It was too late, however. Using his position as **gensek**, Stalin organized the **CPSU** to his advantage by promoting to key posts only those personally loyal to him. It was this organizational spadework that gave Stalin the edge over his rival, Leon Trotsky, organizer of the Red Army and a far more intelligent Marxist. Stalin beat him in party infighting and had him expelled from Russia in 1929 and murdered in Mexico in 1940. Reviled as a deviationist traitor, Trotsky did try to organize an anti-Stalin opposition within the CPSU, a point that fed Stalin's natural **paranoia** and contributed to his ruthlessness in exterminating officials on the slightest suspicion of disloyalty.

Stalin, an uncanny manipulator, played one faction against another until, by the late 1920s, he was the Kremlin's undisputed master. Like Peter the Great, Stalin was determined to modernize regardless of human cost. In 1928 he instituted the first Five-Year Plan, beginning the forced industrialization of Russia. Farmers, very much against their will, were herded into collectives and forced to produce for the state, sometimes at gunpoint. Better-off farmers, the so-called *kulaks,* were "liquidated as a class," a euphemism for killed. Economic development was defined as heavy industry, and steel production became the chief goal of the man of steel.

In 1934, during the second Five-Year Plan, Stalin became obsessed with "Trotskyite" disloyalty in party ranks. Thus began Stalin's **purges**: up to one million party comrades killed, some after they confessed to being British spies or Trotskyite "wreckers." People in positions of prominence trembled that they would be next—and many were. Stalin ordered all managers to train two replacements. Stalin even had all his generals shot, a blunder that hurt the Soviet Union in the 1941 German attack. Perhaps another ten million ordinary citizens, arrested on fake charges, also perished, many in Siberian forced-labor camps. In total, Stalin's orders led to the death of over fifteen million people during collectivization and the purges.

Was Stalin mad? There was some Trotskyite opposition to him, but he exaggerated it. It was Plato who first observed that any tyrant, even one who starts sane, must lose his mind in office because he can trust nobody. More than a question of personality, Stalin shows what happens when one person assumes total power. The Communists did not like to admit it, but it was their *system* that was at fault more than any particular individual.

During his lifetime Stalin was deified as history's greatest linguist, art critic, Marxist theoretician, engineer, agronomist, you name it. His communization of East Europe led to the **Cold War**. By the time he died in 1953—while preparing yet another purge—Stalin had turned the Soviet Union into *his* system, and, in basic outlines, it never did change much. When Mikhail Gorbachev attempted to seriously reform it, the system collapsed.

These three St. Petersburg graves of victims of Stalin's Great Purge convey some of the horror of Stalin's "cleansing" of people he supposed were unreliable. The family of the victim on the right, by erecting a life-size statue of a man in Bolshevik Young Guard uniform, meant to show that he was a faithful Communist all along. (Michael Roskin)

GEOGRAPHY

A TALE OF TWO FLAGS

In late 1991 the familiar communist red flag (with gold hammer and sickle) came down as the Soviet Union dissolved. Red had been the color of socialist movements (taken from the red shirts of Italian unifier Garibaldi) since the nineteenth century; the Bolsheviks made it the national flag in late 1917. The old tsarist flag was developed by Peter the Great, who brought the Netherlands tricolor back with him from his stay in Dutch shipyards in 1699, but changed the stripes from the original Dutch (from the top: red-white-blue) to white-blue-red, sometimes with an imperial double-headed eagle (from Byzantium) on it. The Provisional Government removed the eagle in 1917; this is what the Russian Federation revived as its flag in 1991.

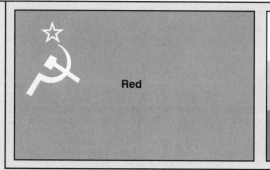

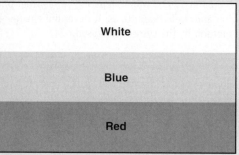

prisoners of war. Faced with extinction, the Soviet Union pulled together. Stalin, like Lenin, recognized the force of Russian nationalism beneath the Communist surface. Reviewing troops marching from Moscow to the front, Stalin mused: "They aren't fighting for communism or for Stalin; they're fighting for Mother Russia." In Russia today, World War II is known as the Great Patriotic War. By the time he died in 1953, Stalin had transformed a backward country into a gigantic empire and major industrial power. He also founded a system that in the long run proved to be inefficient and unreformable and finally collapsed in 1991.

KEY TERMS

gensek   Russian abbreviation for "general secretary," powerful CPSU head (see page 116).

CPSU   Communist Party of the Soviet Union (see page 116).

paranoia   Unreasonable suspicion of others (see page 116).

purge   Stalin's "cleansing" of suspicious elements by firing squad (see page 117).

Cold War   Period of armed tension and competition between the United States and the Soviet Union, approximately 1947–1989 (see page 117).

Key Terms

autocracy (p. 105)

Bolshevik (p. 112)

caesaropapism (p. 107)

capital goods (p. 115)

Cold War (p. 118)

communism (p. 110)

Constantinople (p. 103)

constitutional monarchy (p. 109)

consumer goods (p. 115)

CPSU (p. 118)

Cyrillic (p. 103)

Duma (p. 112)

Enlightenment (p. 103)

exclave (p. 107)

Five-Year Plans (p. 115)

gensek (p. 118)

imperialism (p. 110)

Narodniki (p. 109)

New Economic Policy (p. 115)

paranoia (p. 118)

proletariat (p. 110)

purge (p. 118)

revolution (p. 109)

Siberia (p. 102)

Slavophiles (p. 109)

Tatar (p. 103)

tsar (p. 103)

tyranny (p. 102)

Ukraine (p. 108)

war communism (p. 115)

Westernizers (p. 108)

zemstvo (p. 109)

Further Reference

Conquest, Robert. *The Great Terror: A Reassessment*. New York: Oxford University Press, 1990.

Dukes, Paul. *A History of Russia: Medieval, Modern, Contemporary, c. 882–1996*, 3rd ed. Durham, NC: Duke University Press, 1998.

Figes, Orlando. *Natasha's Dance: A Cultural History of Russia*. New York: Metropolitan Books, 2002.

Fitzpatrick, Sheila. *Everyday Stalinism: Ordinary Life in Extraordinary Times*. New York: Oxford University Press, 1999.

Gilbert, Martin. *The Routledge Atlas of Russian History: From 800 B.C. to the Present Day*, 3rd ed. New York: Routledge, 2002.

Gooding, John. *Socialism in Russia: Lenin and His Legacy, 1890–1991*. New York: Palgrave, 2002.

Hosking, Geoffrey. *Russia and the Russians*. Cambridge, MA: Harvard University Press, 2001.

Kort, Michael G. *Russia*. New York: Facts on File, 2004.

Lieven, Dominic. *Empire: The Russian Empire and Its Rivals*. New Haven, CT: Yale University Press, 2001.

Montefiore, Simon Sebag. *Stalin: The Court of the Red Tsar*. New York: Knopf, 2004.

Read, Christopher. *The Making and Breaking of the Soviet System: An Interpretation*. New York: Palgrave, 2001.

Riasanovsky, Nicholas V., and Mark D. Steinberg. *A History of Russia,* 7th ed. New York: Oxford University Press, 2005.

Service, Robert. *Lenin: A Biography.* Cambridge, MA: Harvard University Press, 2001.

———. *Stalin: A Biography.* Cambridge, MA: Harvard University Press, 2005.

Ulam, Adam B. *The Bolsheviks: The Intellectual and Political History of the Triumph of Communism in Russia.* Cambridge, MA: Harvard University Press, 1998.

8

Russia:
The Key Institutions

Russia now exemplifies the **weak state**, one that cannot effectively collect taxes, pass laws, administer justice, and help its citizens. One characteristic of the weak state, typical of Latin America, is the penetration of crime into government. Corruption, lawlessness, and insecurity are the norm. In such a climate, citizens flock to a leader who rules with a strong hand: Putin.

Russia is sliding back to its authoritarian past, and democracy is unlikely in the near term. Accordingly, we must consider two models, the old Soviet system formed under Stalin and a post-communist system that tried to break with the past but did not quite make it. The dramatic end of the Soviet Union in late 1991 and the birth of a new Russia, we now realize, was less than a **system change**. The new Russian government was not a new broom, and it did not sweep clean. Virtually all of the current leadership has roots deep in the old Soviet system; Russia's constitution overconcentrates power in the presidency, and President Putin has concentrated it more. Much of the old Communist system underlies today's Russia, so we must consider it. As Faulkner said, "The past is not dead. In fact, it's not even past."

THE STALIN SYSTEM

The Soviet system started by Lenin and perfected by Stalin lasted into Gorbachev's tenure. The system changed over time, but not much. Its main structural features were as follows.

Questions to Consider

1. What were the main points of the Stalin system?
2. Why did all three Communist federal systems fail?
3. Is socialism possible without a large bureaucracy?
4. What is the CIS?
5. How is the Russian executive borrowed from France?
6. In what ways did Yeltsin resemble Gorbachev?
7. Putin was elected, so how can he be an authoritarian?
8. Describe the Russian party system. Does it resemble any of the others in this book?

KEY TERMS

weak state   One unable to govern effectively; corrupt and crime-ridden.
system change   Displacement of one set of political institutions by another.

The Communist Party in Command

Said Lenin: "The Communist party is not a party like other parties." Lenin meant that the Bolsheviks would not play the normal political games of democratic parties, contesting elections and leaving office when voted out. The CPSU was going to run Russia without opposition, and it did, for seven decades.

The CPSU was constitutionally defined as "the leading and guiding force of Soviet society." No other parties were permitted, and no factions were allowed inside the Party. The Party did not run things directly but was a central brain and nervous system that transmitted policy lines, oversaw the economy, reported discontent, and selected, promoted, and supervised the system's personnel. There was much overlap between Party and state system, so that at the top, most government ministers were also on the Party's **Central Committee**.

Party membership was tightly controlled. Less than seven percent of the Soviet population (at one point, about nineteen million out of 285 million) were Party members, selected on the basis of good records as workers, students, or youth leaders. The CPSU aimed to skim off the best of Soviet society. The Party was organized like a giant pyramid, with primary party organizations at the bottom; district, province, and republic party conferences in between; and an all-union party conference at the top. Presiding over each conference was a committee. Each level "elected" delegates to the next highest level (actually, they were handpicked from above) in what was called "democratic centralism." Party administrators, **apparatchiki**, held the *apparat* together.

The All-Union Party Congress of some five thousand delegates would meet for a few days every few years, ostensibly to elect the Central Committee of about 300 full and 150 candidate members. The Central Committee would meet twice a year, usually just before the meeting of its government counterpart, the Supreme Soviet, since the membership of the two bodies overlapped.

Above the Central Committee and really running things was the **Politburo**, a full-time decision-making body with about a dozen full members and six candidate members. Politburo decisions were automatically approved by the Central Committee, whose decisions were approved by the Party Congress, and so on down the line. Running the Politburo was a general secretary (*gensek*), called in the West the "party chief." This person in practice usually became supreme boss of both Party and state and assumed dictatorial powers. In most Communist systems, the party chief is the most powerful figure, for he controls the apparat and selects *apparatchiki* who are personally loyal to him.

A Less-Important State Structure

Outside observers agreed that the gigantic Supreme Soviet, with 1,500 members, was not a real parliament. Its members met for only a few days a year to rubber-stamp laws that were drafted by the top echelons of the Party. Nominally bicameral, the Supreme Soviet

---

Central Committee   Large, next-to-top governing body of most Communist parties.

apparatchik   "Man of the apparatus," full-time CPSU functionary.

Politburo   "Political bureau," small, top governing body of most Communist parties.

KEY CONCEPTS

SECURITY POLICE

Security police—sometimes called secret police, after the Nazi Gestapo—are what make dictatorships work and last. In 1991, defeat of the Iraqi army mattered little; Saddam Hussein could not be toppled because he still had his security police, the guardians of his system. Unlike regular police, security police are highly political and focus on preventing any criticism, dissent, or movements that might harm the regime. They often use terror, "the linchpin of the Soviet system," the key element that held it together.

During Stalin's time there was much truth to this, but after Stalin, terror—the fear of being arbitrarily arrested, imprisoned, sent to Siberia, or shot—receded as a means of political control. The security police, later called the KGB (Committee on State Security) were active until the end (and still are), but their methods were more refined and subtle than the Cheka of Lenin's tenure or the NKVD of Stalin's.

Some three-quarters of a million KGB agents were everywhere: guarding the borders, in factories, hotels, and universities, informing on anyone who contacted foreign tourists, handled classified materials, or dissented against the Soviet system. Millions of Soviet citizens had KGB dossiers, and some found out that the KGB was able to recite even trivial incidents from years earlier. Part-time informers, called *stukachi* (squealers), were everywhere.

While the KGB could not actually try most cases—which went to a regular court—they still had the power to frighten by selectively intimidating dissidents. Citizens could lose jobs, get sent to psychiatric hospitals, be denied university entrance, have their rooms bugged, lose the right to live in a city, and generally be made uncomfortable by a word from the KGB.

Although the KGB was formally dissolved with the Soviet Union, its chief component reappeared as the Federal Security Service (FSB in Russian), which is staffed by old KGB hands and carries on with the same tasks: supporting the authorities and eliminating any threat to their power. President Putin handpicked his security police heads and is personally friendly with them. The FSB has strong powers to investigate and arrest, even based on anonymous accusations. Murder and corruption run rampant, but the FSB arrests few. The implication: They are in on the crooked deals and are building *kompromat* (compromising materials) with which to blackmail anyone influential.

Three of Yeltsin's prime ministers in a row were high up in the old KGB and then in the FSB. President Putin was a KGB officer and then head of the FSB, and many of his top appointees—known as *siloviki*, the powerful men—are drawn from the two organizations. The more it changes, the more it stays the same.

"elected" a governing Presidium of twenty members that overlapped with the Politburo. The Presidium simply decreed whatever laws it wished. The Presidium also served as a collective presidency, and its chairman was often called the "president" of the Soviet Union. Since Brezhnev, the Party general secretary was also named president, so as to make clear he headed both state and Party.

Who Was When: Soviet Party Chiefs

Party Chief	Ruled	Main Accomplishments
Vladimir I. Lenin	1917–1924	Led Revolution; instituted War Communism, then NEP.
Josef Stalin	1927–1953	Five-Year Plans of forced collectivization and industrialization; purges; waged World War II; self-deification.
Nikita Khrushchev	1955–1964	Destalinized; experimented with economic and cultural reform; promised utopia soon; ousted.
Leonid Brezhnev	1964–1982	Partially restalinized; refrained from shaking up system; let corruption grow and economy slow.
Yuri Andropov	1982–1984	Cracked down on corruption and alcoholism; suggested major reforms but soon died.
Konstantin Chernenko	1984–1985	*Nichevo.*
Mikhail Gorbachev	1985–1991	Initiated sweeping change, unwittingly collapsed Soviet system.

The Supreme Soviet also chose a sort of cabinet, the mammoth Council of Ministers, with some eighty-five highly specialized ministries, mostly concentrated on branches of the economy (for example, Ministry of Machine Building for Animal Husbandry and Fodder Production). The Council of Ministers rarely met for collective deliberation. Only Politburo members served as prime minister, or minister of state security (KGB), **interior**, defense, and foreign affairs, the "power ministries."

A Centralized Federal System

The Soviet Union was a federation—like the United States, Canada, and Germany—but one long dominated by the center. What the Politburo in Moscow laid down was implemented throughout the country by the Party. The Soviet Union had some two dozen major nationalities and many more minor ones—104 in all. The fifteen largest got their own Soviet Socialist **Republic** (for example, the Uzbek SSR), which together made the USSR (Union of Soviet Socialist Republics). The nationalities, however, are somewhat dispersed; there are ethnic Russians in every newly independent republic—one-third of the populations of Latvia and Kazakhstan are Russian—and this has sharpened a dangerous nationalities question.

The Russian Federative Republic was by far the biggest and is still today a federation of numerous autonomous regions for the bewildering variety of ethnic groups within it. The chief purpose of Soviet federalism was preservation of language rights. Stalin, who developed Soviet nationality policy, recognized that language and culture are potential political dynamite, so it was best to let each nationality feel culturally autonomous while in fact they were politically subordinate. Stalin's formula was: "National in form, socialist in content." This deception turned out to be unstable.

Key Terms

interior ministry   In Europe, department in charge of homeland security and national police.
republic   First-order civil division of Communist federal systems, equivalent to U.S. states.

GEOGRAPHY

GOVERNMENT IN A FORTRESS

Many cities were founded as fortresses, but few still have their walls. The Kremlin (from the Russian *kreml*, "fortress") is a walled city dating back centuries. (The present walls were built in 1492.) Triangular in shape and a mile and a half around, the ancient Kremlin houses government buildings and cathedrals (now public museums). Right next to the Kremlin wall is Lenin's tomb, once used as a reviewing stand by the Politburo for parades in Red Square on May 1 (International Workers' Day) and November 7 (anniversary of the revolution). Also facing Red Square: the colorful onion-shaped domes of St. Basil's Cathedral.

A Gigantic Bureaucracy

Karl Marx argued that after socialism eliminated class differences, the state would "wither away." German sociologist Max Weber countered that socialism required much more state power and a much larger bureaucracy. Marx was wrong; Weber was right. The Soviet bureaucracy became monstrous, with some eighteen million persons administering every facet of Soviet life. **Bureaucratization** spelled the ruination of the Soviet Union, whose civil servants were slow, marginally competent, inflexible, indifferent to efficiency, corrupt, and immune to criticism except from high Party officials. This bureaucracy, carried over largely intact from Soviet days, still delays and blocks important reforms. Getting bureaucrats to change is one of Putin's hardest tasks.

The Party, in fact, interpenetrated and guided the bureaucracy, what the Party called its *kontrol* function. The Party appointed and supervised all important officials, and this kept them on their toes. If they fouled up or were egregiously crooked, they could get demoted or transferred to a remote area. This tended to make officials extremely cautious and go strictly by the book. On the other hand, if officials were effective and successful, the Party could recommend them for higher positions. The key tool in this was the **nomenklatura**, a list of some 600,000 important positions and another list of reliable people eligible to fill them, nearly all of them Party members, and they generally stayed on the list until retirement.

Central Economic Planning

The State Planning Committee, **Gosplan**, was the nerve center of the Soviet economic system, attempting to establish how much of what was produced each year and setting longer-term targets for some 350,000 enterprises. Central planning produced both impressive

KEY TERMS

bureaucratization   Heavily controlled by civil servants.

nomenklatura   Lists of sensitive positions and people eligible to fill them, the Soviet elite.

Gosplan   Soviet central economic planning agency.

GEOGRAPHY

FEDERATIONS

Diversity is the advantage of **federalism**, a system that yields major autonomy to their **first-order civil divisions**, be they U.S. or Brazilian states, German **Länder**, or Russian republics. The components cannot be legally erased or split or have their boundaries easily changed; such matters are grave constitutional questions. Certain powers are reserved for the **center** (defense, money supply, interstate commerce, and so on) while other powers are reserved for the components (education, police, highways, and so on). Large countries or those with particularistic languages or traditions lend themselves to federalism.

The advantages of a federal system are its flexibility and accommodation to particularism. Texans feel Texas is different and special; Bavarians feel Bavaria is different and special; Québécois feel Quebec is different and special; and so on.

If one state or province wishes to try a new formula for funding health care, it may do so without upsetting the state-federal balance. If the new way works, it may be gradually copied. If it fails, little harm is done before it is phased out. U.S. states in this regard have been called "laboratories of democracy": You can try something in one state without committing the entire nation to it. Governments at the Land or state level also serve as training grounds for politicians before they try the national level. Examples: Texas Governor George Bush and Guanajuato Governor Vicente Fox.

The disadvantage is the inconsistent and sometimes sloppy administration among components. Many federal systems cannot achieve nationwide standards in education, environment, welfare, or health care. One state wants something and can afford it; another state cannot. One state says a certain type of person is eligible for a program; another says he or she is not. Federal systems are less coherent than unitary systems. To correct such problems, many federal systems have granted more power to the center at the expense of the states. The United States is a prime example of this; compare the relative powers of the states and of Washington over the course of a century. In unitary systems there is a tugging in the direction of federalism, whereas in federal systems there is a tugging in the direction of unitary systems. This does not necessarily mean that the two will eventually meet in some middle ground; it means that neither unitary nor federal systems are finished products and that both are still evolving.

A federal system may also achieve a stable balance between local and national loyalties, leading gradually to a psychologically integrated country, as the United States, Germany, and Switzerland. This

KEY TERMS

federalism   System in which component areas have considerable autonomy.

first-order civil division   Main territorial unit within countries, such as Canadian provinces.

Land   (plural *Länder*) Germany's first-order civil division, equivalent to U.S. state.

center   In federal systems, powers of nation's capital.

does not always work, though. Soviet, Yugoslav, and Czechoslovak federalism actually fostered resentments of the republics against the center. When Communist party strength weakened, local nationalists took over and declared independence. All three of the world's Communist federal systems failed—messy in the Soviet Union, bloody in Yugoslavia, but peaceful in Czechoslovakia—and the huge Russian Federation still has problems with unity.

The tsarist system imposed a unitary pattern on the empire that was so hated that old Russia was called "the prison of nations." With the Bolshevik Revolution, Finland and the Baltic states of Lithuania, Latvia, and Estonia happily escaped to independence. (In 1940, Stalin swallowed the Baltics and treated their citizens cruelly.) Stalin thought he could retain the tsarist empire in a Soviet Union that, on paper, granted each republic great autonomy.

With Gorbachev's *glasnost* (openness) policy of relative freedom of speech and press, out came the nationalities question with a vengeance. Amid economic uncertainty, many republics prohibited shipment or sale of scarce commodities to other republics, thus nullifying the main point of a federation: economic integration of a large area. In 1991, all fifteen republics departed from the union and legally dissolved it.

Many ex-Soviet nationalities fear, hate, or resent other nationalities. Attitudes border on racism. Particularly delicate is the question of the 25 million Russians who now live outside of Russia. The Russian army has made clear that it will use force to protect them and has already done so in Moldova, where several hundred Romanian-speakers were gunned down. The newly independent republics are cautious about antagonizing Russia.

Why did Soviet federalism fail to integrate its peoples? There are many factors. First, there are so many national groups that not all could have their own territories. Second, the nationalities are dispersed; in Uzbekistan, for example, there are Tajiks, Russians, Jews, Tatars, Koreans, and many others in addition to Uzbeks. It would not be possible to draw a clean line separating nationalities.

Third, the Soviet federal system was devised by Stalin, who drew the borders deliberately to make sure there would be ethnic tension. This gave Stalin the ability to arbitrate disputes and thus increase his own power, the old "divide and rule" technique. Every republic would depend on Stalin. Fourth, the center held too much power, chiefly through the Communist party and KGB, so the federalism was less than genuine.

The Soviet Union paid the price for Stalin's fake federal system. Can a Russian federalism now be devised that will hold the Russian Federation with its eighty-nine component parts together by bonds of trade, laws, and mutual respect? Some feared the endless war in Chechnya was a taste of things to come.

growth and massive dislocations. Under Stalin, it enabled the Soviet Union to industrialize quickly, albeit at terrible human cost. But it also meant chronic shortages of items the Gosplan ignored. One year no toothbrushes were produced in the entire Soviet Union, a Gosplan oversight.

Soviet leaders claimed that a planned and centrally directed economy was more rational than a Western market economy. Actual results refuted that, but Soviet bureaucrats were reluctant to surrender central planning, an article of faith of "scientific socialism." In Gosplan the hopes, aims, fears, and sometimes caprices of the Soviet system converged and struggled. Gosplan, itself quite sensitive to the wishes of the Politburo, determined who got what in the Soviet Union, whether steel grew at x percent this year and plastics at y percent next. Heavily computerized, Gosplan was the steering wheel of the Soviet economy.

THE NEW SYSTEM

In the months after the failed coup of August 1991, the old Soviet system collapsed, and from the rubble emerged a new system that looks democratic on paper but does not function that way.

No More Soviet Union

All of the fifteen Soviet republics took advantage of the turmoil of late 1991 and declared their independence. The Baltic republics especially—Lithuania, Latvia, and Estonia—led the way to full and immediate independence. They expelled Soviet police, issued their own passports and visas, and took control of their borders. The other republics soon followed suit, and now all are independent, some more so than others. Although Ukraine had been part of tsarist Russia for centuries and was the breadbasket of the Soviet Union, many Ukrainians resented being ruled by Moscow, especially after they read about what Stalin's farm collectivization had done to them—deliberately starved six million people to death. They voted for independence and, in 2004, for a pro-Western democracy.

Belarus (formerly Belarussia, the area between Russia and Poland), which had never been an independent country or harbored much separatist feeling, voted for independence, too. But Belarus still uses the Russian ruble as currency and gets sweetheart trade deals with Russia. Its army is closely linked to the Russian army. Belarus in reality never cut its Russian ties and is ruled by Europe's last dictator.

The most alarming problem was the ethnic tension that came out in the republics. Minorities who had lived in peace for generations (because the KGB was watching) became the target of nationalist resentment. In the Caucasus, blood flowed. Many politicians at the republic level played the nationalist card, and this easily led to violent behavior within the republics. Their messages were simple and effective: Georgia for the Georgians, Uzbekistan for the Uzbeks, Armenia for the Armenians, even Russia for the Russians.

All of the Central Asian republics plus Azerbaijan have a Muslim majority and speak a Turkic language except the Tajiks, who speak a type of Persian (like Iran). There has been Muslim-Christian violence between Azeris and Armenians and in Georgia. Inside the Russian Federation, Muslim Chechnya, brutally crushed by the Russian army, produces murderous terrorists. All together, however, more were killed in ex-Yugoslavia. A big question: In which direction will the ex-Soviet Muslim republics go—toward the modern and secular example of Turkey, toward the Islamic fundamentalism of Iran, or back to an economically and militarily dominant Russia?

DEMOCRACY

1991: THE COUP THAT FAILED

In August 1991, as Gorbachev was on vacation in the Crimea, most of his cabinet tried to overthrow him. An eight-man **junta** (Russians used the Spanish word) of conservatives, calling themselves the "Emergency Committee," said Gorbachev had taken ill and declared his vice-president acting president.

Some Western experts had been predicting a **coup** for three years. Gorbachev's reforms, cautious as they were, threatened the Soviet system and the jobs and comforts of the Soviet ruling elite. Gorbachev had been warned repeatedly of their anger. In December 1990 Foreign Minister Eduard Shevardnadze resigned in public protest at what he said was a coming dictatorship.

Gorbachev zig-zagged between promising major reforms and reassuring Party conservatives that he would not reform too much. In 1991 Gorbachev again favored reform and with the leaders of nine of the Soviet republics drafted a new union treaty that would give the republics great autonomy within a market economy. This was the last straw for the conservatives. The day before the treaty was to be signed they staged their coup.

For three days the world held its breath. Would the coup by not-very-bright Kremlin apparatchiks succeed? The apparatchiks seemed to hold the upper hand. Among them were the head of the military, the KGB, and the interior ministry. The following are some of the reasons the coup failed:

- Few supported the coup. Tens of thousands of citizens favoring democracy publicly opposed the coup. Gorbachev was not very popular, but the junta was much worse.
- Boris Yeltsin stood firm. Approximately a mile and a half from the Kremlin is the parliament of the Russian Republic, then presided over by reformist Yeltsin. Yeltsin and his helpers holed up in the building and declared the junta's decrees illegal. A tank column sent to take the building instead sided with Yeltsin and defended the building. Thousands of Muscovites came to stand guard and protest the coup. Yeltsin's toughness galvanized opposition.
- The Soviet armed forces started to split. Many commanders either stood on the sidelines or opposed the junta. Facing a bloody civil war, the junta lost its nerve.
- International pressure opposed the coup. All major countries made it clear that the Soviet economy, desperate for foreign help, would get none if the coup succeeded. Foreign broadcasts (heard by Gorbachev himself) heartened the anti-junta forces.

A haggard Gorbachev returned to Moscow vowing further reform. The junta was arrested (one committed suicide). The coup attempt actually hastened the end of the Soviet Union. After it, Gorbachev was revealed as an indecisive failure. Yeltsin bumped him out of power and proclaimed an independent Russia. Democracy got a chance.

KEY TERMS

junta   Pronounced Spanish-style, "khun-ta"; group that pulls military coup.

coup   Extralegal seizure of power, usually by military officers.

GEOGRAPHY

THE FIFTEEN EX-SOVIET REPUBLICS

We should learn the names and approximate location of each of the fifteen former Soviet republics; they are now independent countries, but many are under Russian influence. (See the map at the beginning of Chapter 7). To help you remember the republics, note that there are three groups of three, plus a **Central Asia** group of five (the five -stans), plus one oddball.

Slavic	Baltic	Caucasian	Central Asian	Romanian-Speaking
Russia	Lithuania	Georgia	Turkmenistan	Moldova (formerly Moldavia)
Ukraine	Latvia	Armenia	Kazakhstan	
Belarus	Estonia	Azerbaijan	Kyrgyzstan	
			Uzbekistan	
			Tajikistan	

A Commonwealth of Independent States

Is anything left of the old Soviet federal system? As it officially ceased to exist at the end of 1991, most of its component republics agreed to form a "Commonwealth of Independent States" (CIS), with headquarters in Minsk, Belarus. Conspicuously missing were the three Baltic republics and Georgia. Georgia was later forced, in the middle of a civil war abetted by Moscow, to sign the CIS treaty. No one quite knows what the powers of the CIS are, but most now think it is a Moscow plan to regain control over the ex-Soviet republics, in effect, to rebuild the Russia of Peter the Great.

There are reasons for some republics retaining ties with giant Russia. First, eight of the twelve CIS member republics are landlocked and need Russia for access to the outside world. Industrially, all are tied to the Russian economy for manufactured goods and energy. Financially, over the decades many of these republics benefited from major Soviet aid.

A New Constitution

Along with voting for a new parliament, in late 1993 Russians also approved a new and completely different constitution, one modeled on de Gaulle's 1958 French constitution.

KEY TERM

Central Asia   Lands between Caspian Sea and China, formerly part of Russia and Soviet Union.

DEMOCRACY

RUSSIA'S 2004 PRESIDENTIAL ELECTIONS

Russian presidential elections, held every four years, are modeled on the French two-round system. The 2004 results resembled those of 2000 except Putin won a bigger majority on the first round of 2004, so in neither case was there a second round. In 2004 Putin had less opposition—few dared run against him—and won with more than 70 percent. Russians were happy with the stability and economic growth Putin had brought.

Turnout was an unenthusiastic 64.4 percent, as many Russians knew Putin would easily win. Three and a half percent voted for "none of the above," allowed on the Russian ballot. The 2004 results:

Candidate	Party	Percent
Vladimir Putin	United Russia	71.3
Nikolai Kharitonov	Communist	13.7
Sergei Glazev	Motherland	4.1
Against all candidates		3.5

If no one had won a majority, a runoff would have been held two weeks later between the top two, as was done in 1996. Between the two rounds in 1996, deal-making rounded up majority support for incumbent President Boris Yeltsin. In both 1996 and 2000, most of the Russian mass media, owned by newly rich *oligarchs,* supported the incumbents, and voting irregularities were reported. By 2004, almost all of the media was back in state hands and fawned on Putin. The 2004 election was not democratic. There was nominal competition, but several candidates endorsed Putin. And competition is the crux of democracy. Putin, who could have won a fair election, likes to control everything.

A Strong President   Many observers now say that the presidency, borrowed from French **semipresidentialism**, started too strong, got stronger, and is being misused. The Russian president—elected for a maximum of two four-year terms—sets basic policy, names the prime minister and other top officials, and can veto bills and dissolve parliament. In many areas the president can simply rule by decree. The president can give himself strong emergency powers. The president's power could theoretically be offset by opposition parties in the Duma, but President Putin owns the Duma. There is no vice-president; if the

KEY TERMS

turnout   Percentage of those eligible who vote in a given election.

semipresidentialism   Strong president aided by a prime minister.

PERSONALITIES

PUTIN: THE KGB PRESIDENT

Russian President Vladimir Putin is hard to read and likes it that way; he keeps his emotions and upcoming moves to himself. At first, many dismissed him as a mediocre mid-level KGB bureaucrat (which he was) without the color, intellect, or vision to lead Russia. But he soon emerged as a cold, secretive authoritarian, who cleverly stabilized Russia and his own power. Unlike his predecessor Yeltsin, Putin is rational, sober, and healthy.

In four months, Putin (pronounced POOH-tin) rose from obscurity to powerful president of the Russian Federation, first as acting president and then elected on his own in 2000. In August 1999, Yeltsin named Putin, then forty-six years old, as his fifth prime minister in seventeen months. Many thought Putin was another temp, but Yeltsin soon designated him as successor. Yeltsin, extremely unpopular by that point, resigned at the end of 1999, and Putin constitutionally became acting president.

Putin's KGB connections brought him one good job after another, and his taking of power represents a quiet KGB coup. Nothing else explains how he could rise so fast from obscurity. Putin graduated law school in 1975 and went right into the KGB, where he became a lieutenant colonel in spy operations in East Germany. As the Soviet Union collapsed, Putin worked in St. Petersburg's municipal government, where he became vice mayor in 1994. In 1996, Yeltsin brought him to the Kremlin to supervise relations among Russia's regions and in 1998 made him head of the FSB. In 1999 Putin was named secretary of the powerful Security Council and then premier, his first substantial exposure to the public. His election to president in 2000 (on the first round) was his first run for any office.

Putin is reasonably bright, but his great strength is his background and sponsors in the KGB (now FSB), who have *kompromat* (compromising materials) to control Russia's most powerful people. They know exactly who is corrupt and who stashes money overseas, including politicians and oligarchs.

Many call Putin authoritarian, but Russians have always rallied to a strong ruler in times of danger and decay, precisely what the Yeltsin years brought. No pure democrat could survive and govern Russia at this stage of its development. By new laws, threats, demotions, or criminal trials, Putin controlled the bureaucracy, media, Duma, regional governors, and oligarchs and now, unlike Yeltsin, is fully in charge.

Putin created mass support by renewing the war in Chechnya (see page 176). Chechen bombs in several Russian cities blew up apartment houses and schools and killed hundreds. The Russian people and army wanted revenge. Putin's orders to crush Chechen rebels drew nearly complete support and let him easily win the presidency in 2000.

Putin allowed President Bush to portray him as a warm friend, especially after 9/11, but by 2003 turned hostile over the Iraq war and alleged U.S. meddling in Russian and Ukrainian politics. Putin's economic views are vague. He passed some long-overdue legal and commercial reforms but brought Russia's oil and gas—its major exports—back under Kremlin control. Putin's goals are those of a KGB officer: restore Russia's power and old borders. Democracy just gets in the way.

GEOGRAPHY

RUSSIA'S COMPLEX FEDERALISM

Unlike U.S. states or German *Länder*, Russia's subdivisions are not the same or equal. Instead, there are a confusing four types:

- twenty-one republics, homelands of the major non-Russian nationalities. For example, Tatars have Tatarstan, and Buryats have Buryatia.
- fifty-two *oblasts* (regions), mostly populated by Russians.
- six *krais* (territories).
- ten autonomous *okrugs* (districts), ethnic portions of oblasts or krais that claim special status.

On paper, the republics have more autonomy. For a few years local strongmen carved out personal fiefdoms. Putin ended that by taking the power to personally appoint governors and new "super governors," thus recentralizing power in Moscow.

president dies or is incapacitated, the prime minister serves as acting president until elections are held within three months. This happened when Yeltsin suddenly resigned at the end of 1999.

A Prime Minister　Again on the French model, Russia has a prime minister as well as a president, and their relative powers are not completely clear or fixed. The president can name and fire prime ministers at will, but they must be confirmed by the Duma, and Yeltsin had some trouble doing this. Putin has no such trouble; the Duma simply obeys. If the Duma rejects the president's nominee for prime minister three times, the president can dissolve the Duma and hold new parliamentary elections. In 2004, President Putin named an experienced administrator, Mikhail Fradkov, as his prime minister with solid Duma approval. Fradkov speaks English and Spanish.

A Federal System　The federal system is carried over from the old Soviet structure. The country's true name is the Russian Federation; it consists of eighty-nine regions—most of them "republics"—twenty-one of which are predominantly non-Russian. Each region is supposed to be bound by treaty to the Federation, but not all have signed, and they do not all like Moscow's rule. One Caucasian Muslim republic, Chechnya, which had resisted Russian rule since its original tsarist conquest, won temporary **de facto** autonomy but was then shelled into ruin.

KEY TERM

de facto　In fact, even if not formally admitted.

DEMOCRACY

1993: THE SECOND COUP THAT FAILED

The 1991 coup attempt was carried out by members of Gorbachev's own executive branch and was stopped by members of the Russian (not Soviet) parliament in its White House some distance from the Kremlin. The October 1993 coup attempt was by a paralyzed parliament that occupied the White House and was crushed by armed forces under President Yeltsin, who was now in the Kremlin.

The trigger of the 1993 attempt was Yeltsin's order to dissolve the Russian parliament and hold new elections. (The old Soviet Congress of Peoples Deputies disappeared with the USSR at the end of 1991.) The Russian parliament had been elected in 1989 under the old regime, when the CPSU still held sway; accordingly, it was incoherent and incapable of passing a new constitution. Yeltsin could no longer govern with this parliament, and, indeed, it was high time for free and fair parliamentary elections.

But the old parliament did not like being put out of business and called Yeltsin dictatorial. A majority of deputies declared the dissolution illegal and holed up in the White House, hoping that the country and especially the army would side with it. They did not; instead, tanks shelled the White House until it caught fire.

Yeltsin won but he lost. New elections were held in December 1993, but by then so many Russians were disillusioned with reforms that brought crime, inflation, and unemployment that they voted in a parliament, now called the State Duma, that was heavily antireformist and anti-Yeltsin. Yeltsin had to dump many reformist ministers.

Russian Parliament, the "White House" some distance from the Kremlin, was the scene of two dramatic showdowns. In 1991 Boris Yeltsin stood here and faced down the junta that attempted to oust Gorbachev, but in 1993 it was Yeltsin who ordered the building shelled to break a coup attempt by parliamentarians. The White House was quickly restored and now houses Russia's State Duma. (Michael Roskin)

DEMOCRACY

RUSSIA'S 2003 OBEDIENT PARLIAMENTARY ELECTIONS

Russia's 2003 Duma elections were far less competitive than the previous ones in 1999. Basically, Putin's United Russia party took over the Duma, turning Russia from a fragmented party system into a dominant-party system. Two small liberal parties were wiped out. Fewer Russians bothered voting; turnout was only 56 percent. International observers called the elections flawed because of the state-controlled media and ballot-box stuffing.

In 1999, of the twenty-six parties that ran for the State Duma, six cleared the 5-percent threshold to win some of the 450 seats. In 2003, only four parties cleared the 5-percent threshold.

Party	Orientation	% PR Vote	Total Seats
United Russia	Pro-Putin	38	306
Communists	Socialist	13	52
Liberal Democrats	Right Nationalist	11	36
Motherland	Left Nationalist	9	38
Yabloko	Democratic	4	0
Union of Right-Wing Forces	Reformist	4	0

Total seats are not proportional to party vote because half of the seats are filled in 225 single-member districts. In 2004 fifteen independent deputies were elected on that basis. Several seats were unfilled, either because of voting irregularities or the war in Chechnya. To change the Russian constitution requires a two-thirds majority in the Duma, which Putin now has.

A Bicameral Parliament   The bicameral parliament resembles the U.S. Congress but has little power to contradict the Russian presidency. The lower house, the **State Duma** (reviving the old tsarist name), consists of 450 deputies elected for up to four years (but not in sync with presidential elections). The Duma passes bills, approves the budget, and confirms the president's nominees for top jobs. It can vote no confidence in a cabinet and, along with the upper house, can override a presidential veto with a two-thirds majority. The upper house, the Federation Council, consists of two members named by each of the

KEY TERM

State Duma   Lower house of Russia's parliament.

eighty-nine regional governments of the Russian Federation. Since Putin names the regional governors, he indirectly also picks the regions' deputies for the Federation Council. The Council's duties are somewhat different than the Duma's. Only the Federation Council can change internal boundaries and ratify the use of armed forces abroad. It appoints top judges and prosecutors and can remove them. Putin controls both houses of parliament, and they pass any law he wants, including laws that give him more power.

A Constitutional Court   The constitutional court is borrowed chiefly from the United States but with some French and German features. The Russian Constitutional Court has nineteen judges appointed by the president and confirmed by the upper house. These judges are supposed to be independent and cannot be fired. They may act on citizens' complaints as well as on cases submitted by government agencies. The court is supposed to make sure all laws and decrees conform to the constitution. Putin however, put it back under political control so that it does little to promote the rule of law in Russia.

A Split Electoral System   This system is borrowed from Germany. Half of the Duma's 450 seats are elected by proportional representation (with a 5-percent threshold), half by single-member districts with plurality win. This "mixed-member" system may be short-lived. Putin reportedly wishes to go to straight PR by party list in order to squeeze out any independent candidates who might win in the single-member districts.

A Party System under Construction

From a one-party system under the Soviets, Russia went to a fragmented system of many weak parties to what is now effectively a dominant-party system (see page 239). Several of Russia's political parties sprang up quickly but were weak, divided, constantly changing, and personalistic, like Latin American parties. Russia's top parties aimed chiefly at getting their leaders elected. In the 1999 Duma elections, five parties had present or former prime ministers as leaders. Putin invented the United Russia party, his vehicle to win the presidency twice and dominate the Duma. And not all Russian parties are democratic; some preach **chauvinism** or a return to communism.

The party system is perhaps the foundation of political stability in the modern world. Britain is basically a two-party system, France a multiparty system, and Germany a "two-plus" system. All have achieved stability. A system with too many parties, some of them extremist, poses a serious threat to democracy. Some thought Russia was headed that way, but the 2003 Duma elections show Russia going the other way, to a dominant-party system (see chapter on Mexico) with no democratic checks or balances on an all-powerful president. Yes, Russians could theoretically elect a Duma to offset the president, but with the Russian preference for a strong hand at the top and the media back in government hands, this will not soon happen.

KEY TERM

chauvinism   Extreme nationalism.

KEY TERMS

apparatchik (p. 122)

bureaucratization (p. 125)

center (p. 126)

Central Asia (p. 130)

Central Committee (p. 122)

chauvinism (p. 136)

coup (p. 129)

de facto (p. 133)

federalism (p. 126)

first-order civil division (p. 126)

Gosplan (p. 125)

interior ministry (p. 124)

junta (p. 129)

Land (p. 126)

nomenklatura (p. 125)

Politburo (p. 122)

republic (p. 124)

semipresidentialism (p. 131)

State Duma (p. 135)

system change (p. 121)

turnout (p. 131)

weak state (p. 121)

FURTHER REFERENCE

Andrews, Josephine T. *When Majorities Fail: The Russian Parliament, 1990–1993*. New York: Cambridge University Press, 2002.

Barry, Donald D. *Russian Politics: The Post-Soviet Phase*. New York: Peter Lang, 2001.

Brown, Archie, ed. *Contemporary Russian Politics: A Reader*. New York: Oxford University Press, 2001.

Hahn, Jeffrey W., ed. *Democratization in Russia: The Development of Legislative Institutions*. Armonk, NY: M. E. Sharpe, 1996.

Knight, Amy. *Spies without Cloaks: The KGB's Successors*. Princeton, NJ: Princeton University Press, 1996.

Marsh, Christopher. *Russia at the Polls: Voters, Elections, and Democratization*. Washington, D.C.: CQ Press, 2002.

Medish, Vadim. *The Rise and Fall of the Soviet Union*, 5th ed. Upper Saddle River, NJ: Prentice Hall, 2002.

Nichols, Thomas M. *The Russian Presidency: Society and Politics in the Second Russian Republic*. New York: Palgrave, 2001.

Orttung, Robert W. *The Republics and Regions of the Russian Federation: A Guide to Politics, Policies, and Leaders*. Armonk, NY: M. E. Sharpe, 2000.

Remington, Thomas F. *The Russian Parliament: Institutional Evolution in a Transitional Regime, 1989–1999*. New Haven, CT: Yale University Press, 2001.

Sakwa, Richard. *Russian Politics and Society*, 3rd ed. New York: Routledge, 2002.

Smith, Steven S., and Thomas F. Remington. *The Politics of Institutional Choice: The Formation of the Russian State Duma*. Princeton, NJ: Princeton University Press, 2001.

Sperling, Valerie, ed. *Building the Russian State: Institutional Crisis and the Quest for Democratic Governance*. Boulder, CO: Westview, 2000.

9

Russian Political Culture

As the Soviet regime declined and collapsed in the late 1980s and early 1990s, the word *democracy* had a positive ring among Russians. It stood for a new beginning, for justice and prosperity, and for joining the Western world. The leading political party was *Demrossiya*, Democratic Russia. Now, after living through several years of economic decline, lawlessness, and national weakness, few Russians care about democracy. They want food on the table, order, and stability, and most think the authoritarian Putin has given it to them. A 2004 poll found that only 30 percent of Russians said democracy is always best; 34 percent said autocracy is sometimes better; and 26 percent said they would vote for Stalin. Poor soil for democracy.

Ignoring the crucial factor of political culture, we naively assumed the collapse of the Communist regime would unleash **liberal democracy** and free-market prosperity. Instead it brought monumental lawlessness and poverty. A handful of **oligarchs** got very rich buying state business (especially oil) at giveaway prices. Mafia gangs were into everything, including the government. Some called the system, half in jest, a **kleptocracy**. The breakdown demonstrated what some scholars long suspected, that under the law-and-order surface of Soviet rule, Russian society was very weak—indeed, it had been made deliberately weak—and could not sustain a free democracy, at least not for some time.

KEY TERMS

liberal democracy   Combines tolerance and freedoms (liberalism) with mass participation (democracy).

oligarchy   Rule by a few.

kleptocracy   Rule by thieves.

1. How can democracy grow in a country where "democracy" has brought decay and poverty?

2. Why is democracy harder in Russia than in ex-Communist Central Europe?

3. Was Solzhenitsyn right about American culture? Why then has it spread worldwide, especially among young people?

4. How to tell if a system is based on ideology? Was the Soviet system? What empirical indicators could you look for?

5. What is "civil society" and how do you get it? Is it the same as "pluralism"?

6. Has Russia stabilized, or is it still "Weimar Russia"?

7. What is the difference between immoral business behavior in America and Russia?

8. Why did we think Russia after communism would quickly become like us?

GEOGRAPHY

HUNTINGTON'S "CIVILIZATIONAL" DIVIDE IN EUROPE

In an influential but controversial article in the Summer 1993 *Foreign Affairs*, Harvard political scientist Samuel P. Huntington argued that with the Cold War over, profound differences of culture were dividing the world into several "civilizations" that have trouble understanding each other. What Huntington called "civilizations" mostly follow religious lines: the West European (with a North American branch), the Slavic/Orthodox, Muslim, Hindu, Confucian, Japanese, and Latin American.

In Europe, said Huntington, the key geographic line is still where Eastern Orthodoxy meets the two branches of Western Christianity, Catholicism and Protestantism, a line running south from the Baltic republics (Lithuania is mostly Catholic, Latvia and Estonia Protestant) and along the eastern borders of Poland, Slovakia, Hungary, and Croatia. West European civilization, initially in Protestant countries, led the way to democracy and capitalism. The Catholic countries followed more recently. Poland, the Czech Republic, and Hungary turned quickly to market systems and democracy after ousting their Communist regimes in 1989.

But notice the difficulty experienced by Slavic/Orthodox countries such as Russia, Ukraine, Serbia, and Romania in making this transition. Basic assumptions about individual freedom and choice, private property, personal rights, and the rule of law that are widespread in West Europe have not developed in the same way in Slavic/Orthodox Europe. One key point: Orthodox culture is much less individualistic, and this helps account for economic behavior.

Economic *shock therapy* (the sudden introduction of a free market) soon brought rapid growth to Poland. Applied in Russia, it simply collapsed the economy: *shock without therapy*. Many observers suggest the differences between Poland and Russia are cultural, that Poland has always faced west and Russia not. Huntington's theory does not mean that other civilizations cannot become free-market democracies, just that it may take some time.

THE RUSSIAN DIFFERENCE

Central Europe discarded its Communist regimes in 1989, and within five years Poland, the Czech Republic, and Hungary were functioning democracies with mostly private market economies. During this time, the Soviet Union, trying to make the same transition, collapsed economically and politically. Why the difference between Central Europe and Russia?

First, there are cultural differences between the mostly Roman Catholic countries of Central Europe and Eastern Orthodox Russia (see box above). Second, the Communists succeeded in capturing Russian **nationalism**, so that a Russian could take a certain pride

KEY TERM

nationalism   Belief in greatness and unity of one's country and rejection of rule by foreigners.

GEOGRAPHY

BOUND SERBIA AND MONTENEGRO

Serbia and Montenegro (ex-Yugoslavia) is bounded on the north by Hungary;
on the east by Romania and Bulgaria;
on the south by Macedonia and Albania;
and on the west by the Adriatic, Bosnia, and Croatia.

In 2003 Yugoslavia, a **rump state**, changed its name to Serbia and Montenegro. The old Yugoslavia of 1918–1941 and 1945–1991 included Slovenia, Croatia, Bosnia, and Macedonia, all of which are now independent. Why not just call it Serbia? Its government wished to preserve the boundary agreements that used the name Yugoslavia. If Montenegro (Black Mountain), which is restless, should depart from the federation, Serbia would lose its outlet to the sea and would probably be called just Serbia, which it was before World War I. In 1999, Serbia lost Kosovo and its largely Albanian population. With the bounding exercises you have now done, you should be able to locate most countries of Europe. Which European lands have not been named in our bounding exercises?

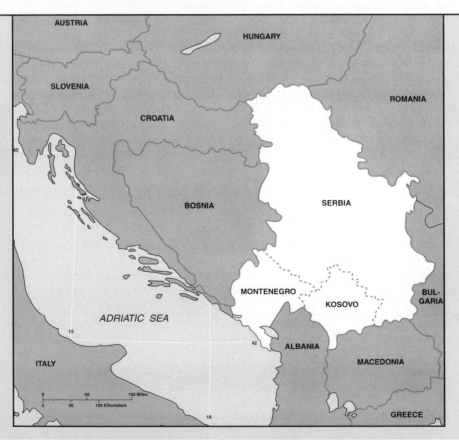

in communism. For Central Europeans, communism was put and kept in place by Soviet bayonets and was profoundly at odds with local nationalism.

Perhaps more basically, communism had been implanted in Central Europe much later (after World War II) than in the Soviet Union; it did not have as much time to take hold. Russians had nearly three-quarters of a century of Communist rule (1917–1991), enough for three generations to know only one system. Furthermore, the previous tsarist system had not been democratic either and was just in the early stages of capitalist economic development.

The system Russians were used to provided them with jobs (constitutionally guaranteed) and a low but generally predictable standard of living. An apartment, once you got one, was tacky by Western standards but cost only a few dollars a month. Few Russians worked hard; there was little point to it. Now, suddenly Russians are told their jobs are not guaranteed and that reward is linked to individual achievement.

The result was psychological disorientation and fear. The economy declined, inflation grew, unemployment increased, and parents worried over how to feed their children. The old legitimacy of Party and leadership collapsed, and nothing took its place. First Gorbachev and then Yeltsin lost their early credibility; they had indecisively zigged and zagged so long on the economy that few saw them as leaders.

In the vacuum of belief, cynicism and despair reign. Some Russians rediscovered their Orthodox Church, which grew after the Communist collapse but has not kept growing. Few attend Orthodox services (but Catholicism and Protestantism are expanding in Russia). Many Russians believe in nothing and say everything is going wrong. Most are politically numb and care nothing for democracy. But people have to believe in something; cynicism cannot sustain a society. Western values of a free society, of morality rooted in religion, of civil rights, and of individual achievement in a market economy are talked about by some intellectuals but not widely held. Seven decades of Communist rule stomped them out; they are being painfully relearned.

The Mask of Legitimacy

For decades, the CPSU tried to pound into Soviet skulls the feeling that the regime was legitimate—that is, it had the right to rule—and was leading the country through the difficulties of "building socialism" to the working utopia of communism. It is impossible to say how many really believed this. At various times, many did. Foreigners were treated to performances of marchers, youth delegations, and seemingly frank conversations with officials that were designed to show that Soviets believed in the system. In private, Western journalists were sometimes able to establish contacts who told them otherwise: dissident intellectuals, bitter workers, and even Party members who had come to doubt the worth of the system.

When Gorbachev permitted increased freedom of expression in the late 1980s, **glasnost**, torrents of criticism poured out. Freed from fear of the police, the media bitterly criticized the bureaucracy, the Party, and the corruption of both. The mask of Soviet legitimacy

Key Terms

rump state   Leftover portions of a country after dismemberment (see page 140).

glasnost   Gorbachev's policy of media openness.

POLITICAL CULTURE

SOLZHENITSYN, A RUSSIAN MYSTIC

In 1963 a short, grim novel, *One Day in the Life of Ivan Denisovich,* burst on the Soviet literary scene. In detailing the horrors of Siberian forced labor, its author spoke from intimate experience: Alexander Solzhenitsyn had lived in such a camp from 1945 to 1953 and then in Siberian exile for another three years. His crime: As an artillery captain he criticized Stalin in a letter to a friend.

But the nightmare conditions did not break Solzhenitsyn; they made him stronger. Freed during Khrushchev's brief period of liberalization, Solzhenitsyn resolved to tell the whole story of Soviet repression through novels and nonfiction. But *One Day* was about as much of the truth as the regime allowed—and that was under the unusual circumstances of Khrushchev's destalinization drive—and Solzhenitsyn was soon expelled from the official writers' union and unable to publish.

His works were smuggled to the West and there were celebrated. Solzhenitsyn had a boundless love for Russia and believed communism was a temporary mistake, imported from the West, that could be cured. Like a nineteenth-century Slavophile, Solzhenitsyn wrote a long letter to the Kremlin's rulers urging them to abandon communism, world empire, heavy industry, and domination over non-Slavic nationalities and to return to the Orthodox faith, a simple agricultural life, and the spiritual roots of old Russia.

In 1973 his monumental *Gulag Archipelago* was released in Paris. A massive compilation of the reports of 227 other camp survivors, *Gulag* showed that capricious terror was built into the Soviet system, that by the 1940s there were from 12 to 15 million people in the **Gulag** at any one time, and that most had committed no crime. That was the last straw for Soviet authorities, who bundled Solzhenitsyn onto a plane in 1974 and did not let him back.

Solzhenitsyn was not merely anti-Communist. He also hated anything Western: rationality, technology, materialism, legality, even personal freedom (which, he said, had degenerated into license). He was not particularly impressed by the United States and lived as a recluse on a Vermont estate. At the 1978 Harvard commencement, he thundered:

> Should someone ask me whether I would indicate the West such as it is today as a model to my country, frankly I would have to answer negatively. Through intense suffering our country [Russia] has now achieved a spiritual development of such intensity that the Western system in its present state of spiritual exhaustion does not look attractive. After the suffering of decades of violence and oppression, the human soul longs for things higher, warmer, and purer than those offered by today's mass living habits, introduced by the revolting invasion of publicity, by TV stupor, and by intolerable music.

Although Solzhenitsyn became a U.S. citizen, he never became culturally American. Instead, he returned to Russia in 1994 with his mystical Russian nationalism. There his TV show flopped, and he was ignored. Things had changed since Solzhenitsyn last lived in Russia; material longing trumped spiritual longing. The materialist West had won.

KEY TERM

Gulag   The Soviet central prisons administration.

slipped away to reveal a system that satisfied few. The trouble was that there was no consensus on what should replace it. The broad masses (Russian: *narod*) generally wanted a cleaned-up socialism that guaranteed everyone a good standard of living. They showed little understanding of democracy or a market system. Many of the better-educated, on the other hand, understood that socialism was defective and should be scrapped in favor of free politics and free economics. Those whose jobs depended on the old system saw change as a threat. And many Russians simply did not know what to think. They had never before been asked for their opinions.

Many Russians have turned to Russian nationalism, a powerful impulse long manipulated by the Communists, and to newly freed Russian Orthodox Christianity, which enjoyed an upsurge for a few years. Russian nationalism and the Orthodox faith, however, cannot cement Russia together: Twenty-one ethnic republics are non-Russian, mostly Tatar and Muslim (roughly 10 percent of Russia's population), and harbor their own nationalism and separatism. No symbols unite Russians. Some like the new tricolor flag (based on a tsarist design); others want to bring back the red flag with hammer and sickle. National day is no longer November 11 to celebrate the revolution (although thousands, out of nostalgia, still parade) but June 12 to celebrate Russia's declaration of independence in 1990 (for which few parade). Many Russians deplore the breakup of the Soviet Union.

THE ILLUSION OF IDEOLOGY

Some studies of the Soviet Union paid great attention to Marxism-Leninism, the ideology of communism. In truth, ideology counted for little in the Soviet Union for many years; with *glasnost* it disappeared from sight. Much of Soviet *ideology* was little more than Russian national pride masking feelings of inferiority. Marxism, by predicting the collapse of the capitalist West, tried to reassure Russians that they would eventually emerge superior. They were "building socialism," which at a certain point would surpass the United States and turn into a Communist utopia with no social or economic problems. In earlier decades some Soviets believed it, but many American academics went way overboard in supposing ideology was the basis of the Soviet system. The Soviet system turned people into **opportunists**. Young people joined the Party to get into universities, to win job promotions, to become military or civilian officials. Most were cynical and cared nothing for Marxism-Leninism. They were motivated by careers, not ideology.

Marxism is basically a method of analysis, one that stresses social classes and their conflicts. As such, it stayed far livelier in the West, where it faced constant argument and challenge. In the Soviet Union, it atrophied. Applying this tool of analysis to Soviet society was the last thing the *apparat* wanted, as it would have revealed a pampered Party elite lording it over a wretched proletariat. Soviet Marxists thus focused on the West and cranked out the standard clichés, such as the "sharpening of contradictions" and "increasing tempo and magnitude of crises." The West was supposed to collapse any minute. After some decades, few took it seriously. Soviet students took required classes on Marxism-Leninism with the enthusiasm of American students going to compulsory chapel.

KEY TERM

opportunist   Unprincipled person out for self.

POLITICAL CULTURE

HOW TO BUILD A CIVIL SOCIETY: THE PHILOSOPHICAL GAP

One of the key differences between us and the Russians is philosophical; namely, we are the children of John Locke and they are not. Although few Americans study the philosopher who is at the root of much of our thinking, most have assimilated what the seventeenth-century English thinker had to say: People are rational and reasonable; they have a natural right to life, liberty, and property. Government is good if it preserves these rights and bad if it infringes on them. If this sounds like the Declaration of Independence, it is; Jefferson was an ardent Lockean, as were most of the Founding Fathers. Ever since, Americans have taken to Locke like a duck takes to water; we love his common-sense emphasis on small government and individuals working for the good of themselves and their families. To Russians, this is not common sense.

Russian thought comes out almost the opposite of Locke and traces back to the geographical dilemma of living on a defenseless plain: Either build a strong state or perish. Plugging into the Russian tradition of a strong state is Jean-Jacques Rousseau, the radical eighteenth-century French thinker whose theory of the "general will" rejected Lockean individualism in favor of using state power to "force men to be free." With Locke, people form society, and then society sets up a state, all with an eye to preserving property. With Rousseau, the flow goes the other way: The state, guided by the general will, molds society and then redoes individuals. Marxists added a class-struggle gloss to this; Lenin bought the package and then sold it to the Russian people.

Many Americans thought that once communism was overthrown Russians would rapidly become like us: capitalist entrepreneurs and democrats. This neglected the centuries of philosophical underpinning that is utterly lacking in Russia. If there is to be a Peace Corps in Russia, the teaching of the philosophical basis of markets, pluralism, and limited government might be one of its first and most urgent tasks. Without a new philosophical outlook, one taken mostly from the West, the Russians will likely stay trapped in their statist frame of mind.

The constant mouthing of a dead doctrine created a climate of cynicism, hypocrisy, and opportunism. With the collapse of the Soviet system, Marxism-Leninism collapsed like the house of cards it always was. Marxist ideology was always a defective foundation, but what kind of society can they build with no foundation?

THE REDISCOVERY OF CIVIL SOCIETY

Some analysts hold that the crux of the Soviet system was the stomping out of society by the state. Nothing was to be autonomous; everything in society was to be under strict state supervision. There were to be no independent enterprises, churches, associations, clubs, educational institutions, or morality. State power, in turn supervised by the Party, ran amok. The Communist system partly succeeded in crushing civil society, and its collapse has left a kind of vacuum where there should be society. Some thinkers argue that Russia must urgently reconstruct the **civil society** that the Soviet state annihilated.

The concept of civil society starts with the notion that state and society are two different things, although they clearly influence each other. Society over time evolves informal manners, usages, and customs that make living together possible. The *civil* (as in civilized) indicates a reasonable level of trust, politeness, public spirit, and willingness to compromise. A civil society through parents, churches, and schools **socializes** its members to right behavior and "rules of the game" that continue even when the state, through its police and bureaucrats, is not watching.

The state, the formal institutional structures that wield power, cannot substitute or replace civil society, although the Communists tried. Attempting such a substitution creates a system where people lack basic civility and see no need to play by informal rules of the game. Businessmen cheat and mafia gangs muscle into all sectors of the economy. Politicians attack each other hysterically, immoderately, with no possibility of compromise; they have never learned restraint. Citizens feel little need to obey the law if they can get away with breaking it. Legitimacy is terribly weak.

The West has had centuries to build up its civil societies. Philosophers such as Hobbes and Locke explained rationally why civil society is necessary. Churches, often with threats of eternal damnation, inculcated right behavior. The market system generated usages aimed at keeping dealings fair and predictable. Laws and courts enforced this with a system of contracts, both written and unwritten. All of this has been missing in Russia since the 1917 Revolution. Americans tended to take their civil society for granted until the corporate misdeeds of 2002 reminded them that businesses without ethics undermine the whole system. All civil societies need maintenance and reform from time to time when unscrupulous cheats take advantage of the trust that has been built up.

In Russia, unscrupulous cheats are the norm, and Russian corporations do things far worse than Enron or Worldcom. When communism fell, we thought the sudden imposition of democratic institutions and a market economy in Russia would quickly bring a civil society. We now see that without the philosophical, moral, economic, and legal understandings of civil society, Russia trends back to authoritarianism. One key question for Russia, then, is can a civil society be built in a condition of chaos and quasi-authoritarianism?

NATURAL EGALITARIANS?

Marxism-Leninism may have vanished in Russia, but many Russians display a tendency toward extreme equality, a natural socialism. Russians resent differences of wealth or income and enviously try to bring the better-off down to their level. Most Russians hated the new-rich oligarchs and were delighted to see Putin break and jail them. Some observers argue that the Russian peasantry, who for centuries tilled the soil in common and shared the harvest, developed highly egalitarian attitudes, which the Communists nourished. Perhaps so,

KEY TERMS

civil society   Everything bigger than the family but smaller than the government: churches, businesses, associations, and the pluralistic values that come with them.

socialize   To teach political culture, often informally.

POLITICAL CULTURE

HOW TO BUILD A CIVIL SOCIETY: THE MORAL GAP

America has its share of corporate crooks and cheats, but what would America be like if one could go back over three generations and systematically strip out most moral teachings? What if parents, churches, and schools did not attempt to inculcate a sense of innate right and wrong in young people? What if no one could trust anyone else? The result, I suspect, would be rather like Russia today. This is another area we overlooked in thinking that once communism ended, Russians would quickly become like us.

Russians had ethical training, but it was relativistic, superficial, and based on Marxist theories of social class. That which helps the working class is good, went the litany. The Communist party helps the working class, so it must be good. The Soviet state is totally devoted to the working class, so it must be very good. The Party and the state must therefore be obeyed, respected, and defended. Anyone who goes against them is insane, a wrecker, or a spy. Crime is something that happens only in capitalist countries, where the poor are forced to steal. Private property is inherently wicked, because it has been stolen from the workers who produced it. Under communism, there were no moral absolutes. The Russian Orthodox Church, tightly controlled by the government, confined itself to religious ritual and avoided moral instruction. By contrast, the Polish Catholic Church, for centuries the pillar of Polish civil society, stayed free of state control and critical of communism, always trying to face Poland westward. Religion matters.

Communist rhetoric aside, Soviet citizens soon learned to treat the system with cynicism. With the KGB and its informants everywhere, no one could trust anyone else, and they still do not. With no individual responsibility, stealing, especially from the state, was okay. After all, it really belonged to no one. Under communism, monstrous rip-offs became standard: Everyone stole and bribed.

When the Soviet Union collapsed, things got worse. Knowing the Party and KGB were watching restrained some Soviets to small rip-offs. Once these external controls vanished, a spirit of "anything goes" was unleashed. Nothing happens without bribes. People who were smart, ruthless, or well-connected grabbed whole industries. Russia was robbed from within by its own bureaucrats. Since Soviets had always been taught that capitalists and *biznesmeny* (long a term of derision, now adopted as a loan word) were crooks and their gains were ill-gotten, many Russians went into business with that image as their norm. The crime rate shot up; only Colombians are more likely to be murdered than Russians. Massive protection rackets, enforced by professional *keelers* (another loan word), were alright because they were just stealing from capitalist thieves.

What escaped both Russians and Americans is that a modern capitalist culture has a considerable moral basis; people have to be able to trust each other. Such a system draws from religious and ethical teachings, legal enforcement, a spirit of trust, and the knowledge that cheating businesses get few repeat customers. It may take a long time to build up this moral consensus. We made the mistake of thinking it would automatically arrive with the free market, which we suppose to be generally self-policing. In 2002, we discovered that U.S. financial institutions are not self-policing but need some outside controls. For most Russians, a free market means legal cheating. (Some American CEOs think so too.) For capitalism to work right, both in Russia and America, the moral gap must be filled.

but attitudes are not genetic; they are learned and can be unlearned, given the right conditions. Until new attitudes are learned, however, the old ones can trip up the best-laid plans of reformers.

Americans also favor equality, but it is "equality of opportunity": Everyone has a chance; the results are up to you. An American who gets ahead is usually applauded for his or her ability and hard work. Most Russians do not understand this kind of equality; they expect "equality of result," with each person collecting the same rewards. Those who get ahead are presumed to have cheated, exploited, or bribed (actually, many have). "The rich are living on our poverty," said one elderly Russian lady. In polls, most Russians say the free market and small state are wrong for Russia; only a few favor them. American values of individual work and achievement lend themselves to capitalism; Russian values generally do not.

RUSSIAN RACISM

With glasnost, hate-filled racist attitudes latent among Soviet nationalities came into the open. Under Soviet law, citizens had their nationality stamped in their internal passports, and, contrary to U.S. usage, nationality throughout East Europe and the ex-Soviet Union does not equal citizenship. For example, one can be a Russian citizen of the Komi nationality. This approach is asking for trouble, because it encourages people to demand an independent state. Educated Russians admire the U.S. approach, which prohibits the official identification of citizens by race or national origin.

And Russians tend to pigeonhole everyone on the basis of their nationality. Some nationalities are acceptable, others despised. Russians, for example, respect the Baltic peoples as European, civilized, and "cultured." On the other hand, Russians speak scathingly of the Muslim-Turkic peoples of the **Caucasus** and **Central Asia** as lawless and corrupt mafiosi (the loan word *mafiya* is much used) who do nothing but make babies. The theme of the differential birthrate comes up often. Most Russian families nowadays have one child (also the norm in much of West Europe.) Muslim families have many children, sometimes eight or more. Some Russians fear that their stagnant numbers will be swamped by a tide of inferior peoples. When bombs blew up apartment houses in 1999, killing close to 300 people, the Russian government and the people eagerly blamed alleged Chechen terrorists and supported a new war to crush them. People from the Caucasus and Central Asia were often the victims of ethnic violence by Russians.

The non-Russian nationalities feel little affection or affinity for the Russians. In Central Asia, several republics have made their local language the only official language. Educated Uzbeks, for example, know Russian perfectly, but now they speak only Uzbek as a way of making local Russians feel unwelcome. Many Russians are getting the message and leaving Central Asia. Virtually none have fled from the Baltic republics, however, and some Russians there even support independence. They feel they would be treated fairly by the cultured Balts. They fear the Muslims of the Caucasus and Central Asia.

KEY TERMS

Caucasus   Mountainous region between Black and Caspian Seas
Central Asia   Region between Caspian Sea and China.

POLITICAL CULTURE

HOW TO BUILD A CIVIL SOCIETY: THE ECONOMIC GAP

In addition to the philosophical and moral foundations of a civil society, another basic point has been overlooked in the eager assumption that Russians would quickly become like us: People have to learn capitalism. A market economy may be something that occurs naturally (whenever buyers and sellers meet), but it is not understood naturally. You have to take courses in market economics and read books and articles about it. Soviet courses covered "bourgeois economics" as part of the history of economic thought but gave it short shrift as a doomed system riven with contradictions, unfairness, and depressions. When their system collapsed, only a minority of economists had a decent grasp of what makes market economies work.

Especially missing was any appreciation of how money plays an autonomous role in the economy. In Communist countries, there simply was no theory of money. For example, I have tried the following mental experiment on a seminar of U.S., Central European, and Russian colonels, all bright and well-educated. Imagine, I tell them, a miniature country with ten citizens, each of whom works in one hamburger shop. The ten workers make a total of ten hamburgers a day and each is paid $1 a day. Then each buys one hamburger a day with their $1. The government decides to raise the pay of each to $2 a day (by printing an extra ten $1-bills). The output of the workers is still ten hamburgers a day. Within a day or two, what is the price of a hamburger?

The Americans respond fast and almost instinctively: $2! The East Europeans and Russians do not get it. "You haven't given us enough data," they say. Well, how would you explain it to them? It is not so simple. Phrases like "supply and demand" by themselves do not explain much. What we accept as basic and self-evident, Russians do not. (By the way, once you can explain the parable, you have a rudimentary theory of money.)

Mini-capitalism: A Russian peasant woman sells fruit near Moscow. (Ashley Barnes)

Antisemitism, deliberately cultivated in tsarist Russia, is back but unofficial and played down in public statements. Russian nationalists and Communists point to the handful of Russians of Jewish or partly Jewish origin who made big money and see a sinister international conspiracy called "Zionism." Small nationalist parties of skinheads urge violence against Jews, and tens of thousands of Russian Jews have moved to Israel. Most Russians, however, condemn antisemitism, and in 2002 President Putin got the Duma to pass a law against ethnic extremism.

A CULTURE OF INSECURITY

Average Russians are terribly insecure. Crime, corruption, and economic decay dominate their lives. Some compared the 1990s to the Time of Troubles in the early seventeenth century. Others used the phrase "Weimar Russia" to suggest a coming fascism. Before Putin took power, most Russians described the situation as "tense," "critical," or "explosive" and expected anarchy. Many feel Putin made things a bit more secure; they liked his increased power and paid no attention to his undemocratic methods.

Ultimately, Russia can become as democratic as Germany or Spain, but not under conditions of chaos. Putin did restore some order and is much better than Communists, extreme nationalists, and gangsters, but he has no plans for full-fledged democracy.

We now realize that in the early 1990s, when Communist rule cracked and then collapsed, we were expecting too much. We paid insufficient attention to crucial factors of political culture and assumed that capitalism and democracy bring their own political culture with them. They do, but it takes a long time. Thrust onto an unprepared population in the midst of economic decline, democracy and capitalism have not yet taken root in Russia. Spain under Franco was a police state, but strong economic growth made a majority of Spaniards middle class, and in the late 1970s Spain moved easily to democracy. If Putin can do something similar for Russia, he may be remembered favorably.

RUSSIA: PARANOID OR NORMAL?

"We could have been contenders," Russians seem to be saying. We once had a great empire that challenged the Americans; suddenly it vanished. Although support of client states around the globe was a net drain on the Soviet economy, many Russians were proud of their empire. Some analysts argue that the feeling of belonging to a mighty empire served to quiet discontent over shortages and poor living conditions. Every time a new client signed up—Cuba, Vietnam, Ethiopia, Angola—Russians could say, "See, we really are the wave of the future." The loss of empire was a psychological letdown for many Russians.

Russians used to feel they were the equals—maybe the superiors—of the Americans; now the arrogant Americans sneer at Russia. Indeed, it was they who craftily engineered the fall of the Soviet Empire and the collapse of the Soviet Union. Now they are moving in for the kill: the destruction of Russia. What else could the extension of NATO eastward—by adding first Central Europe and now the Baltic states—mean? See what they are doing to our little Slavic brother Serbia. The Americans gave little money and a lot of bad economic advice, making sure our economy collapsed. Now that we are starving, they cut us off.

POLITICAL CULTURE

HOW TO BUILD A CIVIL SOCIETY: THE LEGAL GAP

Much of Russia is lawless, one characteristic of the weak state. Russian police and courts are chaotic and easily bribed. Law is used selectively: Regime opponents get arrested and convicted, but major assassinations go unsolved, and corrupt officials are untouched. Said one Russian law expert ruefully, "The only lawyer around here is a Kalashnikov," a favorite weapon of *keelers*.

The Soviet legal structure broke down almost completely, and it was deficient to begin with. Soviet law paid minimal attention to property. Any big property (land, factories) automatically belonged to the state, and stealing state property could be harshly punished as a form of treason. The Lockean notion that property is a natural right and basis for human freedom was rejected out of hand. Russians, having been inculcated with the Marxist notion that "all property is theft," have trouble grasping the democratic and capitalist notion that "private property means personal freedom."

Weak or absent in the old Soviet socialist legal code, which Russia inherited, are such basics of the Common Law as ownership, contracts, torts, and bankruptcy. If you set up a business in the United States, Canada, or much of West Europe, you are reasonably confident your property and earnings will not be taken from you. In Russia, you have little confidence. Not only are business and property laws brand new, there is no legal culture built up over the years that regards these areas as important. One result is that foreigners and Russians alike are reluctant to invest in Russia; they may lose everything.

By way of contrast, Poland adopted its excellent Commercial Code in 1935, borrowed heavily from the Italian. The Polish Communist regime never repealed this code and after the Communists' ouster in 1989, Polish jurists simply dusted it off and put it into practice. Both Poles and foreigners who invest in Poland enjoy legal protections. Result: The Polish economy was for most of the 1990s the fastest growing in Europe. Russia finally passed commercial and criminal codes in 2002, based in part on Western legal concepts.

Remembering the definition of paranoia—unreasonable suspicion of others—observers were distressed at the signs of paranoia that grew as the Russian economy worsened. The images carried by many Russians are terribly untrue. The Soviet and later Russian systems collapsed from their own chiefly economic weaknesses; it was not a U.S. plot. Moscow rejected most Western economic urgings and then got angry when Western banks refrained from investing. Such a victim mentality contributed to the growth of nationalist authoritarianism.

The September 11, 2001, terrorist strikes on America produced a remarkable (but short-lived) shift in Kremlin policy. Putin declared solidarity and cooperation with America. Presidents Bush and Putin exchanged warm visits. Putin decided that Russia's

DEMOCRACY

FREE MEDIA

One of the basic components of democracy—in addition to competitive elections—is a free press. The easiest way to tell if a country is democratic is to see whether its mass media are controlled or muzzled. If television, radio, newspapers, and magazines routinely criticize the regime and remain open, you probably have a democracy. The government closing them down or taking them over is one of the first signs of authoritarianism. Freedom of information is indispensable to democracies but undermines dictatorships.

As Robert Mugabe consolidated his grip on Zimbabwe, critical newspapers were closed and critical journalists were jailed or expelled. Mugabe's definition of critical: Anyone not supporting his regime and its policies. The struggle for democracy in Iran is inseparable from the struggle of independent publications to stay open. Conservatives close them every few months, but they reopen under new names. Russia is now in a "grey zone," with much national media taken over by government-linked corporations and the rest cowed into "self-censorship," afraid they will be next. The Kremlin, never stating its intentions, forced some "oligarchs" to relinquish their television networks and newspapers—which had supported first Yeltsin and then Putin in elections. Moscow also prosecutes Russian writers and journalists for critical views. Although not as bad as in Communist times, all of Russia's national media now praise President Putin.

modernization lay with the West, especially with America, and 9/11 gave him the opportunity to put it into practice. Hostility to America in the Russian Duma, media, and military declined—Putin ordered it so. Paranoia can be turned up or down by government policy. By 2003, Russia was cool toward the United States over Iraq.

One of the leading studies of Nazi Germany blamed its rise on "the politics of cultural despair," a situation where everything seems to have failed, where the bonds of civil society have dissolved and nothing has taken their place. How far can despair go before something snaps? Under Yeltsin, Russia was headed for the abyss; Putin seems to have pulled it back just in time.

There are hopes for political stability—but not necessarily democracy—in Russia. Under Putin, the economy began to grow again. Voting patterns resemble those of stable democracies. City dwellers and young people tend to vote for continued reforms leading to a market economy. In other countries, we would call this a "liberal" or "left" vote, typical of urban areas. The Communists score best among old Russians, whose pensions have disappeared with inflation, and country dwellers, who fear a market system.

Russians are no more inherently ungovernable or authoritarian than Germans or Spaniards, both of whom grew to democracy after World War II. With some decades of stability and prosperity, Russians can do the same. Can Putin deliver these?

Key Terms

Caucasus (p. 147)

Central Asia (p. 147)

civil society (p. 145)

glasnost (p. 141)

Gulag (p. 142)

kleptocracy (p. 138)

liberal democracy (p. 138)

nationalism (p. 139)

oligarchy (p. 138)

opportunist (p. 143)

rump state (p. 141)

socialize (p. 145)

Further Reference

Alexander, James. *Political Culture in Post-Communist Russia: Formlessness and Recreation in a Traumatic Transition*. New York: St. Martin's, 2000.

Brudny, Yitzhak M. *Reinventing Russia: Russian Nationalism and the Soviet State, 1953–1991*. Cambridge, MA: Harvard University Press, 1999.

Bugajski, Janusz. *Cold Peace: Russia's New Imperialism*. Westport, CT: Praeger, 2004.

Chulos, Chris J., and Timo Piirainen, eds. *The Fall of an Empire, the Birth of a Nation: National Identities in Russia*. Brookfield, VT: Ashgate, 2000.

Colton, Timothy J. *Transitional Citizens: Voters and What Influences Them in the New Russia*. Cambridge, MA: Harvard University Press, 2000.

Kramer, Mark. *Travels with a Hungry Bear: A Journey to the Russian Heartland*. Boston, MA: Houghton Mifflin, 1996.

Lukin, Alexander. *The Political Culture of the Russian "Democrats."* New York: Oxford University Press, 2000.

Merridale, Catherine. *Night of Stone: Death and Memory in Russia*. London: Granta, 2000.

Pipes, Richard. *Property and Freedom*. New York: Knopf, 1999.

Randolph, Eleanor. *Waking the Tempests: Ordinary Life in the New Russia*. New York: Simon & Schuster, 1996.

Schmemann, Serge. *Echoes of a Native Land: Two Centuries in a Russian Village*. New York: Knopf, 1997.

Smith, Kathleen E. *Mythmaking in the New Russia: Politics and Memory in the Yeltsin Era*. Ithaca, NY: Cornell University Press, 2002.

10

Russia:
Patterns of Interaction

Going back two centuries, Russian politics has been a tug-of-war between reformist and conservative forces. Post-Communist Russian politics reflects, and to some extent continues, Soviet and even earlier Russian patterns. Since tsarist times Russia has been a system that cries out for reform but contains many conservative forces able and happy to block reform. A hundred years ago educated Russians could recognize the problem: How to reform the unreformable system? Many have tried, and ultimately all failed to both reform and preserve the system.

REFORMERS VERSUS CONSERVATIVES

The trouble with Russia is that there are few rules or institutions to regulate and moderate political clashes. Without experience in multiparty competition, a free press, voluntary associations, tolerance, and simple politeness, the new forces freed by the ending of Party control started to play a new game without rules. Their clashes were bound to be chaotic, and they were made worse by insiders who used the unregulated privatization to grab state enterprises cheap.

Earlier editions of this book argued that under the uniform surface of political life in the old Soviet Union existed a permanent struggle between liberals and conservatives, the former for major change toward Western models, the latter for standing pat with the essentially Stalinist system. It is here argued that this conflict continues in the post-Soviet era. In the 1990s, how to build democracy was discussed openly, but now discussions are more subdued, as Putin has deepened and extended his power.

Questions to Consider

1. How are we watching an old problem in Russia?
2. What did Khrushchev attempt to do and why? Why did he fail?
3. What is the difference between totalitarian and authoritarian?
4. What did Gorbachev attempt to do and why? Why did he fail?
5. Explain *conservative* and *liberal* in the Russian context.
6. Who were Russia's *oligarchs* and what became of them?
7. Why did reforms work in Central Europe but not in Russia?
8. Is *semipresidentialism* inherently unstable? Why?
9. Is Putin building an authoritarian system?

DEMOCRACY

DEFINING DEMOCRACY

Democracy is not something that automatically falls into place once authoritarian or totalitarian regimes fall. We were naïve about stable democracy coming soon to Russia and Iraq. Democracy is a complex balancing act, requiring a political culture with the right philosophical, moral, economic, and legal underpinnings. Most definitions of democracy include the following:

Accountability   Elected officials must face a real possibility of losing reelection. This induces them to adopt Friedrich's "rule of anticipated reactions" (see page 81).

Equality   One person, one vote. No citizens can be excluded.

Competition   Several candidates and parties compete in free and fair elections. No one-party system can be democratic.

Alternation   Occasional turnovers in power replace the "in" party with the "out" party.

Representation   "The room will not hold all," so a few fairly represent the many. The electoral system does this, either by single-member districts or proportional representation.

Free Media   Only democracies permit the press to criticize the government. This is the quickest check for democracy.

Harvard political scientist Samuel P. Huntington suggested a "two-turnover test" for stable democracy. Two alternations of government—the "outs" replacing the "ins"—suggest a firmly rooted democracy. Since the Polish Communist regime fell in 1989, Poland has had several turnovers from left to right and back again, indicating stable democracy. Russia has not had a turnover since 1991 and is not soon likely to. Russia's democracy is dubious.

Freedom House in New York City uses a seven-point scale to annually rank countries on how much they accord citizens political rights and civil liberties. FH calls 1 to 2.5 "free," 3 to 5.5 "partly free," and 5.5 to 7 "not free." Russia has slid lower during the Putin years. Some of FH's 2005 findings:

United States	1	(free)
Canada	1	(free)
Britain	1	(free)
South Africa	1.5	(free)
Mexico	2	(free)
Brazil	2.5	(free)
Turkey	3	(partly free)
Nigeria	4	(partly free)
Russia	5.5	(not free)
Iran	6	(not free)
China	6.5	(not free)
Cuba	7	(not free)

Key Concepts

Totalitarian versus Authoritarian

Since the 1930s, political science has debated the existence and nature of modern dictatorships. Some political scientists developed theories and models of **totalitarianism** to explain Mussolini's Italy, Hitler's Germany, and Stalin's Soviet Union. Carl J. Friedrich and Zbigniew Brzezinski argued that totalitarian dictatorships have these six points in common:

1. An official ideology
2. A single, disciplined party
3. Terroristic police control
4. Party monopoly of the mass media
5. Party control of the armed forces
6. Central direction of the economy

Widely accepted for years, the totalitarian model gradually came under criticism as unrealistic and over-simplified. Far from total, the systems of Mussolini, Hitler, and Stalin were quite messy. Many citizens knew the regimes were frauds; plans were often just improvisations. The dictators like their systems to *look* total. Totalitarianism was an attempt at total control that always fell short.

The word *totalitarianism* fell into disfavor; instead **authoritarianism** was used to describe modern dictatorships. It can be quite brutal but does not aim for total control of society. Politics is in the hands of a dictator, such as Spain's Franco or Chile's Pinochet, but wide areas of the economy and cultural life are open. Most or all of the above six points are missing.

Political scientist Jeane J. Kirkpatrick in 1980 argued there are still useful distinctions between the two words. Authoritarian regimes, more loose and open, can change and reform themselves into democracies. This happened throughout Latin America in the 1980s. Totalitarian systems, especially Communist ones, she argued, cannot reform; they are too rigid. In a way, Kirkpatrick was right. The Communist regimes of East Europe and the Soviet Union never did reform; they collapsed.

Most of the reformers who rallied to Gorbachev and then to Yeltsin resigned or were dismissed from high office. In many respects they hearkened back to the Russian Westernizers of the nineteenth century who wanted to import Western ways nearly wholesale: a market economy, free democracy, and individualistic philosophy. This led

Key Terms

totalitarianism   Attempts to totally control society, as under Stalin and Hitler.

authoritarianism   Dictatorial rejection of democracy, as Spain under Franco and Chile under Pinochet.

PERSONALITIES

FAILED REFORMERS: NIKITA KHRUSHCHEV

The Soviet Union had petrified under Stalin, and Nikita Khrushchev attempted to revitalize the system and get it moving toward communism again. He was only partly and briefly successful, for much of the Soviet party and bureaucracy resisted him. We now realize Khrushchev was far from the undisputed master of the Kremlin that Stalin was and had to overcome opposition. Like Gorbachev, he failed.

Born in 1894 of an ethnic Russian family in Ukraine, Khrushchev joined the Bolsheviks shortly after the revolution and worked his way up through party jobs. A protégé of Stalin, Khrushchev did some of the dictator's dirty work in the 1930s, which earned him a full Politburo membership in 1939. During the war he was a political general on the Ukrainian front. After the war he organized party work in Ukraine and then the Moscow region, and carefully packed the party leadership with his supporters, the key to success in Soviet politics.

Stalin's death in 1953 opened a period of jockeying for power. All the Politburo had feared Stalin and longed for stability and personal security. Accordingly, they immediately had the head of the secret police, Lavrenti Beria (like Stalin, a Georgian) shot, putting the KGB under Party control. The first post-Stalin premier was Georgi Malenkov, who advocated relaxing the Stalin system and producing more consumer goods. But Khrushchev was made party first secretary, a post that was always more powerful, and craftily built a coalition against Malenkov, who in 1955 was demoted to minister for power stations. The Soviet leadership abandoned violent death as a way to run a political system.

To consolidate his power and trounce his enemies within the Party, Khrushchev took a dramatic step: He denounced Stalin to a Party congress. A Party that was still Stalinist was immobile, incapable

the new reformists to attempt the economic **shock therapy** recommended by Harvard economist Jeffrey Sachs, which earlier worked in Bolivia and Poland. In Russia, such therapy was never fully and correctly applied, and the economy plunged downward. (See next chapter.)

What we are calling here "conservatives" covers a broad swath from moderates to extremists. What they have in common is their opposition to the thorough restructuring of the Russian economy. Russia may need reforms, some concede, but they must be our reforms tailored to our conditions. Some old-line Party types would go back to a centralized command economy. Like the old Russophiles of the nineteenth century, they reject Western models and would turn inward, to Russia's roots; accordingly, they are nationalistic, some rabidly so.

These two general camps are halves of the Russian political spectrum that contains several gradations and combinations. Some worried that the two extremes of the political

KEY TERM

shock therapy   Sudden replacement of socialist by market economy.

of reform or innovation and blocking the productive potential of the Soviet Union under a blanket of fear and routine. At the Twentieth Party Congress in February 1956, Khrushchev delivered a stinging, hours-long tirade against the "crimes of Stalin" who, he said, had murdered thousands of Party comrades and top military officers. Stalin had built a **cult of personality** that must never be allowed again.

Communist parties the world over had based themselves on Stalin-worship, and when the speech leaked out, all hell broke loose. A Hungarian uprising was crushed by Soviet tanks; Poland nearly revolted. In the West, longtime Communists resigned from the party. In China, Mao Zedong was horrified at Khrushchev for undermining the Communist camp by denouncing its symbol. Thus began the Sino-Soviet split.

To revitalize the Soviet economy, Khrushchev proposed decentralization. Outvoted in the Politburo, he called a 1957 Central Committee meeting packed with his supporters and backed by the army, which forced his opponents, the "antiparty group," to resign. CPSU leaders, however, grew increasingly irritated at his "harebrained schemes" to boost production (especially of consumer goods), eliminate class differences (everyone would have to work before college, even the children of big shots), and outfox the Americans by placing missiles in Cuba. They considered him a reckless experimenter and liberalizer, and in October 1964 the Politburo *voted* him out of office, a rare thing in Communist systems. He went into retirement and died in 1971.

The Khrushchev era brought major changes in both domestic and foreign policy. A generation of young Party members—including Gorbachev—came of age wanting and planning economic reform. These people, "Khrushchev's children," later staffed the Gorbachev reform effort. Khrushchev was a flamboyant, can-do character, who promised major change. He stressed consumer goods over heavy industry, and this infuriated both managers and the military. He permitted publication of anti-Stalin works (such as Solzhenitsyn's *One Day*), then backed off when he felt things were getting out of hand. We now see that Khrushchev was trying to reform against the interests of the Party *apparatchiki,* the same people who brought down Gorbachev.

spectrum could form a **"red-brown"** coalition of old Party supporters plus lunatic nationalists. Moderate conservatives cluster in the Communist party. Putin's takeover prevented that, so we should not be too critical of him.

Under the label "centrist," another group seeks a middle ground of moderate reforms cushioned by continued state subsidies and ownership. Unfortunately, under Yeltsin this approach led to incredible corruption. Thoroughgoing reformers and democrats, such as Yabloko, are weak because few Russians share their Western-type thinking. One interesting possibility emerged with the 1999 Duma elections. Prime Minister and later President Putin, whose Unity (later United Russia) catchall spanned all political views, indicated he could work with the economic reformers of the Union of Right-Wing Forces. Putin, however, has been cautious about pursuing economic reforms. He prefers control.

KEY TERMS

cult of personality   Dictator who has himself worshiped.

red-brown   A possible combination of Communists and Fascists, the brown standing for Hitler's brownshirts.

PERSONALITIES

FAILED REFORMERS: MIKHAIL GORBACHEV

"Life punishes those who delay," said the Soviet president in 1989 as he urged the East German Communist regime to reform before it was too late. The East Berlin regime ignored Gorbachev and collapsed. But Mikhail Sergeyevich Gorbachev did not grasp that he too was engaging in delayed and halfway reforms that collapsed the Soviet regime and led to his own ouster from power.

Amid great hopes Gorbachev assumed the top Soviet political position—Party general secretary—in 1985. The Soviet Union had gradually run down during Brezhnev's eighteen-year reign; growth slumped while cynicism, alcoholism, and corruption grew. Two elderly temporaries, Andropov and Chernenko, followed as the Soviet system atrophied. Gorbachev—age fifty-four, a mere kid in Politburo terms—announced wide-ranging reforms to shake up the Soviet system.

Born into a peasant family in the North Caucasus in 1931, Gorbachev graduated in law from Moscow University in 1955 and returned to his home area for Party work. As Party chief of Stavropol province in 1970, he impressed Brezhnev, who summoned him to Moscow in 1978 to oversee agriculture. (Gorbachev had taken a degree in agronomy by correspondence.) Gorbachev now was under the wing of Andropov, head of the KGB, and Mikhail Suslov, a Politburo kingmaker from Stavropol. Gorbachev was elected to the Party's Central Committee in 1971, to candidate member of the Politburo in 1979, and to full member in 1980. When Andropov took over in 1982, Gorbachev assisted him and implemented his anticorruption policies.

In 1985 Gorbachev began his reforms with great fanfare, as the hero who would turn the Soviet Union into a modern, possibly democratic, system. He announced "new thinking" in foreign policy that led

PRESIDENT VERSUS PARLIAMENT

Executive and legislative branches have been at serious odds in Russia recently, and their competing claims have led to anger and violence. The initial problem, as noted earlier, was the carryover from Soviet times of a Russian parliament elected under the old rules and under the Communists in 1989. Most members of this parliament stood firm with Yeltsin during the abortive coup of 1991.

But then Yeltsin gathered more power into the office of the presidency. The Russian parliament reacted, claiming Yeltsin was becoming dictatorial. They also disliked seeing their own power and perquisites diminished. Some deputies who had earlier counted themselves as reformers began to discover the negative side of reforms and to slide into the conservative camp. To make clear who was in charge, in 1993 Yeltsin sponsored and won a referendum that endorsed both reform and the power of the presidency. Later that year, he pushed through a new constitution with Gaullist-type presidential powers. The last straw was Yeltsin's dissolution of parliament in order to hold new elections; that produced the parliamentary coup attempt of 1993.

to arms control agreements with the United States and to the freeing of East Europe from the Communist regimes imposed by Stalin after World War II. With these steps, the Cold War ended.

Gorbachev ordered *glasnost* in the Soviet media, which became more pluralist, honest, and critical. Corrupt big shots were fired. Gorbachev also urged *demokratizatzia;* competitive elections were introduced, and a partially elected parliament convened.

Gorbachev at first tried to fix the economic system with old remedies: verbal exhortations, anti-alcohol campaigns, "acceleration," and importing more foreign technology. Then, after having hesitated too long, he ordered **perestroika**, which slowly began to decentralize and liberalize the Soviet economy. Farms and factories made more of their own decisions and kept more of their own profits. Private businesses called "cooperatives" were permitted and grew. But it was too little, too late. By 1989 economic disaster loomed. Economic dislocations lowered Soviet living standards and angered everyone.

With a freer press, the many nationalities (including Russians) demanded greater autonomy or even independence. Violence between ethnic groups flared. The *apparat* and *nomenklatura* sabotaged economic reforms by hoarding food and raw materials. Some generals and the KGB indicated they would not stand for the growing chaos, which would have soon led to the dismemberment of the Soviet Union, so Gorbachev pulled back from reforms and tightened up in late 1990.

In early 1991 Gorbachev appeared to favor reform again. In opposition, conservative hardliners in his own cabinet—hand picked by Gorbachev—attempted a coup against him in August 1991. The coup failed due to splits in the Soviet armed forces and the stubbornness of Russian President Boris Yeltsin, who then pushed a weakened Gorbachev from office and broke up the Soviet Union by pulling the vast Russian federation out of it.

In part, Gorbachev had himself to blame for the Soviet collapse. He dawdled too long and changed course too many times. He sought to preserve the Party and "socialism" and never did adopt an economic reform plan. Life indeed punished him who delayed.

Then parliamentary elections turned into slaps at Yeltsin. Some of the biggest votes were for the Communists and other antireform parties. Yeltsin backed down, jettisoned his main reformers, and made cautious reformers, several of them briefly, his prime ministers.

But is this not just democracy in action? An executive starts showing dictatorial tendencies and implements policies that go farther and faster than citizens want, so the citizens, through their elected representatives in parliament, put on the brakes. That is the way the State Duma liked to see itself, but the problem in Russia is trickier. Without major economic reforms, democracy in Russia does not stand a chance. But such reforms are seldom initiated by purely democratic means because they inflict too much pain, at least temporarily. Major reforms need strong executive leadership; a fragmented parliament cannot do it. If the executive is blocked, the result will likely not be democracy but chaos, and out of chaos grows dictatorship.

KEY TERM

perestroika   Russian for "restructuring," Gorbachev's proposals to reform the Soviet economy.

COMPARISON

SEMIPRESIDENTIALISM IN RUSSIA

Borrowing the French model, which has both an executive president and a premier, Russia borrowed its problems as well. President Yeltsin, in eight years in office, had six prime ministers, some lasting just a few months. An erratic drunk, Yeltsin tried to deflect blame away from himself for Russia's economic collapse and to appease an opposition-dominated Duma. But there were other, deeper causes for the mess.

Semipresidential systems may be inherently unstable. The French partway remedied the defects by the device of *cohabitation*, where the president, faced with a parliament dominated by his opposition, names an opposition figure prime minister and takes a cut in presidential power. It worked in France, but Yeltsin would stand for no cut in his presidential power. He really did have dictatorial tendencies. His throwaway prime ministers were a crude attempt at cohabitation that made no one happy and hurt Russia's chances for democracy. One solution: Get rid of this crazy semipresidential system. In effect—without rewriting the constitution—Putin has done this by tilting virtually all power into his own hands.

THE TAMING OF THE OLIGARCHS

Moscow privatized ("piratized" might be more accurate) the Russian economy in such a way as to make a few people incredibly wealthy. Clever wheeler-dealers, some of them members of the *nomenklatura*—who understood the value of state-owned firms, chiefly in the oil and natural-gas industries—bought them at giveaway prices. Most of what they did was legal because there were few laws in these areas. Russia privatized badly.

These oligarchs, as they were soon called, either had or quickly developed ties to leading politicians. One of the best-known oligarchs was Boris Berezovsky, a former math professor turned used-car king and then media and oil magnate. Berezovsky's money, newspapers, and TV network helped first Yeltsin and then Putin win election. Putin then had Berezovsky prosecuted and shorn of most of his properties. Berezovsky now lives in exile.

Russia's oligarchs did not act like the old U.S. *robber barons*, who invested and then reinvested to make the economy and jobs grow. Russian oligarchs simply stripped assets from their companies—for example, selling oil abroad—and did not reinvest the money but stashed it in foreign (Swiss, Cayman Islands, Cyprus) banks. They did not like paying taxes or competing in a free market. As they got rich, the Russian economy got poor.

How to fix? Stop subsidizing industries and let the money-losers go bankrupt. Institute a Polish-type commercial code to regulate banks and businesses. Force the oligarchs to behave like real capitalists. But the oligarchs were well-connected and had many politicians on their payroll. They ousted a reform-minded cabinet in just five months, as well as those who vowed to collect taxes. In the name of keeping a vital industry alive and of not increasing unemployment, the subsidies, sweetheart contracts, and tax breaks continued. Another name for the process is corruption. Western executives call Russia one of the most corrupt countries in the world.

KEY CONCEPTS

THE TIMING OF REFORMS

In addition to the cultural factors we have already discussed, the timing or *sequencing* of reforms can make a crucial difference to the successful founding of democracy. The differences in timing between what happened in Central Europe and what happened in Russia are instructive.

First, in Central Europe (Poland, Czechoslovakia, and Hungary) a broad anti-Communist movement formed while the Communists were still in power. By the time liberal Communists held free elections in 1989 or 1990, an aware electorate completely voted the Communists out of power, from the president's and prime minister's office to the main parties of parliament. It was a new broom sweeping clean. The initial winner was the broad catchall of anti-Communist forces, the leader of which became either the president (Walesa of Poland and Havel of Czechoslovakia) or the prime minister (Antall of Hungary). Later, these catchalls fell apart, but they had done their job: Communism was out, and democracy and market economics were established. Soon these countries joined NATO and the EU.

In Russia, there was no new broom and the old one did not sweep clean. There was no nationwide anti-Communist catchall movement like Solidarity or Civic Forum. The Communists never allowed that. Instead, the Communists held semifree elections but did not allow themselves to be voted out of power. Gorbachev, who was never elected anything, stayed in office believing he was supervising major reforms.

But Gorbachev still faced major conservative (that is, Party) forces and continually changed course in the face of them. Sensing his weakness, Party conservatives attempted to overthrow him. After their defeat, the Party was finally ousted from office (late 1991) but was still influential in parliament, industry, and the countryside. Yeltsin, with no mass movement behind him, attempted serious reform but was still blocked by conservative forces, some of them remnants of the Party.

If Russia had done it like Central Europe, there would have been multiparty elections in late 1991 instead of late 1993. At the earlier date, there might have been sufficient enthusiasm to elect a proreform majority; by the latter date, the declining economy had produced despair and a backlash. This happened in Central Europe as well; in both Poland and Hungary economic hardship gave electoral wins to their Socialist parties (ex-Communists). But by then both democracy and the market economy were established and could not be rolled back. The Socialists had no intention of dismantling a working market system; instead, they made minor adjustments in the *social safety net* of Poland and Hungary.

The desirable sequence, as illustrated by Central Europe: First, form a broad mass movement; second, thoroughly oust the Communists in parliamentary elections; third, institute political and economic reforms. The Russians tried to do it backward.

Russians, with their penchant for equality, hated the oligarchs and liked how President Putin cracked down on them. Most are in jail or in exile. His *siloviki* targeted some for tax evasion (in a system where everyone cheats on taxes) and forced them to turn over their companies—including oil and gas industries, television networks, and newspapers—to government fronts. Under Putin, most of the big Russian media came under state control, and few dared criticize him. Several oligarchs, fearing prosecution, fled abroad. One, Mikhail Khodorkovsky was jailed and shorn of his huge (and well-run) Yukos oil firm, allegedly for

Key Concepts

Runaway Systems

We earlier (Chapter 8) referred to President Putin as authoritarian, a strong ruler who concentrated much power in himself but preserved democratic forms. Is it likely that Russia and Putin will tend to greater authoritarianism? The process seems to be already underway.

Yale political scientist Robert Dahl noted that powerful people tend to use their resources (legal, political, economic) to gain more resources. If there are no counterbalancing institutions or strong laws to check them, some amass power without limit: Stalin. Engineers call this a **runaway system**, which keeps concentrating power until it breaks. (Example: The New York Yankees use their resources to buy more top ballplayers, who win more games, which net them even more resources, which enable them to buy . . .) This probably comes less from unbalanced personalities than from lawless systems in which any loss of control leads to overthrow. The presidents of Syria or the Congo cannot be nice, easygoing guys. Leaders in such lands must be control freaks; relaxation soon ends in their deaths.

Putin is a test case for the runaway-systems theory. Gradually and skillfully—never revealing his ultimate intentions—he amasses power. Will he reach a point where he has "enough" power, or will he always seek more? One indicator to watch: Will Putin step down in 2008 after his two four-year terms, or will he alter the constitution to stay longer? Or will the Duma, which Putin controls, alter the constitution to keep Putin in power? Putin keeps his plans to himself, but he will likely stay powerful.

not paying taxes but more likely for trying to bring in U.S partners. Putin brought Yukos under state control. Like many Russians, he felt that something as important as oil should never have been privatized. Putin also wanted to stop Khodorkovsky from dabbling in politics in a way that rivaled Putin. A few smaller oligarchs, who do things Putin's way and stay out of politics, survive. The oligarchs were egregious, greedy, and sometimes criminal, but their television stations and periodicals gave Russia a brief period of freedom of information.

The Mafia

The **mafia** (Russians use the loan word *mafiya*) is an important interest group in Russia, for it stands for much more than the criminal underworld. In Russia, the word covers a multitude of meanings, ranging from local strong-arm rackets (virtually all businesses

Key Terms

runaway system   Influential people use their powers to amass more power.

mafia   A criminal conspiracy.

pay protection money) to the sophisticated takeover of natural resources by the Communist *nomenklatura* that used to run industry. Anyone in their way gets murdered—bankers, journalists (including American Paul Klebnikov in 2004), old people (for their apartments), American businessmen, and Duma members. Most "banks" are simply money-laundering operations. And no one is brought to justice, indicating the police are either connected to crime or ordered not to interfere. The FSB could solve such crimes but does not. Putin controls the FSB.

Russian mafiosi flaunt their new wealth, flashy cars (any make you can name, often stolen), clothes, lady friends, and parties. The average Russian hates those who have rapidly enriched themselves as they have degraded Russia, and this hatred feeds support for politicians who vow to crack down on them. Thus, lawlessness helped President Putin consolidate his power. Russians have long argued that without strict supervision and draconian controls they are the most lawless of peoples. Americans, they say, have internal controls that Russians have not. Historically, freedom in Russia meant chaos and bloody anarchy, and many Russians have welcomed rule by a strong hand, however harsh.

THE ARMY

In chaotic times the army becomes a major player, sometimes injecting itself directly into the political system. The Soviet army played a role in the process of attempted reform; namely, some sectors of the Red Army saw the need for economic changes in order to boost military technology to catch up with the Americans. In 1983 the Chief of the Soviet General Staff, Marshal Nikolai Ogarkov, told *New York Times* editor Leslie Gelb that the Soviet military was falling behind technologically. He was later pushed out of high office for his outspokenness. "Modern military power is based upon technology," he told Gelb, "and technology is based upon computers," an area where the Americans were well ahead. His conclusion:

> We will never be able to catch up with you in modern arms until we have an economic revolution. And the question is whether we can have an economic revolution without a political revolution.

The price of military backwardness became clear with the quick U.S.-led victory over Soviet-equipped Iraq in early 1991. Late that year, portions of the Soviet army participated in a coup.

The new Russian armed forces are much smaller (nominally 1.2 million members) than the old Soviet armed forces (some 4 million) but still in a wretched condition. Many soldiers and officers have to work off-base. (In comparison, U.S. armed forces total 1.4 million and are superbly fed and led.) Russian armed forces are absurdly top-heavy, with as many officers as enlisted soldiers (U.S. ratio: 1:6). Officers, fearful of losing their jobs and starved for decent housing, are angry. Soldiers go unpaid for months and have to grow much of their own food. Hundreds of conscripts, hazed and starved, commit suicide each year. Most young men ignore the twice-yearly draft calls.

Several leading generals either supported the 1991 coup or did not oppose it. Many Soviet higher officers were fired. One, Marshal Sergei Akhromeyev, committed suicide. The Soviet armed forces had been consuming a quarter of the country's gross domestic product,

Veterans, like these in Moscow, wear war medals on their suits, a Soviet custom. Generally conservative, most veterans oppose reforms leading to capitalism. (Michael Roskin)

a figure that was cut drastically. The army is still one of the few semistable institutions in Russia and may yet play a direct political role.

When a political system starts falling apart, whatever groups are best organized amid growing chaos are most likely to seize power. This usually means the army. (See the box entitled "Praetorianism," on page 279.) In much of the Third World, military coup is the standard way to change governments. Some believe the Russian army could play such a role, although historically it never has. In 1991 and 1993 the military was divided and most of it hung back, afraid of being used by politicians and of starting a civil war among army units.

The army is surely an interest group within Kremlin politics, and it is an angry one, having suffered several humiliations. Gorbachev tried to limit its size. In 1988 he admitted that the Soviet invasion of Afghanistan had been a mistake and withdrew Soviet forces. In 1989 he gave up East Europe, which the Soviet military defined as a defensive shield. In 1994–1996 Chechen "bandits" beat them; in revenge in 1999 the army began the merciless demolition of Chechnya. Many high officers resent the retreat of Russian power and their shrinking defense budget and manpower. They are also highly nationalistic and see an American plot in the eastward expansion of NATO and U.S. presence in Central Asia. Putin's defense minister, former KGB colleague Sergei Ivanov, wanted to move from a draftee army to a professional one.

PERSONALITIES

FAILED REFORMERS: BORIS YELTSIN

Gorbachev was the first *prezident* (they use the loan word) of the Soviet Union. Boris Yeltsin was the first prezident of the Russian Federation. As with Gorbachev, both Russians and the world initially hailed Boris Yeltsin as the great reformer who would make a prosperous and peaceful Russia. Both disappointed with halfway, half-hearted reforms that ruined the economy and their approval ratings. Neither were convinced democrats; by background and training both acted like Party big shots. Yeltsin, however, was a gutsy risk taker who put his career and even life on the line.

Born in 1931 (as was Gorbachev) near Sverdlovsk (now Yekaterinburg) in the southern Urals of a poor peasant family, Yeltsin studied engineering and worked in the housing industry in his hometown. Joining the Party in 1961 at age thirty, Yeltsin was promoted to the Central Committee in 1976. He was noticed as an energetic manager and reformer, and Gorbachev elevated him to head the Moscow Party organization in 1985 and made him a candidate member of the Politburo. A natural populist, Yeltsin, unlike other Soviet leaders, mingled with the people and denounced the privileges of the nomenklatura. The common people rallied to him.

Then came a bizarre series of events that, if the Soviet system had not been collapsing, would have led to Yeltsin's permanent banishment if not imprisonment. In a 1987 speech to the Central Committee, Yeltsin attacked Party conservatives by name for dragging their feet on reform. For that, he was relieved of his Party posts and demoted.

But he bounced back. In the first partly competitive election in 1989, he ran on his populist credentials and easily won election to parliament, where he criticized Gorbachev for dawdling on reforms. Shifting his attention to the Russian (as opposed to the Soviet) government, Yeltsin won election to the Russian parliament in 1990. Yeltsin sensed that the Soviet Union was doomed, but Russia would survive. In July 1990 Yeltsin resigned from the Party and was now free to be as critical as he wished. As a non-Communist, he won fair elections to become president of the Russian Federation in 1991. This gave him another edge on Gorbachev, who had never been popularly elected to anything.

In the attempted coup of 1991, Yeltsin became a hero, standing firm on a tank in front of the Russian parliament. Mocking Gorbachev as an indecisive weakling, Yeltsin pulled the Russian Federation out of the Soviet Union in late 1991, thus collapsing the entire structure. Conservatives think it was a terrible mistake to break up the Soviet Union.

As president, Yeltsin went from bad to worse. Frequently drunk or ill, Yeltsin and his ministers bungled privatization, the economy tanked, corruption soared, and Russians turned bitterly against him. Consulting with no one, Yeltsin ordered the crushing of breakaway Chechnya (see page 176). Although reelected in 1996 as the lesser of two evils, during his last years in office Yeltsin's public approval rating was under 5 percent. The Duma tried to impeach him but was too divided. One of Yeltsin's favorite stunts was, every few months, to blame his prime ministers for economic failures and replace them. One of the questions of today's Russia is whether a first president other than Yeltsin could have done things differently or better.

DEMOCRACY

TRANSITIONS TO DEMOCRACY

The spread of democratic regimes in the late twentieth century—what Harvard's Samuel Huntington called democracy's "third wave"—provoked much theorizing and attempts to find common patterns. Some thinkers saw democracy arising after economic growth produced a large, educated middle class (see page 218). Some saw it as going through similar stages—opening, breakthrough, and consolidation—but others saw "multiple paths" to democracy. Several said it needed agreement among elites—a "pacted transition"—to work. Many found that early institutional choices produced "path-dependent development": As the twig was bent, so the tree inclined.

By the early twenty-first century, however, doubts arose about "transitology," as it was derisively dubbed. Some theories of transition explained the coming of democracy in one cultural area (such as Latin America) but not others (such as East Asia). Even in the Communist lands of East Europe, the relatively smooth transition to democracy in Central Europe was not duplicated in the Balkans. One size did not fit all. None of the theories fit Russia.

The toughest criticism asked: "Do all transitions lead to democracy?" Transitologists tended to assume that they did, but this was not always the case. Some countries enjoyed only brief democratic interludes (Peru, Ecuador, Venezuela) but became unstable or quasi-authoritarian. Huntington noted long ago that after every wave of democracy washes in, a reverse wave washes out, as in the rise of the totalitarian dictatorships between the two world wars. Many countries, including Russia, stalled in a *semi-authoritarianism* between dictatorship and democracy.

Theories in political science seldom last more than a generation. They can yield new insights, provided we do not **reify** them. Theories are only attempts to get a handle on reality; they are not reality itself. Take all theories with a grain of salt. (For more on the dangers of theorizing too much, see the next chapter, page 170.)

TRANSITION TO WHAT?

In the last quarter of the twentieth century, democracy spread, leaving about half the world's nations (close to a hundred) democratic to some degree. Starting in the mid-1970s, democracy replaced dictatorships in Portugal, Spain, and Greece, and then in Latin America, East Asia, and finally, in late 1989, in East Europe. Soon academics developed theories to explain the growth of democracy (see box above). Some applied them to the collapse of the Soviet Union and to the new institutions of a democratic Russia. They did not fit.

The collapse of the Soviet system was unique, one of a kind. Much of the old system carried over into the new, stunting the growth of democracy. Culturally, only a minority

KEY TERM

reify   From the Latin *res,* thing; to take a theory as reality.

understood or wished genuine democracy. Economically, Russia tanked under Yeltsin; people feared chaos and breakup of the federation. Putin was the necessary if authoritarian corrective to this slide. As a friend and supporter of democracy, I am sad to admit this, but if it had not been Putin, it would have been someone worse.

KEY TERMS

authoritarianism (p. 155)

cult of personality (p. 157)

mafia (p. 162)

perestroika (p. 159)

red-brown (p. 157)

reify (p. 166)

runaway system (p. 162)

shock therapy (p. 156)

totalitarianism (p. 155)

FURTHER REFERENCE

Beissinger, Mark R. *Nationalist Mobilization and the Collapse of the Soviet State*. New York: Cambridge University Press, 2002.

Breslauer, George W. *Gorbachev and Yeltsin as Leaders*. New York: Cambridge University Press, 2002.

Brown, Archie, and Lilia Shevtsova, eds. *Gorbachev, Yeltsin, and Putin: Political Leadership in Russia's Transition*. Washington, D.C.: Carnegie Endowment, 2001.

Gill, Graeme, and Roger D. Markwick. *Russia's Stillborn Democracy?: From Gorbachev to Yeltsin*. New York: Oxford University Press, 2000.

Golosov, Grigorii V. *Political Parties in the Regions of Russia: Democracy Unclaimed*. Boulder, CO: L. Rienner, 2004.

Hahn, Gordon M. *Russia's Revolution from Above, 1985–1999: Reform, Transition, and Revolution in the Fall of the Soviet Communist Regime*. New Brunswick, NJ: Transaction, 2001.

Hoffman, David. *The Oligarchs: Wealth and Power in the New Russia*. New York: PublicAffairs, 2003.

McFaul, Michael, Nikolai Petrov, and Andrei Ryabov. *Between Dictatorship and Democracy: Russian Post-Communist Political Reform*. Washington, D.C.: Carnegie Endowment, 2004.

Ottaway, Marina. *Democracy Challenged: The Rise of Semi-Authoritarianism*. Washington, D.C.: Carnegie Endowment, 2003.

Polsky, Yury. *Russia During the Period of Radical Change, 1992–2002*. Lewiston, NY: Mellen, 2002.

Ross, Cameron, ed. *Russian Politics under Putin*. New York: Palgrave, 2004.

Shevtsova, Lilia. *Putin's Russia*, rev. ed. Washington, D.C.: Carnegie Endowment, 2005.

Varese, Federico. *The Russian Mafia: Private Protection in a New Market Economy*. New York: Oxford, 2001.

11

What Russians Quarrel About

We are interested in why the Soviet Union collapsed not out of purely historical curiosity but to serve as a warning about what can go wrong again. Whatever happened to the Soviet Union can happen to Russia; the problems and resistance Khrushchev, Gorbachev, and Yeltsin faced, Putin still faces. The question is also part of current Russian politics.

WHY THE SOVIET UNION COLLAPSED

Many Russians, especially strong nationalists, refuse to believe that the Soviet Union collapsed largely because of the inherent economic inefficiency of socialism. They blame sinister forces, especially the Americans, the functional equivalent of the *stab in the back* myth that so harmed Weimar Germany.

The real explanation is that socialist economies—meaning state-owned and centrally planned, "Communist," if you prefer—work poorly. They do not collapse overnight but over time slowly run down. Under certain circumstances, to be sure, centrally planned economies can grow very fast, as did the Soviet Union under Stalin's Five-Year Plans in the 1930s. A backward country borrowed capitalist technology and threw all its resources, including labor, into giant projects, chiefly into making steel and then making things from steel. From the 1930s through the 1960s, many observers assumed that the Soviet Union would catch up with and eventually overtake the United States in terms of economic production.

As the Soviet Union tried to catch up, however, its economy became more complex and harder to control.

Questions to Consider

1. What is to blame for Russia's current troubles?
2. Why did political scientists fail to grasp the decay of the Soviet Union?
3. Is it fair to compare Poland's economic "shock therapy" with Russia's?
4. Does Russia now have capitalism? Why or why not?
5. What happened to Russia's economy in 1998? How does it compare to Mexico?
6. What happened in Chechnya? Could similar things occur?
7. What is the "near abroad" and why do Russians want it?
8. What are the difficulties of "middle ways"?

Input-output tables required hundreds of mathematicians to make the thousands of calculations necessary to set the targets of the Soviet economy on a centralized basis. Product quality was poor, as only quantity was calculated and required. Designs, often copied from old Western products, were out of date. Efficiency counted for nothing; there was not even a Russian word for efficiency (the closest was effective). Many factories produced things nobody wanted.

The consumer sector, deliberately shortchanged, offered too few products to motivate Soviet workers, who had to wait years for an apartment or a car. Accordingly, workers did not exert themselves but chuckled; "They pretend to pay us, and we pretend to work." Many took afternoons off to shop for scarce goods; standing in lines took hours each week. These and other factors made Soviets angry with the system. By the early 1970s, the Soviet economy slowed, especially in comparison to the surging economies of West Europe and the Pacific Rim.

But this by itself was not enough to bring down the system, which could have lumbered on in shabby decay. The real killer was technological backwardness, especially as it impinged on the Soviet military. The computer age had arrived, and thinking machines were spreading fast into Western businesses, research labs, and military systems. The Soviets fell behind in computerization, and the Soviet military knew what that meant: getting beat. With U.S. President Ronald Reagan came an even worse technological menace: a "Star Wars" shield in space that would make America invulnerable. An important sector of the Soviet military thus turned to economic and technological reform out of the fear of falling behind.

Many thinking Soviet Party people, especially younger ones, knew by the 1980s that economic reforms were necessary and were eager for someone like Gorbachev to lead the way. But by themselves, they could not prevail against the conservative forces of managers and *apparatchiki*, many of whose jobs were at stake. It took, I believe, the high-tech sections of the armed forces to ally themselves with Gorbachev and give the green light to economic reforms in the expectation that these would lead to military technology to equal the Americans.

Oil plays a roller-coaster role in first keeping afloat and then sinking the Soviet/Russian economy. The rapid increase in oil prices in the 1970s meant that Soviet petroleum exports—at that time the USSR was the world's biggest oil producer and exporter—could for a few years pay for Soviet imports of food and technology. When oil prices fell, so did the Soviet Union. Now Russia is too dependent on oil exports. The 2004–2005 jump in world oil prices brought great earnings and taxes, but oil-price spikes never last, and ultimately neither will Russia's oil

How to Reform?

At no time did Mikhail Gorbachev adopt a thoroughgoing plan of economic reform. His advisors presented him with several, each bolder than the previous, but he never implemented any. He never wanted capitalism; instead, he sought a middle path or "third way"

Key Term

input-output table   Spreadsheet for economy of entire nation.

KEY CONCEPTS

LACKING FACTS, THEY THEORIZED

The most stupendous change of the late twentieth century took political scientists by surprise. Why did we fail to anticipate—notice that I am not asking for prediction—the collapse of the Soviet Union? Only a handful of historians and economists sounded warnings. Curiously, it was a demographer who made the best prediction. Nicholas Eberstadt examined the statistical decline of Soviet health and saw doom years in advance. Political scientists tended to see more of the same, with some reforms.

Why did we miss it? I see several mental blocks we built for ourselves, mostly by reading each others' books and articles—what intelligence officers call *incestuous amplification*.

1. *Lousy Empirical Data.* Much of the Soviet system was secret; we had to piece together flimsy indicators and infer how things worked. We filled the informational vacuum with theory, much of it misleading. In Yugoslavia, by way of contrast, you could get accurate data and candid interviews. As early as the 1960s some saw cracks in the Yugoslav federation. Little theory came out of studies of Yugoslavia, as researchers did not need to theorize; they had facts. Lacking facts, Soviet specialists theorized. The moral: We are only as good as our data.

2. *Systems Theory.* Since the 1960s, political scientists have been trained to see all countries as *political systems* that have varying structures but perform the same functions. Whenever the system is thrown off balance, it always corrects itself, by new governments, parties, or reforms. Systems were thus presumed to be highly durable, possibly immortal. Systems theorists could simply not envision system collapse.

3. *Anti-Anticommunism.* The anticommunist hysteria of the early Cold War years, especially McCarthyism, was so primitive that some thinkers gave Communist systems the benefit of the doubt. Specialists tended to accept Communist systems as givens (as did systems theorists) and to conduct detailed studies of how they worked. Anyone who suggested Communist systems were inherently flawed and doomed was read out of the profession as speculative, right wing, and unscholarly.

4. *Undervaluing Economics.* Many Soviet specialists paid little attention to economics; they assumed politics dominated economics. (Economists assume the opposite.) Few appreciated that a deteriorating economy eventually drags the entire country down with it. Some economists noted Soviet economic decline for years, but political scientists largely ignored them.

5. *System Reformability.* Political scientists supposed Soviet problems could be fixed with reforms. (This too derives from systems theory.) If the system has an economic or structural problem, it will correct it, was the bland assumption. Eventually, some thought, the Soviet system would reform itself into a social-democratic welfare state. The brittleness of the Soviet system occurred to few.

6. *Fixation on Personalities.* Because reforms are necessary, they will be carried out; they just need the right personality. Ah! Here comes Gorbachev, the man both we and Russian liberals have been waiting for. His reforms will produce a much nicer Soviet Union. In this way, we read into Gorbachev heroic and reformist qualities he never had. Clueless would be more like it.

Apartment houses in Russia are prefabricated and small. There is a terrible housing shortage, so flats like these in a Moscow suburb are eagerly sought. (Michael Roskin)

between capitalism and socialism. Gorbachev hesitated and changed his mind more or less annually, one year for economic reform, the next year against. Later he admitted several mistakes. First, he now says, he should have liberalized agriculture, as the Chinese did under Deng (see Chapter 12). Instead, Gorbachev tried a couple of timid steps he inherited from his mentor, the late Andropov: "intensification" and an anti-alcohol campaign. Both failed.

When it came to real reforms, Gorbachev choked, both out of fear for the consequences and in the face of massive resistance by conservative Soviet forces. Gorbachev finally freed most prices, but he did not privatize industry. The result was far too many rubles chasing too few goods: inflation. Everyone wanted dollars as the ruble dwindled in value. Worried citizens muttered that things could not go on like this. It was against this background that Gorbachev's own cabinet plotted a coup in 1991. Before the year ended, the Soviet Union was dissolved, Gorbachev was a private citizen, and Yeltsin was president of the Russian Federation. At last, reform started looking serious, but Yeltsin too faced opposition from conservative forces.

FROM THE RUBBLE OF THE RUBLE

Finally the Russian economy is growing. With the right policies, it could have happened much sooner. Gorbachev never restructured the Soviet economy. Yeltsin did not fully restructure the Russian economy. Are we asking for the impossible? Poland initiated a "shock therapy" at the beginning of 1991 and within two years had gone through the worst of its inflation and industrial decline and for several years was the fastest growing economy of Europe.

KEY CONCEPTS

THE TERMINOLOGY OF ECONOMIC REFORM

- *liberalize:* Cutting prices free to find their own level. Instead of centrally designated prices, factories may charge whatever they can get on the free market (thus sometimes called to "marketize").
- *privatize:* Putting state-owned enterprises and land into private hands by selling them to local investors, foreign investors, their own workers, or the citizenry at large through vouchers. In Russia, only a few benefitted.
- *shock therapy:* Liberalizing and privatizing simultaneously and rapidly. This proved successful in Central Europe but not in the ex-Soviet Union.
- *currency convertibility:* The ending of fake, imposed exchange rates by letting the local currency be exchanged for foreign currency at whatever rate the market sets. Convertibility makes it impossible to disguise inflation.
- *stabilization:* Controlling the amount of currency in circulation, both by limiting the printing of money and by denying government loans to industry, so as to slow inflation and make currency worth predictable.
- *tradeoff:* The choice between inflation and unemployment, allowing one to rise in order to keep the other low. Most ex-Soviet type economies elect to let inflation roar in order to hold down unemployment.

Yeltsin's first prime minister (until late 1992) and later finance minister, the dynamic reformer Yegor Gaidar, tried to induce shock therapy as he privatized the large, obsolete industrial enterprises the Communists had built. Terribly inefficient and overstaffed and with no concern for consumer needs, many Soviet plants actually *subtracted* value from the raw materials they processed. But these industries were the wealth and power of the bureaucrats and *apparatchiks* who took them over and gave employment for those who listlessly worked in them. Accordingly, they were able to pressure Moscow to keep the subsidies flowing. In any rational system, they would have been declared bankrupt immediately. But you cannot throw millions of people out of work all at once, protested many Russians.

Privatization in Russia (and some other ex-Communist lands) was carried out badly. A handful of clever operators bought up factories and raw materials cheap and turned themselves into a new class of capitalists. Many of these industries still get government subsidies (such as cheap energy), which allows the new owners to reap enormous profits as they export oil, natural gas, and minerals. Much of the profit does not return to Russia, though; it goes into foreign banks, a pattern typical of South America. Because this capital was not recycled back into the Russian economy, the rest of the economy

Traveling Salesmen: These young Russians make a niche in the economy by buying Russian medicines (in the big bags) and selling them in outdoor markets in Sofia, Bulgaria. After a few days at the market, they return home for more, bribing their way across borders. They showed me how to catch a train from Romania to Bulgaria without a ticket: "Just bribe the conductor," they shrugged, "It's a Russian train." (Michael Roskin)

declined, making poor people poorer. Capitalism in Russia began as **asset-stripping**, which is no basis for long-term future. Only recently has it begun to work like capitalism elsewhere, with capitalists reinvesting their money inside Russia.

August 1998 showed what bad policies can bring. Some observers saw trouble coming well in advance, in the area of **public finances**. Russia was collecting less than half the taxes it was supposed to. Everyone cheated on taxes. As a result, the budget went dangerously into deficit, so the Yeltsin government simply printed more money. Banks—and anyone in Russia could open a bank—were unregulated and made unsecured loans to friends.

KEY TERMS

asset-stripping Selling off firm's property and raw materials for short-term profit.
public finances What a government takes in, what it spends, and how it makes up the difference.

GEOGRAPHY

WILL RUSSIA FALL APART?

Russia is an extreme case of center-periphery tensions, one that could have led to the breakup of the Russian Federation. As starvation loomed and Russia's eighty-nine republics and regions got no help from Moscow, many ignored the center and set up their own economic systems, with price controls, limits on "exports" to other parts of Russia, and barter systems. Some talked about introducing their own currency. Some ethnic groups claimed sovereignty; a few even declared independence. Many regions refused to pay taxes to Moscow. Many of the republics are authoritarian dictatorships where opposition candidates or media are not tolerated.

Trying to rein in unruly republics, Putin in 2000 created seven super-regions and named mostly KGB and FSB officials as super-governors. Since then, things have stabilized somewhat under Moscow's tighter control. This may be undemocratic, but what would the fragmentation of the giant Russian Federation lead to? As we mentioned in Chapter 7 (page 102), its very size means Russia must be ruled with a firm hand from the center.

The chief monetary instrument of Russian banks was U.S. $100 bills, some of them counterfeit. Knowing the perils of the Russian economy, Russian oligarchs stashed between $150 billion and $350 billion in **flight capital** offshore. Eventually, this system had to crash, and when it did, in 1998, the ruble lost some three-quarters of its value in relation to **hard currencies**. Many banks closed, leaving depositors with nothing. Russia's fledgling stock markets dived. Some industries collapsed. Russia **defaulted** on its loans (biggest losers: German banks, with over $30 billion loaned to Russia) and had to beg for new credit. Badly burned, foreign investors fled Russia.

Russians felt angry and betrayed. We had told them that the free market is the path to prosperity, but it brought them only misery. A third now fell below the official (very low) poverty line. Actually, Russia had never fully implemented a functioning market system. Much Western advice was ignored. Most of the $66 billion in Western aid disappeared. There were too many government subsidies and tax breaks and too few rules and regulations that keep a market economy steady. Money, always a weak point with Russians (see page 148), was just something you printed. In the words of one Russian reformer, it was "the most expensive economic education in history."

KEY TERMS

flight capital   Money owner sends out of country in fear of losing it.

hard currency   Noninflating, recognized currencies used in international dealings, such as dollars and euros.

default   Not being able to pay back a loan.

Before the 1998 collapse, some people got rich fast while many went hungry. Having long been taught by the Communists that material equality is good and just, Russians witnessed the explosive growth of inequality. (Income inequality in Russia is now greater than in the United States.) Some *biznesmeny* and mafiosi (the two words are linked in the Russian mind) enjoyed new wealth while most Russians lived worse than ever.

Good emerged from the rubble of the ruble. Fake businesses collapsed, and entrepreneurs started investing their profits in Russia. Russia's economy, helped by the runup in world oil prices and cheap currency, has recently grown by several percent a year. The federal budget is in balance, and inflation eased from 80 percent in 1998 to a few percent. Russia's trade balance, again thanks to oil, has been very positive (in contrast to big U.S. deficits). Putin's reforms of taxes, banks, and land sales could promote growth. Said Putin in 2002: "Our economy must grow much faster." (Stalin said the same in 1931.) The big test: Will Russia's economy be honest enough to let it join the World Trade Organization, which it very much wants to do?

Two clouds of uncertainty hang over the Russian economy, and Russians live in fear of a major downturn. The first is oil prices, which at times soared to over $60 a barrel. Russia is a major oil (and natural gas) exporter, and cash poured in. But oil prices are volatile and cannot be counted on. The second is Putin's persecution of oligarchs such as Khodorkovsky (see previous chapter), which panicked foreign investors. Fearing that Putin was returning Russia to state-ownership of industries, foreign investment plunged, and it is an important component of economic growth. Russia's economy is not yet stable.

RECOVER THE LOST REPUBLICS?

So far, we have been talking about the complex Russian Federation, a difficult situation itself. But what of the non-Russian republics that departed from the Soviet Union, what Russians call the **near abroad**? Most of them had been incorporated into the tsarist empire, and many Russians still think of them as belonging to Russia. Some want to restore the Russian empire, especially the Russian army, which still has troops in most of the ex-Soviet republics. For U.S. policy, Moscow's influence in Central Asia is not all bad. Putin helped establish U.S. bases in Uzbekistan and Tajikistan to overthrow the Afghan Taliban after 9/11. Until landlocked Central Asia gains access to the outside world through Iran, Afghanistan, and Pakistan, it will remain dependent on Russia for trade and transportation.

In many ex-Soviet republics, the "new" leaders are old Party big shots, and rule by a corrupt and authoritarian Party elite continues uninterrupted and intact. Not counting the Baltic republics, Russia had the most progressive and most reform-minded leadership. Other republics lagged behind. A particularly tragic example was Ukraine, potentially rich and European, whose ex-Communist leaders instituted no economic reform program. The result was a hyperinflation that made the Russian economy look good.

One crucial fact in Russian thinking concerns the 25 million ethnic Russians who live in the near abroad. (The term does not refer to the former satellites of East Europe, such as Poland or Hungary.) Some Russians in these republics feel threatened. Any outright violence

KEY TERM

near abroad   Non-Russian republics of old Soviet Union.

GEOGRAPHY

THE UNRAVELING OF THE NORTH CAUCASUS

Mountainous regions, because they are hard to control, permit small ethnic and religious groups to develop into distinct cultures that resist outside rule. Russia's **North Caucasus** illustrates this well. The rugged region—home to more than 6 million people, mostly Muslim—is a crazy quilt of ethnic groups, most consolidated into their current borders by Stalin. From west to east they are Karachayevo-Cherkess, Kabardino-Balkaria, North Ossetia, Ingushetia, Chechnya, and Dagestan.

The tsarist army finally subdued the region only in the early nineteenth century. Emblematic was the tsarist fortress built in 1784: Vladikavkaz (Master of the Caucasus), now the capital of North Ossetia. Few locals liked Russian rule, and Russians despised them as bandits. In 1944, Stalin accused several Caucasian nationalities, Chechens among them, of collaborating with the German invaders and brutally exiled them to Central Asia.

Decades later, Chechen Jokar Dudayev became a general in the Soviet air force. Assigned to an Estonian airbase in the 1980s, Dudayev sympathized with the Estonians, who, like Chechens, hated Russian rule. Dudayev blocked the landing of Soviet troops in early 1991, helping Estonia win independence. He then retired, won an election in Chechnya, and proclaimed its independence as the Soviet Union broke up in late 1991. But Chechnya, unlike Estonia, had never been a *union republic;* it was part of the Russian Federation, and Moscow fears unrest spreading to all the North Caucasus, which is happening. Crime and insurgency are met with police brutality. Gunfights are frequent.

Yeltsin, in late 1994—with no discussion among military professionals, parliamentary debate, or publicity—gave the order to quickly crush Chechen independence. But the military campaign stalled; the Russian army was pathetic, and Chechens fought boldly and tenaciously. Some 80,000, mostly civilians, were killed, and the capital, Grozny, was shelled into ruin. Most Russians, even military officers, hated the war; partly because of it, Yeltsin's popularity plummeted. Ex-General Alexander Lebed worked out a shaky peace with Chechen fighters in 1996, leaving them an undefined autonomy.

In 1999, Chechen-led Muslim fundamentalists attempted to take over neighboring Dagestan. Moscow retaliated sharply, pursuing the guerrillas back into Chechnya. In Russian cities, several apartment houses were blown up, killing nearly 300. Some suspect it was a put-up job, but Moscow immediately blamed Chechen terrorists and launched a major invasion of Chechnya. This time the Russian army was in much better shape, and the Russian people were behind them. Putin's tough stance boosted his popularity. Putin declared victory in 2002, but guerrilla warfare, banditry, and terrorism continue and have spread through the North Caucasus. Theatergoers and schoolchildren have been victims. Putin used Chechen terrorism to concentrate more power in his hands, and most Russians accepted it.

Chechnya's two bloody wars could be just the first stage of the unraveling of the North Caucasus region. In the first war, 1994–1996, Chechen rebels pushed the Russian army out. In the second, 1999–2002, Russians bloodily occupied Chechnya but did not end the Muslim-nationalist rebellion. Foreign leaders condemn the horror, but no one offers a plan to solve it and none wish to antagonize Russia. Putin, angry at U.S. criticism, asked: Just what is the United States doing in Iraq? Putin vowed to wipe out terrorism in Russia. "We showed weakness," he said of the Chechen problem, "and the weak are trampled upon." Stalin couldn't have said it better.

GEOGRAPHY

YUGOSLAVIA: A MINIATURE SOVIET UNION?

The former multiethnic Balkan federal system of Yugoslavia resembles the ex-Soviet Union. Both countries had a Slavic core nationality: Russians in the Soviet Union and Serbs in Yugoslavia. Serbs and Russians are both Eastern Orthodox Christians and use the Cyrillic alphabet. Both defined themselves as the founders and guarantors of their respective nations. They regarded breakaway republics as traitors to the nation.

The other nationalities resent this overbearing attitude. In each country an advanced northwest (the Baltic republics in the Soviet Union and Slovenia in Yugoslavia) grew tired of being held back by the less-developed core nationality, which economically drained the advanced area. Interestingly, the Baltics and Slovenia declared their independence first.

The second largest nationality in each country is also Slavic but with a distinctive culture and resentments against being bossed by the center; thus, Ukraine and Croatia quickly broke away. In the south, feisty Muslim nationalities demand greater autonomy and fight neighboring Christian nationalities (the Azeris against the Armenians and the Bosnian Muslims and Kosovar Albanians against the Serbs). In most of the newly independent republics in both the ex-Soviet Union and ex-Yugoslavia, the "new" leaders had been local Communist bosses prior to independence.

A final touch: Russians and Serbs, respectively, formed the bulk of the officer corps of the old Soviet and Yugoslav armies and now of the Russian and Serbian armies. The top officers are conservative and dedicated to keeping their countries intact. They are not adverse to using force to do so. In 1991, both armies started intervening directly in politics. The key difference so far is that conservative Communists took over in Belgrade and, with the army's general staff in agreement, attempted to hold Yugoslavia together by force. When that quickly failed, they turned to building a *Greater Serbia* by military conquest, coupled with *ethnic cleansing*. In the ex-Soviet Union, the death toll has not been as large, but it too experienced wars in the Caucasus region.

against them, however, provokes the Russian army, which feels it has a duty to come to the rescue. This could someday be used as an excuse to seize all or part of neighboring republics.

Recovery of the lost republics could come about by more subtle means as well: economics. As the economies of other republics plunged downward, some turned desperately to Moscow for help. Under the banner of the Commonwealth of Independent States, Moscow delivers some aid (e.g., a good deal on oil and natural gas) but in return gets trade concessions and general obedience. Moscow successfully used this approach on Belarus—which now uses the Russian ruble as currency—and seems to be trying it on Ukraine.

KEY TERM

North Caucasus   Mountainous region north of Georgia and Azerbaijan; includes Chechnya (see page 176).

GEOGRAPHY

RUNNING OUT OF RUSSIANS

Almost all industrialized countries produce few babies, but Russia is in serious **demographic** decline. In 1989, before the Soviet collapse, an average Soviet woman (many non-Russian) bore 2.17 children. Now an average Russian woman bears only 1.1 children, one of the world's lowest **fertility rates**, which is not the same as the *birth rate,* a different measure. In comparison, an average American woman bears 1.95 children; a French woman, 1.6; a British woman, 1.7; a Japanese woman, 1.45; and a German woman, 1.2. Replacement level is 2.1, the rate at which a population will hold steady, found in no advanced industrialized countries. Large families are not prized, and women have increased educational and career options.

In Russia, the situation is worse. Declining health standards have worsened the **infant mortality rate** to around 20 per thousand live births (recently improved), much worse than West or Central Europe. Expectant mothers are poorly nourished and so are their babies, many of whom suffer protein deficiency. There have been isolated reports of children starving to death. Most Russian families have only one child. Meanwhile, the Russian death rate climbed; life expectancy of adult men dropped to fifty-eight years, lower than in much of the Third World. Result: Russia's population shrinks by nearly 700,000 a year.

One of the causes of death is prodigious alcohol consumption (some of it poisonous home-brew) leading to industrial accidents. Russian environmental poisoning, both chemical and nuclear, is among the world's worst, and environmentally caused diseases are common. (Russia's closest rivals: East Europe.) The air in Russia's industrial cities is dangerous. "To live longer," said one official, "we should breathe less." Many factories just dumped toxic and nuclear wastes into shallow landfills. Once-pristine Lake Baikal, long revered as a symbol of Mother Russia, is now polluted.

A tricky third way appeared in Georgia, which itself is home to many non-Georgian nationalities. The Muslim Abkhazians of western Georgia broke away by force of arms, many of them supplied quietly by the Russian army. Georgia had originally refused to join the CIS in 1991 but, faced with military defeat, did so in 1994. Then the Russians changed sides and began supporting Georgia with arms and troops. They called it "peacekeeping," but it was more like a protection racket.

KEY TERMS

demography Study of population growth.

fertility rate How many children an average woman bears.

infant mortality rate Number of live newborns who die in their first year, per thousand; standard measure of nation's health.

COMPARISON

SCANDINAVIAN-TYPE SOCIALISM FOR RUSSIA?

Confusion surrounds the term *socialism*. Many Russians and East Europeans now tell you they no longer know what the word means. Some call the welfare states of Scandinavia "socialist" because freely elected Social Democratic governments have gradually introduced elaborate medical, unemployment, educational, housing, and other programs to lift up the lower rungs of society: *cradle-to-grave welfare*. These Social Democratic parties started out Marxist but all of them shed it. They are all based on large labor-union federations. The aim of these parties is to wipe out poverty without resorting to coercion or state control.

And here's where Scandinavian *welfarism* differs sharply from Communist-style socialism. The Scandinavian lands have little nationalized industry, and what was nationalized was done so for non-ideological reasons (for example, to hold down unemployment). The bulk of the economy is private and capitalist. Swedish managers especially developed a ferocious reputation for efficient, money-making plant operation. Taxes, to be sure, are high, but the economy is otherwise free.

In sum, Scandinavia is not socialist; it is a variation on capitalism called welfarism. If you wish to call it socialism, of course, you may. But please note that it was developed after and on top of Scandinavia's capitalist industrial base. First came capitalism, then came welfare. It is doubtful if the order can be reversed or if they can be built simultaneously.

No one has yet found a way to combine capitalism and socialism on a long-term, stable basis. For a while, such a combination sometimes seems to work. Then the private sector starts bumping into the restricted, slow-moving state sector. The private sector needs raw materials, labor, infrastructure, and transportation on a flexible, ever-changing basis. The state sector, still run by a central plan, cannot possibly deliver and has no incentive to. If you allow state enterprises to enter the private-sector market, you are gradually desocializing the economy. It gets more efficient but less socialist. Eventually you come to a point where you must either bury the socialist sector as a bad experiment or curb and recontrol the private sector. The mix will not hold steady; you must go one way or the other. China is caught up in this dilemma.

Many Russians, including Putin, still think they can find a middle way that is uniquely Russian. Experience suggests that if they try to build a middle way, it will lead to an unstable, declining system with high inflation.

Should we as Americans criticize Russians for wishing to recover the near abroad? What did President Lincoln do when faced with the breakup of the Union? Americans should have a bias toward holding unions together. And has not West Europe turned itself into the EU? If Moscow can build a CIS similar to the EU by economic means, it should not bother us, provided the trade deals are voluntary. If, however, Russia attempts to regain the lost republics by military force, it will mean that a dangerous crowd has taken over in the Kremlin, and that should concern us greatly.

A MIDDLE WAY FOR SOCIALISM?

Putin's ultimate problem—which was inherited from his predecessors—was that he thought there was a **middle way** between a centrally planned socialist economy and a free-market economy. Reforms, some argue, can blend a market economy with a socialist economy. They do it in Sweden, do they not? (No, they do not. See the box on Scandinavian-type socialism on page 179.) Some Russians think that they can reserve the "commanding heights" of heavy industry for the state while permitting small enterprises to operate in a free market. This is what Lenin did under the NEP in the early 1920s, and the NEP was frequently mentioned as a model by Gorbachevites. The NEP, however, was inherently flawed and was running down in the late 1920s when Stalin dropped it in favor of forced industrialization.

WHICH WAY RUSSIA?

Observers of Russia divide into two camps: optimists and pessimists. Pessimists see a botched job. Capitalism has not taken root. At first the oligarchs looted state enterprises and stashed the money abroad; then Putin stole it back from them. The oil and gas industry has returned to state control. Corruption and lawlessness link authorities (including the police) and mafias. Many Russians live worse than ever. And it had to happen. No country can take the kind of chaos and decay the Yeltsin era brought. Either Russia was going to collapse or be taken over by an authoritarian. Many expected that authoritarian to be an ex-general, but it was a KGB man, Putin.

The optimists point to the fact that most of Russia's economy is private and, ever since the collapse of 1998, is growing nicely. Inflation is dropping, and **current-account balances** are very positive, thanks to high oil prices. The remaining oligarchs have shifted from asset stripping to production and reinvestment, a healthy sign. Privatization was chaotic and crooked, but now owners have a stake in rule of law to keep their gains. Reasonably free elections have been held in which most Russians rejected both Communists and extreme nationalists. Putin is a bit of a control freak, but he is better than many alternatives one can imagine. A market is now being built in Russia, argue optimists, and in a few years it may lead to democracy. (We will hear similar rosy projections on China's evolution.)

Which way will Russia go? The stakes for us are enormous. We hoped to have a friendly, democratic Russia as a trading partner but now face growing Russian hostility. Many Russians blame America for their decline, and Putin accuses critics of working for foreign interests. True, American economists gave advice that overlooked the lack of cultural and institutional bases for capitalism in Russia. They casually assumed that Russia was a big Poland. But Russia never really swept out the old system.

KEY TERMS

middle way   Supposed blend of capitalism and socialism; also called "third way."
current-account balance   A country's exports minus its imports.

GEOGRAPHY

FEAR OF INVASION

Russians are unhappy and fearful because their former Central European satellites (Poland, the Czech Republic, Hungary) joined NATO in 1999 and the former Soviet republics of Lithuania, Latvia, and Estonia joined NATO in 2004, along with Bulgaria, Romania, Slovakia, and Slovenia. NATO, the enemy during the long Cold War, keeps getting closer. No Russian likes this, but Putin knows there is nothing he can do about it now.

Geopolitics has always been important to the Kremlin's rulers. Starting under the tsars but reemphasized by Stalin during and after World War II, it became an article of Kremlin faith that Russia needed Eastern Europe—which Moscow organized as the **Warsaw Pact**—as a defensive shield against attack from the west. There have indeed been many such invasions; the Nazi invasion of 1941 was the most recent. Until Gorbachev, all Soviet civilian and military leaders accepted this argument. To prevent East Europe's departure from the Soviet orbit, Khrushchev crushed the 1956 Hungarian uprising and Brezhnev crushed the 1968 Prague Spring. Both nearly invaded Poland.

But East Europe was a major economic and military drain on the Soviet Union, and it blocked improved relations with the West. By 1989, Gorbachev had decided to no longer support the Communist regimes of East Europe, and the regimes fell. Central Europe quickly became democratic with free markets. Russia's strategic situation actually improved, for the end of the Cold War removed the military threat from the West. NATO, with declining defense budgets and small armies, poses no danger. Costs to Russia, in garrison troops and subsidized trade deals, have been drastically cut. Instead of selling Russian gas and oil at sweetheart prices to their satellites, Russia can get world-market prices for them, and in hard currency. Potentially, Russia is now open for trade with and investment from the West, the ticket to prosperity. Still, many Russian conservatives argue that Gorbachev gave away Russia's defensive shield; a few want it back. The very old fear of invasion from the West played into the hands of demagogic Russian politicians.

Russia is frosty to the West, but this will not be a new Cold War, because Russia is too poor and weak to stand up to the West. In the rigged 2004 Ukrainian elections Putin charged Western interference (he favored the pro-Russian authoritarian candidate) but he backed down, and new elections were held. Moscow has to take external pressures into account. To attract foreign investment, Russia needs rule of law. To get major loans it must adhere to austere IMF limits on budget deficits. With NATO expanded eastward and Russia's military terribly weak, Moscow must be strategically cautious; few fear Russia any more.

KEY TERMS

geopolitics   Influence of geography on policy.
Warsaw Pact   Soviet-led alliance of Communist countries, defunct.

Is Russia now a democracy? No. Freedom House (see page 154) downgraded Russia to "not free," closer to dictatorship than to democracy. There is competition, but control of the mass media skews elections. Institutions are unbalanced, the presidency too powerful and the legislature too weak. Corruption dominates everything. A democratic sprit of tolerance and fair play is absent. Some scholars argue that Russia is comparable to several developing countries in an "in-between" stage. We do not expect instant democracy from them, and neither should we expect it from Russia.

Can Russians eventually govern themselves in a moderate, democratic fashion? I think they can, but it will take many years. There is nothing genetically authoritarian about Russians. Earlier in the twentieth century Germans and Spaniards were deemed unfit for responsible self-government, but now they are practicing democracy as well as any Europeans. I believe Russia will eventually turn democratic, in your lifetime if not in mine.

KEY TERMS

asset-stripping (p. 173)

current-account balance (p. 180)

default (p. 174)

demography (p. 178)

fertility rate (p. 178)

flight capital (p. 174)

geopolitics (p. 181)

hard currency (p. 174)

infant mortality rate (p. 178)

input-output table (p. 169)

middle way (p. 180)

near abroad (p. 175)

North Caucasus (p. 177)

public finances (p. 173)

Warsaw Pact (p. 181)

FURTHER REFERENCE

Åslund, Anders. *Building Capitalism: The Transformation of the Former Soviet Bloc.* New York: Cambridge University Press, 2001.

Birgerson, Susanne M. *After the Breakup of a Multi-Ethnic Empire: Russia, Successor States, and Eurasian Security.* Westport, CT: Praeger, 2002.

Breslauer, George W., and Victoria E. Bonnell, eds. *Russia in the New Century: Stability or Disorder?* Boulder, CO: Westview, 2001.

Cox, Michael, ed. *Rethinking the Soviet Collapse: Sovietology, the Death of Communism, and the New Russia.* New York: Pinter, 1998.

Goldman, Marshall I. *The Piratization of Russia: Russian Reform Goes Awry.* New York: Routledge, 2003.

Herspring, Dale R., ed. *Putin's Russia: Past Imperfect, Future Uncertain.* Blue Ridge Summit, PA: Rowman & Littlefield, 2002.

Jack, Andrew. *Inside Putin's Russia: Can There Be Reform without Democracy?* New York: Oxford University Press, 2004.

Kempton, Daniel R., and Terry D. Clark. *Unity or Separation: Center-Periphery Relations in the Former Soviet Union.* Westport, CT: Praeger, 2001.

Kuchins, Andrew C., ed. *Russia After the Fall*. Washington, D.C.: Carnegie Endowment, 2002.

Meier, Andrew. *Chechnya: To the Heart of a Conflict*. New York: Norton, 2004.

Reddaway, Peter, and Dmitri Glinski. *The Tragedy of Russia's Reforms: Market Bolshevism against Democracy*. Herndon, VA: U.S. Institute of Peace, 2001.

Shlapentokh, Vladimir. *A Normal Totalitarian Society: How the Soviet Union Functioned and How It Collapsed*. Armonk, NY: M. E. Sharpe, 2001.

Trenin, Dmitiri, and Aleksei V. Malashenko. *Russia's Restless Frontier: The Chechnya Factor in Post-Soviet Russia*. Washington, D.C.: Carnegie Endowment, 2004.

Xenakis, Christopher I. *What Happened to the Soviet Union? How and Why American Sovietologists Were Caught by Surprise*. Westport, CT: Praeger, 2002.

PART III

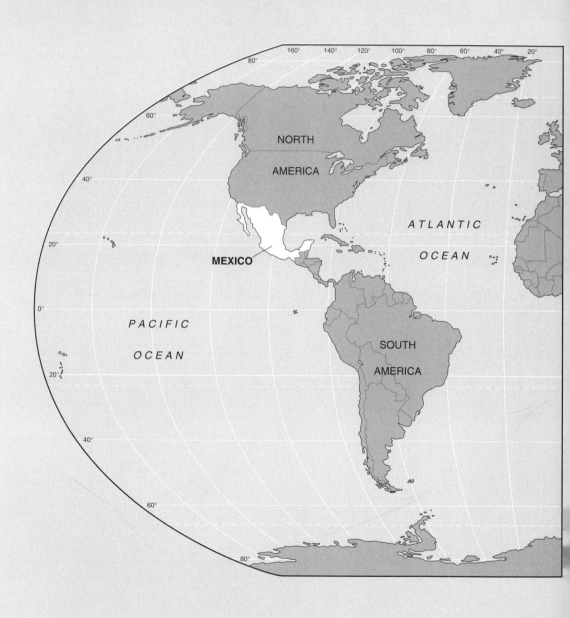

THE THIRD WORLD

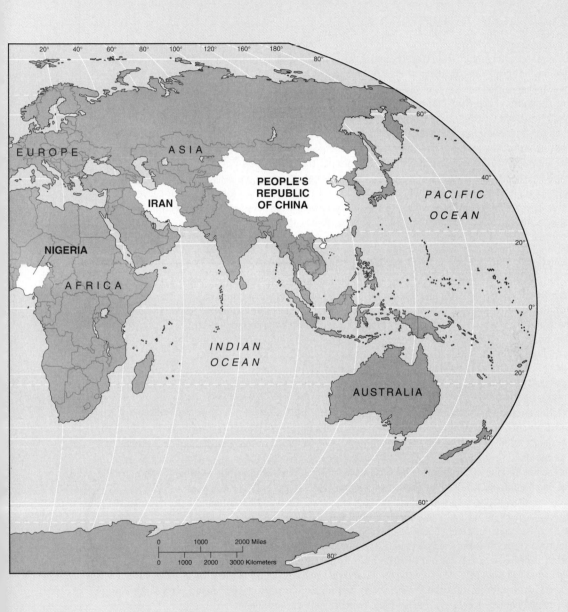

GEOGRAPHY

THE GEOGRAPHY OF IMPERIALISM

We understand much about Third World countries by knowing who its former imperial masters were, who left behind borders (most of them artificial), languages, legal codes, transportation lines, and styles of governance. Notice how few non-European lands stayed free of imperial rule: Afghanistan, Ethiopia, Japan, Thailand, and Turkey. China and Iran were reduced to semi-colonial status.

Much has been written about Europe's imperial impulse. Marxists see it as a race for riches, but in the long run administering and defending colonies often cost the imperial power more than they gained. Europe's richest countries never had colonies, but its poorest, Portugal, was drained by colonial expenses. Private interests, to be sure, profited from the colonial trade. Some see imperialism as a race for security: "If we don't take it, someone else will." Spain, Britain, France, and others competed for colonies out of fear they would be at a strategic disadvantage if they had none. A *contagion* or *copycat factor* was also at work, as colonies brought prestige. Only powers with colonies were respected. This helps explain the U.S. push for colonies in 1898. Roughly, here is who had what:

Spain, starting with Columbus, had most of Latin America (almost all of it lost in the 1820s) and the Philippines (lost to the United States in 1898).

Portugal's was the longest-lived empire. Portugal had Brazil (independent in 1822) but kept Goa until India took it in 1961; Angola, Mozambique, and Guinea-Bissau in Africa until 1975; East Timor until invaded by Indonesia in 1975; and Macau (near Hong Kong), ceded to China in 1999.

Britain's was the biggest empire—"The sun never sets on the British Empire"—and included Canada, Australia, New Zealand, India (which then included Pakistan and Bangladesh), Sri Lanka, Burma, Malaya, South Yemen, much of Africa below the Sahara (including South Africa and Nigeria), and Hong Kong, plus temporary arrangements in Egypt, Israel, Jordan, and Iraq.

France's was the second-biggest empire, including Vietnam, Laos, Cambodia, most of North and Equatorial Africa, and bits of the Caribbean and South Pacific. France and Britain gave up their colonies from 1947 to 1964.

The Netherlands held the rich Dutch East Indies from the seventeenth century to 1949 and South Africa's Cape area in the eighteenth century, plus specks on the Caribbean.

Belgium brutally exploited the vast Congo from 1885 to 1960, initially as the personal property of King Leopold.

Latecomer Germany in 1885 got some leftover pieces of Africa (Tanganyika, Namibia, Cameroon) and half of Samoa but lost them all at the close of World War I.

Italy, another latecomer, took Somalia in 1889, Eritrea in 1890, and Libya from the Ottomans in 1912, and Ethiopia in 1935 but lost everything in World War II.

Imperialism was not solely a European thing. The Ottoman Turkish Empire took the Balkans in the late fourteenth century and held parts until the early nineteenth. They also took the Middle East in the sixteenth century until pushed out by Britain in World War I.

Japan took Taiwan in 1895, Korea in 1910, and Manchuria in 1931 but lost them all in 1945.

And let us not forget that the United States had an empire too. In 1898 America took the Philippines (independent since 1946), Puerto Rico, Hawaii, Midway, and Guam.

GEOGRAPHY

WHAT IS THE THIRD WORLD?

Coined by French writers in the 1950s, *le Tiers Monde* (**Third World**) referred to the majority of humankind that was in neither the Western capitalist First World nor the Communist Second World. It is an awfully broad term that permits few firm generalizations. Now, with the collapse of communism in East Europe and the ex-Soviet Union, the Third World is simply everything that is not "the West," meaning Europe, the United States, Canada, Australia, and now Japan. Some say the only meaningful dividing line is now "the West and the rest."

The Third World is mostly poor, but some oil-producing countries are rich, and some of its lands have industrialized so fast that they are already affluent. It is mostly nonwhite. Almost all of it was at one time or another a colony of a European imperial power. Most of it is hot and closer to the equator than the rich countries, so some writers call it the Global South. The U.S. State Department and some international banks call it the LDCs (less-developed countries). The ones making fast economic progress are called NICs (newly industrializing countries). Business calls them the "emerging markets."

Call it what you will, one generalization stands up fairly well: It is politically unstable. The political institutions of almost all of its 120-plus countries are weak, and this is their chief difference from the West. Most Third-World lands are wracked by political, social, and economic tensions that sometimes explode in revolution, coups, and upheavals, and often end in dictatorship. Crime and **corruption** penetrate most Third World lands; rule of law is usually weak. Few have yet made it into the ranks of stable democracies, the characteristic now of all of the West. India is an amazing exception—although it went through a bout of authoritarian rule under Indira Gandhi. Pakistan is more typical: unstable elected governments alternating with military rule.

Scholars find an imperfect correlation between economics and democracy. Most countries with per capita GDPs above $6,000 (middle-income countries and higher) are able to found stable democracies that do not revert to authoritarianism. Countries with per capita GDPs below $5,000 have trouble establishing and sustaining democracy; they often revert to authoritarianism. Notice how some of the countries discussed here are in this borderline area.

We should really come up with a better name than Third World to describe the complexity of the lands that are home to five-sixths of the human race, but until such a term has established itself, we use Third World.

KEY TERMS

Third World   Most of Asia, Africa, and Latin America.

corruption   Use of public office for private gain.

12

China

THE IMPACT OF THE PAST

China's population is 1.3 billion and slowly growing, even though the regime promotes one-child families. Less than one-third of China's territory is arable—rice in the well-watered south and wheat in the drier north. China's **man-land ratio**—now only one-quarter acre of farmland (and currently shrinking) for each Chinese—long imposed limits on politics, economics, and social thought.

With little new territory to expand into, Chinese society evolved **steady-state** structures to preserve stability and make the peasants content with what they had rather than encourage them to pioneer and innovate. Labor-saving devices would render peasants jobless and were not encouraged. China's achievements in science and technology—far ahead of medieval Europe's—remained curiosities instead of contributions to an industrial revolution.

Commercial expansion was also discouraged. Instead of a Western mentality of reinvestment, growth, and risk taking, Chinese merchants sought only a steady-state relationship with peasants and government officials; they depended heavily on government permits and monopolies.

Neither was there interest in overseas expansion; China's rulers saw no use for anything foreign. All outlying countries were inhabited by barbarians who were

KEY TERMS

man-land ratio How much arable land per person.

steady-state A system that preserves itself with little change.

permitted to **kow-tow** and pay tribute to the emperor. China had all the technology for overseas expansion but did not bother. Gigantic naval expeditions—one of which visited Africa—reported back that there was nothing worthwhile beyond the seas. Thus, for centuries, China remained a stay-at-home country.

THE BUREAUCRATIC EMPIRE

China unified very early in a sequence nearly the reverse of Europe's. After a period of **Warring States**, in 223 B.C. the Qin dynasty (earlier spelled Ch'in, origin of the name China) established the first unified empire, the **Middle Kingdom**, and that has been the Chinese ideal ever since. Europe had a great empire (Rome), but it collapsed, leading to centuries of feudalism (also the case in Japan). During roughly this same time China was a prosperous, unified, and bureaucratic empire, complete with impartial civil-service exams to select the best talent. The resulting Mandarin class—schooled in the Confucian classics, which stressed obedience, authority, and hierarchy—was interested in perpetuating the system, not changing it. A gentry class of better-off people served as the literate intermediaries between the Mandarins and the 90 percent of the population that were peasants. The words of one peasant song:

> When the sun rises, I toil;
> When the sun sets, I rest;
> I dig wells for water;
> I till the fields for food;
> What has the Emperor's power to do with me?

Dynasties came and went every few hundred years in what is called the **dynastic cycle**. As the old dynasty became increasingly incompetent, water systems were not repaired, famine broke out, wars and banditry appeared, and corruption grew. In the eyes of the people, it looked as if the emperor had lost the *Mandate of Heaven*, that is, his legitimate right to rule. A conqueror, either Chinese or foreign (**Mongol** or **Manchu**), found it easy to take over a delegitimized empire. By the very fact of his victory, the new ruler seemed to have gained the Mandate of Heaven. Under vigorous new emperors, things went well;

KEY TERMS

kow-tow   Literally, head to the ground; to prostrate oneself.

Warring States   China's early period (475–221 B.C.), before unification.

Middle Kingdom   China's traditional name for itself, in the middle of the heavens.

dynastic cycle   Rise, maturity, and fall of an imperial family.

Mongol   Central Asian dynasty, founded by Genghis Khan, that ruled China in thirteenth and fourteenth centuries.

Manchu   Last imperial dynasty of China, also known as *Qing*; ruled from seventeenth century to 1911.

GEOGRAPHY

BOUND CHINA

China is bounded on the north by Russia, Mongolia, and Kazakhstan;
on the east by Korea and the Yellow, East China, and South China Seas;
on the south by Vietnam, Laos, Myanmar (formerly Burma), India, Bhutan, and Nepal;
and on the west by Pakistan, Afghanistan (minutely), Tajikistan, and Kyrgyzstan.

By knowing China's boundaries, you can label most of mainland Asia. Only Cambodia, Thailand, and Bangladesh do not border China.

The People's Republic of China. (The solid black line shows the approximate route of the 1934–1935 Long March.)

GEOGRAPHY

RAINFALL

A focus on Europe may cause us to overlook one of the most basic physical determinants of a politico-economic system. Rainfall in Europe is generally sufficient and predictable, but in much of the world it is not. There is plenty of land in the world; water for humans and crops is the limiting factor. Over one billion people do not have clean drinking water, a number that is growing rapidly. An average Chinese has available less than a third of the water of the global average.

Irrigation and conservation can compensate for lack of rain, but they require a high degree of human organization and governmental supervision. This may explain why high civilizations arose early in China and Iran. Large desert or semi-desert areas of our four Third World examples—China, Mexico, Nigeria, and Iran—cannot sustain much development.

the breakdowns were fixed. After some generations, though, the new dynasty fell prey to the same ills as the old, and people, especially the literate, began to think the emperor had lost his heavenly mandate. The cycle was ready to start over.

Two millennia of Chinese empire left an indelible mark on the China of today. Not a feudal system like Japan, China early became a unified and centralized system, with an emperor at the top setting the direction and tone, Mandarins carrying out Beijing's writ, gentry running local affairs, and peasants—the overwhelming majority of the population—toiling in the fields. For centuries China was the world's greatest civilization and biggest economy, far ahead of Europe. By around 1500, however, Europe was surging ahead (for some of the factors, see page 6), while China stagnated. European empires soon controlled most of the Third World. Chinese today are well aware that China was a great civilization, one humiliated by the West.

THE LONG COLLAPSE

For some 2,000 years China absorbed invasions, famines, and new dynasties. The old pattern always reasserted itself. But as the modern epoch impinged on China, at least two new factors arose that the system could not handle: population growth and Western penetration.

In 1741, China's population was 143 million; just a century later, in 1851, it had become an amazing 432 million, the result of new crops (corn and sweet potatoes from the Americas), internal peace under the Manchu dynasty, some new farmland, and just plain harder work on the part of the peasants. Taxation and administration lagged behind the rapid population growth, which hit as the Manchus were going into the typical decline phase of their dynastic cycle in the nineteenth century.

POLITICAL CULTURE

CONFUCIANISM: GOVERNMENT BY RIGHT THINKING

The scholar Confucius (551–479 B.C.) advised rulers that the key to good, stable government lay in instilling correct, moral behavior in ruled and rulers alike. Each person must understand his or her role and perform it obediently. Sons were subservient to fathers, wives to husbands, younger brothers to elder brothers, and subjects to rulers. The ruler sets a moral example by purifying his spirit and perfecting his manners. In this way, goodness perpetuates the ruler in power. Japan picked up **Confucianism** from China.

The Confucian system emphasized that good government starts with thinking good thoughts in utter sincerity. If things go wrong, it indicates rulers have been insincere. Mao Zedong hated everything old China stood for, but he could not help picking up the Confucian stress on right thinking. Adding a Marxist twist, Mao taught that one was a proletarian not because of blue-collar origin but because one had revolutionary, pure thoughts. Confucius would have been pleased.

At about the same time the West was penetrating and disorienting China. It was a clash of two cultures—Western dynamism and greed versus Chinese stability—and the Chinese side was no match. In roughly a century of collapse, old China went into convulsions and breakdowns, which ended with the triumph of the Communists.

The first Westerners to reach China were daring Portuguese navigators in 1514. Gradually, they and other Europeans gained permission to set up trading stations on the coast. For three centuries the Imperial government disdained the foreigners and their products and tried to keep both to a minimum. In 1793, for example, in response to a British mission to Beijing, the emperor commended King George III for his "respectful spirit of submission" but pointed out that there could be little trade because "our celestial empire possesses all things in prolific abundance."

But the West, especially the British, pushed on, smelling enormous profits in the China trade. Matters came to a head with the Opium Wars of 1839 to 1842. The British found a product that Chinese would buy, opium from the poppy fields of British-held India. Opium smoking was illegal and unknown in China. The British, however, flouted the law and popularized opium smoking. When at last a zealous Imperial official tried to stop the opium trade, Britain went to war to keep the lucrative commerce open. Britain

KEY TERM

Confucianism   Chinese political philosophy of social and political stability based on family, hierarchy, and manners.

KEY CONCEPTS

CYCLICAL VERSUS SECULAR CHANGE

China offers good illustrations of the two kinds of change that social scientists often deal with. Cyclical change is repetitive; certain familiar historical phases follow one another like a pendulum swing. China's dynastic cycles are examples of cyclical change; there is change, but the overall pattern is preserved.

Secular change means a long-term shift that does not revert to the old pattern. China's population growth, for example, was a secular change that helped break the stability of traditional China. One of the problems faced by historians, economists, and political scientists is whether a change they are examining is secular—a long-term, basic shift—or cyclical—something that comes and goes repeatedly. (Discussions of global warming face the same problem.)

easily won, but the Chinese still refused to admit that the foreigners were superior. Moaned one Cantonese: "Except for your ships being solid, your gunfire fierce, and your rockets powerful, what good qualities do you have?" For the Chinese, war technology was not as important as moral quality, a view later adopted by Mao Zedong.

The 1842 Treaty of Nanjing (Nanking in the now-obsolete Wade-Giles transcription) wrested five **treaty ports** from the Chinese. Britain got Hong Kong as an outright possession. In the treaty ports the foreigners held sway, dominating the commerce and governance of the area, and enjoying **extraterritoriality**, meaning they were not subject to Chinese law but had their own courts, a point deeply resented by both Chinese and Japanese. In the 1860s, nine more Chinese treaty ports were added.

Around the treaty ports grew **spheres of influence**, understandings among the foreign powers as to who really ran things there. The British, French, Germans, Russians, and Japanese in effect carved up the China coast with their spheres of influence, in which they dominated trade. China was reduced to semicolonial status. With many U.S. missionaries in China, America saw itself as China's "big brother" and in 1900 issued the **Open Door** notes to stop the dismemberment of China.

KEY TERMS

treaty ports   Areas of China coast run by European powers.

extraterritoriality   Privilege of Europeans in colonial situations to have their own laws and courts.

sphere of influence   Semicolonial area under control of major power.

Open Door   U.S. policy of protecting China.

FROM EMPIRE TO REPUBLIC

Internally, too, the Empire weakened. Rebellions broke out. From 1851 to 1864, the **Taipings**—espousing a mixture of Christianity (picked up from missionaries), Confucianism, and primitive communism—baptized millions in South China and nearly overthrew the Manchu (Qing) dynasty. In 1900, with the backing of some reactionary officials and the empress dowager, the antiforeign **Boxer** movement, based on traditional temple-boxing exercises, killed missionaries and besieged Beijing's Legation Quarter for fifty-five days. An international expedition of British, French, German, Russian, American, and Japanese troops broke through and lifted the siege. The foreigners then demanded indemnities and additional concessions from the tottering Imperial government.

Could the Qing (pronounced "Ching") dynasty have adapted itself to the new Western pressures? The Japanese had; with the 1868 **Meiji** Restoration they preserved the form of empire but shifted to modernization and industrialization with spectacular success. Many young Chinese demanded reforms to strengthen China, especially after their humiliating defeat by Japan in 1895. In 1898 the young Emperor Guangxu gathered reformers around him and in the famous Hundred Days issued more than forty edicts, modernizing everything from education to the military. Conservative officials and the old empress dowager would have none of it; they carried out a coup, rescinded the changes, and put the emperor under house arrest for the rest of his short life. (He was probably poisoned.)

A system that cannot reform is increasingly ripe for revolution. Younger people, especially army officers, grew fed up with China's weakness and became militant nationalists. Many Chinese studied in the West and were eager to westernize China. Under an idealistic, Western-trained doctor, San Yatsen (Sun Yat-sen in Wade-Giles), disgruntled provincial officials and military commanders overthrew the Manchus in 1911. It was the end of the last dynasty but not the beginning of stability. In the absence of central authority, so-called **warlords** fragmented China from 1916 to 1927.

The **Nationalist** party, or Guomindang (in Wade-Giles, Kuomintang, KMT), gradually overcame the chaos. Formed shortly after the Manchu's overthrow, the Nationalists were guided by intellectuals (many of them educated in the United States), army officers, and the modern business element. Their greatest strength was in the South, in Guangzhou (Canton), especially in the coastal cities where there was the most contact with the West. It was no accident that they made Nanjing their capital; the word in fact means "southern capital." (North-South tension exists to this day in China.)

Power gravitated into the hands of General (later Generalissimo) Jiang Jieshi (Chiang Kai-shek), who by 1927 had succeeded in unifying most of China under the Nationalists. While Jiang was hailed as the founder and savior of the new China—publisher Henry Luce, son of a China missionary, put Jiang ten times on the cover of *Time*—in reality, the Nationalist rule was weak. The Western-oriented city people who staffed the Nationalists did

KEY TERMS

Taiping   Religion-based rebellion in nineteenth-century China.

Boxer   Chinese antiforeigner rebellion in 1900.

Meiji   Period of Japan's rapid modernization, starting in 1868.

warlord   Local military chief who runs province.

Nationalist   Chiang Kai-shek's party that unified China in late 1920s, abbreviated KMT.

not reform or develop the rural areas where most Chinese lived, usually under the thumb of rapacious landlords. Administration became terribly corrupt. And the Nationalists offered no plausible ideology to rally the Chinese people.

Still, like Kerensky's provisional government in Russia, the Nationalists might have succeeded were it not for war. In 1931 the Japanese seized Manchuria and in 1937 began the conquest of the rest of China. By 1941 they had taken the entire coast, forcing the Nationalists to move their capital far up the Changjiang (Yangzi) River from Nanjing to Chongqing. The United States, long a supporter of China, embargoed trade with Japan, a move that led to Pearl Harbor. For the Americans in World War II, however, China was a sideshow. Jiang's forces preferred fighting Communists to Japanese, while waiting for a U.S. victory to return them to power.

The Communist Triumph

One branch of Chinese nationalism, influenced by Marx and the Bolshevik Revolution, decided that communism was the only effective basis for a nationalist revolution. The Chinese Communists have always been first and foremost nationalists, and from its founding in 1921 the Chinese Communist party (CCP) worked with the Nationalists until Jiang, in 1927, decided to exterminate them as a threat. The fight between the KMT and CCP was a struggle between two versions of Chinese nationalism.

While Stalin advised the Chinese Communists to base themselves on the small proletariat of the coastal cities, Mao Zedong rose to leadership of the Party by developing a rural strategy he called the "mass line." Mao concluded that the real revolutionary potential in China, which had little industry and hence few proletarians, was among the poorest peasants. It was a major revision of Marx, one that Marx probably would not recognize as Marxism.

In 1934, with KMT forces surrounding them, some 120,000 Chinese Communists began their incredible Long March of more than 6,000 miles (10,000 km) to the relative safety of Yan'an in the north. It lasted over a year and led across mountain ranges and rivers amidst hostile forces. Fewer than twenty thousand survived. The Long March became the epic of Chinese Communist history. Self-reliant and isolated from the Soviets, the Chinese Communists had to develop their own strategy for survival, including working with peasants and practicing guerrilla warfare.

While the war against Japan drained and demoralized the Nationalists, it strengthened and encouraged the Communists. Besides stocks of captured Japanese weapons from the Russian takeover of Manchuria in 1945, the Chinese Communists got little help from the Soviets and felt they never owed them much in return. Mao and his Communists came to power on their own, by perfecting their peasant and guerrilla strategies. This fact contributed to the later Sino-Soviet split.

After World War II, the Nationalist forces were much larger than the Communists', and they had many U.S. arms. Nationalist strength, however, melted away as **hyperinflation**

Key Term

hyperinflation   Very rapid inflation, more than 50 percent a month.

KEY CONCEPTS

MAO AND GUERRILLA WAR

In what became a model for revolutionaries the world over, the Chinese Communists swept to power in 1949 after a decade and a half of successful guerrilla warfare. During these years, Mao Zedong, often in his Yan'an cave, developed and taught what he called the **mass line**. His lessons included the following:

1. Take the countryside and surround the cities. While the enemy is stuck in the cities, able to venture out only in strength, you are mobilizing the masses.
2. Work very closely with the peasants, listen to their complaints, help them (for example, getting rid of a landlord or bringing in the harvest), propagandize them, and recruit them into the army and Party.
3. Do not engage the enemy's main forces but rather probe for his weak spots, harassing him and wearing him out.
4. Do not expect much help from the outside; be self-reliant. When in need of weapons, take the enemies'.
5. Do not worry about the apparent superior numbers and firepower of the enemy and his imperialist allies; their strength is illusory ("paper tigers") because it is not based upon the masses. Supreme willpower and unity with the masses are more important than weaponry.
6. At certain stages guerrilla units come together to form larger units until at last, as the enemy stumbles, your forces become a regular army that takes the entire country.

destroyed the economy, corrupt officers sold their troops' weapons (often to the Communists), and war weariness paralyzed the population. The Nationalists had always neglected the rice roots of political strength: the common peasant. The Communists, by cultivating the peasantry (Mao himself was of peasant origin), won a new Mandate of Heaven. In 1949, the disintegrating Nationalists retreated to the island of Taiwan while the Communists restored Beijing ("northern capital") as the country's capital and proceeded to implement what is probably the world's most sweeping revolution. On that occasion, Mao, reflecting his nationalistic sentiments, said: "Our nation will never again be an insulted nation. We have stood up."

KEY TERM

mass line   Mao's theory of revolution for China.

Chairman Mao Zedong proclaims the founding of the People's Republic of China on October 1, 1949. (Xinhua)

THE KEY INSTITUTIONS

THE SOVIET PARALLEL

The institutions of China's government are essentially what the Soviet Union had—interlocking state and Party hierarchies—but China adds a Third-World twist: The army is also important, at times intervening directly into politics, as happens in other developing countries. China, no less than Nigeria (see Chapter 14), has experienced upheaval and chaos, which has led to army participation in politics, the mark of a Third-World country.

As in the old Soviet model, each state and Party level ostensibly elects the one above it. In China, production and residential units elect local People's Congresses, which then elect county People's Congresses, which in turn choose provincial People's Congresses. China, organized on a unitary rather than federal pattern, has twenty-one provinces. The provincial People's Congresses then elect the National People's Congress (NPC) of nearly 3,000 deputies for a five-year term.

As in the ex-Soviet Union, this parliament is too big to do much at its brief annual sessions. Recent NPC sessions, however, have featured some lively debate, contested committee elections, and negative votes—possibly indications that it may gradually turn into a real parliament with some checks on the executive. This would be a major step to democracy. A Standing Committee of about 155 is theoretically supreme, but it too does not have much power in overseeing the executive branch. The chairman of the Standing Committee is considered China's head of state or president. Party general secretary Hu Jintao became president in 2003, as is usual in Communist countries.

PERSONALITIES

TANDEM POWER: MAO AND ZHOU

For over a quarter of a century, until both died in 1976, power in Beijing was not concentrated in the hands of a single Stalin-like figure but divided between Party Chairman Mao Zedong and Premier Zhou Enlai. This Chinese pattern of tandem power may now be sufficiently deep to continue into the future.

Both men were of rural backgrounds, but Mao was born in 1893 into a better-off peasant family, while Zhou was born in 1898 into a gentry family. As young men, both were drawn to Chinese nationalism and then to its Marxist variation. Neither of them went much further than high school in formal education, although both studied, debated, and wrote in Chinese leftist circles. Zhou was in France from 1920 to 1924, ostensibly to study but actually to recruit Chinese students in Europe. Mao had no experience outside of China.

As instructed by the Soviets, the young Chinese Communist party worked closely with the Nationalists. Zhou, for example, was in charge of political education at the Nationalist military academy. In 1927, when Chiang Kai-shek turned on the Communists, both Mao and Zhou barely escaped with their lives. (Zhou was the model militant Chinese revolutionary for French writer André Malraux's novel *Man's Fate*, set in 1927 Shanghai.)

The next decade set their relationship. Mao concluded from his work with peasants that they were the means to China's revolution. Zhou, who briefly remained loyal to Moscow's proletarian line, by 1931 had changed his mind and joined Mao in his Jiangxi redoubt. From there, the two led the arduous Long March to the north. By the time they arrived in Yan'an, Mao was clearly the leader of the CCP, and his "mass line" of basing the revolution on the peasantry prevailed.

Mao dominated mainly by force of intellect. Other CCP leaders respected his ability to theorize in clear, blunt language. Mao became the Party chief and theoretician but did not supervise the day-to-day tasks of survival, warfare, and diplomacy. These became Zhou's jobs; he was the administrator of the revolution. Never bothering to theorize, Zhou was a master at shaping and controlling bureaucracies, smooth diplomacy, and political survival amidst changing lines.

There was some tension between the two, but Zhou never showed it. Publicly Zhou dedicated himself to fulfilling Mao's desires, although at times, in the shambles of the Great Leap Forward (1958–1960) and the Cultural Revolution (1966–1969), he tried to hold things together and limit the damage.

Mao was the abstract thinker, Zhou the pragmatic doer. This made Mao more radical and Zhou more conservative. Mao could spin out his utopian dreams, but Zhou made the bureaucracy, military, and economy function. Different roles, different personalities.

The top of the executive branch is the State Council, a cabinet of approximately forty ministers (specialized in economic branches) and a dozen vice-premiers led by a premier, China's head of government, since 2003 Wen Jiabao.

The formal structure of the executive does not always correspond to the real distribution of its power. In 1976, after the death of both Party Chairman Mao and Premier Zhou, a relative unknown, Hua Guofeng, was installed in both their offices. On paper, Hua appeared to be the most powerful figure in the land.

But an elderly, twice-rehabilitated Party veteran, Deng Xiaoping, named to the modest post of senior vice-premier in 1977, was in fact more powerful than his nominal boss, Hua. When Deng toured the United States in 1979, he acted like a head of state. Deng's power grew out of his senior standing in the Party and the army. In 1980, he demoted Hua and assumed power himself, still without taking over the job titles, which he left to others. By 1982, Hua was out of the Politburo and out of sight.

THE PARTY

Like the old Soviet Communist party, the Chinese Communist party (CCP) is constitutionally and in practice the leading political element of the country. With 66 million members, the CCP is large, but relative to China's population it is proportionately smaller than the CPSU was. As China's economy has decentralized and marketized, the Party now admits private businesspeople. The CCP has lost authority and sense of mission. Said one longtime Party member: "What does the Communist party stand for now? Nothing. Stability, maybe. But really no ideals at all." Communist officials now use their positions for personal gain; massive corruption has set in.

In organization, the CCP parallels the defunct CPSU. Hierarchies of Party congresses at the local, county, provincial, and national levels feed into corresponding Party committees. At the top is the National Party Congress; composed of some 2,100 delegates and supposed to meet at least once in five years, this congress nominally chooses a Central Committee of about 200 members. Since both bodies are too big to run things, real power is in the hands of a Politburo of about twenty Party chiefs. But this too is not the last level. Within the Politburo is a Standing Committee of five to nine members who really decide things. Power is extremely concentrated in China.

The CCP's structure used to be a bit different from the classic Soviet model. Instead of a general secretary at its head, the CCP had a Party chairman, Mao's title, which he passed on to Hua Guofeng. By then, however, the office was robbed of meaning, and Hua was eclipsed by Senior Vice-Premier Deng Xiaoping, who, to be sure, also held important Party and army positions. In 1982, under Deng's guidance, the Party abolished the chairmanship—part of a repudiation of Mao's legacy—and upgraded the position of general secretary, so that now the CCP structure more closely matches that of the old CPSU. Deng arranged to have his protégé Hu Yaobang named general secretary. Hu, however, proved to be too liberal and unpredictable. He also failed to win approval of the army (see next section) and was dropped in 1987. His place was taken by another Deng protégé, Zhao Ziyang, who in turn was ousted in 1989 for siding with student demonstrators. Replacing him was the hard-line mayor of Shanghai, Jiang Zemin, who retired as head of the Party but retained important influence for several years, just as Deng Xaioping did (see box on page 200).

China's nervous system is its Party **cadres**. There are 30 million CCP cadres, and whoever controls them controls China. In 1979, Deng Xiaoping began the ticklish job of

KEY TERM

cadre French "framework," used by Asian Communists for local Party leader.

PERSONALITIES

THE INVISIBLE PUPPETEER: DENG XIAOPING

Deng Xiaoping was a strange leader. He had been purged from Chinese politics twice before becoming "senior vice-premier" in 1977, a deliberately deceptive title to cover the fact he was China's undisputed boss. And Deng sought no fame or glory; unlike Mao, he built no personality cult. Deng seldom appeared in public or in the media but governed in the ancient Confucian tradition: quietly, behind the scenes, chiefly by picking top officials. MIT political scientist Lucian Pye called him the "invisible puppeteer." This former protégé of Zhou Enlai—who, like Zhou, was a pragmatic administrator rather than a theorizer—set China on its present course and gave China its current problems.

Deng was born in 1904 into a rural landlord family. Sent to study in France, Deng was recruited by Zhou Enlai and soon joined the Chinese Communists. As a political commissar and organizer of the People's Liberation Army, Deng forged strong military connections. Rising through major posts after 1949, Deng was named to the top of the Party—the Politburo's Standing Committee—in 1956.

Deng was not as adroit as Zhou and kept getting into political trouble. An outspoken pragmatist, Deng said after the Great Leap: "Private farming is alright as long as it raises production, just as it does not matter whether a cat is black or white as long as it catches mice." During the Cultural Revolution this utterance was used against Deng to show he was a "Capitalist Roader." Although not expelled from the Party, Deng dropped out of sight and lost his official position. His son was crippled by a mob during the Cultural Revolution.

But the little man—Deng was well under five feet tall—bounced back in 1973 when moderates regained control. In 1975, he seemed to be ready to take over; he spoke with visiting U.S. President Ford as one head of state to another. But just a month later Deng was again in disgrace, denounced by the radicals of the **Gang of Four** as anti-Mao. Again, he was stripped of his posts, but an old army buddy gave him sanctuary in an elite military resort.

But the adaptable Deng bounced back yet again. With the arrest of the Gang of Four in 1976, moderates came back out of the woodwork, among them Deng. In July 1977, he was reappointed to all his old posts. Many Chinese state, Party, and army leaders, badly shaken by the Cultural Revolution, looked to old comrade Deng to restore stability. In 1978 Deng, then already seventy-four, started China on its present course by splitting economics from politics. In effect, he offered the Chinese a new deal: Work and get rich in a partly market economy but leave politics to the Communist party. This started China's amazing economic growth. But will not massive economic changes eventually influence politics? Apparently Deng never gave much thought to this contradiction, which is now China's chief problem.

Deng was no "liberal." He encouraged economic reform but blocked any moves toward democracy, as have his successors. In 1989, Deng brutally crushed the prodemocracy movement in Beijing's Tiananmen Square. Although weak and reclusive in the 1990s, Deng still quietly controlled Beijing's top personnel and main policy lines until he died in 1997 at age ninety-two.

KEY TERM

Gang of Four   Mao's ultraradical helpers, arrested in 1976.

Generations of Chinese Communist Rulers			Accomplishments
First	Mao and Zhou	1949–1976	Won revolution, brutally communized, destructive upheavals
Second	Deng	1977–1989	Calmed China, allowed private enterprise, crushed Tiananmen
Third	Jiang, Li, Zhu	1989–2002	Foreign investment, rapid growth
Fourth	Hu and Wen	2002–	

easing out both the incompetent old guard—whose only qualification, in many cases, was having been on the Long March—and the extreme leftists who wormed their way into the cadre structure during the tumultuous Cultural Revolution. Quietly, Deng brought in younger, better-educated cadres dedicated to his moderate, pragmatic line.

THE ARMY

Until recently, all top figures in the Chinese elite held both high state and high Party offices, as in the old Soviet Union. In China, though, they also held high positions atop the military structure, through the important Central Military Commission, which interlocks with the CCP's Politburo. Mao, Hua, Deng, and Jiang were all chairmen of the Military Commission. In addition, the CCP Standing Committee usually has at least one top general. Indeed, from the beginning, the People's Liberation Army (PLA), earlier known as the Chinese Red Army, has been so intertwined with the CCP that it is hard to separate them. Deng named an active-duty general to the elite Politburo Standing Committee, and nearly a quarter of the Central Committee is PLA. Fighting the Nationalists and the Japanese for at least a decade and a half, the CCP became a combination of Party and army. The pattern continues to this day. Political scientist Robert Tucker called the Chinese system "military communism."

Mao wrote, "Political power grows out of the barrel of a gun," but "the Party commands the gun, and the gun must never be allowed to command the Party." Where the two are nearly merged, however, it is hard to tell who is on top. As the Communists took over China in the 1940s, it was the PLA that first set up their power structures. Until recently, China's executive decision makers all had extensive military experience, often as political commissars in PLA units. Said Zhou Enlai: "We are all connected with the army." When the Cultural Revolution broke out in 1966, as we shall see, the army first facilitated, then dampened and finally crushed the Red Guards' rampages. By the time the Cultural Revolution sputtered out, the PLA was in de facto control of most provincial governments and most of the Politburo. Several Politburo members are still active military men. At various times during mobilization campaigns, the army is cited as a model for the rest of the country to follow, and heroic individual soldiers are celebrated in the media.

What does PLA influence mean for the governance of China? Armies, as guardians of their countries' security, define whatever is good for them as good for the country. Anyone who undermines their power earns their opposition. During the Cultural Revolution, for example, the army under Defense Minister Lin Biao supported Mao's program to shake up the Party and state bureaucracy. (The army was not touched.) As the chaos spread,

PERSONALITIES

HU IS NEXT, AND WEN

In 1989, when Deng Xiaoping at age eighty-five gave up his last formal post—chairman of the powerful Central Military Commission—he made sure two protégés took over: Party General Secretary Jiang Zemin and Premier Li Peng. They were, respectively, sixty-three and sixty-one years old, the *third generation* of Beijing's Communist rulers. In 1998, when Li's two five-year terms were up, he was replaced as premier by Zhu Rongji, then seventy.

All three of these leaders kept firm central control of politics while allowing a partial market economy. All silenced troublesome intellectuals. All were graduate engineers—still the case today—giving their rule a technocratic bent. None were popular, nor did they seek popularity. None returned to the visions of Mao, but all were cautious about major change. None suggested democracy in China's future. In late 2002, Jiang gave up his Party position, and in 2003 Premier Zhu retired.

China got its *fourth generation* of Communist leaders at the Sixteenth Communist Party conference in late 2002. Succeeding Jiang was Vice President Hu Jintao, then fifty-nine, picked by Deng Xiaoping before he died. An engineer, Hu was typed as an obedient technocrat. Jiang tried to stay influential, as chair of the Central Military Commission, but in 2004, at age seventy-eight, he reluctantly stepped down, and President Hu became China's military chief, thus completing his hold on power. Succeeding Premier Zhu in 2003 was Deputy Premier Wen Jiabao, then sixty. Wen trained as a geologist but is experienced in finance and agriculture. We do not know who will replace them, or when.

however, military commanders worried that it was sapping China's strength and military preparedness. Lin became increasingly isolated within the military. In 1971 Beijing released the amazing story that Lin had attempted a coup and fled to the Soviet Union in a plane that crashed. Outside observers suggest Lin died by other means. His supporters were purged from the military. The PLA thus helped tame Maoist radicalism.

China's leaders seem to have decided that the army is not a good way to control domestic unrest. (They are right.) The PLA did not like mowing down students in Tiananmen in 1989. To deal with such situations, Beijing built up the People's Armed Police (PAP), now over 1 million strong. This paramilitary police could also be used as a counterweight to the PLA in case there is political infighting.

China's leaders pay special attention to the PLA and increase its budget, but the PLA, with 2.3 million soldiers, is still poor and underequipped. Trying to supplement its meager budget, the PLA went massively into private industry, running some 15,000 businesses. Worried about the PLA's corruption, smuggling, and loss of mission, President Jiang ordered the army to get out of business and get back to soldiering. They complied, indicating that the Party still commands the gun. In general, the PLA has been a conservative force in Chinese politics, for almost axiomatically, an army stands for order and sees disorder as a security problem. In China, when chaos threatens, the army moves.

CHINESE POLITICAL CULTURE

TRADITIONAL CULTURE

Mao used to say that his countrymen were "firstly poor, secondly blank," meaning that the Communists could start with a clean slate and create the Chinese citizens they wished. Mao was wrong. Many of traditional Chinese attitudes have carried over into the People's Republic. Indeed, even Mao's vision of perfecting human nature by thinking right thoughts is a Confucian notion.

When the Communists restored Beijing as the capital in 1949, they were restoring an old symbol; Beijing had been the capital for centuries until Jiang's Nationalists moved it to Nanjing. Some government offices and elite living quarters now directly adjoin the old Forbidden City of the emperors, just as the Soviets made the Kremlin their home. Tiananmen (Gate of Heavenly Peace) Square is still Beijing's parade and demonstration area, much like Red Square is in Moscow.

The Communists' bureaucrats and cadres perform much the same function as the old Mandarins and gentry. Reciting the latest Party line instead of Confucius, the new elites strive to place a huge population under central control and guidance. Their aim now, to be sure, is growth and modernization, but still under a central hand. Mao himself recognized the similarity of old and new when he denounced the bureaucrats as the "new Mandarins" during the Cultural Revolution. Deng Xiaoping governed in the old Confucian style.

To become one of the new Mandarins, Chinese youths must undergo twelve and a half hours of grueling university entrance exams. Only about 12 percent of China's youths go to college (as opposed to some 40 percent in the United States). The three days of exams resemble the Imperial examination system of old China. The new exams, given simultaneously throughout China, include Chinese, English, math, science, history, and politics. China's Harvard is (and for a century has been) Beijing University (*Beida*); its MIT is Qinghua. As in old China, study is the key to personal advancement.

Mao argued against the examinations and had them dropped during the Cultural Revolution; they were restored only in 1977. Mao thought the exams were elitist and unrevolutionary, that they created a class of privileged bureaucrats. Mao was quite right, but without competitive exams, educational standards slid, and incompetents got into universities based on their political correctness. Inferior graduates retarded China's progress in industry and administration, so the post-Mao moderates restored the examinations. It was another example of a long-functional process reasserting itself.

Another carryover from Old China: Age confers special qualities of wisdom and leadership in the People's Republic. Mao died at eighty-two and Zhou at seventy-eight, both in office. When he returned to power in 1977, Deng Xiaoping was seventy-three. In his early nineties he was still politically influential although weak and deaf. Former President Jiang and Prime Minister Zhu still governed in their seventies. Trying to break the tendency to gerontocracy, the Party now does not appoint anyone over seventy to a new position.

NATIONALISM

Overlaying traditional Chinese values is a more recent value, the nationalism that has dominated China's intellectual life for more than a century. Chinese nationalism, like Third World nationalism in general, is the result of a proud and ancient civilization suffering penetration, disorientation, and humiliation at the hands of the West and Japan. This can induce explosive fury and the feeling that the native culture, although temporarily beaten by foreigners, is morally better and more enduring. In our day, Chinese, Russians, and Iranians still act out their resentment of the West, especially of America. Much of what Beijing does today—from economic growth to space launches to hosting the 2008 Olympics—is out of a sense of nationalism. For the sake of Chinese power, Beijing has even accepted capitalism.

In Asia, Chinese and Japanese nationalists vowed to beat the West at its own game, building industry and weaponry but placing them at the service of the traditional culture. The Japanese modernizers, starting with the 1868 Meiji Restoration, were able to carry out their designs; the Chinese are still caught up in this process, which from time to time leaps out in self-destructive campaigns. All of the founding generation of Chinese Communist leaders, including Mao and Zhou, began as young patriots urging their countrymen to revitalize China and stand up to the West and to Japan.

As in the old Soviet Union, the prevailing Chinese attitude is the nationalist drive to catch up with the West. During their good economic-growth years—the mid-1950s and since 1980—Chinese leaders were proud of their rapid progress. The Great Leap Forward and the Cultural Revolution ruined the economy. A pragmatic moderate such as Zhou or Deng always has a powerful argument against such disruptions: They harm growth and weaken China. Basically, this is a nationalist argument, and one used by pragmatists today.

Anti-U.S. Chinese nationalism is growing. Part is deep and genuine, part is hyped by the regime. Tension with the United States over Taiwan and American pressures over human rights and copyright violations sparked a government-approved anti-U.S. campaign. A popular book (modeled on an earlier Japanese book), *China Can Say No*, portrayed a vast conspiracy led by America to keep China down (the same line put out by extreme Russian nationalists). Well, America better watch out, the book said, because China will defend itself. Chinese got angry when U.S. jets mistakenly bombed the Chinese embassy in Belgrade in 1999 and a U.S. surveillance plane entered Chinese airspace in 2001. In 2005 Beijing sponsored anti-Japanese protests. Observers suggest China's decaying regime is using nationalism to prolong its hold on power.

Maoism

Maoism, or Mao Zedong Thought, as Beijing calls it, has faded. It draws from both traditional and nationalistic values, despite its claim to be totally new and revolutionary. From traditional China, it takes the Confucian emphasis on thinking right thoughts, based on the idea that consciousness determines existence rather than the reverse: Willpower is more important than weaponry in wars; willpower is more important than technology in building China. The unleashed forces of the masses, guided by Mao Zedong Thought, can conquer anything. This extreme form of **voluntarism** comes from China's past.

Key Term

voluntarism   Belief that human will can change the world.

Mao's portrait still looks out from Beijing's Forbidden City onto Tiananmen Square. (Lisa Caputo)

From nationalism, Mao took the emphasis on strengthening and rebuilding China so that it could stand up to its old enemies and become a world power. The trouble is that these two strands are partly at odds with each other. Traditional values call for China to ignore the West and its technology, but nationalistic values call for China to learn and copy from the West. The continuing, unresolved conflict of these two streams of thought spell permanent trouble for China.

Maoism is an outgrowth of Mao's thoughts on guerrilla warfare (see page 196). According to Maoist doctrine, what the PLA did to beat the Nationalists, China as a whole must do to advance and become a world leader: Work with the masses, be self-reliant, and use more willpower than technology to overcome obstacles. Mao can be seen as a theorist of guerrilla warfare who continued to apply his principles to governance—with catastrophic results.

In the Great Leap Forward from 1958 to 1960, Mao tried guerrilla warfare tactics on the economy, using raw manual labor plus enthusiasm to build earthen dams and backyard blast furnaces. Engineers, experts, and administrators were bypassed. The Soviets warned Mao it would not work and urged him to follow the Soviet model of building the economy by more conventional means; Mao refused. In 1960, the Soviets withdrew their numerous foreign-aid technicians, and the Sino-Soviet split became public.

For the Soviet Communists, the revolution was over; the proletariat triumphed in 1917 and moved Russia into the most advanced stage of history. For Mao, the revolution never ends. Mao held that at any stage there are conservative tendencies that block the path to socialism: bureaucratism, elitism, and opportunism. Mao resolved to combat these tendencies by means of *permanent revolution*, periodic upheavals to let the force of the masses surge past the conservative bureaucrats.

Socialism and bureaucratism are closely connected—as Max Weber saw long ago—but Mao thought he could break the connection. He saw China settling into the bureaucratic

POLITICAL CULTURE

SLOGANS FROM THE CULTURAL REVOLUTION

- "Put destruction first, and in the process you have construction."
- "Destroy the four olds—old thought, old culture, old customs, old habits."
- "Once all struggle is grasped, miracles are possible."
- "Bombard the command post." (Attack established leaders if they are unrevolutionary.)
- "So long as it is revolutionary, no action is a crime."
- "Sweep the great renegade of the working class onto the garbage heap!" (Dump the moderate chief of state, Liu Shaoqi.)
- "Cadres step to the side." (Bypass established authorities.)
- "To rebel is justified."

---

patterns he hated and was determined to reverse it by instituting a permanent revolution. The result was the Great Proletarian Cultural Revolution from 1966 to 1976, during which young people were encouraged to criticize, harass, and oust all authority except the army. Chaos spread through China, the economy slumped, and the army took over. Shortly after Mao's death, power returned to the bureaucrats; they won and Mao failed.

Mao refused to recognize the unhappy truth that if you want socialism you must accept the big bureaucracy that comes with it. By trying to leap directly into a sort of guerrilla socialism without bureaucrats, Mao nearly wrecked China. On balance, Mao Zedong Thought is inherently inapplicable, and in post-Mao China, Mao is no longer much quoted.

CROUCHING ANGER, HIDDEN DISSENT

There is growing unrest in China—among rural people, unemployed rust-belt workers, journalists, academics, medical doctors, and Muslim Uighurs in Xinjiang province in the west. There are protests but no organized dissent, as the regime crushes protests and jails leaders. Brave souls who criticize corruption and incompetence are fired, harassed, and arrested. The doctor and editor who first reported the SARS virus were jailed. A nervous regime and Party, afraid that criticisms will undermine their rule, try to deny and cover up problems.

As ever, China's cities are the hotbeds of criticism and reform. Although a small minority, the urban educated classes have often taken the lead in changing China. Student protests in Beijing, for example, go back more than a century and contributed much to the overthrow of the Empire and the rise of first the Nationalists and then the Communists.

GEOGRAPHY

REGION AND LANGUAGE

China illustrates the close connection—and problems—between a country's languages and its regions. All but small countries have regions, often based on language. In some cases, as between Serbs and Albanian-speaking Kosovars, the country splits apart. China is populated mostly by Han Chinese (there are important non-Han minorities in Tibet, Xinjiang, and elsewhere), but even Han do not all speak the same language.

Chinese rulers have always proclaimed the unity of China, but China has eight main language groups—mutually unintelligible—and hundreds of dialects, making it the world's most linguistically diverse country. The biggest by far is Mandarin, dialects of which are spoken by 800 million in a broad swath from north to south, but not in the important southern coastal provinces, where 90 million speak some form of the Wu language (including Shanghai) and 70 million speak Cantonese.

The regime has always feared that separate languages could lead to breakup. Since 1913 under the KMT, Beijing has tried to make Mandarin standard and universal, and the CCP carried this on, now pushing a largely Beijing dialect, *Putonghua* (common language), as the language of government and education. Most urban Chinese can now sort of speak it, but not country folk. The new prosperity in China's southern coastal provinces has actually boosted the use of their local dialects. Beijing is not pleased.

During the twentieth century, educated Chinese generally had a cause to believe in. At first it was building a new republic that would not be carved up by foreigners. Then it was in repelling the Japanese invaders. With the Communist takeover, many Chinese idealistically believed that Mao offered them a blueprint for a prosperous, socialist China. After Mao, Deng Xiaoping offered the image of a prosperous, semicapitalist China. After the June 1989 massacre of prodemocracy students in Tiananmen Square, many Chinese fell into despair. For most, Marx, Mao, and Deng have been discredited, and the Party now has nothing to offer.

Religion, both old (including Christianity) and new, is growing rapidly despite the arrest, imprisonment, and torture of believers. A new religion, *Falun Gong* (Buddhist Law), attracts all kinds of Chinese with faith healing and traditional exercises. As one can see in Japan, Buddhism generates offshoots without limit. Beijing understands that religion can bring upheaval—the Taipings and Boxers in the nineteenth century—and in 1999 denounced Falun Gong as a brainwashing cult, outlawed it, and arrested thousands of its followers. This is the reaction of a nervous regime.

Some educated Chinese have discovered classic liberalism—the philosophy of small government and personal and economic freedom of Locke, Adam Smith, Jefferson, Hayek, and Friedman. This could challenge the stale Marxism of the regime and lead to democracy, but proponents are often arrested.

KEY CONCEPTS

THE GREAT LEAP FORWARD

In 1958 Mao Zedong launched one of the strangest efforts in the Third World's struggle to move ahead: the Great Leap Forward. Vowing to progress "twenty years in a day" and "catch up with Great Britain in fifteen years," all of China was urged to "walk on two legs" (use all possible means) to industrial-ize rapidly. Most peasants—then a majority of Chinese—were herded into gigantic communes, some with as many as 100,000 people. Deprived of their private plots, they were ordered to eat in communal din-ing halls, leave their children in nurseries, and even sleep in large dormitories.

The communes were ordered to participate in engineering and industrial projects. Relying on "labor-intensive" methods to compensate for lack of capital, millions were turned out to move earth with baskets and carry poles to build dams and irrigation works. Backyard blast furnaces were ordered built so that every commune could produce its own iron.

Within a year the failure was plain for all to see. Even Mao had to admit it; he resigned as presi-dent of the PRC but kept his chairmanship of the CCP. Peasants—as in the Soviet Union—failed to pro-duce without private incentives. Labor was wasted in foolish projects. Major food shortages developed, and over 30 million Chinese died of malnutrition. To meet Party quotas, peasants melted down their good tools to produce implements of miserable quality. The communes were phased out, broken first into *production brigades* and then into *production teams*, which were in fact the old villages. Private farming was again permitted. Mao lost; old China won.

Over the decades, Chinese became politically numb. They had to mouth slogans and participate in mass campaigns—one year anti-Confucius, the next anticapitalist roaders, then anti-Gang of Four, then anti-"spiritual pollution," then anti-"bourgeois liberaliza-tion"—without end. Chinese are fed up with this nonsense and mentally tune out.

The great hope for Chinese students is to go abroad. Many study English and dream of joining the 54,000 Chinese students already in the United States. Many, of course, do not return to China. The regime, aware of this brain drain, now restricts their numbers. Chi-nese university graduates must first work five years before they can apply for graduate study overseas. The great prize: a graduate degree, often an MBA, from a prestigious U.S. uni-versity. Some high-ranking Chinese get their children into such programs.

The Chinese way of handling the latest government crackdown on freedom and democ-racy is called *biaotai*, "to express an attitude." Chinese know how to crank out the current line while concealing their true feelings. This leads to what Chinese call *nei jin, wai song*, "tranquility outside, repression within." Everything looks calm, but only because people know they are being carefully watched. Just below the surface, though, repressed anger waits to erupt. Some of this shows up in the constant flow of nasty rumors about repression, economic incompetence, and the corruption of officials. This has been called a struggle between the Big Lie and Little Whisper: The government tries to fool people with big lies, but the people fight back with little whispers. Chinese, knowing that all foreigners are

KEY CONCEPTS

THE GREAT PROLETARIAN CULTURAL REVOLUTION

If the Great Leap Forward was strange, the Great Proletarian Cultural Revolution was downright bizarre. In it, an elderly Mao Zedong tried to make his revolution permanent by destroying the very structures his new China had created. Of the many slogans from the Cultural Revolution, "bombard the command post" perhaps best summarizes its character. Mao encouraged young people, who hastily grouped themselves into ragtag outfits called Red Guards, to destroy most authority, even the CCP. They did, and Chinese progress was set back years.

The Cultural Revolution began with a 1965 flap over a Shanghai play some radicals claimed criticized Mao by allegory. Mao turned a small literary debate into a mass criticism that led to the ouster of several Party officials. Then university and high-school students were encouraged to air their grievances against teachers and school administrators. Behind their discontent was a shortage of the kind of jobs the students thought they deserved upon graduation.

By the fall of 1966, most schools were closed as their students demonstrated, humiliated officials, wrote wall posters, and traveled to "share revolutionary experiences." China was in chaos. Hundreds of thousands of victims of the Red Guards committed suicide. A much larger number were "sent down" to the countryside to work with the peasants and "learn from the people." This included physical abuse and psychological humiliation. An unknown number were murdered. Worried officials set up their own Red Guard groups to protect themselves. Different Red Guard factions fought each other.

Even Mao became concerned, and in early 1967 he ordered the army to step in. By the end of 1967 the People's Liberation Army pretty much ran the country. To replace the broken governmental structures, the army set up "revolutionary committees" on which sat PLA officers, Red Guard leaders, and "repentant" officials. By 1969, the worst was over, although officially the Cultural Revolution did not end until 1976 when Mao died and the ultra-radical Gang of Four (headed by Mao's wife, Jiang Qing), was arrested.

The effects of the Cultural Revolution were all bad. Industry suffered. Education, when it resumed, was without standards, and students were chosen on the basis of political attitudes rather than ability. The more moderate and level-headed officials, whom the Red Guards sought to destroy, laid low and pretended to go along with the Cultural Revolution. When it was over, they reasserted themselves and made sure one of their own was in charge: Deng Xiaoping.

And what became of the Red Guards? Claiming their energy was needed on the farm, the army marched more than sixteen million young city people to rural communes for agricultural labor and forbade them to return to their cities. By hook or by crook, many of them managed to get back to their homes to try to continue their studies. Some, utterly disillusioned with the way they had been used, turned to petty crime or fled to the British colony of Hong Kong. Some eventually became capitalist millionaires in the burgeoning Special Economic Zones of the South.

closely monitored, discuss nothing political (or religious) with visitors. The Chinese Internet filters e-mails with key words such as "democracy," "Tiananmen," and "Taiwan" and jails bloggers for "subverting state power."

Such a tightly controlled system is frightened and unstable. A fraction of China's population dislikes and distrusts the regime, especially in the South, which has long resented rule by the North. Many Chinese are frustrated that China's progress is blocked by a Party elite that simply wants to cling to its power and good jobs. They know that in the southern coastal zones, where capitalism and foreign investment began, the economy is booming. Why then not just expand free enterprise until it covers all of China? They also know that Taiwanese enjoy five times the per capita income and far more freedom than mainlanders. Some Chinese students speak with shame that they did not have the guts to do what the Romanians did in 1989: stand up to the government's guns and overthrow the regime. In time, Chinese student frustration could boil over again.

In the right situation—for example, a split in Beijing leadership over personnel and policies—China's peasants, workers, and students could make common cause and overthrow the regime. Needless to say, the police work hard to prevent a Chinese equivalent of Poland's Solidarity. Political repression, of course, solves nothing; it merely postpones the day of reckoning. What happened in East Europe could happen in China.

PATTERNS OF INTERACTION

CYCLES OF UPHEAVAL

Since the Communists came to power in 1949 there have been three major upheavals plus several smaller ones. Among major upheavals are the *agrarian reforms* (that is, execution of landlords and redistribution of land) of the early 1950s, the Great Leap Forward from 1958 to 1960, and the Cultural Revolution from 1966 to 1976. Smaller upheavals include the brief Hundred Flowers liberalization of 1956, the antirightist campaigns of 1957 and the early 1970s, the crushing of the Gang of Four and their supporters in the late 1970s, and the 1989 repression of alleged *counterrevolutionary rebellion* of prodemocracy students.

The big upheavals and most of the smaller ones can be traced to the same underlying problem: Beijing's leaders, having inherited a poor and backward land, want to make China rich, advanced, and socialistic. Mao Zedong Thought taught that everything is possible: China can leap into the modern age and even beyond it. But the old, stubborn, traditional China does not yield; it frustrates the bold plans and tugs the system back toward the previous patterns and problems.

Observers used to label CCP figures as "radicals" or "moderates" according to their willingness to support the kind of upheavals previously described. China's moderates were and still are those high up in the Party, government, or army. Almost axiomatically, anyone who is part of the establishment will not be a radical. Mao was right: Bureaucrats are by nature conservative. China's radicals were drawn largely from those peripheral to power but ambitious for it: students, junior cadres, and some provincial leaders. The old radical-moderate split faded with the death of Mao, replaced with a conservative-liberal split.

One of the prime motivations for radicals, especially during the Cultural Revolution, was the scarcity of job openings in Party, state, army, industrial, and other offices. For the most part, positions until recently were staffed by aging Party comrades who go back to the 1949 liberation or even the Long March. They never retire, and their longevity in office breeds impatience and resentment among younger people with ambitions of their own. A further element fueling youthful discontent was the difficulty of getting into a university.

CONSERVATIVES AND LIBERALS IN CHINESE POLITICS

Conservatives	Liberals
selectively quote Mao	forget about Mao
keep Party Communist	admit business people
control media closely	freer media
demand purity	demand modernization
central economic controls	largely market economy
oppose foreign influence	open to foreign influence
minimize mass input	expand local elections
take over Taiwan	tolerate Taiwan
ideological	empirical

Such tensions underlay the radical outburst of the Cultural Revolution. Those who aspired to power enthusiastically attempted to carry out Mao's designs. Those who held power pretended to go along with it, often by mouthing the correct slogans and self-denunciations. In Mao's words, they "waved the red flag to oppose the red flag." When the campaign burned itself out, the bureaucrats and cadres took over again, and it appeared that the moderates had won.

CHINESE LIBERAL AND CONSERVATIVE POLITICS

With the Maoist demon back in the bottle, a gradual split between liberal and conservative forces appeared, similar to what the Soviets went through before their system collapsed. Conservatives tend to be older people, with secure positions in the Party, army, and bureaucracy, much like Soviet *apparatchiks*. They want socialism on the Soviet model, with centralized control over the economy, politics, and cultural life.

Liberalizers, usually younger people, see the unfairness and inefficiency of central control. They point to the record-setting growth in output that came with private and cooperative enterprises and the SEZs. "See, the market system works," they say in effect. They also want Western-style political democracy and cultural freedoms. Chinese conservatives, just like their old Soviet counterparts, fear that such a system would no longer be Communist, would collapse into chaos (a possibility) and, worst of all, would cost them their jobs.

As we discussed in connection with the old Soviet Union, ideology is often a mask for self-interest. The people who have the cushy jobs warn that democracy and liberalization mean "abandoning socialism." In analyzing Communist (and many other) systems, take ideology with a grain of salt; follow the jobs. (Think the jobs explanation is an exaggeration? What motivates you?)

The liberal-conservative split caused Deng and his successors much grief. They are prepared to liberalize cautiously, hoping to confine it to the economic sector. But demands keep bubbling up to go farther and faster. In the spring of 1989, tens of thousands of Chinese university students staged giant protests and hunger strikes in favor of democracy. Deng fired his handpicked and liberal-minded successor, Zhao Ziyang, and had the PLA

POLITICAL CULTURE

ANTI-WESTERN CAMPAIGNS

Every few years China is hit with a campaign aimed at making the Chinese pull away from the Western model of economic and political freedom. The work of conservatives within the CCP, these campaigns warned that decadent Western ideas such as free enterprise, open discussion, and a loosening of Party control would mean the end of socialism in China.

In late 1983, the catchword was *spiritual pollution*, meaning that Western styles in clothes, music, and thought were ruining China. Deng, fearing the campaign was being used to block his economic liberalization, called it off after only four months.

In 1986, a somewhat longer campaign against *bourgeois liberalization* appeared, ruling out any discussion of ending the CCP monopoly on power and replacing it with Western-style liberalism. After the 1989 Tiananmen Square massacre, conservatives charged that it was a "counterrevolutionary rebellion" inspired by Western influences, which had to be curbed. We have not seen the last anti-Western campaign.

mow down the students in Tiananmen Square. Several hundred died, and some ten thousand were imprisoned. A chill settled over Chinese life. Conservatives also launched anti-Western campaigns (see box above). The conservatives had one serious drawback: Most were elderly. Time seemed to be on the side of the liberalizers, but not without rear-guard conservative actions.

RICE-ROOTS DEMOCRACY

With the new millennium, scattered across China thousands of village-level competitive elections appeared, like rice shoots just poking out of the soil. Such things cannot happen without tacit Party approval. Some believe it is the work of liberalizers in the Party ever-so-slowly introducing democracy. Others say it comes from the bottom up, from villagers' anger at corrupt local officials who pocket arbitrary "taxes." In some villages and townships, the Party candidate loses.

So far, the scope of these elections is limited. Elected village and township chiefs are still controlled by local Party secretaries. But gradually, local Party secretaries are also being chosen by more open methods among Party members. Since 1999, a few urban neighborhoods have had direct, competitive elections for minor offices. Some Chinese political scientists predict the level of elections will climb to include mayors and eventually even national office. A clever regime could expand democratic elections as a way to defuse anger, but if it does not let democracy go all the way to top national offices it could end up increasing mass anger. There could be other Tiananmens.

DEMOCRACY

THE TIANANMEN MASSACRE

During the early morning of June 4, 1989, more than 100,000 Chinese troops opened fire on young demonstrators camped out in Beijing's Tiananmen (Gate of Heavenly Peace) Square, killing hundreds and injuring thousands. (The regime never released figures.) Much of the killing, including tanks crushing protesters and bicyclists shot at random, took place outside the Square, but the horror went down in history as "Tiananmen."

Tiananmen marked the point at which China's Communist chiefs choked over letting China's 1980s experiment with a partially free market economy spill over into political democracy, never the intention of Beijing's rulers. The massacre illustrates the danger of halfway reform: It gets people thinking of democracy.

Trouble began with the death of the liberal ex-Party chief Hu Yaobang in April 1989. Students began mourning him and protesting the current CCP leadership. On April 18, thousands began to occupy the Square. While the regime pondered how to handle the demonstration, the students organized, gave speeches, and built a Goddess of Democracy statue that resembled New York's Statue of Liberty. Around the country, many sympathized with the demonstrators, and criticism of the regime mounted.

If prodemocracy demonstrations had kept going, the regime would have been in trouble. The regime knew that and struck back. Zhao Ziyang, who succeeded Hu in 1987, went out to talk with the students and took their side. Politburo hardliners immediately ousted Zhao from office. (Zhao was under house arrest until his death in 2005, and his funeral was nearly secret so as not to give mourners another occasion to demonstrate for freedom. Even funerals are touchy events in China.) Deng Xiaoping, still the real power at age 84, ordered the army to crush the demonstrators. "We do not fear spilling blood," he said.

Troops and tanks poured into Beijing. The soldiers, mostly simple country boys, felt little in common with the urban students. In one memorable videotaped confrontation, a lone protester blocked a tank column; when the tanks tried to go around him, he quickly stepped in front of them again. It seemed to symbolize the individualism of democracy standing up to the coercion of dictatorship. After the bloodbath, thousands were arrested. The top protest figures received sentences of up to thirteen years, less for those who "repented." Hundreds were held for years without trial. China's elite decided to keep going with economic change but to keep the lid on political change. The ingredients for new upheavals in China are already present.

WHAT CHINESE QUARREL ABOUT

A MARKET ECONOMY FOR CHINA?

Starting in 1978, the Chinese economy grew at amazing rates. China, like all Communist countries, faced the question of how centralized the economy should be and decided on decentralization while retaining central political control. This, as in other countries that tried it, is an unstable combination.

KEY CONCEPTS

PURCHASING POWER PARITY

Traditional per-capita GDP (GDPpc) figures that used the *market exchange rate* were deceptive because they did not figure in prices in each country. China's GDPpc at exchange rate, for example, is only about $1,100. But exchange rates overvalue or undervalue currencies and change rapidly. To correct for this, economists now calculate GDPpc in **purchasing power parity** (PPP) by measuring what it costs to live in each country. This makes Chinese a lot richer, about $5,000.

	GDPpc at PPP	Big Mac Index
United States	$37,800	3.06
Canada	29,800	2.63
Japan	36,000	2.34
Britain	27,700	3.44
France	27,600	3.58*
Germany	27,600	3.58*
South Africa	10,700	2.10
Mexico	9,000	2.58
Russia	8,900	1.48
Brazil	7,600	2.39
Iran	7,000	—
China	5,000	1.27
Nigeria	900	—

*average of euro-area prices
Sources: First column CIA, second column *The Economist*.

   PPP is hard to calculate because economists must find a market basket of goods and services that is the same in each country. A quick and cheeky way to approximate PPP was devised by the British newsweekly *The Economist*: Compare the price of a Big Mac sandwich at the local McDonald's with its U.S. (big-city) price. These Big Macs are big-city prices from mid-2005. Since a Big Mac requires the same ingredients, labor, and overhead wherever it is produced, it is actually a mini-market basket that reflects local costs fairly accurately. A Big Mac that is more expensive than the U.S. price indicates the local currency is overvalued, the case with the British pound and the euro. A cheaper Big Mac indicates the local currency is undervalued, the case in Mexico, Brazil, China, and Russia. The Big Mac Index is a quick way to check currency parities, which can change rapidly as the dollar rises and falls.

KEY TERM

purchasing power parity (PPP)   GDP figures that take cost of living into account.

The earliest changes came in the countryside, where most of China's population always lived. Collectivized farms were broken up, and families were permitted to go on the "responsibility system," a euphemism for private farming. Peasants lease land from the state for up to fifteen years—still no private owners—and must deliver a certain quota to the state at set prices. Beyond that, they can sell their produce on the free market for the best price they can get. They can choose their own crops and decide how to use fertilizer and farm machinery, which they buy at their own expense. Farm production soared, Chinese ate better, and farmers' incomes went up; some even got rich.

By the 1990s, things were not going so well in the countryside, where over 60 percent of Chinese still live. The government held down farm prices and paid peasants IOUs for their grain. Farm incomes declined as inflation soared. In many rural areas, order broke down as people rioted and attacked local authorities, who extort illegal "taxes" from them. In a pattern very typical of the Third World, millions of rural Chinese leave every year for jobs in the coastal cities where market economies flourish, a destabilizing tide the regime cannot control.

The partly free market spread to the cities. Faced with growing unemployment, the regime let individuals open small stores, restaurants, repair shops, and even manufacturing facilities. It was even permissible to hire workers, something any Marxist would call capitalist exploitation. But it worked. The Chinese applied individual hustle to produce and sell more and better products than the indifferent state factories and stores ever could. Hole-in-the-wall "department stores" had customers waiting in line to buy the fashionable clothing and footwear Mao used to scorn. People swarmed to outdoor markets to buy home-produced chairs and sofas.

Starting with the area around Hong Kong, parts of coastal China were declared "Special Economic Zones," open to private and foreign investors. Capital poured in (much of it from Taiwan and Hong Kong) to take advantage of low Chinese wages (for unskilled, 50 cents an hour, but rising), and production soared. These firms compete in a world market to make profits. Because of these firms—which now account for half of China's economy—in a quarter century China's GDP grew at an amazing average of 9.5 percent a year to become the world's second largest overall economy (but not per capita) and third biggest exporter (after America and Germany). China's economy was twenty times bigger in 2002 than it had been in 1980. By comparison, one-third of some 100,000 state-run enterprises lose money and have to be propped up by subsidies. Of these, half are reckoned to be hopeless. Whether to close the losers (and create unemployment) is one of the great questions facing Beijing.

As modern, high-rise boomtowns sprang up on the coast, some Chinese business people became millionaires, and a substantial middle class began to form. Most Chinese liked their taste of the free market, but many cadres did not. If you really go to a market system, what do you do with the cadres who make a good living by supervising a controlled economy? They dig in their heels and try to block major change. Deng purged or retired the old guard and replaced them with young technocrats—such as current Party chief Hu and Premier Wen—who pursue capitalist-style economic growth and call it "socialism with Chinese characteristics."

But market economies produce problems of their own (see box on page 216) and awaken resentments and jealousies. China's leaders fear the economy is careening out of control and attempted to slow it, aiming for a "soft landing." In the longer term, the system needs democracy, but Beijing vows China will have only one party. What will happen when a destabilizing economic system escapes the bonds of a dictatorial political system? Think: bucking bronco (China's economy) throwing its rider (the Party).

KEY CONCEPTS

THE TROUBLE WITH MARKETS

The trouble with bringing a market economy into Communist countries, such as Yugoslavia, Hungary, or China, is that it grows too fast, runs out of control, and destabilizes. China has seen major increases in the following:

Unemployment   Communist systems disguised unemployment by gross labor inefficiency, but once China's firms had to make profits, they let go 24 million workers. Urban unemployment is estimated at 8–10 percent. Rural joblessness is much higher, and 150 million rural Chinese, most without permission, have left to seek work in the Special Economic Zones (SEZs). An equal number are ready to do the same.

Inequality   Foreign direct investment began in the SEZs of the southern coastal provinces, and they got rich fast. Inland provinces stayed poor, and resentments grew. To head off regional tensions, China is now extending its industrial zones deep inland, along the Pearl and Yangzi Rivers.

Worker protest   Treated unfairly and arbitrarily, some Chinese workers attempt to form unions, but they are jailed. Beijing denies that they even exist. Ironically, a Communist regime is more anti-labor than anti-capitalist.

Currency distortion   Beijing fixed the **yuan** too low in relation to the dollar and kept it there. Most other countries let their currencies "float" (rise against the dollar), which is what Washington urged Beijing to do. The cheap yuan let China become the "workshop of the world" but caused a property bubble and inflation. Historically, all bubbles pop.

Corruption   Corruption grows at the interface of the private and governmental sectors. Economic liberalization multiplies such interfaces as entrepreneurs need permits from government officials, obtained by under-the-table payments. Transparency International rates China as one of the world's most corrupt countries. Chinese business is based on *guanxi* (connections).

Crime   With all the above plus weakened social controls, crime grows, along with campaigns to stop it. Firing squads execute thousands each year. China leads the world by far in capital punishment (Iran is second).

Pollution   With few pollution controls, China has the world's worst environmental problems. City air is unbreathable, ground water is contaminated, and diseases spread rapidly. Environmental and health activists are jailed for speaking out.

How to solve these problems? A start is democracy, which permits people to organize interest groups and parties and holds officials accountable.

KEY TERM

yuan   China's currency, worth 12 U.S. cents.

KEY CONCEPTS

SECOND- AND THIRD-ORDER EFFECTS

China's program to limit population growth shows what can go wrong with coercing society into what the government has decided is desirable. It also illustrates the problem of second- and third-order consequences, that is, how hard it is to predict the longer-term effects of a policy.

In the early 1980s China carried out a ferocious program to curb births. Urban women were ordered to have only one child and were fined and lost benefits if they had more. Many women were forced to have abortions. The first-order consequence, as might be expected, was to bring down China's rate of population increase to under 1 percent a year, similar to Europe but very low for the Third World, much of which grows at 3 percent.

A second-order effect, however, was a large excess of boy over girl babies, both by abortion and female infanticide. About 5 percent of the girls expected to be born from 1979 to 1995 are missing, 10 percent in the 1990s. In 2000, 118 males were born for 100 females. Cheap ultrasound scans permit selective abortions. Like many Third World cultures, Chinese value boys above girls, both to work on the farm and to support the parents in old age. So, if they are allowed only one child, many Chinese strongly prefer a son.

Third-order effects flow from the second. The surplus of males over females means that millions of Chinese men will never find brides. Further, the drastic restriction in fertility rates—from 2.29 per births per average woman in 1980 to 1.69 in 2004—means that China's retired generation—now much bigger and living much longer thanks to improved nutrition and health care—will not have nearly enough working Chinese to support it. Chinese speak of "4-2-1": four grandparents and two parents supported by only one child, the logical result of the one-child policy. China, still a poor country, will thus face exactly the same problem as the rich countries. China's State Family Planning Commission, which now emphasizes education and contraception, never considered the second- and third-order consequences.

How then to handle the serious Third World problem of too-rapid population growth? Economic growth solves the problem without coercion. As the economy grows, more people become urban and middle class and decide for themselves to limit their number of children, as Japanese have done. As more women are educated they postpone marriage in favor of work and have fewer children. No rich country has a problem of too many babies (in fact, it is just the opposite), and newly industrializing lands show a dramatic falloff in births. China's demographic debacle is one example of Mao's (and, earlier, Stalin's) thinking that society can be forced into any shape the Party decrees.

A MIDDLE WAY FOR THE MIDDLE KINGDOM?

The basic supposition of Beijing's recent rulers is that there is a middle way between capitalism and communism, between a controlled and a free-market economy, between the Soviet and American models. (Soviet President Gorbachev entertained similar notions, and

DEMOCRACY

DO MARKETS LEAD TO DEMOCRACY?

Economic liberalization tends to encourage political participation. You cannot reform the economy alone, for economic reform generates demands for political reform, namely, democracy. As political scientist Peter Berger put it: "When market economies are successful over a period of time, pressure for democratization inevitably ensues." A market economy generates a large, educated middle class and interest groups. People start resenting a corrupt government treating them like small children. They want democracy. If the regime is intelligent and flexible, it gradually opens up, usually by permitting a critical press, then opposition parties, and finally free and fair elections.

Taiwan is the textbook example of this transition from authoritarianism to democracy. Some argue that China will follow a similar path, but there are differences. Taiwan's elite, many of them educated in the United States, led the way to democracy in the late 1970s. One of their motives: Show the Americans they are a democracy in order to win U.S. support against Beijing's demands to take over Taiwan. We must be careful in supposing the Taiwan model fits mainland China.

China's elite is still firmly Communist, has no desire for democracy, and is not trying to please the Americans. Much of China's economy that looks private is actually still controlled by the state or army. China's leaders are not planning for capitalism; they are planning for Chinese power. China's middle class is rapidly growing, but it is tied to the state, which also blocks the growth of "civil society," the autonomous groups that underlay pluralist democracy. Calls for democracy are ruthlessly crushed. Do not count on China moving to democracy automatically or peacefully, no matter what its economic growth.

you know what happened to him.) By bringing in elements of a market economy while retaining a large state sector, they sought a middle way. Is there one? Not really, and some observers think the Chinese elite has quietly admitted it, at least among themselves.

When a Communist country introduces a bit of market economics—supply and demand, competing producers, profits, family farming, prices finding their own level—the first few years are usually good. Farm output especially grows, and people eat well. Consumer goods become far more available, and people live and dress better. New industries produce clothing and consumer electronics for the world market. Statistically, growth rates shoot up. It looks like they found the happy balance: a market economy at the *micro* level to provide for consumer needs under the benevolent guidance of a state-run economy at the *macro* level (see pages 281–282 for the distinction). The farmers, shoemakers, and tailors are mostly private; many big industries, as well as banking and planning systems, are state-owned and under Party control.

But after a few years things start to go wrong. Shortages, distortions, and bottlenecks appear. China's growth has slowed compared to the early 1990s. The private sector keeps bumping into the state sector. Every time it does, there is a "crisis" that can be resolved only by expanding the private sector and shrinking the state sector. After some years of this, there is little socialism left, and this Beijing's rulers do not like.

GEOGRAPHY

THE HONG KONG EXAMPLE

In 1997 the British colony of Hong Kong reverted back to China. Most of Hong Kong actually consisted of leased territory on the mainland—the source of the colony's water supplies—and the lease was up in 1997. Britain decided to give the whole package back to Beijing. Many prosperous and hardworking Hong Kongese did not want to be part of China, although Beijing guaranteed, under the formula *one nation, two systems*, that Hong Kong can keep its autonomy for fifty years. Beijing's intention, many believed, was to show Taiwan that it could rejoin the mainland and still keep its political and economic system. Few Taiwanese are buying.

Beijing slowly introduced new laws in Hong Kong on "security" and "information" to punish dissent. Beijing court decisions eroded Hong Kong's special status. Critical Hong Kong editors lost their jobs. Corruption grew, as certain cooperative Hong Kongese got special deals. Beijing favors Shanghai as China's financial hub, as it once was before World War II. Prime Minister Zhu—like President Jiang, a former mayor of Shanghai—said in 1999, "Shanghai will be China's New York." Hong Kong will be its "Toronto." Hong Kong, one of the world's great financial centers, did more and more business with mainland China and less and less with other Pacific Rim countries. As Hong Kong lost its glitter, Singapore tried to move into its place as the great trading post of the Pacific Rim.

The Chinese—like the Yugoslavs and Hungarians—found that a little bit of capitalism is like being a little bit pregnant. The choice Communist countries faced was difficult. If they went part of the way to a market economy, they experienced a few years of growth followed by dangerous distortions. If they called off the liberal experiment, they returned to the centralized, Stalinist system that was slowly running down, leaving them further and further behind the capitalist world. If they went all the way to a market system, they admitted they had been wrong all these decades.

Another problem cropped up with the financial problems that hit other East Asian lands in 1997: China's banks also loan recklessly and crookedly; the whole banking system is fragile. Some loans were under government orders, to prop up money-losing state industries. The central government itself was deeply in debt from subsidizing too much and collecting too little in taxes. With a faulty and foolish financial system, China's growth is threatened. Like America, China has a debt bomb ticking away.

Some observers argue that China's reforms were far more clever than the Soviet Union's and have a much better chance to succeed. First, China permitted private farming. The Soviet Union was still debating private farming when it collapsed. Then China permitted small businesses. Next, China designated SEZs for foreign investment. Missing in China is the political liberalization that blew up in Gorbachev's face. No Beijing ruler wants to be China's Gorbachev, hence they tolerate no democracy, competing parties, or free press, precisely the reforms that Gorbachev did first. Did the Chinese do it right, sequencing their reforms so as to build an economic basis for democracy before reforming their political system?

Other observers fear that China could collapse, that its economic reforms without political reforms will blow up. With increasing corruption and inequality (see box on page 216) there is increasing mass unrest. So far, the only successful transitions from communism to free-market capitalism have come in Central Europe—Poland, the Czech Republic, and Hungary—where anticommunists completely threw out the communist regimes. No controlled, middle-way transition has worked.

CRUNCH TIME

Several destabilizing forces are hitting China all at once. The easy economic reforms—independent farming and manufacturing and foreign investment—have been done. The really tough parts remain: dangerous government, banking, and state-industry debts; inefficient agriculture; and the need to add some nine million new jobs every year. Any global economic slowdown cuts China's export-led growth. As Japan discovered, exports cannot be the sole basis of an economy.

Now there is a new, unpredictable factor: In 2001 China won membership in the **World Trade Organization** (WTO), which it had long sought in order to boost China's exports. But in joining the WTO, China also had to open up its own economy to all manner of foreign investments and companies, including hitherto protected sectors like banking. Many weak Chinese firms will fail. Imported foods will be cheaper than Chinese farm products. How will Beijing handle the foreign competition and new ideas? The Internet—with its ability to communicate and inform instantly—poses a threat to the regime, which blocks some sites. (They briefly blocked Google but found the country needed it.)

China has not really been stable in more than a century and could go off the tracks again. China, hard to govern in good times, now has a split and uncertain Party, corrupt local officials, weakening central authority, and growing discontent. Some observers fear Beijing is deflecting discontent outward by promoting an angry nationalism, a common practice of nervous regimes, and this is a very nervous regime.

Beijing aims to become the number-one military power of East Asia, eclipsing Japan. Said Party chief Jiang: "There will only be two superpowers by around 2020—China and the United States." One of China's priorities is its navy, with which it has claimed and fortified islets far from its shores in the East and South China Seas. This angers other countries in the region—Japan, the Philippines, Malaysia, Indonesia, and Vietnam. And Beijing proclaims the right to seize Taiwan, which it regards as a renegade province, at any time. By a 1979 law, the United States is committed to a peaceful, voluntary reunification. If Beijing applies force or intimidation to Taiwan, how should we react?

Underlying everything is China's deep craving for dignity and respect for what was once the world's greatest civilization but one that was brought low by Western and Japanese imperialists. How China achieves this recognition will be one of the great chapters of twenty-first century history.

KEY TERM

World Trade Organization   120-plus members open selves to trade and investment; has quasi-judicial powers.

KEY WEB SITES

Statements from U.S. State Department
state.gov/www/current/debate/china.html

News Sources
South China Morning Post
scmp.com

Hong Kong Standard (business)
standard.com.hk

Far East Economic Review
feer.com

KEY TERMS

Boxer (p. 194)
cadre (p. 199)
Confucianism (p. 192)
corruption (p. 187)
dynastic cycle (p. 189)
extraterritoriality (p. 193)
Gang of Four (p. 200)
hyperinflation (p. 195)
kow-tow (p. 189)
Manchu (p. 189)
man-land ratio (p. 188)
mass line (p. 196)
Meiji (p. 194)
Middle Kingdom (p. 189)

Mongol (p. 189)
Nationalist (p. 194)
Open Door (p. 193)
purchasing power parity (p. 214)
sphere of influence (p. 193)
steady-state (p. 188)
Taiping (p. 194)
Third World (p. 187)
treaty ports (p. 193)
voluntarism (p. 204)
warlord (p. 194)
Warring States (p. 189)
World Trade Organization (p. 220)
yuan (p. 216)

FURTHER REFERENCE

Buruma, Ian. *Bad Elements: Chinese Rebels from Los Angeles to Beijing.* New York: Random House, 2001.

Chang, Gordon G. *The Coming Collapse of China.* New York: Random House, 2001.

Chase, Michael S., and James C. Mulvenon. *You've Got Dissent! Chinese Dissident Use of the Internet and Beijing's Counter-Strategies.* Santa Monica, CA: RAND, 2002.

Economy, Elizabeth C. *The River Runs Black: The Environmental Challenge to China's Future.* Ithaca, NY: Cornell University Press, 2004.

Fairbank, John King. *China: A New History*. Cambridge, MA: Harvard University Press, 1994.

Fewsmith, Joseph. *China since Tiananmen: The Politics of Transition*. New York: Cambridge University Press, 2001.

Gamer, Robert E., ed. *Understanding Contemporary China*, 2nd ed. Boulder, CO: L. Rienner, 2003.

Gilley, Bruce. *China's Democratic Future: How It Will Happen and Where It Will Lead*. New York: Columbia University Press, 2004.

Huang, Jing. *Factionalism in Chinese Communist Politics*. New York: Cambridge University Press, 2000.

Li, Cheng. *China's Leaders: The New Generation*. New York: Rowman & Littlefield, 2001.

Lü, Xiaobo. *Cadres and Corruption: The Organizational Involution of the Chinese Communist Party*. Stanford, CA: Stanford University Press, 2000.

Perry, Elizabeth, and Mark Selden, eds. *Chinese Society: Change, Conflict and Resistance*, 2nd ed. New York: Routledge, 2003.

Saich, Tony. *Governance and Politics of China*, 2nd ed. London: Palgrave, 2004.

Spence, Jonathan. *Mao Zedong*. New York: Viking, 2000.

Studwell, Joe. *The China Dream: The Elusive Quest for the Greatest Untapped Market*. Boston, MA: Atlantic Monthly Press, 2002.

Zhao, Hongwei. *The Political Regime of Contemporary China*. Lanham, MD: University Press of America, 2002.

Zheng, Yongnian. *Discovering Chinese Nationalism in China: Modernization, Identity, and International Relations*. New York: Cambridge University Press, 1999.

13

Mexico

THE IMPACT OF THE PAST

Roughly 12,000 years ago hunter-gatherers, probably pursuing game, walked across the Bering Strait from Asia into North America. The ice age lowered the sea level and formed ice bridges across the Strait. In a few centuries the hunter-gathers had spread the length of the Western Hemisphere. Some of them founded **civilizations**, but several thousand years later than the first civilizations of the Middle East.

Several civilizations rose and fell in Mexico long before the Spaniards arrived. The first, the Olmec, flourished around present-day Veracruz a thousand years before Christ and set the pattern for subsequent **Mesoamerican** civilizations. In the first centuries A.D. the Zapotec and Teotihuacán constructed palaces and pyramids tourists visit today. During the first millennium the Mayas built a high civilization in the Yucatán. From the tenth to twelfth centuries the Toltec held sway in Central Mexico until destroyed by nomadic invaders, the Aztecs among them.

The Aztecs or Mexica, who originated in the northwest of Mexico, pushed into the Valley of Mexico around 1300. They made their capital on an island where they had sighted a prophetic eagle with a snake in its beak, later the symbol of Mexico. In 1376 the first Aztec king was crowned. Aztec kings had absolute power and ran their empire through a huge bureaucracy, characteristics

Questions to Consider

1. What is civilization? Did Mexico have civilizations?
2. How did Mexico's colonial period differ from ours?
3. Why were Calles and Cárdenas so important?
4. In what ways was the PRI reign undemocratic?
5. What ideologies did Mexico import? Do any fit Mexico?
6. Was the breakdown of PRI accidental or necessary?
7. What role did the Catholic Church play in Mexico?
8. Why do elections not equal democracy?
9. What is the impact of globalization on Mexico?
10. Has Mexico become a true democracy? How can you tell?

KEY TERMS

civilization   City-based culture with writing, social classes, and complex economic and political organization.

Mesoamerica   (Spanish for Middle America) Southern Mexico and northern Central America.

GEOGRAPHY

CITIES AND CIVILIZATIONS

The root of *civilization* is the Latin word *civitas,* city, and it is indeed the early cities that created high cultures of art, architecture, writing, money, social classes, and specialized economic functions. Cities arrived only after the domestication of plants and animals, which enabled humans to grow more food than their families needed. Growers traded their food surplus for utensils and clothing produced in towns. Food and other production were taxed to support rulers' courts and a professional officer class, who became nobles.

Humans began the several-thousand-year transition from hunter-gatherers to settled farmers around 10,000 years ago in the **Neolithic** age, which progressed to the founding of cities around 3,500 years ago in the **Bronze Age**, when metal-working began. Both shifts occurred first in Mesopotamia (present-day Iraq), followed shortly by Egypt. Scholars believe that civilization began there because the Middle East was home to more plants and animals that could be domesticated—including wheat and sheep—than anywhere else on the planet. The domesticated species spread to Europe and Asia but never crossed the Bering Strait. The Americas had few domesticable plants (corn) or animals (llamas in Peru), so their civilizations lagged behind Europe's, leaving them easy prey for the greedy Europeans.

---

still present in Mexican politics. The Aztecs kept expanding because they needed more land, serfs, and captured warriors to sacrifice for their deities. As a result, subordinate peoples did not love the Aztecs. The Aztec kingdom was complex and highly developed but not terribly old by the time Columbus sailed.

NEW SPAIN

Portugal actually started the voyages of discovery, initially aimed at direct access to the wealth (especially spices) of the "Indies" that bypassed the Arab traders and the Moors, whom Spain and Portugal had just expelled. Prince Henry the Navigator saw himself as a religious crusader against Muslims. Over a century, Portuguese navigators worked their way down Africa's west coast until they rounded the Cape of Good Hope, Africa's southern tip, in 1488. They quickly crossed the Indian Ocean and set up forts and trading posts in Asia. Spain's Ferdinand and Isabella, aware that Portugal was far ahead in opening the Asia trade,

KEY TERMS

Neolithic   New Stone Age, beginning of agriculture, about 10,000 years ago.
Bronze Age   Beginning of metal-working and cities, about 3,500 years ago.

GEOGRAPHY

MEXICO'S MOUNTAINS

Mexico's geography is distinctive and helped mold its current politics, which is highly regional. Two mountain chains, the Sierra Madre Oriental on the east and Sierra Madre Occidental on the west, connect at Mexico's narrow neck, forming a kind of Y. Between the Y's two arms is the Mesa Central, an upland that includes the Valley of Mexico with its rich volcanic soil and abundant rainfall. Mexico City, at 7,500 feet (a mile and a half), is one of the highest capitals in the world.

Like other mountainous areas (Spain, Colombia, and the Caucasus), mountains can make a country hard to unify. With communication slow and difficult, some tribes and ethnic groups live in *patrias chicas* (little countries) outside central control. As the West Virginia motto says, *Montani Semper Liberi* (Mountaineers are always free). Mexico was never well integrated—neither by the Aztecs nor the Spaniards—and still retains important regional differences and politics. In remote mountain villages, many still speak Indian languages. Mexico's crumpled geography forced any national government to work through and with **caciques**. Current Mexican voting patterns (and cuisine) are still regional.

accepted Columbus's argument that Spain could reach Asia directly across the Atlantic. (Yes, even then, educated people understood—from the ancient Greeks—that the world was round.) Columbus's 1492 voyage was to be a quick way to catch up with Portugal.

Columbus thought he had nearly reached India and called the inhabitants of Hispaniola "Indians." The name stuck, although some now prefer Native Americans, Amerindians, First Nations (Canada), or *índigenas* (Latin America). Initially based in Cuba, the Spaniards charged quickly into the New World for "gold, God, and glory," serving respectively the royal treasury, the Catholic Church, and the *conquistadores*, who had just won a struggle of eight centuries to expel the Arabs from Spain. They treated the Indians with the same contempt they held for the Moors. Indian lives meant nothing to them.

The Aztecs had a large population—their capital was probably larger than any European city at that time—and were well-organized into a bureaucratic empire. Why could they not send the Spaniards packing? Several factors doomed the Aztecs. First, the Spaniards brought with them smallpox, against which Native Americans had no immunity. Mexico's population plunged from about 20 million at the time of the conquest to barely 1 million by 1600. Only in 1940 did Mexico reach the population it had under the Aztecs. Next, the Spaniards had steel; their swords sliced up the Aztecs (and later the Incas) as their armor minimized their own casualties. They also had horses and guns, which the Aztecs had never

KEY TERM

cacique   (Originally Indian chief) local political boss.

GEOGRAPHY

BOUND MEXICO

Mexico is bounded on the north by the United States;
on the east by the Gulf of Mexico and the Caribbean;
on the south by Belize and Guatemala;
and on the west by the Pacific.

Geographically, Mexico is considered part of North America. To its south is **Central America**, consisting of Belize, Guatemala, Honduras, El Salvador, Nicaragua, Costa Rica, and Panama. **South America** is south of that. Everything south of the United States, including Mexico, is called **Latin America**.

seen before. Many of the peoples the Aztecs had subjugated aided the Spaniards. Finally, the Aztecs had a legend that the white god Quetzalcóatl would return from the east and destroy them.

Based in Cuba, Spanish ships explored Mexico's coast and brought back news of fabulous wealth in the interior. Partly at his own expense, Hernán Cortés equipped eleven ships and sailed from Havana in late 1518. After founding the city of Veracruz, he pushed inland with a force of 500 Spanish soldiers and several thousand Indians. The Aztec emperor Moctezuma (known to Americans as Montezuma) at first welcomed the Spaniards to his capital of Tenochtitlán, but they soon arrested him, and fighting broke out. Cortés retreated from the city but returned in 1521 after smallpox had killed much of its population. After three weeks of fierce battle, the Spaniards captured and killed the last emperor, Cuauhtémoc (a name that reappears with a current Mexican politician). Mexico today celebrates Aztec heroes but no Spanish ones, and many **pre-Columbian** traditions remain in Mexican culture.

On the ruins of Tenochtitlán the Spaniards built a new capital and called it Mexico. Upon the ruins of the main Aztec temple they built a huge cathedral. With little resistance, they soon took over most of Southern Mexico. Rich silver mines moved the Spaniards to expand over Central Mexico, but takeover of Northern Mexico, arid and

KEY TERMS

Central America   Countries between Mexico and Colombia.
South America   Continent south of Panama.
Latin America   All countries south of the United States.
pre-Columbian   The Americas before Columbus arrived.

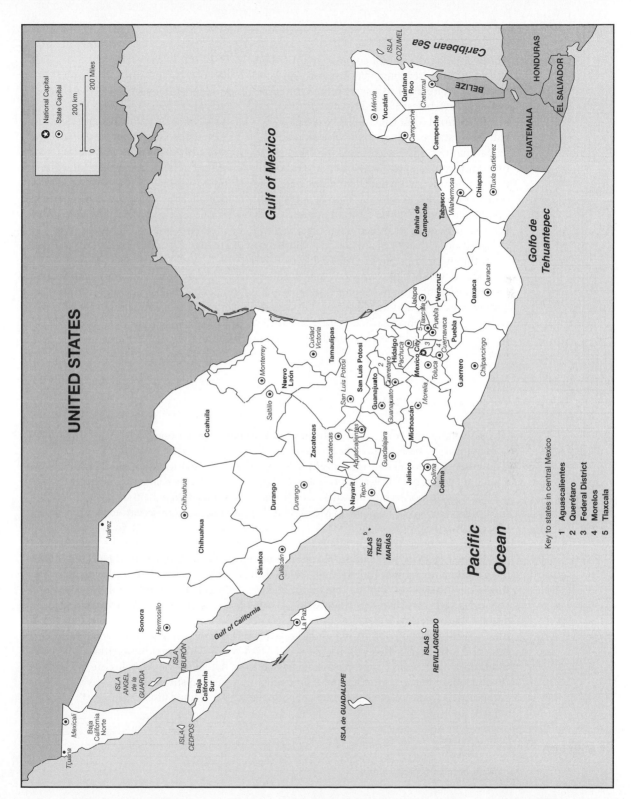

UNITED STATES

Gulf of Mexico

Caribbean Sea

ISLA COZUMEL

Quintana Roo

Mérida
Yucatán

Chetumal

Campeche
Campeche

HONDURAS

BELIZE

EL SALVADOR

GUATEMALA

Tuxla Gutiérrez
Chiapas

Tabasco
Vilahermosa

Bahia de Campeche

Golfo de
Tehuantepec

Oaxaca
Oaxaca

Veracruz
Jalapa
Puebla
5 *Tlaxcala*
Puebla
Cuernavaca
3 4
Hidalgo
Pachuca
Mexico City 1
Querétaro 2
Guanajuato
Guanajuato
Toluca
Morelia
Michoacán
G.uerrero
Chilpancingo

Cuidad Victoria
Tamaulipas

San Luis Potosi
San Luis Potosi

Monterrey
Nuevo León

Ccahuila
Saltillo

Zacatecas
Zacatecas

Aguascalientes 1

Guadalajara
Jalisco
Colima
Colima

Nayarit
Tepic

Durango
Durango

Chihuahua
Chihuahua

Juárez

Sinaloa
Culiacán

ISLAS TRES MARIAS

Pacific
Ocean

ISLAS REVILLAGIGEDO

ISLA de GUADALUPE

Sonora
Hermosillo

Gulf of California

La Paz

Baja California Sur

ISLA TIBURON

ISLA ANGEL de la GUARDA

ISLA CEDROS

Baja California Norte
Mexicali

Tijuana

National Capital
State Capital

0   200 km
0   200 Miles

Key to states in central Mexico

1   Aguascalientes
2   Querétaro
3   Federal District
4   Morelos
5   Tlaxcala

227

thinly populated, was not completed until about 1600. North of the present U.S.-Mexico border Spanish settlement was sparse and late—Texas in 1716 and California in 1769—which ultimately led to war with the United States and loss of the vast territories that became the southwest United States.

To control what they called New Spain, Spain used a Roman institution, *encomiendas*, grants of land and the people who worked on it, to Spanish soldiers and settlers. In the feudal manner, the *encomendero* was the lord and master of Indian serfs. They worked for him, and he looked after their welfare and Christianized them. Actually, the setup was not much different than what the Indians were used to under the Aztecs. The *encomienda* system soon produced a feudal type of social stratification. At the top were those born in Spain, *peninsulares*, who held all administrative positions and a social edge over *criollos* (**creoles**). Persons of mixed parentage, *mestizos*, became artisans and foremen, often in competition with poor Spaniards. The Indians worked the land on the *encomiendas* or stayed up in the mountains out of Spanish control.

The Spanish Habsburgs ran out of heirs; in 1707 a French Bourbon became king. (Spain's present monarch, Juan Carlos, is a Bourbon.) The Spanish Bourbons improved administration by dividing New Spain into twelve *intendencias*, each supervised by a French-style *intendente*, who reported to a central authority. Economic liberalization boosted Mexico's economy, and more Spaniards settled there. Bourbon reforms thus helped wake up Mexico.

Mexican Independence

The late eighteenth century brought new ideas to both Spain's and Portugal's Latin American colonies. The Enlightenment and the U.S. and French Revolutions inspired some to seek independence. The trigger event was Napoleon's occupation of Spain in 1808. Spanish King Ferdinand VII was imprisoned, and Spain's Cortes (parliament) passed the liberal 1812 constitution, which Mexico's elite feared would spread French atheism and liberalism into their realm. The impulse to Mexico's independence was conservative, not liberal, as in the United States.

A parish priest, Miguel Hidalgo, on September 16, 1810, proclaimed Mexico's independence. It got nowhere but is still commemorated as Mexico's Independence Day. Hidalgo led a strange uprising of Indians that presaged the confused turmoil of the Mexican Revolution a century later. On the one hand, Hidalgo demanded equality of all Mexicans and the redistribution of land for the Indians. But he also fought against French-style atheism and for Catholicism. Hidalgo's band ran out of control and massacred Spaniards and Creoles. Royalist forces soon captured and executed Hidalgo. Another priest of similar persuasion, José Maria Morelos, in 1814 and 1815 led a widespread guerrilla uprising in Southern Mexico until he too was caught and shot. Hidalgo and Morelos are considered revolutionary heroes who founded the populist nationalism sill very much alive in Mexican politics. Mexico's states of Hidalgo and Morelos are named after them.

Key Term

creole   Spaniard born in the New World.

Another trigger of Mexican independence was the liberal 1812 constitution, which Ferdinand VII had rejected upon returning from exile in 1814. An uprising of Spanish liberals got him to reinstate it in 1820. Again, Mexican conservatives feared it threatened their privileged status. To preserve it, they reasoned, they must declare independence from Spain, which they did, in 1821. It was an elite thing with no mass participation and no fighting with Spain to achieve it. Only Brazil's 1822 independence from Portugal was as painless.

Between Monarchy and Republic

Mexico, like Brazil, began as a conservative monarchy, but that lasted only a year and a half (Brazil's lasted until 1889). Immediately Mexico's elite—and politics was an exclusively elite thing—split into two camps: conservative centralizers and liberal federalists, a split that has never fully healed. For much of the nineteenth century Mexico, like most of Latin America, was led by **caudillos**.

The key figure in the first decades of the Republic of Mexico was Antonio López de Santa Anna, Mexico's off-and-on president, general, and dictator who played both sides of every conflict and continually broke his word. Santa Anna's big problem was Texas. To populate huge, thinly populated Texas, Mexico in 1821 gave American settlers land there, but they soon outnumbered Mexicans. To discourage further American immigrants—who brought slaves with them—Mexico outlawed slavery in 1828. (Texas was later a slave state and joined the Confederacy.)

By 1833 Texas had some 30,000 American settlers who demanded state's rights to govern themselves (and their slaves) within a Mexican federation. Santa Anna rejected the demand, the Republic of Texas declared independence in 1836, and Santa Anna marched north to reclaim it. He took the Alamo but was captured by the Texans. The United States annexed Texas in 1845, but Mexican and U.S. forces soon clashed, leading to the 1846–1848 War with Mexico. The United States, after occupying Mexico City, took the southwest states and paid Mexico $15 million. Mexico was permanently humiliated.

An especially strange interlude in Mexico's history was its brief occupation by France, 1861–1867. Mexican conservatives in exile convinced Napoleon III that he could reconstruct a Catholic monarchy in Mexico. The ambitious Napoleon III thought Mexico would be the base for a French-led "Latin America" (the first use of that term). With the U.S. Civil War giving Napoleon III a window of opportunity, he used the pretext of Mexico's big European debts to send French troops to install the Austrian Habsburg Maximilian as his puppet emperor of Mexico. The effort found little support in Mexico and collapsed. It cost Paris too much money, and the U.S. Civil War was over. The French left, and Maximilian was shot. The French had committed the common mistake of supposing that Mexico was more or less like orderly Europe, where rational authority is obeyed. Latin America is quite different, more chaotic and rebellious. Few obey and plans seldom work right. The only remnant of the French in Mexico is the word *mariachi*, from the French hiring musicians for a *mariage*.

Key Term

caudillo   Military chief or strongman, specifically one who takes over government.

The iconic figure of nineteenth-century Mexican politics was Benito Juárez (1806–1872), who was remarkable on several counts. First, he was born of Indian parents (who died when he was three) at a time when all power was in Creole hands. Educated in law, Juárez rose in state and national politics and became president in 1858. A classic nineteenth-century liberal, Juárez saw a stagnant Mexico dominated by the old aristocracy and a conservative Catholic church. He wanted to redistribute their lands and institute a market economy, federalism, and separation of church and state. Juárez did not invent Mexican anti-clericalism but gave it a powerful boost. Conservatives forced Juárez to spend 1853–1855 in New Orleans, and later the French forced him to withdraw to the U.S.-Mexico border, to a city later renamed after him. Although not long in power, Juárez set standards of modesty and honesty that few other Mexican leaders have met.

Porfirio Díaz (1830–1915) followed in Juárez's footsteps but turned himself into a military dictator. Like Juárez, Díaz was born in the southern state of Oaxaca (pronounced: wha-haw-ka), but of a mestizo family. Díaz studied law, fought the French, but turned against Juárez. Díaz was "elected" president seventeen times between 1877 and 1910 and personally centralized control over all branches of government. With the **Positivism** then popular in Latin America, Díaz's top bureaucrats, *los científicos,* pushed economic growth, but profits and land ownership went to a wealthy few and to foreign investors. Peasants were forced by debt to sell their land and grew poorer. By 1910 perhaps 95 percent of rural Mexican families were landless and eager to follow Zapata, who preached returning land to them. Díaz's long stay in power, called the Porfiriato, offered Mexicans *pan y palo* (bread and bludgeon), prominent in Mexico's governing philosophy ever since.

THE MEXICAN REVOLUTION

Compared to Mexico's 1910–1920 upheaval, the Bolshevik and Chinese revolutions are clear and easy to understand. They had only two sides; Mexico's had several, and they changed allegiances during the course of it. Mexico's is one of Latin America's few genuine revolutions. Latin America, to be sure, has had scores of military coups and "palace revolutions," but they were among elites. Mexico and much later Cuba and Nicaragua had armies fighting for years to overthrow regimes and replace them with totally different ones. (Castro's Cuban revolution, however, was conducted by law graduates plus one medical graduate, Che Guevara from Argentina.) A revolution is seldom caused by just one problem. It takes a series of mutually reinforcing, insoluble problems. Mexico had been storing up its contradictions until they erupted in the Revolution of 1910.

Under the long Porfiriato, discontent increased at the unfairness and cruelty of the Díaz regime. Anarchist and socialist ideas crept in from Europe. Juárista liberals who organized clubs, parties, and newspapers were jailed; many fled to the United States. Labor unrest was crushed by government troops. Influenced by Russian revolutionary Mikhail Bakunin, in 1906 the Mexican group Regeneration published a manifesto calling for one term for a president, civil rights, public education, land reform, improved pay and working

KEY TERM

Positivism   Philosophy, originally French, of applying scientific methods to analyze and improve society.

conditions, and ending the power of the Catholic Church. These eventually became the program of the party that ruled Mexico for most of the twentieth century.

The trigger for the Mexican Revolution was Díaz having the obedient Chamber of Deputies "reelect" him once again. On November 20, 1910, now celebrated as the start of the Revolution, presidential candidate Francisco Madero, from a wealthy family that owned much of Northern Mexico, proclaimed from San Antonio, Texas, that the election was illegal and urged Mexicans to revolt. Madero used his own fortune to supply rebels such as Pancho Villa. Díaz's decrepit Federalist army fell back, and Díaz resigned and left for Paris. Congress proclaimed Madero the new president. If things had stopped there, Mexico would have had another of its many irregular changes of power.

But Federalist General Victoriano Huerta, encouraged by the U.S. ambassador, had President Madero arrested and shot. Huerta assumed the presidency himself, and full-fledged revolution broke out. Angered by the assassination and believing America could put things right in Mexico, President Woodrow Wilson had the Navy occupy Veracruz in 1914 and sent General Pershing after the bandit and guerrilla chief Pancho Villa in 1916. Wilson announced that America "went down to Mexico to serve mankind," but the effort solidified Mexican opposition to U.S. intervention, and U.S. forces had to fight Mexican guerrillas. (Sound familiar?)

Huerta fell in 1914, but at least four armies then battled for control of the country. Two of them were genuinely revolutionary, that of peasant leader Emiliano Zapata in the south and Pancho Villa in the north. The other two, under moderates Venustiano Carranza and Álvaro Obregón, sought to establish a stable order. The four sometimes collaborated but sometimes fought each other. Zapata was assassinated in 1919, Carranza in 1920, Villa in 1923, and Obregón in 1928. Revolution is a dangerous business. Mexicans still celebrate the revolutionary tradition of Zapata and Villa.

THE REVOLUTION INSTITUTIONALIZED

With the 1917 constitution, Mexican generals and state political bosses started what Peruvian novelist Mario Vargas Llosa called "the perfect dictatorship"—perfect because it looked like a democracy. Others have called it a series of six-year dictatorships because of limits on the presidential term. It was impressive and lasted about as long as Lenin's handiwork in Russia. The system grew out of a deal between Obregón and Calles.

Obregón became president in 1920 and began to implement rural education and land reform, including the granting of **ejidos** to poor villagers. In 1924 he arranged the election of his collaborator, Plutarco Elías Calles, who in turn got Obregón reelected in 1928. But just then a Catholic fanatic assassinated Obregón, part of the bloody 1927–1929 Cristero Rebellion. Calles had implemented the anticlericalism of the 1917 constitution by banning foreign priests and clerical garb. With the cry, "*¡Viva Cristo Rey!*" (Long live Christ the King), militant Catholics rebelled, and government troops crushed them. Mexico's Church-anticlerical split began to heal only with the election of the conservative and Catholic Vicente Fox in 2000.

KEY TERM

ejido   Land owned in common by villages.

POLITICAL CULTURE

POOR MEXICO!

¡Pobre Mexico! Tan lejos de Dios, tan cerca de los Estados Unidos. "Poor Mexico!" exclaimed President Porfirio Díaz. "So far from God, so close to the United States." He voiced the widespread Mexican view that just sharing a long border with us condemns them to be dominated by the powerful United States. Díaz had seen the U.S. invasion of 1846–1847 that robbed Mexico of its northern half in 1848. The sad exclamation also indicates Mexican resentment of their rich, well-run neighbor, a sentiment found throughout Latin America.

Calles, still running things from behind the scenes, decided in 1928 on a law making Mexico's presidency a single, non-renewable six-year term, something Mexicans had wished since Díaz kept reelecting himself. To perpetuate his hold on power, in 1929 Calles organized a coalition of state political bosses, generals, union chiefs, and peasant leaders into the National Revolutionary party (PNR), renamed in 1946 the Institutional Revolutionary party (Partido Revolucionario Institucional, PRI).

The remarkable politician is one who builds lastingly, and Calles did. He founded the political party that brought stability and led Mexican politics for the rest of the twentieth century. It could not, however, last forever. (Well, what can?) The Calles system masked contradictions and concentrated power in the presidency. From its founding until 2000, PRI never lost an election, which, to be sure, were less than democratic. Still, considering what much of Latin America went through in the twentieth century—numerous military coups—the "soft authoritarianism" of the Mexican system was not bad.

Calles was basically a conservative, and his PNR made only moderate reforms until the 1934 election of Lázaro Cárdenas, who took Mexico on a radical path by implementing what the Revolution and 1917 constitution had promised. When Calles opposed him, Cárdenas had Calles exiled to California. Cárdenas was of mestizo descent and had little formal education but joined Carranza in the Revolution, becoming a general in 1920. Cárdenas was one of the PNR's founders and its first president, transforming it from a loose coalition to a cohesive and well-organized nationwide party. Upon taking office, President Cárdenas implemented a serious leftist program, including nationalization of U.S.-owned oil industries, which he turned into Petróleos Mexicanos (Pemex). In doing this, Cárdenas connected to

KEY TERMS

priísmo   Ideology and methods of PRI (see page 233).

sexenio   (from *seis años*) Six-year term of Mexico's presidents (see page 233).

austerity   Drastically holding down government expenses (see page 233).

POLITICAL CULTURE

MEXICO'S POLITICAL ERAS

Few countries have gone through such radical and bloody changes as Mexico. Most political cultures develop slowly and gradually. Mexico's developed in sudden shifts, each jerked back and forth by the introduction of new cultures and ideas, which never blended into a coherent whole (see discussion below).

Era	Years	Remembered for
Aztec	1325–1521	High civilization, bureaucratic empire, human sacrifice
New Spain	1521–1821	Colonialist exploitation, Catholicism
Empire	1821–1823	Conservative independence
Santa Anna	1830s–1850s	Erratic leadership, lost Texas and U.S. war
Juárez	1850s–1860s	Equality, federalism, anti-clericalism
Porfiriato	1877–1911	Dictatorship, economic growth, poverty
Revolution	1910–1920	Complex multisided upheaval
Maximato	1924–1934	Calles, *el jefe máximo,* founds single six–year term and PNR
Cárdenismo	1934–1940	Cárdenas makes PRI socialistic and corporatistic; nationalizes oil
Conservative Priísmo	1940–1964	Favors business and foreign investment; crackdown on leftists
Destabilizing Priísmo	1964–1982	Oil, overspending, and inflation spur unrest; massacre of students
Desperate Priísmo	1982–2000	Technocrats calm economy, promote NAFTA, clean up elections; assassinations
Panismo	2000–	Rejection of PRI; accomplishes little

The three phases of **priísmo** summarize the thrust of the presidents of each period. The four **sexenios** of the conservative period mark PRI's turning away from the Revolution and from *Cárdenismo,* giving lip service to labor and peasants but shifting to business and to stability. The three destabilizing *sexenios* mark the oil boom and government debt plus the 1968 massacre of students in Mexico City and psychological breakdown of President Echevarría. The desperate phase marks the recognition by Presidents de la Madrid, Salinas, and Zedillo that Mexico's economy is in shambles, and the whole system is losing legitimacy. U.S.-trained economic technocrats try to stabilize it with policies of **austerity** to reign in Mexico's runaway economy, but average Mexicans are hurt by it. Two political assassinations under Salinas turn many Mexicans against PRI. Panismo, never really implemented under Fox, may be short-lived.

an old Latin American pattern, **statism**, that Mexico has been reluctant to shed. Cárdenas carried out massive land redistribution and organized peasants and workers, making their unions constituent groups of the huge National Revolutionary party. He left office on schedule, in 1940, but kept a watchful leftist eye on the government until his death to make sure it did not drift under *yanquí* influence. Cárdenas remains a legend of Mexican nationalist radicalism, something that helps his son, Cuauhtémoc Cárdenas, now head of the leftist Party of Democratic Revolution.

Cárdenas also made the party, which he renamed the Party of the Mexican Revolution, into a corporatist one. **Corporatism**, which brings interest groups directly into parties and parliaments, was riding high at the time. Initially a device of Mussolini's fascism, Brazil's Vargas also adopted corporatism into his New State in 1935. Cárdenas organized the PMR with peasant, labor, military, and "popular" sectors. The latter included small businesses, later expanded to include big businesses. He built a large bureaucracy to mediate demands between groups and allocate funds to them—called **clientelism**. Initially, corporatism and clientelism seem to solve the problems of participation, power-sharing, and allocation of funds in chaotic situations. They are, however, not really democratic and over time become rigid and unstable. They are contrived and temporary fixes and leave the system saddled with an overlarge bureaucracy.

THE KEY INSTITUTIONS

The first thing you notice about Mexico's political history is that, prior to 1924, few Mexican presidents either came to power or left office in a regular, legal way. Most were installed and/or ousted on an ad hoc basis by a handful of elites or military coups, sometimes with violence. Mexico has had four constitutions since independence but not much **constitutionalism**. Once in office, Mexico's presidents observed few limits on their powers and tended to construct personalistic dictatorships. This is true of much of the Third World, where politics consists of strong personalities making their own rules.

That changed—but not completely—with the beginning of the single, six year presidency in 1928 and the 1929 founding of what became PRI. A contrived stability settled over Mexico for the rest of the century. There were no more upheavals because all the major reins of power—including the military—passed through PRI into the hands of the president. The personality of the president still counted—some, such as Cárdenas, were radical, others conservative—but the system counted more. Mexico was an example of what political scientists call a "clientelistic system," in which most major groups have been co-opted into cooperation. They feel they have a stake in the system and some input into government policy. Peasants get land reforms and ejidos; workers get unions; and bureaucrats get jobs.

KEY TERMS

statism   Idea (originally French) that a strong government should run things, especially major industries.

corporatism   Direct participation of interest groups in politics.

clientelism   Government favors to groups for their support.

constitutionalism   Degree to which government limits its powers.

KEY CONCEPTS

INSTITUTIONS AND INSTITUTIONALIZATION

Obviously, politics depends on power (see page 7). Power is not necessarily force, which is a subset of power, a coercive one best used sparingly. (Reason: If you use a lot of force, people will hate you and be eager for your overthrow. You will build little legitimacy.) **Political power**, however, is temporary unless it is turned into **political institutions**.

Mexico has had plenty of strong leaders who concentrated a great deal of power into their hands, but it vanished when they left office. Then the new leader had to amass power into his hands. Political power must not be too personal. Franco ruled Spain, sometimes by jail and firing squad, from 1939 to his death in 1975. He built what looked like a stable regime, but it was too much based on his one-man rule and quickly unraveled upon his death. Dictators rarely **institutionalize** their power. Within two years there was essentially nothing left of the Franco setup.

No country is born with functioning institutions; they have to evolve over time, usually in a series of accommodations among groups. An institution is not just an impressive building—although often they are housed in them to foster respect—but relationships of power that have solidified or congealed into understandings—sometimes written into constitutions or statutes, sometimes just traditions (as in Britain)—over who can do what.

Political scientists often speak of Third World governments as "poorly institutionalized," characterized by irregular or extra-legal changes of leaders (such as revolutions and coups) and no clear boundaries as to who can do what. There are no rules; many try to seize power. Long ago, all countries were like that. We admire British government as "well institutionalized," but centuries ago it suffered conquest, massacre, civil war, a royal beheading, a temporary Commonwealth, and attempts at absolutism. British institutions had to evolve, and did not reach their modern form until the nineteenth century. Go back far enough, and Britain resembled Mexico. Thanks to several historical factors, Britain simply institutionalized out of its tumultuous phase a couple of centuries earlier.

Accordingly, let us not ask too much of countries like Mexico too soon. They are bound to be messy and chaotic. Mexico did not begin political institutionalization until the 1920s, with Calles, and has not yet completed the process. Americans often wonder why Mexico cannot be like us—with democracy and rule of law—but Americans too spilled rivers of blood, first for independence, then to hold the country together. And America is no stranger to gangsters, drug traffickers, and crooks in high places.

KEY TERMS

political power   Ability of one person to get another to do something.

political institution   Established and durable relationships of power and authority.

institutionalize   To make a political relationship permanent.

KEY CONCEPT

CLIENTELISM

How can a society as badly fractured as Mexico's hold together? Why is it not stuck in civil wars, up-heavals, and coups (which it was until the 1920s)? Clever political leaders, such as Calles and Cárdenas in Mexico, may calm such situations by making sure important groups have a share not only of seats in parliament but of favors, such as development projects, rigged contracts, subsidies, or just plain cash. In a clientelistic situation, the elites of each major group strike a bargain to obtain resources and restrain their followers from violence. Most major groups get something; no one group gets everything. Clientelism is widely practiced in the Third World (heck, maybe in the First as well), as in the Persian Gulf oil sheikdoms and in Nigeria (see next chapter).

Clientelism has at least three problems. First, it may be fake, with only small payouts to labor and agrarian sectors, which PRI kept in line with the traditional *pan y palo*. Second, it may exclude important groups. In Mexico, the Catholic Church got no part of the deal, and big businessmen got little until some were co-opted into PRI during World War II. (These are among the groups that brought Vicente Fox to power in 2000.) A third problem is rigidity. The allocation of which group gets how much help and money cannot be frozen; it has to change as society and the economy evolve. Village land held in common and state-owned industries can retard economic growth, but the Mexican groups who benefit from these institutions fight change. Fortunately, Mexico loosened up its system in time to avoid an explosion.

THE SIX-YEAR PRESIDENCY

Latin America generally has modeled its institutions on the U.S. pattern, preferring presidential to parliamentary systems (see page 47). Mexico's presidential system, like the United States, combines head of state and chief of government. For most of the twentieth century it was even more powerful than the U.S. presidency. We must qualify that statement by noting that it was powerful when a PRI president dominated a Congress with a big PRI majority. The 2000 election of Vicente Fox of PAN did not give PAN a majority in the Congress, making Fox much less powerful than his PRI predecessors. Starting in 2000 Mexico tasted the "divided government" that often prevails in the United States, when a president of one party faces a Congress dominated by another. Likewise, the French system devised by de Gaulle made the president very powerful, but these powers shrank when opposition parties won a majority of the National Assembly. Then French presidents had to practice "cohabitation" with prime ministers of opposition parties.

Since 1928 Mexico has not deviated from the single, six-year term, although it might have been otherwise. One of the Revolution's goals was "no reelection"—to prevent another Díaz from monopolizing power. Obregón, who already had served from 1920 to 1924, won reelection in 1928, with Calles's support, but was assassinated by a Catholic fanatic (the

COMPARISON

TERM LENGTHS

Some American critics of our two four-year terms for president say we should consider a single six-year term. The theory here is that presidents are so concerned with reelection that they accomplish little their first term and then do irresponsible things their second term, because they do not have to worry about reelection. It is not clear that term lengths cause anything very specific. Both limited and unlimited terms have lent themselves to mistakes and corruption. Here is how our six countries' terms for chief executive compare:

Britain	prime minister	Unlimited terms, each one up to five years (but usually four).
Russia	president	Two four-year terms (which Putin might lengthen).
China	president	Two five-year terms (but this is recent).
Mexico	president	One six-year term.
Nigeria	president	Two four-year terms (barring overthrow).
Iran	president	Two four-year terms (but real power in hands of Islamist Guide).

Too long in office can lead to corruption, but not if chiefs of government must face an informed electorate at regular intervals. Margaret Thatcher served eleven years through three elections until her party dumped her over policy questions and slumping popularity. Term limits in Nigeria, on the other hand, did nothing to curb corruption. A limited term may even encourage officials to grab more sooner. By themselves, term limits do little; it all depends on the institutional and cultural context.

Cristero Rebellion was underway) before taking office. That convinced Calles to support the *sexenio* without reelection, even after an interval.

Under the long PRI reign, succession was actually in the hands of the president, who is also party chief. In consultation with past presidents and other PRI, chiefs would designate the party's nominee for the next election, a process called, half in jest, **dedazo**. Once nominated, of course, until 2000 no PRI candidate lost, and many won by 90 percent. Presidents would pick their successors—not necessarily well-known persons—with an eye to preserving stability and the power of PRI. There may also have been understandings that the new president would not look into corruption. No choice was absolutely predictable, and

KEY TERM

dedazo   (From *dedo,* finger) Tapped for high office.

PERSONALITIES

FOX IN THE PRI HOUSE

Mexico became a lot more democratic when PRI finally lost the presidency in 2000, after seventy-one years and fourteen elections. Alternation in power is one of the hallmarks of democracy. It was as if Mexicans finally said, "We've had enough of PRI's corruption and economic uncertainty. Time for a change."

The winner was Vicente Fox Quesada, then 58, of the conservative National Action party (Partido de Acción Nacional, PAN) from the state of Guanajuato, to the north of Mexico City. The name Fox marks an Irish ancestor. Fox attended the Jesuit-run Iberoamerican University in Mexico City but never graduated. Instead, he worked his way up through Coca Cola, becoming chief of its Mexico operations. Fox won a congressional seat for PAN in 1988 and ran for governor in 1991. Fox lost, but PRI fraud (hardly a new thing) brought reforms that led to a clean election in 1995, which he won. Showcasing himself as an honest and hard-working Catholic businessman, Fox campaigned ferociously in 2000, calling PRI snakes who had retarded Mexico's progress. Fox won the presidency for PAN in 2000 with 42.5 percent of the vote in what was probably Mexico's first clean national election. Francisco Labastida of PRI got 36.1 percent, and Cuauhtémoc Cárdenas of the radical PRD took 16.6 percent.

Fox formed a cabinet that included other parties but could not remotely accomplish his planned "transformation" of Mexico. PRI's continued plurality in the national legislature and its domination of state governments and the civil service blocked most of his reform proposals. Actually, previous PRI presidents proposed similar reforms to clean up elections and free the economy; Fox and PAN were not a totally new departure. PRI and PRD deputies in the Mexican Congress treated Fox rudely when he presented his annual report. Fox and Bush, taking office at the same time, thought they would be close but grew apart when Bush failed to offer a new deal for Mexican immigration to the United States. As Fox's support in polls slumped, PRI vowed to take back the presidency in 2006. Fox had won on PRI's corruption and on his warm and engaging personality, and that was not enough to govern Mexico.

once in office presidents often departed from previous policies. Calles did not know, for example, how far left Cárdenas would veer. When his term was ending, Cárdenas picked an obscure military officer, Manuel Ávila Camacho, who was more conservative.

MEXICO'S LEGISLATURE

Mexico's bicameral Congress (Congreso de la Unión) has been much less important than its presidency. Díaz was famous for simply putting obedient supporters into the legislature, and PRI did much the same. Legislative elections changed with the 1986 Electoral Reform Law, induced by uproar over PRI's habitual election frauds. Inspired by Germany's mixed-member system, Mexico (like Italy) now fills most seats from single-member districts,

Anglo-American style, but allocates additional seats based on each party's share of the popular vote, that is, by proportional representation (PR).

Mexico's upper house, the Senate (Cámara de Senadores), now has 128 seats and six-year terms. Ninety-six of the seats are filled from single-member districts, 32 by PR. The lower house, the Federal Chamber of Deputies (Cámara Federal de Diputados), now has 500 seats with three-year terms. Three hundred seats are filled by district voting, 200 by PR in five regions. In 2005, PRI was the biggest party in both chambers but no longer a majority:

	Senate	Chamber of Deputies
PRI	60 seats	222 seats
PAN	46	151
PRD	16	95

Some smaller parties such as the Greens and Workers parties held a few seats.

Since 1997, after several electoral reforms, PRI lost its majority in the Congress. PAN and PRD together could outvote PRI, but they are from opposite ends of the political spectrum and agree only in their dislike of PRI. Conservative PAN favors a free-market economy and curbs on spending, radical PRD the opposite. That kind of legislative deadlock persuades some voters to return to PRI as the only party that can run the country. Unless PAN can achieve majority status (unlikely) or get cooperation from some PRI senators and deputies (difficult), it can do little in Congress. This deadlock doomed the Fox *sexenio*.

MEXICO'S DOMINANT-PARTY SYSTEM

We mentioned that Britain is a "two-plus" party system: two big parties and several small ones. Some countries might be called "one-plus" party systems, for they are dominated by parties so big that they seldom lose. Mexico's PRI, Japan's Liberal Democrats, and Putin's United Russia are examples. India, under the long reign of the Congress party, used to be, but has since experienced electoral alternation.

In a dominant-party system (see page 136), other parties are perfectly legal, but the dominant party is so well-organized and has so many resources that upstart parties seldom have a chance. In some cases, the party founded the country, as the Congress party under Ghandi did in India. The big parties dominate the media and civil service. Voters may acknowledge that the dominant party is corrupt, but they may also like the stability and prosperity it has brought. Many Japanese voters see the Liberal Democrats in this light. When the dominant party can offer neither, as PRI discovered, it may cease to be dominant.

PRI, founded by Calles in 1929, is Mexico's oldest party. As its name attests, it billed itself as revolutionary and socialist long after it abandoned such policies. PRI presidents such as Cárdenas and Luis Echevarría Álvarez took leftist—especially anti-U.S.—stances, but most have been moderate centrists. Calles and Cárdenas designed the party well, with its four sectors and strong patronage network, but as Mexico gained a large middle class, these sectors became less and less important, making PRI out-of-date. Some Mexican commentators call the PRI sector chiefs "dinosaurs." PRI's share of the vote has shrunk, but it still wins in a broad belt across Central Mexico. PRI victories in many state gubernatorial elections augur well for it in the 2006 presidential contest.

PAN was founded in 1939 to oppose PRI on religious grounds. PAN was a Catholic reaction to Calles's anticlericalism. Mexico's Church-state relations have been bloody at times, and serious Catholics felt martyred by the PRI government. In the 1980s, the modern business community, which disliked state-owned industries and economic instability, found PAN a useful vehicle for their discontents. The two strands, Catholic and business, coexist uneasily within PAN and could pull it apart. PAN makes its best showings in Northern Mexico, where proximity to the United States has contributed to prosperity and a capitalist orientation. PAN, still dominated by Catholic militants, is not nearly as well organized as PRI. Mexicans' big 2000 Fox vote did not indicate that they had become conservative Catholics but that they were fed up with PRI. As disappointment with Fox grew, PAN was not expected to win the 2006 elections.

The south of Mexico is the poorest and most radical part of the country. Zapata, a local boy, is remembered. It is here that the new Democratic Revolutionary party (Partido Revolucionario Democrático, PRD) makes its best showing. In 2005 the PRD won the governorship of the southern state of Guerrero (and of Baja California Sur). Cuauhtémoc (the Aztec name may win him some votes) Cárdenas, son of the oil-nationalizer, might have won the 1988 presidential election if not for PRI rigging. Cárdenas, along with a leftist chunk of PRI, split from PRI in 1988 over its turn to free-market policies. PRI had to split; it had abandoned revolution in favor of business. With some Socialists and Communists, Cárdenas in 1989 formed the leftist PRD, which claims to be true to the ideals of his father, anticapitalist and anti-United States. With a much weaker organization and base of support than PRI or PAN, PRD has an uphill struggle. The PRD's Andrés Manuel López Obrador (known as AMLO), the populist mayor of Mexico City, was seen as the strongest candidate for president in 2006.

At this point we might call Mexico a "former dominant-party system," as the PRI has weakened and now faces **bilateral opposition**, that is, both on its left (PRD) and right (PAN). The key factor in PRI's decline: its corruption and the growth of an educated middle class that no longer stands for it. Mexico may be on its way to becoming a multiparty or two-plus party system. The United States is no stranger to dominant-party systems: Most U.S. congressional districts reliably return the same party to Congress, sometimes without opposition.

MEXICAN FEDERALISM

Most countries are unitary systems, but the Western Hemisphere boasts the largest number of the world's federal systems, partly due to the U.S. model and partly to the sprawling geography of many countries. Argentina, Brazil, Canada, and Mexico are federal systems, some more federal than others. Mexico consists of thirty-one states and the Federal District

KEY TERM

bilateral opposition   Centrist parties or governments undermined from both sides.

POLITICAL CULTURE

MEXICO AND AMERICA AS COLONIES

The Spanish colonies of the New World resembled the declining feudal system of Europe. Society was rigidly stratified by birth and race into privileged and lower ranks. The Catholic Church, supervised by Rome, tried to calm Mexico's Indians by both material help and spiritual uplift. Madrid's chief interest in New Spain was in the amount of gold and silver it could ship to the royal treasury. For this, Spain set up Mexico (indeed, all of its Latin American holdings) as vast bureaucracies, which plague the region to this day. Latin America was born bureaucratic. Mexico was Spain's richest colony; its gold and silver funded the giant Habsburg military effort in the Thirty Years War. Under the mistaken doctrine of **mercantilism**, Spain reckoned it was rich, but gold and silver produce neither crops nor manufactured goods. Ironically, as Spain stole the vast wealth of the New World it grew poorer. The extractive industries impoverished Mexico, too.

The English colonizers of Virginia and New England arrived a century after the Spaniards did in Mexico. By the early seventeenth century the feudal age was over in England, and the immigrants carried little feudal baggage or bureaucracy. The colonies largely ran themselves. No one expected quick gold or silver, either for themselves or for London. Although the English brought ranks of nobility with them, most settlers were farmers or merchants with an **egalitarian** ethos. They concentrated on agricultural production. Their several varieties of Protestantism—none of which had Catholicism's central control— taught hard work, delayed gratification, equality, and individuality. They pushed the Indians westward but did not turn them into serfs.

Samuel Huntington's latest controversial book, *Who Are We?*, posits religion as the biggest determinant of political culture. If French, Spanish, or Portuguese Catholics had originally settled the United States, he argues, we would today resemble, respectively, Quebec, Mexico, and Brazil. The fact that we were first settled by Anglo-Protestants has made all the difference.

(Distrito Federal, DF, the equivalent of our D.C.) of Mexico City. Each state has a governor elected for a single six-year term but only a unicameral legislature.

In actuality, Mexican federalism concentrates most power in the center, a bit like Soviet federalism. For most of the twentieth century PRI presidents handpicked state governors, who then used the office as a tryout for federal positions. As in the United States, many Mexican presidents first served as governors, including President Fox. The states get much of their revenue from the national government and then dispense it to the municipalities, a food chain that keeps subordinate levels of government loyal and obedient.

KEY TERMS

mercantilism   Originally French theory that a nation's wealth is the gold and silver in its treasury.

egalitarian   Dedicated to equality.

MEXICAN POLITICAL CULTURE

Mexican political culture—and this is true of much of Latin America—is hard to comprehend because it is a dysfunctional pastiche of several cultures and ideologies: Indian passivity, Spanish greed, Catholic mysticism, populist nationalism, and European anticlericalism, liberalism, anarchism, positivism, and socialism. Unsurprisingly, these many strands never blended. Mexico is regionally, socially, and culturally badly integrated, never forming a coherent whole. Mexican political culture did not grow slowly and locally over time but was imported in waves, mostly from Europe, none of which really sank in enough to create a coherent Mexican political culture. In comparison, most elements of American political culture blend and reinforce each other: freedom, equality, Protestantism, individualism, pragmatism, materialism, market economics, and rule of law. The U.S. creeds that did not easily blend—slavery, Catholicism, and welfarist liberalism—formed America's political divide for several generations.

MEXICO'S INDIAN HERITAGE

Mexico looks Spanish but, many scholars argue, beneath the surface remains very Indian. Indian cultures and languages still survive in isolated villages. Mexico's cuisine is basically Indian. Mexico's spirituality is a blend of pre-Columbian religions and Spanish Catholicism, which was always dipped in blood. The Indians, of course, were used to blood sacrifice at the hands of the Aztecs and took easily to the blood emphasis of Spanish Catholicism. The Spanish Inquisition, which traveled to Mexico and even to New Mexico, also utilized human sacrifice. Since the Spaniards built their great cathedral on the ruins of the main Aztec temple, it is hard to tell the precise reason why it is a pilgrimage site. Is the impulse purely Christian or an echo of pre-Christian religion?

The Aztecs and earlier Mexican societies were strongly hierarchical. Those at the base, peasants, were taught to defer to their social superiors. Social-class distinctions come with civilization. When the Spanish took over from the Aztecs, Indian peasants were used to subordinate behavior; most accommodated to the forced labor of **haciendas** and silver mines. (In contrast, the Indians of the present-day United States had no cities and were highly egalitarian.) The Spanish, of course, brought their own feudal society with them and imposed it on the Indians.

One important demographic point about Mexico is that its Spanish conquerors were exclusively males; Spanish women did not arrive until much later. (The English settled whole families in America.) Very quickly, a new class of persons appeared in Mexico, mestizos, those of mixed descent. **Mestizaje** was also a cultural and social thing, contributing to Mexican Catholicism and the beginnings of a middle class between the Spaniards (later creoles) and the Indians.

KEY TERMS

hacienda   Large country estate with Spanish owner (*hacendado*) and Indian serfs.
mestizaje   Intermingling of Spanish and Indian.

POLITICAL CULTURE

PERSONALISMO AND MACHISMO

Latin American politicians frequently rely on **personalismo** in politics rather than on parties, ideologies, or laws. Said one Mexican diplomat, "In Mexico we have egos, not institutions." Most Latin Americans like to be perceived as having a strong personality, the men especially as *macho* (male), leading to **machismo**. Latin American leaders traditionally combine personalismo and machismo to gain mass support.

After Cárdenas, Mexican presidents of the PRI era, selected by *dedazo,* did not much utilize these qualities because they did not need them. With the recent arrival of competitive politics, however, personalismo and machismo appeared in Mexico. Vicente Fox, for example, ran on his colorful and outspoken personality. Now future Mexican politicians must do the same.

Latin Americans boast, especially to **norteamericanos**, that they are free of racial prejudice. In Latin America, they say, money and manners count for more than skin color in deciding race. A person with the right culture and language is accepted as essentially European. As they say in much of Latin America, "Money lightens" (one's skin color). There is some truth to it, but money and life chances tend to come with racial origin in Latin America. Whites have a much better chance of going to a university, entering a profession, making lots of money, and living in a nice house. Mexicans of Indian descent run a high risk of infant death, malnutrition, poverty, and the lowest-paying jobs or unemployment.

Still, Mexico has done a better job historically than has the United States at letting at least some nonwhites rise to the top. Juárez, of Indian descent, led Mexico in the mid-nineteenth century. Cárdenas and several other presidents were of mestizo descent. The United States has not yet had a comparable racial breakthrough. Most of Mexico's top leaders, in the economy and politics, to be sure, have been white, a point true of Latin America generally. Because few Mexicans are of purely European descent, all Mexican politicians celebrate the country's Indian heritage. There are no statues of Cortés in Mexico, and the quincentennial of Columbus's 1492 voyage was little noticed.

KEY TERMS

personalismo   Politics by strong, showoff personalities.
machismo   Strutting, exaggerated masculinity.
norteamericanos   "North Americans"; U.S. citizens.

DEMOCRACY

SKEPTICAL DEMOCRATS

Latin America (except Cuba) turned democratic in the 1980s, but Latins remain skeptical about democracy. Like Russians, they expected democracy to bring prosperity, and it did not. About half of Latin Americans tell pollsters they prefer democracy, but half also say that an authoritarian government can sometimes be preferable.

Democratic feeling rises and falls with the economy, as most Latins worry about unemployment and poverty. An authoritarian who puts food on the table is not so bad. Further, many Latin Americans perceive all government, democratic or not, as essentially rigged to favor a few powerful interests. Mexico's numbers are typical: The percent preferring democracy stayed at 53 percent from 1996 to 2004. During the same period, however, the percent saying authoritarian rule can be preferable dropped from 23 to 14 percent.

IMPORTED IDEOLOGIES

Latin America is noted for picking up ideas invented elsewhere, warping them, and then trying to apply them where they do not fit. One Latin America expert called the continent a *reliquiario*, a place for keeping old relics of saints, a piece of the true cross, and so on. Now it is a reliquary for old ideas long passé in the rest of the world. This makes Latin American political thought a sort of remainder sale of old ideologies. The following paragraphs discuss some notions still or recently alive in Latin America.

Liberalism here means the original, nineteenth-century variety that rejected monarchy and opened society to new forces. The United States, with its large middle class, took naturally to this philosophy of freedom, but Latin America, encumbered by inherited social positions, big bureaucracies, and state-owned industries, did not. No middle class, no liberalism. Juárez and Díaz could not make liberalism work in Mexico. Some Latin American countries have recently turned to economic *neoliberalism* by trying to build free markets.

Positivism, as discussed earlier, proposed that experts should improve society through science. It died out in Europe but caught on in Latin America, especially Brazil, where its motto, "Order and Progress," is in the flag. In Mexico, Díaz's *científicos* typified the positivist spirit, which conflicts with the hands-off philosophy of liberalism.

Socialism in Europe made sense, as Europe had much industry and a large working class that was amenable to unionization and social-democratic parties, such as Britain's Labour and Germany's Social Democrats. Latin America, however, until recently had little industry and only a small proletariat; it was precapitalist. No working class, no socialism. Governments such as Mexico's and Brazil's invented and coddled unions to make it look like they had a working-class base. Some idealists still see socialism as the answer to Mexico's vast poverty, but they offer no successful examples of it. Chile prospered after it overthrew the Socialist government of Salvador Allende.

Rural socialism rejects industry in favor of small farms. It proposes returning to a rural idyll of equality and sufficiency based on family farming. Zapata was its hero. It idealizes a past that never existed and cannot be: There is simply not enough land for exploding populations. Peasant farming equals poverty. Zapatista guerrillas in Chiapas state in Mexico's south, however, still pursue this **quixotic** vision.

Anarchism is a sort of primitive socialism that argues the end of national government will erase class differences. A small political movement, it caught on only in Spain in the late nineteenth century, where it became anarcho-syndicalism: No government needed because trade unions will run things. Several Mexican revolutionaries were influenced by anarchism.

Anticlericalism, founded by the French writer Voltaire, caught on strongly in Spain and then spread to Latin America. Anticlericalists such as Calles claim the Church has too much political power, favors the rich, and keeps Mexico backward. Few scholars think the Catholic Church in Latin America really had much power. Now the shortage of priests has marginalized it.

Fascism, founded by Mussolini and copied by Hitler, briefly influenced some Latin American countries, especially those with many German and Italian immigrants. It combines nationalism, corporatism, and fake socialism under a charismatic leader. Vargas's Brazilian "New State" drew the quip "fascism with sugar." Perón's Argentina was not as sweet and welcomed Nazi war criminals. Cárdenas's nationalism and socialism hinted at national socialism.

Communism, revolutionary Marxist socialism under Moscow's control, was for decades popular among Latin American intellectuals. It proposed to end the continent's drastic inequality and poverty by the state taking over production and ending U.S. exploitation, a permanent and popular theme. Some of Mexico's leading artists, such as Diego Rivera and David Siqueiros, were Communists. Castro's Cuba and Che's icon drew much support until Latin intellectuals noticed that Cuba is a stagnant tyranny. Although largely defunct, Marxism lingers in *dependency theory*.

Latin American intellectuals have been so addicted to one ideology after another that they fail to notice the rest of the world has already discarded them. Communism, for example, collapsed in East Europe and the Soviet Union and is meaningless in China but is still alive in Cuba, which will likely be the last Communist country in the world, the reliquary of Marx's bones.

PATTERNS OF INTERACTION

Calles and Cárdenas devised a system of **co-optation** that gave the Mexican government control over groups that might otherwise cause them trouble. They promised peasants and labor a good deal but rarely gave them much in return. When rural and worker unions got demanding, the government crushed them. While professing "socialism," Mexican presidents tolerated no competition from Communists, especially after Stalin

KEY TERMS

quixotic   (From Don Quixote) Romantic, unrealistic efforts to achieve mistaken goals.

co-opt   To enroll other groups in your cause, rendering them harmless.

KEY CONCEPTS

DEPENDENCY THEORY

During much of the Cold War, many Latin American intellectuals subscribed to fashionable leftist views that their region's poverty was the result of exploitation by wicked capitalists, especially by *norteamericanos*. After World War II, radicals worked this up into what they called **dependency theory**, that the Third World is economically dependent on the capital, products, and policies of the First World, especially the United States. (Think: U.S. "shark" feeding on Latin American "sardines.") Only by getting out from under the control of U.S. corporations—who dictated what Latin American lands would produce (bananas and coffee) and what they would consume (Chevrolets and Coca-Cola)—would Latin America eliminate poverty. Accordingly, radical regimes such as Cuba, Nicaragua, and currently Venezuela are praiseworthy, because they broke their dependency on the Yankees and instituted independent economic development that would benefit their own peoples.

Dependency theory contains several disputes. It is a type of Marxist theory, but some orthodox Marxists disliked it. Marx saw class conflict *within* a country as the key to its economic and political development. Many Latin American critics blame their continent's poverty on its "predatory class structure," where a few rich families own everything and there is not much of an industrial proletariat. Latin America's problem, in their view, is that it is still saddled with a feudal social structure. Marx had little to say about relations among countries. Lenin made that leap (see Chapter 7) with his claim that some imperialist countries have redone the globe to suit themselves by exploiting their colonial areas. Dependency theory partakes more of Lenin than of Marx. Mexican dependency theorists use Cárdenas as an exemplar of Mexico's efforts to break *dependencia*.

By the 1990s, many dependency theorists came to doubt the theory. Brazilian President Fernando Henrique Cardoso (1995–2002), for example, had been a radical sociologist and promoter of dependency theory, but by the 1980s had abandoned it. A famous Latin American saying: "If you are not a Communist when you're twenty, you have no heart. If you're still a Communist when you're forty, you have no head." Aging wises you up. The demise of Communist regimes in East Europe and the Soviet Union made many wonder if "socialism" really worked. The economic success of Chile, where a military dictator enforced capitalism, made many appreciate market systems and foreign trade. Other Latin American countries restructured their economies in the early 1990s. The results were generally unimpressive, and we may expect a new wave of Latin dependency theory.

had Trotsky assassinated in Mexico in 1940. Even "leftist" presidents such as López Mateos had no trouble arresting Communists and breaking strikes. There was a large element of fakery in PRI governance. Chiefly, they served themselves.

KEY TERM

dependency theory   Radical theory that rich countries exploit Third World lands and keep them poor.

For decades, the Mexican government tried to co-opt students by giving them a nearly free education and then employing them as civil servants. (Saudi Arabia attempted to do the same.) This cannot work forever; there is simply not enough money. Student numbers and discontent grew. Many turned radical and accused PRI of abandoning its commitments to social justice. President Gustavo Díaz Ordaz was obsessed with order and tolerated no criticism. With the 1968 Mexico City Olympics just weeks away, he feared student protests would mar his picture of a modern, happy Mexico. In October at the Plaza of the Three Cultures in Mexico City, police gunned down as many as 400 student protesters. What PRI could not co-opt it crushed. Some mark this as a turning point in PRI rule, the point at which it visibly began to destabilize.

Politics inside PRI

Any party as big as PRI is bound to have factions. The two most relevant are the *políticos* and *técnicos*, politicians and technicians. The *políticos* are populists seeking elected office; they pay heed to mass needs and demands. As such, they pay little heed to economics and are not averse to running up huge deficits. This pleases the crowd but leads to inflation and outcries from foreign investors and international banks for Mexico to get its economic house in order. Presidents Díaz Ordaz (1964–1970), Echevarría (1970–1976), and López Portillo (1976–1982) typify the *político* approach. The relied too much on Mexico's new oil finds and overspent. Eventually, Mexico's economy crashed.

The *técnicos* (known in much of the world as "technocrats") try to fix economic instability. They are more likely to staff appointive positions and worry less about mass demands. Many have studied modern *neo-classical* economics in the United States and see a free market and fewer government controls as the path to prosperity. They urge for Mexico what much of the world calls **neoliberalism**, the return to Adam Smith's original economic ideas. This confuses Americans, as we call it *conservatism*. For Europeans and Latin Americans, however, Britain's Margaret Thatcher instituted a neoliberal economic program. In Chile under Pinochet, the "Chicago boys" (who studied neo-classical economics at the University of Chicago) put neoliberalism into practice with good results.

Presidents Miguel de la Madrid Hurtado (1982–1988) and Carlos Salinas de Gortari (1988–1994) gave technocrats a chance to stabilize the fiscal chaos wrought by the overspending of their predecessors. Actually, these fiscal technicians in PRI implemented some of the free-market reforms that PAN also sought. But reforms provided insufficient regulation, and Mexico's newly freed banks made bad and even crooked loans. Mexico's financial sector crashed in 1995. The peso lost most of its value against the dollar, Mexico's GDP declined by 6.2 percent in 1995 alone, and Mexicans grew poorer. (In 1997, Asian banks folded from exactly the same sort of *crony capitalism*.) The problem is not a lack of bright, well-educated economists. Both PRI and PAN have plenty. The problem is part-way economic reforms that provide freedom without rule of law. These tend to set up wild expansion followed by crashes. Many Mexican groups fight thorough reform, though, and President Fox could accomplish little.

Key Term

neoliberalism   Rediscovery of classic free-market economics.

DEMOCRACY

ELECTIONS AND DEMOCRACY

Americans are given to the notion that elections equal democracy. PRI won fourteen presidential elections in a row, illustrating that democracy is more complex than just balloting. As we considered in Russia (Chapter 9), it involves a great deal of philosophical, moral, social, and legal underpinning, and these tend to come with a large middle class. Elections are just the visible parts and can mislead foreign election monitors, who see little more than the physical balloting on election day and miss the longer-term and less-visible problems. Monitors are getting better, though, and in 2004 called Ukraine's elections rigged, forcing a repeat. Few elections in the Third World are completely free and fair. There are several ways to rig them:

Media Dominance   The big problem is what happens in the weeks and months before the election. To a considerable extent, he who controls television rules the country, as Putin showed in Russia. A country with one or two government-controlled channels will give much news coverage to the ruling party and little to opposition candidates. Paid-for TV advertising may give opposition parties a chance to reach a broad public, so beware any country that bans it. Newspapers can suffer distribution problems and shortage of newsprint.

Bribery   Poor people are often so desperate for money or jobs that they vote for the party that provides them. Mexico's PRI was notorious for rewarding voters. In the 2000 elections in Yucatán PRI gave voters thousands of washing machines, no doubt to insure a clean election.

Ballot Security   Voting is supposed to be secret, but there are techniques to figure out who voted how. Actually, just telling people you know how they voted is often enough to scare them into compliance. This is especially a problem in unsophisticated rural areas. If a whole village does not vote for the party in power, it may miss out on next year's road-repair hires. Ballot boxes can be stuffed in advance. As they used to say in Chicago: "Vote early and often!"

Ballot Counting   Opposition parties may not have enough poll watchers and counters to insure honest counts. They may be barred from watching. Computers do not necessarily make tabulating votes honest. In the 1988 elections, with Cuauhtémoc Cárdenas mounting a major challenge, Mexico's computers tabulating the vote crashed; when they were back up PRI won with a bare 50.4 percent. Over the sixty previous years PRI had never won less than 70 percent.

Amid major complaints of PRI fraud, especially from PAN and PRD, to its credit the PRI government of Salinas in 1990 abolished the Federal Electoral Commission, widely believed to be crooked. In its place, the Federal Electoral Institute (IFE), autonomous and supervised by representatives of all parties, greatly cleaned up Mexican voting at all levels. Immediately, non-PRI parties started winning more votes. IFE demonstrates that Mexico is getting modern and democratic. Recent problems in U.S. vote counts suggest we could use an IFE.

MEXICAN CATHOLICISM

The real sleeper in Mexican politics has been the Roman Catholic Church. More than 90 percent of Mexicans are professed Catholics, some of them quite serious. Since independence, however, the spirit of the Mexican Republic has been generally secular. The Church was never happy with Mexico's break from Spain and tilted strongly conservative. It was conservative Mexican Catholics who convinced Napoleon III that France could take Mexico. The republic tilted in an anticlerical direction, which became especially pronounced in the 1910–1920 Revolution. Its leaders saw the Church as a bastion of upper-class conservatism and reaction. The 1917 constitution imposed limits on Church lands, educational institutions, and religious orders. Detectives ferreted out secret convents and closed them. Priests had to travel in ordinary clothing, without clerical collar. Calles's anticlericalism provoked the Cristero Rebellion. For much of the twentieth century, the Mexican Church was on the defensive.

But the Church never gave up. Through Catholic teachings, lay organizations, schools and universities, and the 1939 founding of PAN, it methodically set the stage for the return of Catholic politics. These are not the politics of a reactionary past but of a modern, business-oriented future. PAN resembles Italy's postwar Christian Democrats, a catchall party that is Catholic but not pietistic.

CRIME AND POLITICS

We have mentioned several Mexican interest groups—labor unions, peasant associations, business, the Catholic Church—but Mexico's most powerful interest group is crime. (Actually, looking at the world as a whole, crime of all sorts is humankind's biggest economic activity.)This is nothing new. Early in human history, the state gave birth to twins—politics, the means of influencing the state, and crime, the means of avoiding the state. Politics and crime know and understand each other quite well, forming an almost symbiotic relationship, one especially clear in a country like Mexico. Politics needs money to win elections and pays little attention to the sources of this money (for example, Japanese Liberal Democratic politicians and *yakuza* gangsters). And crime needs the protection of politics to continue its enterprises (for example, the inability of the Russian police to solve a single assassination). Corruption occurs at the triple interface of the state, politics, and crime. In a weak state, politics, because it is unrestrained, easily turns violent. Crime, because it has little to fear from the state, ignores state power.

Mexico offers good examples. Pancho Villa seamlessly blended banditry and revolution. As we noted, starting with Madero in 1914, assassination of top leaders was common. Assassinations continue in our day. Nosy journalists, zealous prosecutors, and aides to Cuauhtémoc Cárdenas have been gunned down. A Mexican cardinal, possibly mistaken for a drug lord, was riddled with bullets in his limousine. Frustrated with massive crime that the corrupt police did nothing to control, in 2004 a Mexico City mob lynched two cops.

Two killings in 1994 shocked the world and paved the way to Fox's 2000 victory. Luis Donaldo Colosio, PRI's own presidential candidate handpicked by President Salinas, was killed with a shot to the head at an election rally in Tijuana. The deranged shooter was apprehended, but not the one who ordered the hit. Later PRI party secretary general José

GEOGRAPHY

BOUND BRAZIL

Brazil is bounded on the north by Venezuela, Guyana, Suriname, and French Guiana;
on the east by the Atlantic Ocean;
on the south by Uruguay, Argentina, and Paraguay;
and on the west by Bolivia, Peru, and Colombia.

Bounding Brazil enables us to locate all South American countries except Chile and Ecuador.

Ruiz Massieu was shot dead. President Salinas's brother Raúl, who got very rich with drug connections during the *sexenio* of his brother, got fifty years for ordering the killing (but was freed in 2005). President Salinas, who worked his way up as a brilliant U.S.-educated economist, ended his term in disgrace and went into exile in Ireland. Massieu's own brother, a deputy attorney general, was assigned to investigate but resigned, accusing PRI bosses of complicity and coverup. In 2004 the youngest Salinas brother, Enrique, who was suspected of laundering money in France for Raúl, was strangled to death in Mexico City. Colosio may have had an inkling of his murder. Asked shortly before his death by an interviewer about the Salinas family, he replied, "Have you seen *The Godfather?*"

Some good came of the horrors. The 1994 contract killings brought together two trends that had been growing over the years: (1) PRI was stinking more and more, and (2) Mexicans were sufficiently educated and sophisticated to see the system for what it was. A system of control and co-optation that could work amid ignorance and poverty could not work amid a substantial middle class, and Mexico by now had one. Even top *Priístas*, many with U.S. graduate degrees, were ashamed, and embarrassment can be a powerful motivator. It was almost as if PRI knew the game was up. It implemented serious electoral reforms and, to its credit, lost. In 2000 Mexico got its first turnover in power since the Revolution. A second turnover could mark a stable Mexican democracy.

WHAT MEXICANS QUARREL ABOUT

POPULATION AND JOBS

Mexico's population exploded from 16 million in 1935 to 34 million in 1960, a growth rate of 2.8 percent a year. It is now more than triple that but growing at a reasonable 1.2 percent a year. This itself is testimony to the power of economic development to solve the population explosion. Middle-class people turn naturally and with no coercion to small families. Mexico's rate of population increase is not much bigger than the U.S. rate. The difference is that the Mexican rate is held down by emigration while the U.S. rate grows from immigration, much of it from Mexico.

Mexicans do not quarrel about birth rates—Catholic countries seldom do—but they do quarrel about how to create jobs for the millions of unemployed and underemployed. Mexico's institutions and economy simply cannot keep up with its population growth. The Zapatista dream of land for the poor cannot work because there is simply not enough land to redistribute. State-owned industries grow too slowly and employ too few. A state-owned oil industry like Pemex needs only a few trained technicians. It generates a lot of money but not a lot of jobs. (The same is true of Nigeria and the Persian Gulf petrostates.)

The gap between rich and poor in Mexico is huge, as it is throughout Latin America. Economists estimate that the top 4 percent of Mexicans own half of Mexico's wealth while 40 percent of Mexicans live below the poverty line, which is not very high. (Brazil has even greater inequality of wealth and incomes.) With no land or jobs, millions of Mexicans stream to the cities, where they live in shanties and eke out a living selling small items or stealing. Some 22 million Mexicans work off the books, in the "informal economy" (black market), and pay no taxes, contributing to Mexico's chronic federal budget deficits. Mexico City, with a population of over 10 million, is one of the biggest cities in the world, and with some of the world's worst air pollution.

GEOGRAPHY

SHANTYTOWNS

The Third World is characterized by shantytowns, vast tracts of squatter housing that surround most cities, called *barrios coloniales* in Spanish and *favelas* in Portuguese. Many houses are just shacks, but over time some turn into modest homes. Nearly all occupants do not own the land under their dwellings, so they have no legal claim to them and cannot use them as collateral for loans. One Peruvian economist proposes that just giving legal title would yield loans and rapid economic growth.

Some inhabitants of Mexico's *colonias* hold regular jobs, others sell things on the street, and some steal. Crime bosses hold sway in the *colonias.* Mexico's crime rates are astronomical. PRI claims to look out for the poor, but urban poor are neither farmers nor, for the most part, organized workers. No one represents them.

If life is so wretched in the *barrios,* why do Mexicans move there? Because it is even worse in the countryside. Moving to a city for many is a step up, for there they have access to more education and health services and may even find a job. If the Mexican economy worked right, more businesses would start up in the barrios, taking advantage of the low rent and cheap labor. Historically, cities are the incubators of economic growth, even if they are not pretty.

Poverty is especially horrible in the interior south of Mexico, precisely where the Zapatista rebellion started in 1994. Although the Mexican army quickly drove the guerrillas from the towns of Chiapas, they still operate in the mountainous jungles of the region, where they are very hard to catch. Their leader, "Subcomandante Marcos," who is always interviewed with his face covered, speaks eloquently and accurately about Mexico's history of exploitation and poverty and of PRI's betrayal of its promises to uplift the poor. Marcos, however, has no feasible program of his own. He imbibes of the romanticism of the Revolution, as do many Mexicans.

In addition to its obvious injustice, maldistribution of income has several other negative consequences. Some Mexicans go hungry, and many do not earn even the minimum daily wage of $4.50. Poor people have no money to save, which means insufficient capital for investment and growth. Middle-class people save, generating ample capital for investment, as in Germany and Japan. Without domestic capital, Latin American lands must depend on foreign capital, which not everyone likes. (The U.S. middle class also saves little, and the same thing happens: massive inflows of foreign capital, much of it from China and Japan.) The very poor have trouble acquiring the skills needed to lift themselves into the middle class. Schools are inadequate in rural Mexico and in the vast shantytowns around Mexico's cities. The high crime rate frightens away foreign businesses, whose executives are often kidnapped for ransom. Poverty leads to more poverty until it becomes almost endemic. One of the few escape hatches is *el Norte,* sneaking into the United States.

The cures proposed relate to the neoliberal economics mentioned earlier. Populists, leftists, trade unionists, and nationalists—many now clustered in the PRD—want to keep or restore state-owned industries. Privatization of national treasures such as Pemex is deemed a sellout to the foreign capitalists. Mexico's constitution prohibits any private ownership—foreign or domestic—of the country's energy industry. This means lack of investment and shortages; Mexico, which has vast fields of natural gas, must import it from the United States. Young, U.S.-trained economists, on the other hand, recognize that state-owned industries are stagnant, inefficient, corrupt, and employ too few Mexicans. Such people are Panistas or PRI técnicos. Recent PRI presidents have gingerly liberalized Mexico's economy, and Fox wished to go much further.

Oil is an unreliable fix for Mexico's economic problems. Indeed, some Arab intellectuals now speak of their petroleum as a "curse": It skews development away from long-term and balanced growth, employs few, concentrates wealth, and makes the country dependent on the rise and fall of oil prices. (See the Nigeria chapter for further discussion.) When new oilfields were discovered in the south in the 1970s, Presidents Echeverría and López Portillo went crazy with spending. For a while, some Mexicans felt rich, but inflation and the 1995 crash of the peso soon ended that. Mexico, in effect, followed the path of the oil sheiks in squandering new oil revenues to produce a temporary and unsustainable illusion of wealth. Oil is a kind of drug that induces illusions of grandeur.

If Pemex is ever privatized and foreign firms allowed to develop Mexico's oil—both very hot political issues—it will mark the coming of Mexican economic maturity. Yes, the **gringos** want your oil, Mexico, but they pay good money for it and bring badly needed technological improvements. The untouchable status of Pemex as a fountain of corruption does no good for Mexico's economy or political culture.

THE NAFTA QUESTION

Globalization has been a buzzword for some years. Whole books are written either praising it or denouncing it. We need to ask at least two questions about **globalization**: (1) Does it really exist? (2) Does it uplift the poor countries? Basically, globalization is nothing more than trade, and that has been going on for millennia. World trade increased dramatically with Portugal and Spain's voyages of discovery and their trade with, respectively, Asia and Latin America. World trade grew quickly with the steamship and the British Empire, "Victorian globalization." Current globalization, aided by instant communication and rapid transport, just accelerates earlier upward trends.

But globalization does not really cover the globe. Wide areas—especially the Middle East and Africa—are little involved. Globalization extends in a band across North America and Europe, falls off, and picks up again in East Asia. Some developing countries benefit enormously from free trade, namely the *growth dragons* of East Asia. We could nearly cross out *globalization* and put in *China trade*.

KEY TERMS

gringo   (From the Spanish for "gibberish") Foreigner, specifically *norteamericano*, pejorative.

globalization   The world becoming one big capitalist market.

Latin America plays a relatively minor role and is not sure about globalization, because so far it has enjoyed few of its benefits. Some critics cite Latin America's slow or stagnant economic growth as proof that globalization either does not work at all or at least does not work in Latin America, where a rigid class structure stifles growth. China zooms along at nearly 10 percent growth a year, Latin America at a couple percent. Leftists point out that Latin America's gaps between rich and poor are getting bigger. This is true but incomplete. Inequality grows as an economy modernizes, as some poor people climb into the middle class sooner than others. Statistically, this shows up as increasing inequality. If the economy keeps growing, most make it into the middle class, and inequality diminishes. So far, however, globalization has worked no miracles in Latin America.

NAFTA was both hailed and feared. American fear-mongers said U.S. jobs would make a "vast sucking sound" as they drained down to Mexico. Nothing of the sort happened; U.S. employment reached record heights in the late 1990s. Canadian and Mexican nationalists feared the U.S. economy would dominate their two countries. Free-market optimists foresaw economic growth for all.

Actually, not much happened, and that is the trouble. Mexican trade with the United States, which had been growing for years before NAFTA, slowed. The first three years of the Fox administration saw annual GDP growth at less than 1 percent and the loss of 2.1 million jobs. The problem was so obvious that few saw it coming: No one can compete with China. No one. What we thought would be produced in Mexico is produced in China, because it is much cheaper. China has been able to do all the things Mexico (and much of Latin America) cannot. Chinese culture is flexible and adaptable, and its class structure is egalitarian, giving everyone a chance to rise. It may not have a Protestant work ethic, but it has a Confucian work ethic. China's leadership is united in favor of rapid growth based on foreign investment and trade, and no one opposes it. China's labor costs are low, and its productivity is climbing. Related to loss of manufacturing jobs, Mexico's productivity has been declining.

The globalization paradigm did not ask what would be the effects of free trade when one large producer has incredible advantages over all the others. How many giant, low-cost producers can the world take? Will China's productive capacity snuff out all others? Mexicans might paraphrase Díaz and exclaim, "Poor Mexico! So close to the United States, so far from China."

Much of Mexican politics revolves around NAFTA. The left, including PDR people, want to either scrap the whole thing or seriously modify it. PAN is solidly for it; Vicente Fox, with his Coca-Cola background, exemplifies and celebrates globalization as Mexico's way out of poverty. PRI negotiated and ratified NAFTA but has some doubts. It has not produced its expected effects, but home-made Mexican economic instability ruined its first few years. Give it some time, they say, and NAFTA will work. Mexico does not have much time. Its growing population coupled with slow economic growth spells increased poverty and unemployment. To escape them, Mexicans have two poor choices, both related to the United States: illegal immigration and drug smuggling.

Key Term

NAFTA   1994 North American Free Trade Agreement among the United States, Canada, and Mexico.

DRUGS: A MEXICAN OR U.S. PROBLEM?

Mexico grows some marijuana, but cocaine and heroin come from Colombia, Peru, and Bolivia. Mexico is the most important way station, though. Its long border with the United States makes smuggling relatively easy. By air, tunnels, trucks, or "mules," drugs pour into an eager U.S. market. For every kilo found, perhaps twenty or more get through. For several years, drugs on America's streets have gotten cheaper and purer, indicating an excess of supply over demand. We are not staunching the flow.

Drugs are both a Mexican and a U.S. problem. For Mexico, drugs have led the penetration of crime into the highest levels of power. Mexico's police, judicial system, and army have all been corrupted by drug money. Even President Salinas had a brother in the drug trade. In 2005 a spy for a drug cartel was found in President Fox's office. One of the characteristics of the weak state is its penetration by crime. In Mexico, crime and politics depend on each other; drug money helps politicians, and politicians help the traffickers, a difficult cycle to break.

The real problem is the lucrative U.S. drug market. If no Americans took illicit drugs, a wide layer of Latin American crime would disappear. But there are drug users in every town, campus, and walk of life in America. Some think it's cool. They might pause to consider that the **narcotraficantes** murder hundreds and harm the stability and growth of several Latin American lands. Drugs finance the decades-long guerrilla war in Colombia. Catching traffickers and checking border crossings has little impact on overall U.S. drug consumption. The profits from feeding the U.S. drug habit are so great that many join the trade. Where else can a poor person make so much money so fast? In the words of Walt Kelly's Pogo, "We have met the enemy, and he is us."

ILLEGAL OR UNDOCUMENTED?

We call them "illegal immigrants." Mexicans call them "undocumented workers." The Mexico-U.S. border is the only place on earth you can walk from the Third World into the First. For the millions of Mexicans who have made the risky walk, they merely relocated to the northern portion of their republic that the United States seized in 1848. Many die every year, but few worry about breaking the law. The U.S. Border Patrol arrests over 1 million a year and sends them back. Many immediately try again. How many get through is unknown but probably more than 1 million.

The problem of the *indocumentados* parallels the drug problem. There is both a push and a pull. Unemployment and poverty push Mexicans to leave, and jobs and the opportunity to give their families a decent life pull. And Americans do hire Mexicans (and others from further south) with little thought to their immigration status. Many businesses, especially in the U.S. Southwest, depend on cheap Mexican labor. "Heck, he gave me a Social Security number," say many employers. (True, but it's probably the same number used by dozens of illegals.) Few U.S. families could afford household help—maids and gardeners—

KEY TERM

narcotraficante   Drug trafficker.

if they had to hire Americans. This, however, depresses the wages of Americans who might otherwise take these jobs.

Again, this not really a Mexican problem; it's an American problem. The Mexican government, as a humanitarian service, puts out a comic book showing how to survive the dangers and deserts of crossing the border. Mexico wants a better deal from the U.S. administration to accept more immigrants, as either legal or temporary immigrants, and grant amnesty to illegals already here. Most Americans do not want a flood of Spanish-speakers, but employers in clothing, manufacturing, meatpacking, and agriculture quietly resist limits and back it up with campaign contributions. One of President Fox's biggest defeats was in not getting President Bush to make legal Mexican immigration easier. His PRI and PRD opponents sneered, "Thought you were going to get something from your gringo friend? Ha!" But should they come to power they would try to do exactly the same thing.

Going to the United States is both an escape valve for Mexican unemployment and source of **remittances** from those already working here, who each year send back over $14 billion. Remittances are the best form of foreign aid; they bypass corrupt officials and go right to the families who use them to raise children and start businesses. The best thing we could do for Mexico's development is to make remittances safe and cheap.

Modern Mexico?

Can Mexico serve as an example of modernization for a continent where it seems that nothing works right? Compared to most of the rest of Latin America, Mexico is a model of growth and prosperity. With the right policies it might become the *Latin tiger,* rivaling the growth dragons on the other side of the Pacific.

And what is the right policy for growth? The record of the postwar world shows one combination works: low wages and good productivity. When labor costs—and they include taxes and pensions as well as hourly wages—lag behind productivity growth you can produce more and better and earn a share of the world market. Labor costs over time, of course, rise. The trick is to keep productivity rising even faster. You do this through more technology and higher worker skills. The models for the combination of low wages and high productivity: postwar Germany and Japan and present-day China. When German and Japanese labor costs became some of the world's highest, their economic growth flattened. Negative examples include postwar Britain and present-day Mexico.

How can you tell if a country's labor costs are too high and its productivity too low? You do not need elaborate economic calculations. Just note whether foreign or domestic businesses invest there. If domestic businesses park their money overseas—*flight capital,* as we saw in Russia—you know there are problems. Other factors that foster a "hostile business climate" include too many regulations, high taxes, state takeovers, strike-happy unions, crime, and corruption. Clean these up, and you can have rapid growth. Milton Friedman, winner of a Nobel Prize in economics, long extolled the free market as the basis of economic growth. Asked recently if he still thought so, he said he now realizes it is not; the real basis, he said, is rule of law. He might have been speaking of Mexico.

Key Term

remittance   Money sent home.

Key Web Sites

History
mexconnect.com

Biographies
cidob.org/bios/castellano/lideres

Documents
uwaterloo.ca/~aLópez-o/polind.html

University of Texas Latin American Studies
lanic.utexas.edu/la/mexico/

News sources
mexidata.info

El Norte
elnorte.com

El Universal
el-universal.com/mx/noticiash.html

The Herald (English)
el-universal.com/mx/pls/impreso/ol_miami.html

Reforma
reforma.com

Key Terms

austerity (p. 232)
bilateral opposition (p. 240)
Bronze Age (p. 224)
cacique (p. 225)
caudillo (p. 229)
Central America (p. 226)
civilization (p. 223)
clientelism (p. 234)
constitutionalism (p. 234)
co-opt (p. 245)
corporatism (p. 234)
creole (p. 228)
dedazo (p. 237)
dependency theory (p. 246)
egalitarian (p. 241)

ejido (p. 231)
globalization (p. 253)
gringo (p. 253)
hacienda (p. 242)
institutionalize (p. 235)
Latin America (p. 226)
machismo (p. 243)
mercantilism (p. 241)
Mesoamerica (p. 223)
mestizaje (p. 242)
NAFTA (p. 254)
narcotraficante (p. 255)
neoliberalism (p. 247)
Neolithic (p. 224)
norteamericano (p. 243)

personalismo (p. 243)
political institution (p. 235)
political power (p. 235)
Positivism (p. 230)
pre-Columbian (p. 226)
priísmo (p. 232)

quixotic (p. 245)
remittance (p. 256)
sexenio (p. 232)
South America (p. 226)
statism (p. 234)

FURTHER REFERENCE

Ai Camp, Roderic. *Politics in Mexico: The Decline of Authoritarianism*, 4th ed. New York: Oxford University Press, 2001.

Castañeda, Jorge. *The Mexican Shock*. New York: New Press, 1995.

Chand, Vikram. *Mexico's Political Awakening*. Notre Dame, IN: University of Notre Dame Press, 2001.

Crandall, Russell, Guadalupe Paz, and Riordan Roett, eds. *Mexico's Democracy at Work: Political and Economic Dynamics*. Boulder, CO: L. Rienner, 2004.

Fuentes, Carlos. *A New Time for Mexico*. New York: Farrar, Strauss and Giroux, 1996.

Krauze, Enrique. *Mexico: Biography of Power: A History of Modern Mexico, 1810–1996*. New York: HarperCollins, 1997.

Merrell, Floyd. *The Mexicans: A Sense of Culture*. Boulder, CO: Westview, 2003.

Mizrahi, Yemile. *From Martyrdom to Power: The Partido Acción Nacional in Mexico*. Notre Dame, IN: University of Notre Dame Press, 2003.

Needler, Martin C. *Mexican Politics: The Containment of Conflict*, rev. ed. Westport, CT: Greenwood, 1995.

Peeler, John. *Building Democracy in Latin America*, 2nd ed. Boulder, CO: L. Rienner, 2004.

Peschard-Sverdrup, Armand B. *Forecasting Mexico's Democratic Transition: Scenarios for Policymakers*. Washington, D.C.: Center for Strategic and International Studies, 2003.

Rubio, Luis, and Susan Kaufman Purcell, eds. *Mexico Under Fox*. Boulder, CO: L. Rienner, 2004.

Shirk, David A. *Mexico's New Politics: The PAN and Democratic Change*. Boulder, CO: L. Rienner, 2005.

Tulchin, Joseph S., and Andrew D. Selee, eds. *Mexico's Politics and Society in Transition*. Boulder, CO: L. Rienner, 2003.

Ungar, Mark. *Elusive Reform: Democracy and the Rule of Law in Latin America*. Boulder, CO: L. Rienner, 2002.

Youngers, Coletta A., and Eileen Rosin, eds. *Drugs and Democracy in Latin America: The Impact of U.S. Policy*. Boulder, CO: L. Rienner, 2004.

14

Nigeria

Nigeria is important. It has the largest population in Africa—one fifth of Africans south of the Sahara are Nigerians—and larger than any European country. It is the world's seventh largest oil producer and the fifth largest oil supplier to the United States, so we often treat it as little more than a gas station, like we did the Persian Gulf. Such places do not stay "gas stations" but instead turn into zones of chaos and conflict. Nigeria has much influence in Africa and, along with South Africa, has led peacekeeping operations in several African countries. Nigeria is also attempting, for the third time, to establish democracy in a situation that could explode at any time. Nigerian democracy deserves our support.

THE IMPACT OF THE PAST

Nigeria, like Mexico, was home to civilizations long before the coming of Europeans. The Nok culture, adept at grain farming and iron smelting, created an inland kingdom around the time of Christ at the southern end of the trade route from North Africa. Starting in the eleventh century A.D., the Yoruba built a series of city-states in the southwest under a king in the city of Ife. Only the Igbo (also known as Ibo) appear to have been stateless; they lived in egalitarian, self-contained villages in the southeast. There was never a single kingdom of Nigeria.

Islam arrived from the Sudan region in the Sahel of northern Nigeria in the ninth century A.D. and converted the Hausa and Fulani peoples, who are often known as the Hausa-Fulani. The Borno kingdom and later Songhai empire were seats of Islamic learning and culture. Islam also meant that Nigeria would inherit a tragic split between a Muslim north and a largely Christian south, the

Questions to Consider

1. What and where are Nigeria's religions?
2. What and where are Nigeria's main ethnic groups?
3. What were colonialism's effects on Africa?
4. Nigeria modeled its institutions after which country's?
5. How does Nigeria illustrate "praetorianism"?
6. What do the Igbo and Biafra illustrate?
7. What are the macroeconomy and microeconomy?
8. What did oil do to Nigeria's economic development?
9. Why does not fragmented Nigeria just fall apart?
10. Can corruption be measured objectively?
11. Could Nigeria's PDP become like Mexico's PRI?

GEOGRAPHY

SAHARA, SAHEL, SAVANNA

African geography can be looked at as climate bands running east to west. The northernmost of these bands, the Sahara, is very dry, and the south, close to the equator, is very rainy. The Sahara was not always a desert, but about 5,000 years ago its **desiccation** began, making it difficult to traverse and leaving **sub-Saharan** Africa semi-isolated.

Traders, raiders, and Muslim armies occasionally crossed from North Africa into the **Sahel**, which includes northern Nigeria. With uncertain rainfall, the Sahel can be used for little more than cattle grazing, so human populations are thin. The Sahara has been expanding southward as the Sahel gets drier. Some blame this on global warming, others on ice ages, and still others blame growing populations of cattle growers for drawing too much water from its very limited **aquifer**.

South of the Sahel are Africa's vast **savannas**, characterized by hot wet summers and hot dry winters. Much of Nigeria, indeed much of Africa, is savanna. Here rainfall permits farming. Only the south of Nigeria, along the coast of the Gulf of Guinea, has the lush rain forest that some suppose covers most of Africa. Actually, this region of year-round rainfall occupies only the equatorial band of Africa.

source of much conflict today. Today, 29 percent of Nigeria's population are Hausa-Fulani, 21 percent Yoruba, 18 percent Igbo, and 10 percent Ijaw. These are the largest of Nigeria's approximately 250 ethnic groups.

THE COMING OF THE EUROPEANS

Nigeria, like Mexico, was launched by the voyages of discovery. Portuguese navigators, in their effort to round Africa to tap the wealth of Asia, in 1471 were the first Europeans to reach what was much later called Nigeria. The Portuguese began a pattern later followed by other Europeans. They did not venture far inland—climate and disease made that unpleasant—but set up trading forts along the African coast.

They soon found their chief item of trade: slaves. Slavery had always been practiced in Africa; most were used locally, but some were exported to North Africa. Starting with

KEY TERMS

desiccation Drying out.
sub-Saharan Africa south of the Sahara.
Sahel Narrow band south of Sahara, arid but not yet desert.
aquifer Underground water-bearing layer.
savanna Tropical grasslands south of *Sahel*.

the Portuguese, local African chiefs, by raiding and kidnapping, delivered slaves to the burgeoning European slave trade on the coast, which became known as the *slave coast*. Portugal's colony of Brazil and Spain's colony of Cuba needed labor for their sugarcane fields. England's American colonies needed labor for their cotton and tobacco fields. From the 1530s to the 1850s Portuguese, Spanish, French, English, and later Americans shipped over 3.5 million Africans across the Atlantic, chiefly to Brazil (which took perhaps six times as many as the United States did). Due to this brutal trade, many Americans, Brazilians, and Cubans are of Yoruba or Igbo ancestry.

An Islamic *jihad* from 1804 to 1808 in the northern region was little noticed by Europe but contributed to Nigeria's current difficulties. Islamic scholars, in a familiar pattern, found the Muslim kingdoms there insufficiently pure and demanded their overthrow. That done, they set up what was known as the Sokoto **Caliphate**, a single political system much more powerful than any other in the region, and one motivated by Islamic fundamentalism. In less than a century, it collided with British colonialism.

Famed Scottish explorer Mungo Park, often wracked with fever, explored the Niger River from 1795 to 1806 until he drowned while trying to canoe down it. Few ventured after him until quinine was developed for use against malaria in the 1850s. Christian missionaries arrived to work among the Yoruba, Igbo, and others, setting up missionary posts on the coast. Missionaries were often the advance element of imperial expansion, as protecting them soon required a military presence.

It was Britain's suppression of the slave trade that led to the establishment of Nigeria. Under pressure from British Christians, Parliament in 1807 outlawed the shipping of slaves (but not slavery itself, which Parliament ended in the British Empire in 1834). To enforce the ban, the Royal Navy stationed a squadron in the Gulf of Guinea. To replace the slave trade, Britain encouraged trade in palm oil, used for soaps and lubricants. An example of "unforeseen consequences," the move stimulated the capture of more slaves, who were needed to produce and transport the palm oil. To suppress this internal trade, Britain first shelled Lagos, the Yorubas' island capital, in 1851 and then annexed it in 1861.

THE SCRAMBLE FOR AFRICA

The Niger (from the Latin for *black*) River, the greatest river of West Africa, rises far to the west in Guinea, only 150 miles from the Atlantic, and makes a 2,600-mile semicircle, at first north through Mali, then turning south through Niger and finally Nigeria. During the nineteenth century, trade along the Niger, much of it in cocoa, became more profitable. In response to calls from missionaries, a Scottish explorer made monthly steamboat runs up the lower reaches of the Niger.

British businessman George Goldie, the "father of Nigeria," set up the United Africa Company in 1879 and turned it into the chartered Royal Niger Company in 1886, after the Berlin Conference (see box on page 262) had carved up Africa and assigned borders to European imperial powers. The conference stated, however, that no power could claim what it did not occupy, setting off a race to turn vague claims into colonies. This "scramble for Africa" prompted the British to grab Nigeria before the French could.

KEY TERM

caliphate   Islamic dynasty.

GEOGRAPHY

BOUNDARIES IN AFRICA

The boundaries of Africa are especially artificial. Notice how several of Africa's borders are straight lines, a sure sign that a border is artificial. Many of the ones for Central Africa were settled at a conference in Berlin in 1885, the great "carve-up" of Africa to settle overlapping claims of imperial powers. The British envisioned owning a band of Africa running the entire length of the continent, "from Cairo to the Cape." After pushing the Germans out of Tanganyika in World War I, they achieved this. Their great competitors, the French, turned a great swath of Africa running east-west across the continent's great bulge into French West Africa and French Equatorial Africa. Portuguese, Germans, and Belgians took smaller areas of Africa.

The imperialist-imposed, artificial boundaries cut through tribes and forced together unworkable combinations of tribes. A river in Africa is a poor border because typically people of the same tribe live along both banks. In 1963, however, with most of Africa independent, the new Organization of African Unity (renamed African Union in 2002) decided not to change the Berlin borders and even put them in its charter. The new leaders were afraid both of unleashing chaos and of losing their governing jobs. Best to leave these artificial borders alone, they figured. In Africa, the imperialists' land grabs became permanent boundaries.

THE COLONIAL INTERLUDE

In 1894 real British colonialism took shape with the arrival of Fredrick Lugard, one of a remarkable handful of energetic Englishmen who dedicated their lives to the British colonial service and the vision of a British Empire that brought peace and prosperity to the world. To do this, they often used their new Maxim gun on the natives, as Lugard did in many colonial battles around the world. Lugard consolidated the areas of the Yoruba and Igbo—who fought a guerrilla war against him—into two British protectorates and in 1900 moved into the Muslim north with a military force. By 1903 he had captured Kano and Sokoto to form the Protectorate of Northern Nigeria. In 1914 Sir Frederick (he was knighted) combined Southern and Northern Nigeria into nearly its present form under a governor-general in Lagos. (A piece of the German-ruled Cameroon was added on the east after World War I.) In classic imperial fashion, Lugard invented Nigeria, and his wife, a journalist, invented the name Nigeria.

Lugard used two British colonialist styles, the twin policies of **indirect rule** and **divide and rule**. With only a few hundred white men the British ran colonies as vast as India by

KEY TERMS

indirect rule   British colonial governance through native hereditary rulers.

divide and rule   Roman and British imperial ruling method of setting subjects against each other.

KEY CONCEPTS

COLONIALISM

Colonialism means several things. From the legal point of view, a colony lacks sovereignty; ultimate lawmaking authority resides in a distant capital. London controlled the laws governing Nigeria, Paris those of Senegal, and Brussels those of the Congo. For the most part, the "natives" were kept politically powerless, as the imperial power deemed them too backward and ignorant. The British in Nigeria and other colonies gave chiefs some local responsibility.

From the economic point of view, colonialism involved exploitation by the imperial country. The colonies supplied cheap agricultural and mineral raw materials, which the imperial country manufactured into industrial products that it sold back to the colonies. Marxists argue that colonies were captive markets that were kept poor in order to enrich imperialists. Actually, most colonies cost imperial governments more to administer and defend than they earned. Individual firms, to be sure, often made lush profits in the colonial trade.

Racially, colonies were governed on the basis of skin color on the principle that "the lowest of the Europeans is higher than the highest of the natives." A French policeman directing traffic in Algiers was superior to an Algerian doctor. A Dutch clerk in Jakarta was the social better of an Indonesian professor. Racism was an important part of colonialism; it psychologically enabled the imperialists to govern millions of unlike peoples who did not want them there. It also contributed much to the rage felt by educated subjects, some of whom became leaders of independence movements: "You treat me like dirt in my own country. Well, that will stop!"

In hindsight, colonialism stands condemned as brutal and evil. But it was the unavoidable outcome of the restless, dynamic West encountering the traditional areas of the globe that looked like easy pickings. The imperial powers had no right to conquer and govern others; they simply had guns. Of course, without colonialism there would be no United States. *Colonial* has a nice sound to Americans, connoting hardy settlers, Thanksgiving, and pretty landscapes. It has a bitter ring for most other peoples. Colonialism left a chip on the shoulders of the Third World and helps explain lingering anti-West feelings.

working with and through local chiefs and princes, who were bought off with titles and honors. The French, who practiced a much more direct rule and were reluctant to turn over local responsibilities to natives, needed thousands of Frenchmen to staff their colonies. The British were far more efficient.

Divide and rule is an old technique of the Roman Empire: *divide et impera* in Latin. Its logic: "If you keep them divided you can easily rule them. United they could throw you out." Under this policy colonialist officials emphasized the distinctiveness of cultures, powers, and territories of existing tribes to set them against each other. There were always tribes in

KEY TERM

colonialism   Gaining and exploitation of overseas territories, chiefly by Europeans, related to *imperialism*.

GEOGRAPHY

BOUND NIGER

Bounding Niger (a former French colony easy to confuse with Nigeria) teaches us more African geography than bounding Nigeria.

Niger is bounded on the north by Algeria and Libya;
on the east by Chad;
on the south by Nigeria (a former British colony), and Benin;
and on the west by Burkina Faso (formerly Upper Volta) and Mali.

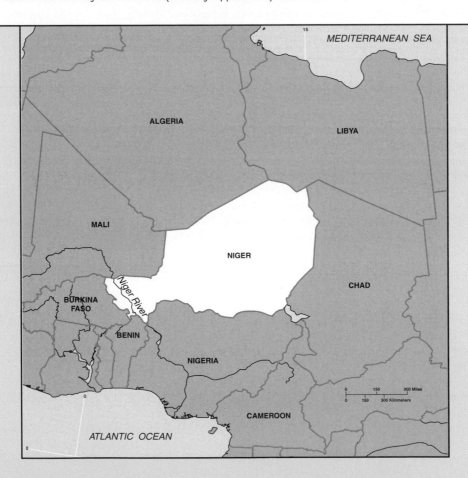

Africa, but some scholars claim the Europeans hyped tribalism to facilitate their rule. The often-murderous tribalism found today owes something to colonialist manipulations.

Colonialism, however, is a wasting asset. The more you organize and educate the natives, the more they want to throw you out. Missionary activity ensured a growing number of educated Africans, some through college level. In the 1920s, especially in the British colonies of Africa, intellectuals developed **pan-Africanism** to liberate the continent from European domination. They argued that without the imperialists to divide them, Africans of all tribes could get along in a united Africa. The British strategy for handling growing political claims from Africans was to cede them local and partial political power in small steps. In 1914 the British established a Nigerian Legislative Council in Lagos and enlarged it with elected members in 1922. It had limited powers and did not include the north. Actually, Britain pursued fairly enlightened colonial policies that may have prevented the worst violence during and after independence. The Belgians, on the other hand, gave the Congolese nothing, trained them for nothing, prepared them for nothing. Result: When Belgium, after some riots, hastily granted the Congo independence in 1960, it erupted into civil war and is still strife-torn.

INDEPENDENCE

World War II weakened the European empires both materially and psychologically. They could no longer afford or justify ruling distant, unlike peoples. **Decolonization** came first as a trickle and then as a flood: India and Pakistan in 1947, Israel (formerly Palestine) in 1948, Indonesia (Dutch East Indies) in 1949, Ghana (Gold Coast) in 1957, then, in 1960, seventeen countries, mostly British and French colonies in Africa. Where there were many European settlers—Algeria, Kenya, and Rhodesia—decolonization was long, hard, and violent, as the settlers wanted to keep their privileged status. Where there were few settlers—West Africa in general, including Ghana, Sierra Leone, and Nigeria—decolonization was easy. By the mid-1960s all the old African colonies had been liquidated except for Portugal's Angola, Mozambique, and Guinea-Bissau. The first European empire was also the last. In 1975, Lisbon too gave way. After white-ruled Rhodesia became black-ruled Zimbabwe in 1980, South Africa was the last white-ruled country in Africa, and this ended in 1994 with the election of a black government under Nelson Mandela. Africa returned to African hands.

To work for independence, the first Nigerian political party was founded in 1923. Herbert Macaulay, grandson of a prominent African Christian minister, founded the Nigerian National Democratic party. Macaulay, whom the British fought, is now called the father of Nigerian independence. The Nigerian Youth Movement was founded as a nationwide party in 1934. Macaulay and Nnamdi Azikiwe ("Zik"), a U.S.-educated Igbo, in 1944 brought together more than forty groups to form the National Council of Nigeria and the Cameroons (NCNC). World War II, in which Nigerian soldiers served in the

KEY TERMS

pan-Africanism   Movement to unite all Africa.

decolonization   The granting of independence to colonies.

GEOGRAPHY

BOUND THE DEMOCRATIC REPUBLIC OF CONGO

The Democratic Republic of Congo (formerly Zaire, earlier the Belgian Congo), is bounded on the north by Central African Republic and Sudan;

on the east by Uganda, Rwanda, Burundi, and Tanzania;

on the south by Zambia and Angola;

and on the west by the Atlantic, the Angolan exclave of Cabinda, and (the formerly French) Congo-Brazzaville.

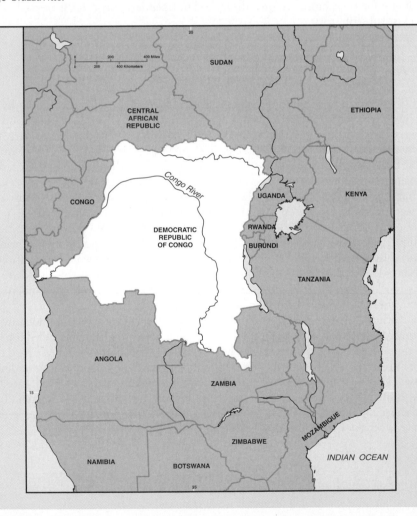

POLITICAL CULTURE

NIGERIA'S POLITICAL ERAS

Even more than Mexico, Nigeria is badly fragmented and lacks a unifying political culture. Consciousness focuses on religions, tribes, and regions. The brief British colonial period had given some Nigerians a modern education and did give a semblance of unity to Nigeria's elites but was not nearly enough to psychologically unify Nigeria as a nation. Nigeria's elites mostly know each other, but they look out more for their tribes than for Nigeria as a whole, as the tribes are their supporters.

Era	Years	Remembered for
Slave trade	1530–1820	Massive export of humans
Pre-Colonial	1820–1894	Suppression of slave trade; British explorers and missionaries
Colonial	1894–1960	By 1914 Lugard consolidates regions into one colony named Nigeria
Independence	1960–1963	Commonwealth member, falls apart
First Republic	1963–1966	Becomes republic
Military rule	1966–1979	Coups, Biafra War
Second Republic	1979–1983	Presidential system, corrupt civilian rule
Babangida	1983–1993	Long military dictatorship
Third Republic	1993	Abortive transition to democracy
Abacha	1993–1998	Cruel and corrupt military dictatorship
Fourth Republic	1999–	Another attempt at democracy under Obasanjo

British army, made subject peoples ask what the struggle against fascism meant when they still lived under authoritarian colonial regimes. The British had no good answer. By now many Nigerians were calling for independence.

The British strategy was to give way piecemeal. In 1947 they set up a federal system—the only plausible solution to Nigeria's regional differences—with Northern, Western, and Eastern regions, corresponding, respectively, to the three largest ethnic groups, the Hausa-Fulani, the Yoruba, and the Igbo. (It is now divided into smaller states.) In 1951 they set up a national House of Representatives, but it fell apart over the question of who represented what, a harbinger of the Nigerian fragmentation that would later wreck the country. In 1954 they made the Nigerian federation self-governing with a Muslim prime minister from the north. Western and Eastern regions got internal self-government, the Eastern under Azikiwe and the NCNC and the Western under Chief Obafemi Awolowo, a lawyer who founded the Action Group, a party for Yoruba. Parties in Africa tend to form along tribal lines.

Nigeria's big problem was clear: How to make the huge Muslim Northern province and the two mostly Christian Southern provinces into one Nigeria. They do not go together easily or naturally. The chief party of the North was the People's Congress, which was always wary that the mostly Christian Eastern and Western peoples and parties would dominate the region. Muslims do not like being ruled by non-Muslims. A parallel happened earlier in India, where in 1906 the Muslim League split off from the Indian National Congress and eventually got a separate Pakistan in 1947.

Britain left Nigeria with a federal constitution and a prime minister that looked pretty good on paper. As in India, the British political position in Nigeria had become impossible to sustain; they had to leave and planned it for years. On October 1, 1960, Britain granted Nigeria independence. It had been a formal colony less than sixty years but had experienced European imperialism for much longer. The imperialists take much blame for Nigeria's troubles. They deranged it with a massive slave trade, took it over at gunpoint, cobbled together an artificial country composed of tribes who disliked each other, and then left. Thus it was not surprising that Nigeria, weak from the start, should collapse into military dictatorships. Nigeria is not unique; it is the story of many nations created by the imperialists.

The Key Institutions

In the first forty-five years of independent Nigeria, civilians ruled only sixteen years, little more than a third of the time. The other two-thirds of the time were military rule under six different generals, some more brutal and greedy than others. The current period of civilian rule, starting in 1999, is the longest one. We hope it will continue but must be forever mindful that Nigeria is still an unstable country with strong tendencies to fall apart. When that threatens the military takes over.

The U.S. Model

Nigerian federalism resembles the U.S. variety. Nigeria's rulers, some of them military dictators, progressively increased the number of states, from twelve, to nineteen, to thirty-one, to the present thirty-six. Every few years the map of Nigeria is redrawn. This is done to calm Nigeria's many ethnic groups, who often feel trapped in a state dominated by another group. When they turn violent, which is often, Nigeria is inclined to carve out a new state for them. It may have worked, as there is less violence between ethnic groups now but never zero.

In 1991 the military dictator Ibrahim Babangida (1985–1993) moved the capital from the old colonial capital of Lagos on the coast to Abuja, a new capital in the precise center of the country. The move resembled Brazil's shift of capital from Rio de Janeiro to Brasília in 1960 to open up the interior. The purpose of the move in Nigeria was to take the capital out of Yoruba hands and put it in more neutral territory. Abuja is now designated the Federal Capital Territory, rather like the District of Columbia. Like Brasilia, Abuja is in the middle of nowhere and has been costly and inefficient.

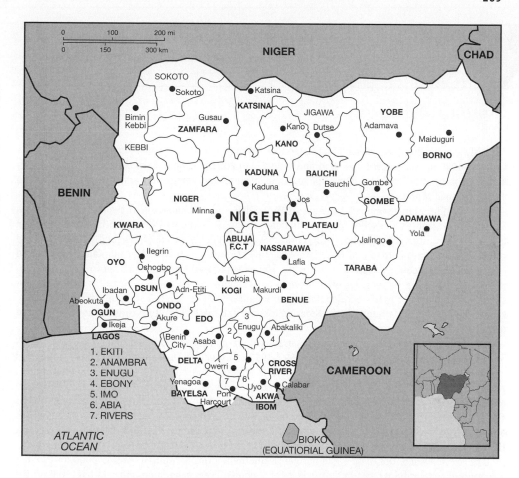

The British set up Nigeria on the Westminster model with a prime minister as chief of government, but the 1979 constitution, now somewhat modified, turned Nigeria into a U.S.-style presidential system, and for a good reason. The British system depends on one party winning a majority of seats in Commons, almost always the case in Britain. But if the legislature is fragmented into many parties, as it was in Nigeria's earlier years, the government must form multiparty coalitions and can fall easily on votes of no-confidence. A U.S.-type presidential system avoids this, as the president can govern with or without majority support in the legislature. Presidents stay until the end of their terms and cannot easily be ousted. Nigeria's president, like the U.S. president, combines head of state with chief of government (see page 39) for a maximum of two four-year terms. Olusegun Obasanjo was the first president of Nigeria's Fourth Republic that emerged after the dictator Sani Abacha died.

THE NATIONAL ASSEMBLY

The U.S. model is again evident in Nigeria's legislative branch, the bicameral National Assembly, which meets in Abuja. The Senate has 109 seats; each of the thirty-six states has three Senate seats plus one for the Federal Capital Territory. The House of Representatives has

PERSONALITIES

OLUSEGUN OBASANJO

Curiously, elected President Olusegun Obasanjo had earlier (1976–1979) been an unelected military president. In 1999 he was elected president and reelected in 2003 as candidate of the centrist People's Democratic party (PDP) on a platform of reducing poverty and corruption and restoring dignity to much-maligned Nigeria.

A Yoruba Christian born north of Lagos in 1937, Obasanjo was educated at the Baptist Boys' High School and worked as a teacher for a year before joining the army in 1958. With further training in England and military cadet school, Obasanjo moved up quickly as an officer and headed an elite commando unit that helped end the Biafra War. In 1975, when Brigadier Murtala Ramat Mohammed seized power in a coup, Obasanjo was deputy. When Mohammed was assassinated in 1976, Obasanjo become military president. He established a good reputation by appointing to his cabinet representatives of all major tribes and leaving power voluntarily to an elected civilian president in 1979, the first time for such a handover in Nigerian history. The 1979 U.S.-style constitution was drafted under Obasanjo.

Obasanjo became a top Nigerian diplomat and at one point was even mentioned as a possible UN Secretary General. Dictator Sani Abacha (1993–1998), suspecting Obasanjo of plotting a coup, had him imprisoned. When Abacha died, Obasanjo was released and ran for the presidency for the PDP, which became Nigeria's biggest and best-organized party. He won in 1999 with 63 percent of the vote and was reelected in 2003 with 62 percent, indicating his ability to attract voters from all regions. His chief opposition in 2003 was another former general who had pulled a coup in 1983, Muhammad Buhari, a Muslim from the North and candidate of the All Nigeria People's party (ANPP), who won 32 percent. Nigeria's civilian government has military roots.

Like Fox in Mexico, Obasanjo could not get nearly the reforms he wanted, even though his PDP has a comfortable majority of seats in both houses of Congress. Every Nigerian group that lives well off the present corrupt setup—state governors, unions, executives of the many state-owned corporations, and the bureaucracy—resists reforms. In another parallel to Mexico, Obasanjo works with a team of young technocrats, many educated in the United States, who understand the urgent need for reforms to the economy. Many think Obasanjo is a genuine patriot and the best president Nigeria ever had, even though he did not accomplish much in office. Many fear what will come after Obasanjo's second term ends in 2007.

360 seats, ten for each state, each representing a single-member district. Both houses are elected for four-year terms at the same time.

The Nigerian setup departs from its U.S. model because its states get the same ten seats regardless of population. It would be like the United States having two Senates. Nigeria feels it must do this to appease smaller ethnic groups with their own states. Appeasing the smaller groups, however, creates resentment in the more populous states that they are underrepresented. The U.S. solution—a Senate to represent states on the basis of equality and a House to represent districts on the basis of population—strikes us as a good compromise, but we do not have Nigeria's touchy ethnic situation. The danger in Nigeria is *hyperfederalism,* a system that tries too hard to represent ethnic groups. It seems to work for a while but can lead to the country falling apart, as it did in Yugoslavia.

NIGERIA'S PARTIES

Freedom House is skeptical about democracy in Nigeria and rates it only 4, "partly free," but better than Russia (which earned a 5.5). The 2003 Nigerian elections were seriously flawed—registration for favored parties, missing ballots, stuffed boxes, and intimidation—but most Nigerians, remembering the years of Abacha's brutal military rule, accepted the officially reported results:

Party	Senate		House	
	Vote	*Seats*	*Vote*	*Seats*
PDP	53.7%	76	54.5%	223
ANPP	27.9	27	27.4	96
AD	9.7	6	8.8	34

The PDP bills itself as a centrist party, but to a considerable extent it is the personalistic vehicle of President Obasanjo. The smaller ANPP gets its strongest following among Northern Muslims; some of its leaders earlier supported the brutal dictatorship of Sani Abacha (1993–1998) and got rich during it. The Alliance for a Democracy (AD) is a Yoruba party that does well on its southwest home turf but is weaker elsewhere. There are other smaller parties, some of them militant Northern Muslim parties, which win one or two seats in the House.

The evolution of Nigeria's party system is a hopeful sign. From many parties—nearly one per tribe—Nigeria seems to have evolved into a "two-plus" party system, a bit like Mexico's. The PDP is a well-funded and well-organized nationwide party and draws votes from all ethnic groups, including many Muslims. The big question: Could the PDP become Nigeria's PRI? Whatever negative one might say about Mexico's dominant party (see the Mexico chapter), it got Mexico out of praetorianism and held it together during times of rapid change and modernization. The PRI analogy may not fit Nigeria, as most Northern Muslims do not support the PDP; some vote for regionalist and Islamist parties. Mexico has troublesome regions, but none with different religions. Nigeria parallels Iraq in its fragmentation. Like Iraq, Nigeria has three major ethnic groups that British imperialists forced into a single artificial state. Some suggest that letting Nigeria and Iraq fall apart into their three main components might not be the worst solution.

The Third World

GEOGRAPHY

Bound Guinea

Guinea, a former French colony in West Africa not to be confused with Guyana in South America, is bounded on the north by Guinea-Bissau, Senegal, and Mali;

on the east by the Ivory Coast;

on the south by Liberia and Sierra Leone;

and on the west by the Atlantic Ocean.

NIGERIAN POLITICAL CULTURE

NIGERIAN FRAGMENTATION

Half of Nigerians are Muslim; another 40 percent are Christian, and 10 percent practice indigenous faiths, for example, the Yoruba religion. In Mexico we spoke of regionalism, but Nigeria's problem is far worse as it tends to fragment along religious and regional lines. Eastern, Western, and Northern regions have trouble living together and exist within Nigeria only because the British colonialists set up an artificial country. The North is especially different—poor, isolated, traditional, and Muslim. It has never liked being ruled by Christians, either British or southern Nigerians. If they had to be in a single country, the northerners always sought to be its rulers. Many especially dislike President Obasanjo for being a born-again Christian who supports the U.S. war on terror. The fundamentalist Islamic Movement of Nigeria has al Qaeda and Iranian ties.

Islam has been the chief religion in Northern Nigeria for a millennium, and, like Islam elsewhere in Africa, has been spreading south by vigorous proselytizing. African Muslims argue that Islam is the natural religion for Africa because it pays no attention to skin color and has deep roots in Africa, whereas Christianity is a recent arrival brought by Europeans with an implicit racism.

Islam, however, can be rigid and intolerant. Some insist on a strictly religious education in Arabic and memorizing the Koran. Muslim preachers insist on Islamic purity, sometimes for all of Nigeria. In the North now a strong fundamentalist movement demands making **sharia** state law, and several Northern states have done so. This does not sit well with Nigerian Christians and federal authorities, because it means states can override national laws. Christians living in the Northern states would also come under *sharia,* which, for example, punishes adulterous women (but rarely men) by stoning to death and thieves by chopping their hands off. A country with two very different legal systems is a house that cannot stand. Compromise might be possible—*sharia* for family law in the North, Nigerian secular law for everything else—but Islamists insist that *sharia* is God's law and must not be mixed with other legal systems.

Fundamentalist Muslim clerics in the North denounced a World Health Organization project to immunize all children against polio. The clerics preached that it was to sterilize Muslim children. Vaccinations were stopped in three Northern states, and polio cases climbed. Muslims took offense at the 2002 Miss World pageant, which was to be held in Abuja, Nigeria. Riots broke out, and the pageant was hastily relocated to London. The smallest incident can touch off Christian-Muslim riots in Northern Nigeria, and thousands have been killed.

Other regions also present problems. The worst was the bitter Biafra War of 1967–1969, in which the Igbo of Eastern Nigeria attempted to break away with their own country, Biafra. In the Niger Delta, Ijaw and Itsekiri tribes fight over control of the oil terminals and even shut them down. Interethnic violence in the Delta can explode any time and takes an average of over a thousand lives a year.

KEY TERM

sharia Muslim religious law based on the Koran.

KEY CONCEPTS

CROSS-CUTTING CLEAVAGES

One of the puzzles of highly pluralistic or multiethnic societies is why they hold together. Why do they not break down into civil strife? One explanation, offered by the German sociologist Georg Simmel early in the twentieth century, is that successful pluralistic societies develop **cross-cutting cleavages**. They are divided, of course, but they are divided along several axes, not just one. When these divisions, or cleavages, cut across one another, they actually stabilize political life.

In Switzerland, for example, the cleavages of French-speaking or German-speaking, Catholic or Protestant, and working class or middle class give rise to eight possible combinations (for example, German-speaking, Protestant, middle class). But any combination has at least one attribute in common with six of the other seven combinations (for example, French-speaking, Protestant, working class). Because most Swiss have something in common with other Swiss, goes the theory, they moderate their conflicts.

Where cleavages do not cross-cut but instead are **cumulative**, dangerous divisions grow. A horrible case is ex-Yugoslavia, where all Croats are Catholic and all Serbs are Eastern Orthodox. The one cross-cutting cleavage that might have helped hold the country together—working class versus middle class—had been outlawed by the Communists. The several nationalities of Yugoslavia had little in common.

Many of Africa's troubles stem from an absence of cross-cutting cleavages. Tribe counts most, and in Nigeria this is usually reinforced by religion. Nigeria does have some cross-cutting cleavages. Not all Nigerian Muslims, for example, are Hausa-Fulani of the North; some are Yoruba in the Southwest, others are Ijaw in the Delta. Social class may also cut across tribal lines, as when a Yoruba businessman knows he has much in common with an Igbo businessman. Nigeria, indeed all of Africa, needs more such connections across tribal lines.

To put things into perspective, though, we might consider what happened in tiny Rwanda, a former Belgian colony east of the Congo. Belgium played classic divide and rule by setting up one tribe, the Tutsis, to be aristocratic masters and another tribe, the Hutus, to be underlings. After the Belgians left in 1962, Hutu-Tutsi fighting and massacres became intermittent and exploded in 1994 as Hutu *genocidaires* massacred an estimated 800,000. The conflict spilled over into eastern Congo where it took an estimated 1.7 million lives, most from starvation and disease. The combined Rwanda-Congo death toll of 2.5 million is the world's worst since World War II. Nigeria has not had anything that bad, but it could.

KEY TERMS

cross-cutting cleavages   Multiple splits in society that make group loyalties overlap.
cumulative   Reinforcing one another.

THE IGBO AND BIAFRA

Nigeria's prime example of interethnic violence is what happened with the Igbo people of southeastern Nigeria in the late 1960s. British explorers and colonial officials noted long ago that the Igbo lacked the cities and culture of the Yoruba of the southwest or the Hausa-Fulani of the north. The Igbo, who lived in scattered villages in the rain forest and Niger Delta, seemed rather primitive in comparison. But the Igbo (also spelled Ibo) harbored a competitive and hustling culture that was not noticed until later. Under the British, the Igbo eagerly took to self-advancement through business, education, the civil service, and military. Igbo, nearly all Christian, also scattered throughout Nigeria. Igbo merchants dominated much of the commercial life of Northern Nigeria, where they were despised for both their wealth and their religion. Some observers called them the "Jews of Nigeria" because they were hard-working, dispersed, better-off, and of a different faith. The Igbo were the most modern and educated Nigerians but were culturally at odds with more traditional Nigerians.

Independent Nigeria started destabilizing almost immediately; unrest and disorder broke out early and often. In response to the fraudulent elections of October 1965, in January 1966 a group of army officers, mainly Igbo, attempted a coup. Prime Minister Abubakar Tafawa Balewa, a Northern Muslim, was assassinated. General Johnson Aguiyi-Ironsi, an Igbo, took over with a plan to save Nigeria by turning it from a federal to a unitary system. Especially to the Muslims of the North, this looked like an Igbo conspiracy to seize the entire country. In July 1966 another coup, under Colonel Yakubu Gowon, a Christian from a small tribe in the center of Nigeria, the Anga, overthrew Ironsi, who was killed.

Nigeria's ethnic pot boiled over. In October 1966 murderous riots against Igbo merchants and their families in the North killed some 20,000 and sent perhaps a million Igbos streaming back to Igboland. After some futile efforts to hold Nigeria together, a consultative assembly of three Eastern states, knowing that they had Nigeria's oilfields, authorized an Igbo colonel, Odumegwu Ojukwu, to set up a separate country. On May 30, 1967, Ojukwu proclaimed the Republic of Biafra. The federal government also knew where the oil was and therefore had to get back the breakaway area. Much of the Biafra War was about oil. At first the Biafran army did well, almost reaching Lagos, until the Nigerian army under Gowon threw them back. For two painful years, the Biafra fighters held out, improvising munitions within a shrinking perimeter, until they finally collapsed in December 1969. Igbo deaths, mostly from starvation, are estimated at half a million.

Gowon was actually quite magnanimous in victory and brought back the Eastern states into Nigeria as equals within the federation, which he had divided into twelve states. It helped that he was from a small tribe that posed no threat to other ethnic groups. The oil boom that soon followed in the 1970s brought jobs and prosperity. Gowon was overthrown by a coup in 1975 by Brigadier Murtala Ramat Mohammed, a Hausa Muslim from the North, who was himself assassinated in 1976. The Biafra War serves as a reminder of just how ethnically fragile Nigeria is and how risky it is to be a Nigerian head of state.

THE TROUBLE WITH NIGERIA

Nigeria has no shortage of smart, educated people. Two-thirds of Nigerians are literate, not bad for a still-poor developing country. Nigeria has considerable numbers of college graduates, some from British or U.S. universities. Many of its army officers were trained in British military academies.

Nigeria, in the theory of Samuel Huntington (see pages 139 and 301), is a **cleft country**—that is, it is split between Islam and Christianity, displaying what he calls *intercivilizational disunity*. The two civilizations rarely live peacefully within one country. Muslims especially tend to break away from such countries. Upon independence in 1947, Muslim Pakistan split from India, which is a majority Hindu. In Yugoslavia, Muslims in Bosnia and Kosovo refused to be ruled by Serbs. The Muslim Central Asian republics of the Soviet Union separated from it in late 1991. Muslim Turks broke away the north of Cyprus in 1974 from the Christian Greeks who held the reins of government. In a parallel with Nigeria, Christians in the south of Sudan—where oil has been discovered—tried to break away from the Muslims of the north. (Do not confuse "cleft countries" in Huntington's terms with **torn countries**, such as Turkey and Mexico, whose leaders wish to make them modern and Western despite mass reluctance.)

Nigeria is not unique in this regard. Most of the coastal nations of West Africa have a Muslim interior and a Christian coastal region. The reason is that Islam came by land from the north and from Sudan; Christianity came by ship from Europe. East Africa, on the other hand, has a Muslim coast and a heavily Christian interior, as in Kenya and Tanzania. Some countries with the two faiths manage to get along tolerably well if they can keep religion in the personal sphere and have adherents of the two faiths dispersed enough to make it hard for either to claim a special area as their own. The overlap of religion with politics in ethnically specific territories, though, can produce breakaway movements.

Political scientists have long celebrated *pluralism* (see page 86) as the basis of modern government and democracy. This is true but only within limits. There must be widespread agreement among groups to not take things too far and to live within certain rules and bounds. Lebanon and Nigeria have plenty of interactions among their many groups, but rules to limit the interactions are weak, so they turn competitive and violent, and the country breaks down. Pluralism without restraint leads to civil war.

DEMOCRATS WITHOUT DEMOCRACY

A majority of Nigerians want democracy. In a 2000 poll, 81 percent expressed support for democracy, a number that, amidst continuing corruption, ethnic strife, and poverty, has since dropped lower. Just wanting democracy does not necessarily make it happen. The problem is not that insufficient numbers of Nigerians understand and desire democracy; there are more than enough educated Nigerians who do. If they were not divided by tribe and religion, Nigerians might have achieved stable democracy. The terrible dilemma for Nigerian democrats is that they know that whenever Nigeria attempts democracy—as it is doing now—it can easily fail amidst tribal and religious animosities, corruption, and military power-grabs. Still, most Nigerians have not given up on democracy.

KEY TERMS

cleft country   In Huntington's theory, a country split by two civilizations.
torn country   In Huntington's theory, one with a Westernizing elite but traditional masses.

DEMOCRACY

THE DEVELOPMENTALIST IMPULSE

The wave of decolonization around 1960 shifted the attention of academics and the U.S. government from Europe to the Third World; it was a fascinating new field and the setting for the big showdown with communism. Many universities offered "area studies" of Southeast Asia, Africa, Latin America, and every other part of the globe. In a parallel to the academic misperceptions of the Soviet Union (see page 170), political scientists were much too optimistic in supposing the Third World would achieve stable democracy and economic growth. Some developing countries, mainly on the rim of Asia, did achieve both, but few academics predicted these success stories in advance. As Princeton economist Paul Krugman points out, no one has successfully predicted the next country or region of rapid economic growth; it always surprises us.

The academics' poor predictions grew out of the pervasive American fear that the Soviets would take over most the Third World. Cuba and the 1962 Missile Crisis were frightening warnings. Kennedy's advisors wrote urgently that either we develop the Third World or the Communists will. The newly independent lands were in a shaky, vulnerable transition, but U.S. help could guide them through it and put them on the path of free-market democracy. This came to be called **developmentalism**. The Kennedy administration responded with the Agency for International Development, the Peace Corps, and Vietnam.

AID, the CIA, and the Ford Foundation funded studies on implementing developmentalist strategies, and academics won grants and built theories to support them. Improving communications was touted as an important technique. But Third World countries developed along the lines of their own internal logic, not ours. Some received lots of U.S. money and advice and bombed. Others received little and prospered. The theories underestimated the impact of culture by assuming that all peoples are culturally ready for development. One key topic was almost totally overlooked: corruption. In an echo of the 1960s, new alarms now urge us to democratize the Middle East before radical Islam takes it over. Review the mistaken developmentalism of the 1960s before you sign up.

PATTERNS OF INTERACTION

Russia and Mexico are weak states, characterized by the penetration of crime deep into politics. Nigeria is even weaker but is not yet a failed state such as Somalia or Afghanistan, where national government effectively ceased. Nigeria has a central government and a strong incentive for most of Nigeria's elites to keep the country intact: graft from the lush

KEY TERM

developmentalism   Early 1960s theory that we could develop Third World lands.

oil revenues. If Nigeria fell apart, only the Niger Delta would have the oil. This was one of the roots of the Biafra War.

COUNT THE COUPS

Weak states often experience repeated military coups, a condition known as **praetorianism** (see box on page 279). It indicates that the normal institutions of government—parliaments, parties, and presidents—have too little legitimacy and authority to stand up in times of stress. Most coups are easy and involve little fighting, because the government has no mass support. Let us count Nigeria's military coups:

Year	Ousted	Installed
1966 (Jan.)	Balewa (Hausa), killed	Ironsi (Igbo)
1966 (July)	Ironsi, killed	Gowon (Anga)
1975	Gowon, deposed	Mohammed (Hausa)
1976	Mohammed, killed	Obasanjo (Yoruba)
1983	Shagari (Fulani), deposed	Buhari (Hausa)
1985	Buhari, deposed	Babangida (Gwari)
1993	Babangida, deposed	Abacha (Hausa)

The best of the lot was Obasanjo, who returned to office as the current president of Nigeria, but now twice democratically elected. In 1979 he turned power over to a civilian government. The worst was Sani Abacha, a cruel supercrook who, with his family to help him, looted between $2 billion and $4 billion of Nigerian oil money and stashed it in Swiss, British, and U.S. banks. Oil revenues give a great incentive for Nigerian generals to think about coups. Another cause of Nigeria's coups is apparent: disputes among ethnic groups, a reflection of Nigeria's fractured political culture. Northern Muslims especially bristle at rule by Southern Christians and vice-versa.

Nigeria still seethes with poverty and violence and could have another coup. Praetorianism tends to become a self-reinfecting illness endemic in the Third World. A country that has had a coup will likely have others. Bolivia has had dozens of coups since independence. Brazil last had a coup in 1964 and was ruled by generals until 1985. Mexico during the nineteenth century was praetorian, but Calles ended it by bringing Mexico's main political forces into one party, the PRI. Nigeria's problem is that it never developed the equivalent of PRI, a dominant nationwide party.

The praetorian tendency raises the question: If these countries slide so easily into military rule, why do they ever slide out? Why does a military dictator ever leave power? The material rewards from control over natural resources could be ample incentives to stay in

KEY TERM

praetorianism   Tendency for military takeovers.

KEY CONCEPTS

THE PRAETORIAN TENDENCY

As the Roman Empire ossified and crumbled, the emperor's bodyguard, the Praetorian Guard, came to play a powerful role, making and unmaking emperors, some of them their own officers. Political scientists now use praetorianism for a situation where the military feels it must take over the government in order to save the country from chaos.

Praetorianism is not just a problem of power-hungry generals but reflects deep conflict in the whole society. In praetorian societies, it is not only the generals who want to take power, but many other groups as well: students, labor unions, revolutionaries, and demagogic politicians would like to seize the state machinery. Institutional constraints and balances have broken down; nobody plays by the rules. In such situations of chaos and breakdown, it is the army among the many power contenders that is best equipped to seize power, so praetorianism usually means military takeover, the case in Nigeria.

office forever. The means for staying in power are well known and widely practiced in the Third World: **patronage** and clientelism (discussed in our Mexico chapter). Mobutu seized power in a 1965 coup and ruled and looted the Congo (which he renamed Zaire) until 1997, with the flimsy cover story that he was the only one who could keep the country together. His real strength was the patronage and clientelistic networks he developed. Sani Abacha of Nigeria set up similar networks and died in office of a heart attack in 1998.

But other forces work against permanent military government. Military officers overthrow governments that have little legitimacy, but the military regime then has even less legitimacy. The military rulers know they are unpopular. A few heads of military regimes may be genuine patriots and professional soldiers who recognize that military government soon turns rotten. Obasanjo in 1979 handed power over to a civilian government. The Brazilian generals who seized power in 1964 boasted how they would end inflation and modernize the Brazilian economy. By the 1980s they were embarrassed as their economic miracle stalled; they left power in 1985.

A more persuasive motive for dictators to leave is their recognition that an angry mob or their own officers could overthrow them. Every general who has seized power in a coup knows that there are several colleagues waiting to do the same to him. With no legitimacy to rely on, the dictator may for a time buy support with pieces of graft, but sooner or later those bought off ask, "Why settle for a piece?" Praetorian systems are rife with conspiracies. The dictator may sense when the time has come to flee with his life and his offshore bank accounts.

KEY TERM

patronage   Giving government jobs to political supporters.

GEOGRAPHY

BOUND KENYA

Kenya is bounded on the north by Sudan and Ethiopia;
on the east by Somalia and the Indian Ocean;
on the south by Tanzania;
and on the west by Uganda.

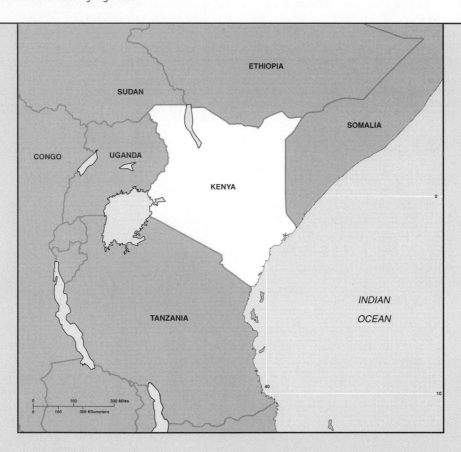

WHAT NIGERIANS QUARREL ABOUT

Upon independence in 1960, Nigeria had roughly the same per capita GDP as several East Asian countries. Forty years later, most of these Asian lands were much richer than Nigeria, even with Nigeria's major oil revenues. Political scientists and economists seek explanations at several levels for this growing gap. They divide into two great camps: explanations from the physical and material world, and explanations from the cultural and psychological realm. The two, of course, are not exclusive; it is likely that one feeds into the other.

The most obvious explanation—that the poor countries have few natural resources—does not hold up. Nigeria and Indonesia have great mineral wealth but are poor. Japan, South Korea, Taiwan, Hong Kong, and Singapore have almost no natural resources and are rich. There may even be an inverse relationship between natural resources and prosperity. Oil may be a curse. With nothing else to rely on, Asian Rimland countries had to get clever, competitive, and productive. It is not natural resources but human resources that pay off in the long run.

Another culprit is imperialism, but it does not provide a complete explanation. In some countries there was a great deal of imperialist exploitation; others, where there was not much to exploit, were left largely alone. The imperialists did not do nearly enough to get their colonies ready for independence. They should have provided more education and training.

But colonialism does not explain success stories in some ex-colonies. Consider what Hong Kong and Singapore had working against them. Both had been British colonies for more than a century. Both are small islands with zero natural resources; they were economically important only for their locations. Both were destroyed in World War II and occupied by the Japanese. That should predict poverty, but now both are thriving economies at the First World level.

In explaining such seeming anomalies cultural factors loom large. Some cultures take quickly to economic development, others not. Those who believe the future can be formed by one's own activities generally do well. Fatalism, on the other hand, keeps people passive; all is God's will. Cultures that instill discipline and a work ethic can grow rapidly. So far, the winners in this cultural race seem to be the Confucian-influenced lands of East Asia, although few predicted their growth. Indeed, some decades ago scholars attributed Asia's *backwardness* to its Confucian heritage. In the right circumstances, a seemingly sleepy culture can wake up and produce an economic miracle. In Nigeria, the Igbo are an example of this; what was latent in their culture became manifest under the British. Do not write off Africa as forever poor. Cultures change.

Some social scientists seek a **strategic variable**, and that is usually in the area of **policy**, a regime's decisions, laws, and programs that may either push or retard growth. Governments have two types of economic policy tools, macroeconomic and microeconomic. Some economists urge governments to get the **macroeconomy**, sometimes called the "fundamentals,"

KEY TERMS

strategic variable   Factor you can change that makes a big improvement.

policy   The specific choices governments make.

macroeconomy   Big picture of a nation's economy, including GDP size and growth, productivity, interest rates, and inflation.

in order—little public debt, plentiful savings, low inflation, sufficient investment capital—and then stand back and let the market do its stuff. The German "economic miracle" followed this pattern. Third World technocrats—who are now as prominent in Nigeria as they are in Mexico—tend, however, to get into the **microeconomy** by choosing which industries to foster or phase out. Postwar Japan used considerable microeconomic management (as well as getting its fundamentals right).

Nigeria shows signs of both macro- and microeconomic mismanagement. The president and finance minister currently propose major reforms, but that means inflicting some of the pain of austerity, at least for the short term. (For the pain of austerity in Mexico, see page 233.) Such reforms could also help clean up corruption. Nigeria's inflation, debt, and unemployment suggest poor choices at the macro level. And the oil industry, in Nigeria as in Mexico, is a constant temptation for microeconomic meddling. Leaving it to market forces would likely produce the best growth. In both countries, that is improbable. Economic rationality often conflicts with political expediency.

The impact of a given policy is hard to judge in advance; you have to see how it works out. Generous public spending (a macroeconomic policy) may keep Nigeria's state governments compliant but unleash inflation, currently around 20 percent a year in Nigeria. Nigeria keeps fuel prices low, because Nigerians demand a special deal on the gasoline they produce. Nigerian subsidies for fuel (a microeconomic policy) mean less to sell on the world market. Nigeria's technocrats understand that the subsidies must be cut, but then you get riots.

THE CORRUPTION FACTOR

One factor trips up the best-laid plans for Third World development: corruption, which makes foreign investors keep away. Corruption can be divided into petty and grand. The petty is the small demands for cash—called "dash" or "sweetbread" in West Africa. A friend of the author once flew into Lagos (then the capital of Nigeria) on an assignment for the World Bank. An airport "health officer" stopped him, saying his inoculation record (often required for travel in the tropics) was missing a stamp (it wasn't), but he could fix it for $20. My friend refused, arguing that he was there to help Nigeria. A higher official came and urged him to pay: "You are a rich man, and he is a poor man." My friend finally paid. Such holdups are still standard at Lagos airport and show the logic of petty corruption. Any time you need a stamp, permit, license, or help from the police—even driving or parking a car—in the Third World, be prepared to pay sweetbread, *la mordida,* or *baksheesh.* It is a normal part of daily life.

Some see petty corruption as an unofficial welfare system to redistribute wealth from the better off to the poor, but it seldom goes to the truly needy and does not spare those with little money. Petty corruption is the demands of underpaid policemen and bureaucrats who are in a position to help or hurt. The historical root of Third World corruption is a less-developed country acquiring a large bureaucracy before it was ready for one.

KEY TERM

microeconomy   Close-up picture of individual markets, including product design and pricing, efficiency, and costs.

Spain set up Latin America with a giant bureaucracy to supervise its extractive economy, and it has been the source of corruption there ever since. One solution is to pay civil servants more, but Third World countries can seldom afford to. Another is to cut the number of regulations and the bureaucrats needed to enforce them. Chile got a lot less corrupt after it did both.

Petty corruption is a minor annoyance compared to grand corruption, the use of official position to siphon money wholesale. There is no clear dividing line between petty and grand corruption, but if the money goes over $1 million or into overseas accounts you can be sure it is the grand variety. Transparency International's CPI (see box on page 284) does not distinguish between the two levels. Theoretically, a country could have grand corruption at the highest levels and still have an honest civil service, and vice versa. But it is unlikely, for one is usually a reflection of the other. If a postal clerk steals your stamps, chances are the minister of communications is stealing far larger amounts. The grand variety does far more damage than the petty variety of corruption, for it eats capital that should go for economic growth, health, and education. It is a major factor in keeping the Third World poor. No Nigerian has been publicly tried for corruption, suggesting that other officials fear what might come out in a trial.

Grand corruption is not simply a matter of crooks in government but of foreign businesses willing to pay them—usually by **kickbacks**—for profitable contracts. Many corporations that would never kick back on contracts in their home countries reckon it is normal in the Third World: If they don't pay, a competing firm that does pay will get the contract. There is no quick, simple cure for corruption, which sometimes feels as if it's rooted in the soil. Some countries have developed an ethos of clean administration, but this may take centuries. A nobleman developed the Swedish civil service in the seventeenth century and hired other aristocrats, thereby stamping the Swedish bureaucracy with traditions of honor and service. Looking at the TI rankings (see box on page 284), we might all wish to become Finns or Singaporeans. There is a hopeful sign here, as Singapore is a new country (independent only in 1965) that started poor but cultivated, under draconic penalties, an ethos of clean administration in a part of the world known for the opposite. With enough will at the top, it can be done.

OIL AND DEMOCRACY

There is an unhappy correlation between petroleum wealth and nondemocratic government. One of the few democratic oil-producing countries is Norway, but it has many other industries and a long history of democracy. Note how the four major oil-producing countries of this book—Russia, Mexico, Nigeria, and Iran—are (or recently were) nondemocratic. Russia attempted democracy but has slid back to authoritarianism. Mexico, we hope, is coming out of a long period of one-party domination. Nigeria at this moment has an elected government but for two-thirds of its history did not. And Iran overthrew one tyrant but now has worse ones.

KEY TERM

kickback   Fee paid to government official for a contract.

COMPARISON

CORRUPTION INTERNATIONAL

If you think corruption is bad in Mexico, take a look at Nigeria. Indeed, corruption is nearly everywhere, finds Transparency International, a Berlin-based organization that polls business people on their perceptions of having to pay off government officials. TI ranks countries on a ten-point scale, ten being totally clean, one totally corrupt. Some of their 2004 Corruption Perception Index (CPI) findings:

Finland	9.7
Singapore	9.3
Britain	8.6
Canada	8.5
Germany	8.2
United States	7.5
France	7.1
Japan	6.9
South Africa	4.6
Brazil	3.9
Mexico	3.6
China	3.4
Iran	2.9
Russia	2.8
Nigeria	1.6
Bangladesh	1.5

Source: Transparency International

TI founder Peter Eigen was a World Bank official in charge of making loans to East Africa but concluded that so much was skimmed off in graft that the loans did little good. To call attention to the massive problem—and to put pressure on governments for **transparency** in their financial dealings—he formed TI in 1993. A poor TI ranking chastises a corrupt country by scaring away business, hopefully pushing it to get clean.

Skeptics doubt the accuracy of the CPI (not to be confused with the U.S. Consumer Price Index), because it is just a compilation of subjective perceptions. These can change from year to year—depending on which businessmen are interviewed—and countries often trade positions on the TI rankings even though little in their behavior has actually changed. That weakness is built into TI's methodology, but there is no other way to measure corruption, even approximately. Corruption (along with drugs and crime) does not show up in GDP calculations, and crooked officials do not list "earnings from kickbacks" on their income tax. TI's CPI is the best measure we have. The big question is, will TI's efforts over time increase rule of law and boost economic growth?

DEMOCRACY

CORPORATE SOCIAL RESPONSIBILITY

A current business buzzword is *corporate social responsibility* (CSR). According to CSR doctrine, large firms must recognize that they owe more than profits to shareholders; they owe fairness and justice to *stakeholders*—their workers, the community, and the environment. Now most corporations' annual reports trumpet their CSR activities, although critics charge they are little more than public relations.

Nigeria offers a good example of CSR—or lack of it—in action. Shell, Chevron, and other oil companies make immense profits from the Niger Delta, but their operations befoul soil and water. Some local people get good jobs in the oilfields, but greater numbers of fishermen and farmers have lost their livelihood. Poverty feeds rising ethnic tensions in the Delta, where well-armed Ijaw gangs demand "self-determination," that is, control of the oil. Strikes and sabotage are common, and violence, some involving the Nigerian army, takes an estimated thousand lives a year in the Delta. Ken SaroWiwa, a writer and environmental activist from the small Ogoni tribe in the oil region, was hanged in 1995 on trumped-up murder charges. His real crime was calling attention to the ecological damage uncontrolled oil pumping had done to his people. The Nigerian government depends on oil revenues and did not like that kind of criticism.

Most agree that the oil companies have a responsibility, but carrying it out is difficult. The oil companies pay the Nigerian government billions a year in taxes and royalties, but much of it disappears into private pockets; little gets back to the Delta. Trying to practice CSR, the oil companies have also given millions to the Niger Delta Development Commission, but it too is corrupt and inefficient. The companies, aware of the poverty and resentment, also build health clinics in the Delta, but many of them are either empty (because the government will not staff them) or burned down by neighboring tribes who are jealous that they did not get a clinic.

There is no way CSR can deliver help to poor Nigerians; it will always get skimmed. The best thing would be to get the Nigerian government to adopt accountability and transparency standards, but the oil companies have no leverage for this. Said one Chevron executive in Nigeria: "It's very difficult for the private sector to replace government. It's not our role." Some economists argue that corporations should just produce income, out of which come wages and taxes. Stakeholders have real grievances, but they must act through democratic governments to obtain pollution laws, fair wages, public health, and so on. These things need force of law, not corporate generosity. Do not expect CSR to solve vast problems of poverty and corruption.

What is there about oil that works against democracy? True, it produces vast wealth, but the wealth is terribly concentrated, mostly in government hands, and seldom benefits the whole society. Oil often becomes the great prize of politics in that country, for he who

KEY TERM

transparency   Exchanges of money open to public scrutiny. (See page 284.) Opposite: *opacity*.

controls the oil monopolizes power. One of Putin's main efforts (successful) was to bring back most petroleum production into state hands. The oil industry employs relatively few, and its wealth is squandered in corruption, overlarge bureaucracies, showcase projects, and rewards for supporters of the regime. The oil bonanza lets rulers avoid investing in infrastructure, industry, and other long-term growth mechanisms. The petrostates' vast incomes have netted them little that can be sustained after the oil runs out. When that happens, the elites will still have their secret overseas bank accounts to live well forever. Their citizens will be poor.

Such is the story of Nigeria, a country with major oil revenues but where a majority of the people live in **absolute poverty**. And even with its oil wealth, Nigeria still has an international debt of $30 billion. Some oil was found long ago in the Niger Delta around Port Harcourt, but major oilfields came on line in the 1970s, just as oil prices were quadrupling. Like Iran, Nigeria is a member of OPEC (see page 295), which assigns quotas to member states to keep oil production down and its price up. The good thing about Nigeria here is that it is one of the easiest OPEC members to bribe to get officials to (secretly) produce above Nigeria's quota.

What to do with the oil has thus become one of Nigeria's most difficult political problems: How to make sure oil serves the long-term good of all Nigerians? Most Nigerian oil is produced through joint ventures between foreign firms and the Nigerian National Petroleum Corporation (NNPC), which gets most of the revenues. Like Mexico's Pemex, the NNPC is corrupt, but nationalizing all Nigerian oil production would simply concentrate more wealth and encourage more corruption. Privatizing Nigeria's oil might help, but only if it were total, that is, with oil companies able to buy the oilfields outright. No Nigerian government is likely to sell the fields; that would eliminate the kickbacks that come from leases. The stated reason for rejecting any such sales, as in Mexico, will always be: "What? Sell Nigeria's sacred patrimony to greedy foreign capitalists? Never!" Nationalism cloaks corruption.

One possibility is a joint Nigerian-international board of supervisors (perhaps staffed by Finns and Singaporeans) with power of oversight and audit. Such a board would make Nigeria's oil deals transparent and take them out of government hands. The oil revenues should not go to Nigeria's federal treasury, where they could be disbursed to favored tribes and officials, but into an internationally supervised bank to make loans for infrastructure, education, and founding and expanding valid enterprises. **Micro-loans** have been effective in encouraging thousands of startup businesses—sometimes just one woman with a sewing machine—at low cost in developing areas. If done well and honestly, oil could give Nigeria a growing economy that would use but not depend on petroleum.

We sometimes forget that there are African success stories. Senegal, Mali, and Botswana are examples of positive development. Effective leadership, sound policies, and the promotion of a national political culture make a difference. Remember, we used to write off Asia as hopeless.

KEY TERMS

absolute poverty   Living on $1 a day or less.
micro-loan   Small unsecured loan (of a few hundred dollars) to beginning businesses.

KEY WEB SITES

University of Pennsylvania African Studies Center
sas.upenn.edu/African_Studies/Country_Specific/Nigeria.html

News Sources
ngrguardiannews.com

nigeria.com

nigeriadaily.com

KEY TERMS

absolute poverty (p. 286)

aquifer (p. 260)

caliphate (p. 261)

cleft country (p. 276)

colonialism (p. 263)

cross-cutting cleavages (p. 274)

cumulative (p. 274)

decolonization (p. 265)

desiccation (p. 260)

developmentalism (p. 277)

divide and rule (p. 262)

indirect rule (p. 262)

kickback (p. 283)

macroeconomy (p. 281)

microeconomy (p. 282)

micro-loan (p. 286)

pan-Africanism (p. 265)

patronage (p. 279)

policy (p. 281)

praetorianism (p. 278)

Sahel (p. 260)

savanna (p. 260)

sharia (p. 273)

strategic variable (p. 281)

sub-Saharan (p. 260)

torn country (p. 276)

transparency (p. 285)

FURTHER REFERENCE

Apter, Andrew H. *The Pan-African Nation: Oil and the Spectacle of Culture in Nigeria.* Chicago, IL: University of Chicago Press, 2005.

Bah, Abu Bakarr. *Breakdowns and Reconstruction: Democracy, the Nation-State, and Ethnicity in Nigeria.* Blue Ridge Summit, PA: Lexington Books, 2005.

Coleman, James S. *Nigeria: Background to Nationalism.* Berkeley, CA: University of California Press, 1963.

Farris, Jacqueline W., and Mohammed Bomoi, eds. *Shehu Musa Yar'Adua: A Biography.* Boulder, CO: L. Rienner, 2004.

Howe, Herbert M. *Ambiguous Order: Military Forces in African States.* Boulder, CO: L. Rienner, 2004.

Laitin, David D. *Hegemony and Culture: Politics and Religious Change Among the Yoruba*. Chicago, IL: University of Chicago Press, 1986.

Larémont, Ricardo René, ed. *Borders, Nationalism, and the African State*. Boulder, CO: L. Rienner, 2005.

Osaghae, Eghosa. *Crippled Giant: Nigeria Since Independence*. Bloomington, IN: Indiana University Press, 1998.

Paden, John N. *Muslim Civic Cultures and Conflict Resolution: The Challenge of Democratic Federalism in Nigeria*. Washington, D.C.: Brookings, 2005.

Rotberg, Robert I., ed. *Crafting the New Nigeria: Confronting the Challenges*. Boulder, CO: L. Rienner, 2004.

Schwarz, Frederick A. O., Jr. *Nigeria: The Tribes, the Nation, or the Race: The Politics of Independence*. Cambridge, MA: MIT Press, 1965.

15

Iran

THE IMPACT OF THE PAST

Much of Iran is an arid plateau around 4,000 feet above sea level. Some areas are rainless desert; some get sufficient rain only for sparse sheep pasture. In this part of the world, irrigation made civilization possible, and whatever disrupted waterworks had devastating consequences. Persia's location made it an important trade route between East and West, one of the links between the Middle East and Asia. Persia thus became a crossroads of civilizations and one of the earliest of the great civilizations.

The trouble with being a crossroads is that your country becomes a natural target for conquest. Indo-European-speaking invaders took over Persia about the fifteenth century B.C. and laid the basis for subsequent Persian culture. Their most famous kings: Cyrus and Darius in the sixth century B.C. The invasions never ceased, though: the Greeks under Alexander in the third and fourth centuries B.C., the Arab-Islamic conquest in the seventh century A.D., Turkish tribes in the eleventh century, Mongols in the thirteenth century, and many others. The repeated pattern was one of conquest, the founding of a new dynasty, and its falling apart as quarrelsome heirs broke it into petty kingdoms. This fragmentation set up the country for easy conquest again.

Iran, known for most of history as Persia (it was renamed only in 1925), resembles China in that it is heir to an ancient and magnificent civilization that, partly at the hands of outsiders, fell into "the sleep of nations." When it awoke, it was far behind the West, which, like China, Iran views as an adversary. If and how Iran will move into modernity is one of our major questions.

Questions to Consider

1. What has geography contributed to Iran's development?
2. How does Iran differ from Arab countries?
3. What is a "modernizing tyrant"? Why do they fail?
4. What factors brought Iran's Islamic Revolution?
5. Explain Iran's dual executive. Who is more powerful?
6. Does secularization always come with modernization?
7. What kind of Iranians wish to liberalize their system?
8. Explain the power struggle in Iran.
9. How is attire a political debate in Iran?
10. How have America and Iran misunderstood each other?
11. Why is the Persian Gulf region strategic?

GEOGRAPHY

BOUND IRAN

Iran is bounded on the north by Armenia, Azerbaijan, the Caspian Sea, and Turkmenistan;
on the east by Afghanistan and Pakistan;
on the south by the Gulf of Oman and the Persian Gulf;
and on the west by Iraq and Turkey.

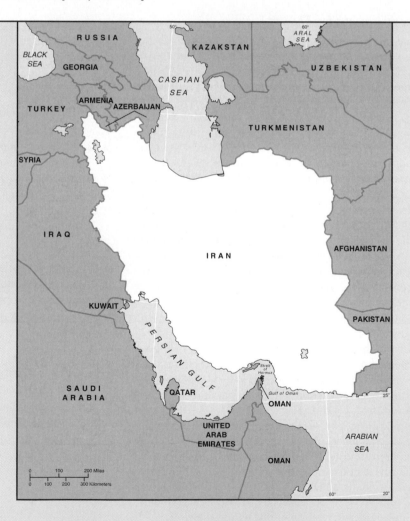

Although it does not look or sound like it, Persian (*Farsi*) is a member of the broad Indo-European family of languages; the neighboring Arabic and Turkic tongues are not. Today, Farsi is the mother tongue of about half of Iranians. Another fifth speak Persian-related languages (such as Kurdish). A quarter speak a Turkic language, and some areas speak Arabic and other tongues. The non-Farsi speakers occupy the periphery of the Farsi-speaking heartland and have at times been discontent with rule by Persians. In Iranian politics today, to be descended from one of the non-Persian minorities is held against politicians.

THE ARAB CONQUEST

Allah's prophet Muhammad died in Arabia in 632, but his religion spread like wildfire. **Islam** means "submission" (to God's will), and this was to be hastened by **jihad**. Islam arrived soon in Iran by the sword. The remnant of the Sassanid empire, already exhausted by centuries of warfare with Byzantium, was easily beaten by the Arabs at Qadisiya in 637 and within two centuries Persia was mostly Muslim. Most adherents of the old religion, Zoroastrianism, fled to India where today they are a small, prosperous minority known as Parsis.

The Arab conquest was a major break with the past. In contrast to the sharp social stratification of Persian tradition, Islam taught that all Muslims were, at least in a spiritual sense, equal. Persia adopted the Arabic script, and many Arab words enriched the Persian language. Persian culture flowed the other way, too, as the Arabs copied Persian architecture and civil administration. For six centuries, Persia was swallowed up by the Arab empires, but in 1055 the Seljuk Turks invaded from Central Asia and conquered most of the Middle East. As usual, their rule soon fell apart into many small states, easy prey for Genghis Khan, the Mongol "World Conqueror" whose horde thundered in from the east in 1219. One of his descendants who ruled Persia embraced Islam at the end of that century. This is part of a pattern that Iranians are proud of: "We may be conquered," they say, "but the conqueror always ends up adopting our superior culture and becomes one of us."

The coming of the Safavid dynasty in 1501 boosted development of a distinctly Iranian identity. The Safavids practiced a minority version of Islam called **Shia** (see box on page 304) and decreed it Persia's state religion. Most of their subjects switched from **Sunni** Islam and are Shias to this day. Neighboring Sunni powers immediately attacked Safavid Persia, but this enabled the new regime to consolidate its control and develop an Islam with Persian characteristics.

KEY TERMS

Islam   Religion founded by Muhammad.
jihad   Arabic for "struggle," also used for Muslim holy war.
Shia   Minority branch of Islam.
Sunni   Mainstream Islam.

WESTERN PENETRATION

It is too simple to say Western cultural, economic, and colonial penetration brought down the great Persian empire. Safavid Persia was attacked from several directions, mostly by neighboring Muslim powers: the Ottoman Turks from the west, Uzbeks from the north, and Afghans from the northeast. In fighting the Ottomans Safavid rulers made common cause with the early Portuguese, Dutch, and English sea traders in the late sixteenth and early seventeenth centuries. As previously in the region's history, the outsiders were able to penetrate because the local kingdoms had weakened themselves in wars, a pattern that continues in our day.

In 1722, Afghan invaders ended the Safavid dynasty, but no one was able to govern the whole country. After much chaos, in 1795 the Qajar dynasty emerged victorious. Owing to Persian weakness, Britain and Russia became dominant in Persia, the Russians pushing in from the north, the British from India. Although never a colony, Persia, like China, slid into semicolonial status, with much of its political and economic life dependent on imperial designs, something Persians strongly resented. A particularly vexatious example was an 1890 treaty giving British traders a monopoly on tobacco sales in Persia. Muslim clerics led mass hatred of the British tobacco concession, and the treaty was repealed.

At this same time, liberal, Western ideas of government seeped into Persia, some brought, as in China, by Christian missionaries (who made very few Persian converts). The Constitutional Revolution of 1906–1907 (in which an American supporter of the popular struggle was killed) brought Persia's first constitution and first elected parliament, the **Majlis**. The struggles over the tobacco concession and constitution were led by a combination of two forces: liberals who hated the monarchy and wanted Western-type institutions and Muslim clerics who also disliked the monarchy but wanted a stronger role for Islam. This same combination brought down the **Shah** in 1979; now these two strands have turned against each other over the future of Iran.

Notice how at almost exactly the same time—1905 in Russia, 1906 in Persia—corrupt and weak monarchies promised somewhat democratic constitutions in the face of popular uprisings. Both monarchies, dedicated to autocratic power and hating democracy, only pretended to deliver, a prescription for increasing mass discontent. A new shah inherited the throne in 1907 and shut down the Majlis with his Russian-trained Cossack bodyguard unit. Mass protest forced the last Qajar shah to flee to Russia in 1909; he tried to return in 1911 but was forced back as Russian troops occupied Tehran. The 1907 Anglo-Russian treaty had already cut Persia in two, with a Russian sphere of influence in the north and a British one in the south. During World War I, Persia was nominally neutral, but with neighboring Turkey allied with Germany, Russia and Britain allied with each other, and German agents trying to tilt Persia their way, Persia turned into a zone of contention and chaos.

KEY TERMS

Majlis   Arabic for assembly; Iran's parliament.

shah   Persian for king.

COMPARISON

ATATURK AND REZA SHAH

During the 1920s, two strong personalities in adjacent Middle Eastern lands attempted to modernize their countries from above: Kemal Ataturk in Turkey and Reza Shah in Iran. Both were nationalistic military officers and Muslims but **secular** in outlook; both wished to separate **mosque** and state.

In economics, both were statists (see page 234) and made the government the number-one investor and owner of major industries. Both pushed education, the improved status of women, and Western clothing. As such, both aroused traditionalist opposition led by Muslim clerics. Both thundered "You will be modern!" but religious forces opposed their reforms, and do to this day.

Their big difference: Ataturk ended the **Ottoman** monarchy and firmly supported a republican form of government in Turkey. He pushed his reforms piecemeal through parliament, which often opposed him. Reza Shah rejected republicanism and parliaments as too messy; he insisted on an authoritarian monarchy as the only way to modernize his unruly country, as did his son. Although Turkey has had plenty of troubles since Ataturk, it has not been ripped apart by revolution. Ataturk built some political institutions; the Pahlavi shahs built none.

THE FIRST PAHLAVI

As is often the case when a country degenerates into chaos, military officers see themselves as saviors of the nation, the *praetorianism* we saw in Nigeria. In 1921 an illiterate cavalry officer, Reza Khan, commander of the Cossack brigade, seized power and in 1925 had himself crowned shah, the founder of the short-lived (1925–1979) Pahlavi dynasty. The nationalistic Reza took the pre-Islamic surname Pahlavi and told the world to start calling the country by its true name, Iran, from the word *aryan*, indicating the country's Indo-European roots. (Nazi ideologists also loved the word aryan, which they claimed indicated genetic superiority. Indeed, the ancient Persian Zoroastrians preached racial purity.)

Like Ataturk, Reza Shah was determined to modernize his country (see box above). His achievements were impressive. He molded an effective Iranian army and used it to suppress tribal revolts and unify Iran. He created a modern, European-type civil service and a national bank. He replaced traditional and Islamic courts with civil courts operating under

KEY TERMS

secular   Nonreligious.

mosque   Muslim house of worship.

Ottoman   Turkish imperial dynasty, fourteenth to twentieth centuries.

Western codes of justice. In 1935 he founded Iran's first Western-style university. Under state supervision and fueled by oil revenues, Iran's economy grew. Also like Ataturk, Reza Shah ordered his countrymen to adopt Western dress and women to stop wearing the veil. But Reza also kept the press and Majlis closely obedient. Troublemakers and dissidents often died in jail. Reza Shah was a classic **modernizing tyrant**.

World War II put Iran in the same situation as World War I had. It was just too strategic to leave alone; it was a major oil producer and conduit for U.S. supplies to the desperate Soviet Union. As before, the Russians took over in the north and the British (later the Americans) in the south. Both agreed to clear out six months after the war ended. Reza Shah, who tilted toward Germany, in September 1941 was exiled by the British to South Africa, where he died in 1944. Before he left, he abdicated in favor of his son, Mohammed Reza Pahlavi.

The Americans and British left Iran in 1945; the Soviets did not, and some argue this incident marked the start of the Cold War. Stalin claimed that Azerbaijan, a Soviet "republic" in the Caucasus, was entitled by ethnic right to merge with the Azeris of northern Iran and refused to withdraw Soviet forces. Stalin set up puppet Communist Azeri and Kurdish governments there. In 1946 U.S. President Truman delivered some harsh words, Iran's prime minister promised Stalin an oil deal, and Stalin pulled out. Then the Majlis canceled the oil deal.

The Last Pahlavi

Oil determined much of Iran's twentieth-century history. Oil was the great prize for the British, Hitler, Stalin, and the United States. Who should own and profit from Iran's oil—foreigners, the Iranian government, or Iranians as a whole? Major oil deposits were first discovered in Iran in 1908 and developed under a British concession, the Anglo-Persian (later Anglo-Iranian) Oil Company. Persia got little from the oil deal, and Persians came to hate this rich foreign company in their midst, one that wrote its own rules. Reza Shah ended the lopsided concession in 1932 and forced the AIOC to pay higher royalties.

The AIOC still rankled Iranians, who rallied to the radical nationalist Prime Minister Muhammad Mossadegh in the early 1950s. With support from Iranian nationalists, liberals, and leftists, Mossadegh nationalized AIOC holdings. Amidst growing turmoil and what some feared was a tilt to the Soviet Union, Shah Muhammad Reza Pahlavi fled the country in 1953. The British urged Washington to do something, and President Eisenhower, as part of U.S. **containment**, had the CIA destabilize the Tehran government. It was easy: The CIA's Kermit Roosevelt arrived with $1 million in a suitcase and rented a suitable mob. Mossadegh was out, the Shah was restored, and the United States won a battle in the Cold War. We thought we were very clever.

Like his father, the Shah became a modernizing tyrant, promoting what he called his "White Revolution" from above (as opposed to a red revolution from below). Under the Shah, Iran had excellent relations with the United States. President Nixon touted the

GEOGRAPHY

CRUISING THE PERSIAN GULF

The countries bordering the Persian Gulf contain two-thirds of the world's proven petroleum reserves. Some of you may do military service in the Gulf, so start learning the geography now. Imagine you are on an aircraft carrier making a clockwise circle around the Gulf. Upon entering the Strait of Hormuz, which countries do you pass to port?

Oman, United Arab Emirates, Qatar, Saudi Arabia, Bahrain (an island), Kuwait, Iraq, and Iran.

Shah as our pillar of stability in the Persian Gulf. We were his source of money, technology, and military hardware. Some 100,000 Iranian students came to U.S. universities, and 45,000 American businessmen and consultants surged into Iran for lucrative contracts. (This point demonstrates that person-to-person contacts do not always lead to good relations between countries.)

The United States was much too close to the Shah. We supported him unstintingly and unquestioningly. The Shah was Western-educated, anti-Communist, and was rapidly modernizing Iran; he was our kind of guy. Iranian unrest and opposition went unnoticed by the U.S. embassy. Elaborate Iranian public relations portrayed Iran in a rosy light in the U.S. media. Under Nixon, U.S. arms makers sold Iran "anything that goes bang." We failed to see that Iran and the Shah were two different things, and that our unqualified backing of the Shah was alienating many Iranians. We ignored how the Shah governed by means of a dreaded secret police, the SAVAK. We failed to call a tyrant a tyrant. Only when the Islamic Revolution broke out did we learn what Iranians really thought about the Shah. We were so obsessed by communism penetrating from the north that we could not imagine a bitter, hostile Islamic revolution coming from within Iran.

What finally did in the Shah? Too much money went to his head. With the 1973 Arab-Israeli war, oil producers worldwide got the chance to do what they had long wished: boost the price of oil and take over oil extraction from foreign companies. The Shah, one of the prime movers of the Organization of Petroleum Exporting Countries (**OPEC**), gleefully did both. What Mossadegh attempted, the Shah accomplished. World oil prices quadrupled. Awash with cash, the Shah went mad with vast, expensive schemes. The state administered oil revenues for the greater glory of Iran and its army, not for the Iranian people, creating resentment that hastened the Islamic Revolution. Oil led to turmoil.

KEY TERM

OPEC   Cartel of oil-rich countries designed to boost petroleum prices.

The sudden new wealth caused great disruption. The Shah promoted education, but the more education people got, the more they could see the Shah was a tyrant. Some people got rich fast while most stayed poor. Corruption grew worse than ever. Millions flocked from the countryside to the cities where, rootless and confused, they turned to the only institution they understood, the mosque. In their rush to modernize, the Pahlavis alienated the Muslim clergy. Not only did the Shah undermine the traditional cultural values of Islam, he seized land owned by religious foundations and distributed it to peasants as part of his White Revolution. The **mullahs** also hated the influx of American culture, with its alcohol and sex. Many Iranians saw the Shah's huge military expenditures—at the end, an incredible 17 percent of Iran's GDP—as a waste of money. As Alexis de Tocqueville noted in his study of the French Revolution, economic growth hastens revolution.

One of Iran's religious authorities, **Ayatollah** Khomeini, criticized the Shah and incurred his wrath. He had Khomeini exiled to Iraq in 1964 and then forced him to leave Iraq in 1978. France allowed Khomeini to live in a Paris suburb, from which his recorded messages were telephoned to cassette recorders in Iran to be duplicated and distributed through mosques nationwide. Cheap cassettes bypassed the Shah's control of Iran's media and helped bring him down.

In the late 1970s, matters came to a head. The Shah's overambitious plans had made Iran a debtor nation. Discontent from both secular intellectuals and Islamic clerics bubbled up. And, most dangerous, U.S. President Jimmy Carter made human rights a foreign-policy goal. As part of this, the Shah's dictatorship came under U.S. criticism. Shaken, the Shah began to relax his grip, and that is precisely when all hell broke loose. As de Tocqueville observed, the worst time in the life of a bad government is when it begins to mend its ways. Compounding his error, Carter showed his support for the Shah by exchanging visits, proof to Iranians that we were supporting a hated tyrant. In 1977, Carter and the Shah had to retreat into the White House from the lawn to escape the tear gas that drifted over from the anti-Shah protest (mostly by Iranian students) in Lafayette Park.

By late 1978, the Shah, facing huge demonstrations and (unknown to Washington) dying of cancer, was finished. Shooting into the crowds of protesters just made them angrier. The ancient Persian game of chess ends with a checkmate, a corruption of the Farsi *shah mat* ("the king is trapped"). On January 16, 1979, the last Pahlavi left Iran. *Shah mat.*

THE KEY INSTITUTIONS

A THEOCRACY

Two and a half millennia of monarchy ended in Iran with a 1979 referendum, carefully supervised by the Khomeini forces, that introduced the Islamic Republic of Iran and a new constitution. As in most countries, the offices of head of state and head of government are split. But instead of a figurehead monarch (as in Britain) or weak president (as in

KEY TERMS

mullah   Muslim cleric.
ayatollah   "Sign of God," top Shia religious leader.

Germany), Iran now has two heads of state, one its leading religious figure, the other a more standard president. The religious chief is the real power. That makes Iran a **theocracy** and a dysfunctional political system.

Theocracy is rather rare and tends not to last. Even in ancient times, priests filled supporting rather than executive roles. Russia's tsar, officially head of both church and state, was way over on the state side; he wore military garb, not priestly. Iran (plus Afghanistan and Sudan) attempted a theocratic system. The principle of political power in Iran—in the system devised by Khomeini—is the **velayat-e faqih**. This leading Islamic jurist, the *faqih*, serves for life. *Jurist* means a legal scholar steeped in Islamic, specifically Shia, religious law. (The closest Western equivalent is **canon law**. In medieval Europe, canon lawyers were among the leading intellectual and political figures.) Allegedly the *faqih*, also known as the "Spiritual Guide," can use the Koran and related Islamic commentaries to decide all issues, even those having nothing to do with religion. (An **Islamist**, of course, would say everything is connected with religion.)

Khomeini, the first and founding *faqih*, died in 1989. He was nearly all-powerful. His successor—the "Leader"—is chosen by an elected Assembly of Experts. These eighty-six Muslim clerics, elected every eight years, choose from among the purest and most learned Islamic jurists. The man they elect (Islam permits no women religious leaders) will likely already be an ayatollah, one of a handful of the wisest Shi'ite jurists, or he will be named an ayatollah.

Iran's *faqih* since 1989, Ayatollah Ali Khamenei, lacks Khomeini's charisma but is still the real power. He names the heads of all major state and religious organizations and may declare war. He controls the judiciary, armed forces, security police, intelligence agencies, radio, and television. He is more powerful than Iran's president and has continually blocked any reform efforts.

IRAN'S EXECUTIVE

Iran's working chief is a U.S.-type executive president, elected by popular vote for up to two four-year terms. The constitution specifies that this president is "the holder of the highest official power next to the office of the *faqih*," indicating he is second in power. Reform-minded President Muhammad Khatami (1997–2005) continually had to defer to the conservative policies of Khamenei. There was no open disagreement between the two, but it meant that Iran was unable to reform and modernize. The cabinet conducts the real day-to-day work of governance. Practically all new laws and the budget are devised by the cabinet and submitted to parliament for approval, modification, or rejection. It does not, however, control the "power ministries" of justice, police, and the armed forces, which are firmly in the hands of the Leader and his conservative helpers.

KEY TERMS

theocracy   Rule by priests.
velayat-e faqih   "Guardianship of the Islamic jurist," theocratic system devised by Khomeini.
canon law   Internal laws of Roman Catholic Church.
Islamist   Someone who uses Islam in political way.

DEMOCRACY

IRAN'S 2005 PRESIDENTIAL ELECTION

The surprise winner of Iran's 2005 presidential election, the ultraconservative mayor of Tehran, Mahmoud Ahmadinejad, age forty-nine, won on his populism and Islamism. Ahmadinejad, a passionate supporter of the 1979 Islamic Revolution, participated in the holding of U.S. hostages. The expected winner, Ayatollah Ali Akbar Hashemi Rafsanjani, who had earlier been president (1989–1997), talked a pragmatic and reformist line but was disliked as corrupt and part of the establishment.

The election was not democratic. The Council of Guardians screened out hundreds of candidates deemed liberal or insufficiently Islamic. Only eight were allowed to run, and one dropped out. Many charged the 2005 balloting was rigged, but they were silenced. Two critical newspapers were closed. Iran's religious hard-liners backed Ahmadinejad and ordered the army and the fanatic *Basiji* militia to turn out and bring their relatives to vote for Ahmadinejad, who was a Basiji and member of the Pasdaran Revolutionary Guards. Iran elects presidents with a French-style two rounds, the first for the two biggest winners, the second a runoff between them. Ahmadinejad won the second round 62–36 percent over Rafsanjani, with a 49 percent turnout. (About 2 percent spoiled their ballots in protest.)

Ahmadinejad had some mass support. Rafsanjani ran an aloof campaign based on his religious rank and political experience (he had also been Majlis speaker). His relatives became very wealthy. Ahmadinejad ran as a man of the people who lived modestly and looked after Tehran's poor in his two years as mayor. Ahmadinejad, the first Iranian president to hold no religious rank, has a doctorate in civil engineering. Some may have voted for him just to protest Iran's corrupt establishment.

Ahmadinejad's victory paralleled that of Muhammad Khatami, who won in a surprise landslide in 1997. Unknown before the election, Khatami hinted at reform and suddenly became a symbol of change. With no liberals allowed to run, Iranians turn to any outsider candidate as a protest. Khatami in office was blocked by Khamenei and the hard-liners and reformed nothing.

Ahmadinejad's young fanaticism does not necessarily predict his policies now. His anti-corruption populism may step on some toes. His vague initial statements mixed hard and moderate lines. He promised to fight corruption and subsidize the poor. He disdained any U.S. ties and will proceed with Iran's "peaceful" nuclear program. Many young Iranians feared a return to Islamic dress codes, but Ahmadinejad foreswore "any kind of extremism." He must still work under Khamenei but as a conservative may have more room to maneuver than Khatami.

IRAN'S LEGISLATURE

Iran has a unicameral (one-house) legislature, the Islamic Consultative Assembly (Majlis), consisting of 290 deputies elected for four-year terms. Iran uses single-member districts, like Britain and the U.S. Congress. Iran is divided into 265 constituencies, and each Iranian sixteen and older can vote. Additional seats are reserved for non-Muslim deputies: five each for Assyrian Christians, Jews, and Zoroastrians, two for Armenian Christians, none for

Baha'is. The Speaker of parliament is a major position. The constitution guarantees MPs immunity from arrest, but the conservative judiciary still jails MPs deemed too reformist.

Electoral balloting is free and fair, but permission to run is totally rigged. The Council of Guardians must approve all candidates, and they disqualify thousands who might be critical. Out-and-out liberals are thus discouraged from even trying to run. The low-turnout 2004 elections gave the Majlis to conservatives because no openly liberal or reformist candidates were allowed, so only half of Iranians bothered to vote.

More powerful than the Majlis is the Council of Guardians, a strange institution combining features of an upper house, a supreme court, an electoral commission, and a religious inquisition. Its twelve members serve six years each, half of them changed every three years. The *faqih* chooses six Islamic clerics; Iran's supreme court (the High Council of Justice) names another six, all Islamic lawyers, who are approved by the Majlis.

The Council examines each Majlis bill to make sure it does not violate Islamic principles. If a majority decides it does, the bill is returned to the Majlis to be corrected. Without Council approval, a bill is in effect vetoed. All bills aiming at reform are blocked in this way. To settle conflicts between the Majlis and the Council, an *Expediency Council* appointed by the Leader, has become like another legislature.

More important, the Council of Guardians examines all candidates and has the power to disqualify them without explanation. The Council scratches most Majlis and presidential candidates. In 2002 President Khatami and the Majlis tried to take this power away from the Council of Guardians, but the Council vetoed the bills. At present, the Council of Guardians makes the Iranian system unreformable.

EMERGING PARTIES?

Parties are legal under Iran's constitution, but the government does not allow them; only individual candidates run. Even Khomenei dissolved his own Islamic Republic party in 1984. Lack of party labels makes Iranian elections less than free, for without them voters cannot clearly discern who stands for what. It is difficult to count how many seats each of the several "tendencies" control; they have to be estimated. In practice, candidates are linked with informal parties and political tendencies. Eventually these may turn into legal parties. Observers see four main political groupings plus many factions and individual viewpoints.

Radicals, the most extreme supporters of the Islamic Revolution, want to adhere to what they perceive as Khomeini's design for an Islamic republic. Socialist in economics, they also favor state control over the economy. They wish to keep out Western influences and continue Islamic supervision of society, such as squads who dictate women's attire. President Ahmadinejad came from this ideological camp.

Conservatives, calmer than the radicals, want a nonfanatic Islamic Republic with special consideration for the economic needs of small merchants. They still oppose any liberalization.

Reformists tend to cluster in the educated middle class. They favor privatization of state enterprises, less Islamic supervision of society, elections open to most candidates, fewer powers for the Council of Guardians, and dialogue with the United States. In the late 1990s they held a majority in the Majlis and formed a sort of party called the Participation Front. With most of their candidates disqualified by the Council of Guardians in 2004, the Front resigned from the Majlis and boycotted elections.

Liberals would go farther. Popular among Iranian students, they emphasize democracy and civil rights and want totally free elections. They want to end all social controls imposed by the Islamists. In economics, however, they are a mixed bag, ranging from free-marketers to socialists. Knowing the Council of Guardians would reject them, no liberals run for office. In effect, there is no longer opposition in Iran's parliament.

A Partly Free System

Iran could be described as a political system longing to be free. The potential is there, but important institutional changes would have to be made. First, the power of the Leader would have to be reduced to that of a purely spiritual guide with few or no temporal powers. Next, the Council of Guardians would have to be abolished. If these two things happened Iran would almost automatically become a democracy, with a real executive president, a critical Majlis, multiparty elections, and a free press. Iran has the greatest democratic potential of any Persian Gulf country.

Iranian Political Culture

As in much of the Third World, many Iranians do not want their traditional culture erased by Western culture. "We want to be modern," say many citizens of the Third World, "but not like you. We'll do it our way, based on our values and our religion." Whether you can be a modern, high-tech society while preserving your old culture is a key question for much of the globe today. Will efforts to combine old and new cultures work or lead to chaos? In some cases, like Japan, it has worked. For Islamic nations, so far it has not. The key factor may be the flexibility and adaptability of the traditional culture, which is very high in the case of Japan. Japan learned to be modern but still distinctly Japanese. Can Muslim countries do the equivalent?

Beneath all the comings and goings of conquerors and kingdoms, Persian society kept its traditions for centuries. As in China, dynastic changes little disturbed the broad majority of the population, poor farmers and shepherds, many of them still tribal in organization. As in much of the Third World, traditional society was actually quite stable and conservative. Islam, the mosque, the mullah, and the **Koran** gave solace and meaning to the lives of most Persians. People were poor but passive.

Then came modernization, mostly under foreign pressure, starting late in the nineteenth century, expanding with the development of petroleum, and accelerating under the two Pahlavi shahs. Iran neatly raises the question of whether you can modernize and still keep your old culture. According to what political scientists call *modernization theory*, a number of things happen more or less simultaneously. First, the economy changes, from simple farming to natural-resource extraction to manufacturing and services. Along with this comes urbanization, the movement of people from country to city. At the same time, education levels increase greatly; most people become literate and some go to college.

Key Term

Koran   Muslim holy book.

POLITICAL CULTURE

IS ISLAM ANTI-MODERN?

Most Middle East experts deny there is anything inherent in Islamic doctrine that keeps Muslim societies from modernizing. Looking at cases, though, one finds no Islamic countries that have fully modernized. Under Ataturk, Turkey made great strides between the two wars, but Islamic militants still try to undo his reforms. In Huntington's terms (see page 276), Turkey is a "torn" country, pulled between Western and Islamic cultures. Recently Malaysia, half of whose people are Muslim, has scored rapid economic progress. Generally, though, Islam coincides with backwardness, at least as we define it. Some Muslim countries are rich but only because oil has brought them outside revenues.

By itself Islam does not cause backwardness. The Koran prohibits loaning money at interest, but there are ways to work around that. Islamic civilization was for centuries far ahead of Christian Europe in science, philosophy, medicine, sanitation, architecture, steelmaking, and more. Translations from the Arabic taught Europe classic Greek thought, which helped trigger the Renaissance and Europe's modernization. A millennium ago you would find Muslims concluding that Christianity kept Europe backward.

But Islamic civilization faltered and European civilization modernized. By the sixteenth century, when European merchant ships arrived in the Persian Gulf, the West was ahead of Islam. Why? According to some scholars, early Islam permitted independent interpretations of the Koran, but between the ninth and eleventh centuries this was replaced by a single, orthodox interpretation; intellectual life atrophied. Islam has never had a reformation.

The Mongol invaders of the thirteenth century massacred the inhabitants of Baghdad and destroyed the region's irrigation systems, something the Arab empire never recovered from. (The Mongols' impact on Russia was also devastating.) Possibly because of this Islam turned to mysticism. Instead of an open, flexible, and tolerant faith that was fascinated by learning and science, Islam turned sullen and rigid. When the Portuguese opened up direct trade routes between Europe and Asia, bypassing Islamic middlemen, trade through the Middle East declined sharply and with it the region's economy.

Islam has a structural problem in its combining of religion and government, making it difficult to split mosque and state. Those who try (e.g., Ataturk) are resisted. Even today, many Muslims want *sharia* (see page 273) to be the law of the land. This creates hostility between secular modernizers and religious traditionalists, who compete for political power, a destructive tug-of-war that blocks progress.

More important, the domination of European (chiefly British) imperialists starting in the nineteenth century created the same resentment we saw in China, the resentment of a proud civilization brought low by unwelcome foreigners: "You push in here with your guns, your railroads, and your commerce and act superior to us. Well, culturally and morally we are superior to you, and eventually we'll kick you out and show you." With this comes hatred of anything Western and therefore opposition to modernity, because accepting modernity means admitting the West is superior. Islam teaches it is superior to all other civilizations and will eventually triumph worldwide. Devout Muslims do not like evidence to the contrary.

If Islamic countries do not discard their cultural antipathy to modernity—which need not be a total imitation of the West—their progress will be slow and often reversed. Millions of Muslims living in the West are modern and still Islamic. Ideas for religious modernization are already afoot in Islam with, ironically, Iranian intellectuals in the lead. Eventually, we could see societies that are both modern and Muslim. One of the best ways to promote this: Educate women.

People consume more mass media—at first newspapers, then radio, and finally television—until many people are aware of what is going on in their country and in the world. A large middle class emerges along with a variety of interest groups. People now want to participate in politics; they do not like being treated like children.

It was long supposed that **secularization** comes with modernization, and both Ataturk and the Pahlavis had tough showdowns with the mullahs. But Iran's Islamic Revolution and other religious revivals now make us question the inevitability of secularization. Under certain conditions—when things change too fast, when the economy declines and unemployment grows, and modernization repudiates traditional values—people may return to religion with renewed fervor. If their world seems to be falling apart, church or mosque give stability and meaning to life. This is as true of the present-day United States as it is of Algeria. In the Muslim world, many intellectuals first passionately embraced modernizing creeds of socialism and nationalism only to despair and return to Islam. (Few intellectuals, however, embraced free-market capitalism, which was too much associated with the West.)

The time of modernization is a risky one in the life of a nation. If the old elite understands the changes that are bubbling through their society, they will gradually give way toward democracy in a way that does not destabilize the system. A corrupt and foolish elite, on the other hand, that is convinced the masses are not ready for democracy (and never will be), hold back political reforms until there is a tremendous head of steam. Then, no longer able to withstand the pressure, they suddenly give way, chaos breaks out and ends in tyranny. If the old elite had reformed sooner and gradually, they might have lowered the pressure and eased the transition to democracy. South Korea and Taiwan are examples of a favorable transition from dictatorship to democracy. Iran under the Shah is a negative example.

The Shah was arrogant: He alone would uplift Iran. He foresaw no democratic future for Iran and cultivated no important sectors of the population to support him. When the end came, few Iranians did support him. Indeed, the Shah scorned democracy in general, viewing it as a chaotic system that got in its own way, a view as old as the ancient Persian attack on Greece. The mighty Persian empire, under one ruler, could surely beat a quarrelsome collection of Greek city-states. (Wrong!) The Shah supposed that Iran, under his enlightened despotism, would soon surpass the decadent West. A journalist once asked the Shah why he did not relinquish some of his personal power and become a symbolic monarch, like the king of Sweden. He replied: "I will become like the king of Sweden when Iranians become like Swedes."

The answer to this overly simple view is that, yes, when your people are poor and ignorant, absolute rule is one of your few alternatives. Such a country is far from ready for democracy. But after considerable modernization—which the Shah himself had implemented—Iran became a different country, one characterized by the changes discussed earlier. An educated middle class resents one-man rule; the bigger this class, the more resentment builds. By modernizing, the Shah sawed off the tree limb on which he was sitting. He modernized Iran until it no longer wanted him.

KEY TERM

secularization   Cutting back role of religion in government and daily life.

KEY CONCEPTS

IS ISLAMIC FUNDAMENTALISM THE RIGHT NAME?

Some object to the term *Islamic fundamentalism*. Coined in the early twentieth century to describe U.S. Bible-belt Protestants, fundamentalism stands for inerrancy of Scripture: The Bible means what it says and is not open to interpretation. But that is the way virtually all Muslims view the Koran, so Muslims are automatically fundamentalists. Some thinkers propose we call it *Islamic integralism* instead, indicating a move to integrate the Koran and sharia with government. *Integralism* too is borrowed, from a Catholic movement early in the twentieth century whose adherents sought to live a Christ-like existence. The Muslim movement for returning to the pure Islam of the founders is *salafiyya*. It has been around for centuries in several forms. The Wahhabi Islam of Saudi Arabia and al Qaeda are *salafi*.

Some political scientists use the term *political Islam*, indicating it is the political use of religion to gain power. The term *Islamism*, a religion turned into a political ideology, won favor for the simple reason that it is short (not a bad reason).

ISLAM AS A POLITICAL IDEOLOGY

Ayatollah Khomeini developed an interesting ideology that resonated with many Iranians. Traditionally Shia Islam has kept away from politics, waiting for the return of the Twelfth Imam to rule (see box on page 304). Khomenei and his followers, departing from this old tradition, decided that while they wait the top Shia religious leaders should also assume political power. Called by some **Islamism**, it was not only religious but also social, economic, and nationalistic. The Shah and his regime, held Khomeini, had both abandoned Islam and turned away from economic and social justice. They allowed the rich and corrupt to live in Westernized luxury while most struggled in poverty. They sold out Iran to the Americans, exchanging the people's oil for U.S. weapons. Tens of thousands of Americans lived in Iran, corrupting Iran's youth with their "unclean" morals. By returning to the Koran, as interpreted by the mullahs, Iranians would not only cleanse themselves spiritually but also build a just society of equals. The mighty would be brought low and the poor raised up by welfare benefits administered by mosques and Islamic associations. Like communism, Islamism preaches leveling of class differences, but through the mosque and mullahs rather than through the Party and *apparatchiks*.

Islamism is thus a catchall ideology, offering an answer to most things that made Iranians discontent. It is a potent mix, but can it work? Probably not. Over time, its several

KEY TERM

Islamism   Islam turned into political ideology.

KEY CONCEPTS

SUNNI AND SHIA

Over 80 percent of the world's Muslims practice the mainstream branch of Islam, called Sunni. Scattered unevenly throughout the Muslim world, however, is a minority branch (of 100 million) called Shia. The two split early over who was the true successor (*caliph*) of Mohammed. Shias claim the Prophet's cousin and son-in-law Ali has the title, but he was assassinated in 661. Shia means followers or partisans, hence Shias are the followers of Ali. When Ali's son, Hussein, attempted to claim the title, his forces were beaten at Karbala in present-day Iraq (now a Shia shrine) in 680, and Hussein was betrayed and tortured to death. This gave Shia a fixation on martyrdom; some of their holidays feature self-flagellation.

Shia also developed a messianic concept lacking in Sunni. Shias in Iran hold that the line of succession passed through a series of twelve *imams* (religious leaders) of whom Ali was the first. The twelfth imam disappeared in 873 but is to return one day to "fill the world with justice." He is referred to as the Hidden Imam and the Expected One. Such believers are sometimes called "Twelver" Muslims.

Shias are no more "fundamentalist" than other Muslims, who also interpret the Koran strictly. Although the origin and basic tenets of the two branches are identical, Sunnis regard Shias as extremist, mystical, and crazy. Only in Iran is Shia the majority faith and state religion. With their underdog status elsewhere, Shias sometimes become rebellious (with Iranian money and guidance), as in Lebanon, southern Iraq, and eastern Arabia. Shia imparts a peculiar twist to Iranians, giving them the feeling of being isolated but right, beset by enemies on all sides, and willing to martyr themselves for their cause.

strands fall apart, and its factions quarrel. Islamism's chief problem is economics (as we shall consider in greater detail later). As Islamism recedes as a viable ideology, look for the reemergence of other ideologies in Iran.

DEMOCRACY AND AUTHORITY

Many observers think rule by the mullahs will be overturned. Western diplomats estimate that only about 15 percent of Iranians support the current regime. But can Iranians then establish a stable democracy, or was the Shah right—do Iranians need a strong hand to govern them? There were two impulses behind the 1979 revolution: secularist intellectuals seeking democracy and Islamists seeking theocracy. The secular democrats, always a small minority, threw in with the more numerous Islamists, figuring they would be an effective tool to oust the Shah and that the two would form an equal partnership. But the Islamists, better organized and knowing exactly what they wanted, used the secular democrats and

POLITICAL CULTURE

ARE IRANIANS RELIGIOUS FANATICS?

Only a minority of Iranians are Muslim fanatics. Not even the supposed Islamic fundamentalists are necessarily fanatic. Many Iranians are perfectly aware that religion is a political tool (more on this in the next section) and are fed up with it. Massive regime propaganda depicts the United States as the "Great Satan," but most Iranians are very friendly to the few Americans who visit. Some have been in the United States or have relatives there; many remember that when Iran was allied with America, Iraq did not dare invade. Iran was the only Muslim country where tens of thousands spontaneously showed sympathy with Americans after 9/11. Do not confuse regime propaganda with the attitudes of ordinary citizens.

Ironically, Iranians pointed to the now defunct Taliban government of neighboring Afghanistan as *salafi* extremists. Far stricter than Iranian Islamists, the Taliban confined women to the home and required all men to have beards. Why the conflict with Iran? Like most of Afghanistan, the Taliban were Sunni and attacked the Shia minority, some 1.5 million of whom fled to Iran. The Taliban killed Iranian intelligence agents who were aiding Afghan Shias. Dangerous stuff, this religious extremism.

then dumped them (in some cases, shot them). Many fled to other countries. Learning too late what was happening to them, some democratic supporters of the Revolution put out the slogan: "In the dawn of freedom, there is no freedom."

But these secular democrats did not disappear; they simply laid low and went along outwardly with the Islamic Revolution. To have opposed it openly could have earned them the firing squad. Among them are the smartest and best-educated people in Iran, the very people needed to make the economy grow. With Iran's drastic economic decline, many lost their jobs and became private consultants and specialists, working out of their apartments. Tens of thousands emigrate each year, preferably to the United States and Canada. Many of them—once they are sure you are not a provocateur for the regime—speak scathingly in private of the oppression and economic foolishness of the mullahs. "I believe in Islam, but not in the regime of the mullahs," said one Iranian.

People like these—who voted for Khatami in 1997 and 2001—believe Iranians are capable of democracy. They argue that the anti-Shah revolution was hijacked by the Islamists but that its original impulse was for democracy, not theocracy, and this impulse still remains. Especially now that people have tasted the economic decline, corruption, and general ineptitude of the mullahs, they are ready for democracy. If the regime ever opens up, the secular democrats will go public to demand open elections with no parties declared ineligible. For now, they lay low and aim their TV satellite dishes to pick up critical views from the large (800,000) Iranian community in the United States.

DEMOCRACY

IRAN'S ANGRY STUDENTS

In the late 1970s, Iranian students, most of them leftists, battled to overturn the old regime. Now Iran's students—who number over one million—again demonstrate for civil rights. Many students are outspoken liberals and want to push for pluralism, a free press, and free elections. As before, they also protest the serious lack of jobs.

Every year hard-line courts—especially the Revolutionary Court—close liberal newspapers and block Web sites. Between 2,000 and 4,000 Iranian editors, writers, professors, public-opinion pollsters, student leaders, and politicians are in jail. Some of them fought in the 1979 Revolution and in the long war against Iraq. At least a hundred dissidents were mysteriously killed. In protest, students demonstrate—chanting "Death to dictatorship"—which leads to arrests and violence. In 2002 Professor Hashem Aghajari, who lost a leg and a brother in the war against Iraq, was sentenced to death (never carried out) for advocating an *Islamic Protestantism* to separate mosque and state. Massive pro-Aghajari student demonstrations swept Iranian campuses.

Could students one day lead the way to democracy? By themselves, probably not. They are too few and not organized. But in combination with other groups, they could push moderates to take stronger reformist stances. In many countries, students have been the spark plugs of revolution.

PERSIAN NATIONALISM

Islam is not the only political force at work in Iran. Remember, Islam was imposed on Persia by the sword, and Iranians to this day harbor folk memories of seventh-century massacres by crude, barbaric invaders. Iranians do not like Arabs and look down on them as culturally inferior and lacking staying power. By adopting Shia, Iranians were and are able to distinguish themselves from their mostly Sunni neighbors. "Yes, of course we are Muslims," is the Iranian message, "but we are not like these other Muslim countries." Accordingly, not far under the surface of Iranian thought is a kind of Persian nationalism, affirming the greatness of their ancient civilization, which antedates Islam by a millennium.

The Shah especially stressed Persian nationalism in his drive to modernize Iran. The Shah was Muslim and had himself photographed in religious devotion, as on his **hajj**, required of all Muslims who can afford it once in their lifetime. But the Shah's true spirit was secular and nationalistic: to rebuild the glory of ancient Persia in a modern Iran. If Islam got in the way, it was to be pushed aside. The Shah was relatively tolerant of non-Muslim faiths; Baha'is (a universalistic and liberal offshoot of Islam), Jews, and Christians

KEY TERM

hajj   Muslim pilgrimage to Mecca.

POLITICAL CULTURE

DOES ISLAM DISCRIMINATE AGAINST WOMEN?

Iran is one of the better Muslim countries in the treatment of women. Unlike the Arab kingdoms on the southern shore of the Gulf, Iranian women drive cars, go to school, work outside the home, and participate in politics. But even in Iran there are tough restrictions on dress, contact with males, and travel.

Devout Muslims swear that women are deeply honored in their societies, but their place is in the home and nowhere else. Women are indeed kept at a subservient status in most Islamic countries; most often they receive little education and do not have personal liberties such as driving a car, and their testimony is worth half of men's in courts of law. But such discrimination does not always come from the Koran. In some Muslim countries (not Iran), such customs as the seclusion of women, the veil, and female genital mutilation are pre-Islamic and were absorbed by Islam (much as Europeans adopted for Christmas the pagan worship of trees). These non-Koranic imports can therefore be discarded with no harm to the faith, maintain Muslim feminists. Yes, there are such people, and increasingly they are speaking out and organizing. If they succeed, they will greatly modernize their societies. The widespread education of Iranian women predicts social and legal change.

were unharmed. Since the Islamic Revolution, non-Muslims have been treated harshly, especially the 300,000 Baha'is, Iran's largest minority religion, who are regarded as dangerous **heretics**. For centuries, Iran's sense of its unique Persianness coexisted uneasily with its Islam. The Shah's modernization program brought the two strands into open conflict.

If you look closely, the Islamic Revolution of 1979 did not totally repudiate the Persian nationalist strand of Iranian thought. Rather, it put the stress on the religious side of Persianness. The long and horrible war with Iraq, 1980–1988, brought out the Persian nationalism of the Islamist regime. They were fighting not only for their faith but for their country and against a savage, upstart Arab country, Iraq, that did not even exist until the British invented it in the 1920s. Iran celebrates two types of holidays, Persian and Muslim. The Persian holidays are all happy, such as New Year (*Now Ruz*). The Islamic holidays are mostly mournful, such as the day of remembrance of the martyrdom of Hussein at Karbala, during which young Shia men beat themselves until they bleed. In analyzing Iranian political attitudes, remember that Persianness is about as strong as Islam, and Iranian regimes typically base themselves on both, although often giving more weight to one. As the Islamic Revolution tires, look for Iran to re-emphasize Persianness.

KEY TERM

heretic   Someone who breaks away from a religion.

Patterns of Interaction

Religion as a Political Tool

Manipulate, use, dump. This is how Khomeini's forces treated those who helped them win the Revolution. Like turbaned Bolsheviks, the Islamists in the late 1970s hijacked the Iranian revolution as it unfolded. First, they captured the growing discontent with the Shah and his regime. By offering themselves as a plausible and effective front organization, they enlisted all manner of anti-Shah groups under their banner—the democratically inclined parties of the National Front, the Iran Freedom Movement, the Marxist (and Soviet-connected) Tudeh party, and Islamic guerrilla movements. They had these groups do their dirty work for them, and then got rid of them, sometimes by firing squad. The flowering of democratic, Islamic, secular, and socialist parties that accompanied the Shah's overthrow was crushed within three years. As an example of revolutionary technique, Lenin would have admired their skill and ruthlessness.

In doing all this, the Islamists used their religion much as the Bolsheviks used Marxism—as a tool, a recruiting and mobilizing device, a means of gaining authority and obedience, and a way to seize and consolidate power. This is not to say they were not serious about Islam, but rather that in a revolutionary situation the instrumental uses of their faith predominated over the devotional. If you want to seize state power, you cannot be otherworldly; you must be very shrewd and practical. There is nothing "crazy" about the Islamists who run Iran; they are perfectly capable of calm and rational decisions calculated to benefit themselves. They only look crazy.

After some time immersed in politics, the power side takes over and the original religious (or ideological) side takes a back seat. As with the Bolsheviks, this soon leads to opportunism and cynicism among the politically involved and ultimately to regime decay. The ruling group turns into a self-serving new class. This is why regimes that base themselves on ideology or religion (Islamism combines both) have finite life spans. After a while, everyone notices the power and greed of the ruling class, and mass disillusion sets in; the regime loses legitimacy. This is happening in Iran. Iran's Islamic revolution will burn out.

An example of this was the seizure of the U.S. embassy in Tehran by student militants in November 1979, which brought American cries of outrage and a complete break in relations. The embassy takeover and holding of fifty-two American officials for 444 days indeed broke every rule in the diplomatic book and seemed to prove that mad fanatics governed Iran.

Looked at more closely, though, the incident was a domestic Iranian power play, cynically manipulated by the Khomeini forces. The ayatollah had no further use for the prime minister he had appointed early in 1979, Mehdi Bazargan, a moderate. How to get rid of him and other moderates? The occasion was the admission of the ailing Shah to the United States for cancer treatment. Khomeini's cadres whipped up mass rage in Iran, claiming that medical help for the Shah proved the United State still supported the ousted regime. Then they had a group of student militants invade and take over the U.S. embassy, which had already been reduced to a skeleton staff. No shots were fired; the U.S. Marine guards were ordered not to shoot. They took sixty-six Americans prisoner—but killed none and released fourteen—and published classified embassy documents (pieced together from the shredder) purporting to show how dastardly the Americans were.

The Islamic activists, using anti-American hysteria ("Death to USA!"), consolidated their hold on the country. Humiliated and powerless, Bazargan resigned. Anyone opposed to the embassy takeover was fired or worse. One foreign-ministry official (who had dropped out of Georgetown University to promote revolution) helped some Americans escape via the Canadian embassy. He was tried and shot. Khomeini's followers seemed to enjoy watching President Carter squirm, especially after the aborted U.S. rescue mission in April 1980. Carter's apparent weakness on Iran hurt him in the 1980 election, which he lost to Reagan.

At that point, the holding of U.S. diplomats had exhausted its utility for Khomeini. Knowing Reagan was not averse to military measures, Tehran released the diplomats just as he was inaugurated. The militants who had seized and held the Americans had also served their purpose. Considered unreliable, some were arrested and executed. Others were sent to the front in the war with Iraq, where they died in the fighting. As a historian of the French Revolution observed, the revolution devours its children.

MODERATES AND ISLAMISTS IN IRAN

After the 1986 Iran-contra fiasco, in which White House aides attempted to secretly sell U.S. missiles to Iranian "moderates," the term *Iranian moderate* disappeared from Washington's vocabulary. The U.S. officials fell for a sucker play by Iranian leaders, who set up the deal and then leaked word that the United States was trading with Iran, illegal under U.S. law. These people never miss a chance to embarrass the United States. There are Iranian moderates, but they have learned to keep their mouths shut and do nothing stupid, like having contact with Americans. Instead, the Iranians who fit under the labels *moderates* and *liberals* discussed earlier play a cautious game, not directly opposing the Islamic revolution while trying to tone it down. They are in a permanent power struggle with conservative forces.

The strongest and most dangerous conservative force is the Islamic Revolutionary Guards (*Pasdaran*). Originally formed in 1979 to support Khomeini, they took many casualties in the war with Iraq and now, with 150,000 members, are separate from and better than the regular army, rather like the SS under Hitler. They get the best weapons, dominate the defense and intelligence ministries, and supervise Iran's nuclear-bomb program, arguing that only with nukes can Iran to stand up to America. They are the "muscle" of the conservative clerics and likely more influential than them. Former Pasdaran hold about a third of Majlis seats and set the agenda and dictate policy to the president. Direct military influence in politics, "praetorianism," as we considered in China and Nigeria, is a hallmark of the Third World. President Ahmadinejad, elected in 2005, was a member of the Pasdaran, suggesting a praetorian element in Iranian politics.

Those who fit under the labels "radicals" and "conservatives" described earlier, want a truly Islamic republic, one based on religious law and presided over by the *faqih*. Anything else means giving in to Iran's enemies—the West in general, the United States in particular—with eventual loss of Iran's independence, culture, and religion. They block any liberalizing reforms, from closing newspapers to voting out ministers to putting allies of Khatami on trial.

In a parallel with what we did earlier for Russia and China, we can construct a list of Iranian moderate and Islamist views (see table on page 310). On at least a couple of points

Moderates	Islamists
end Islamic revolution	maintain it
shift power to Majlis	preserve power of *faqih*
permit all parties	ban non-Islamic parties
free press	censored press
permit Western women's attire	Islamic attire only (veil)
improve relations with West	keep distant from West
dialogue with America	hate America
end nuclear programs	build nuclear bombs
liberalize economy	keep economy statist

there is no clear divergence between moderates and Islamists. First, both groups are Muslim and want to preserve a generally Islamic emphasis in public life, including the judicial system. Second, both groups want economic growth, both for the sake of Iran's national power and to improve the lot of its people. How to do this is the issue: free market or state controlled? In elections no one runs on an opposition platform; all seem to be supporting at least a version of the Islamic revolution. In Iran, direct opposition could be hazardous to your health. It is in the nuances among groupings that differences begin to appear.

There are some Iranians, both inside and outside the country, who would like to get rid of the whole Islamic revolution. A few monarchists would like to restore the son of the last Pahlavi, a young man now living in the West, to the throne, but even Iranians who think the Shah's rule was not so bad do not give this option a chance. The times are against monarchy; every decade there are fewer and fewer ruling (as opposed to figurehead) monarchs.

On the other side, some Marxist-type revolutionaries, the *Mujahedin-e Khalq* (Fighters for the People), who earlier worked with the Islamists to overthrow the Shah now try to overthrow the Islamists. Among them were some of the young militants who seized the U.S. embassy. Subsequently, it is estimated that over 10,000 Mujahedin were executed by the Khomeini forces. Their survivors were sheltered in and sponsored by Saddam Hussein's Iraq, which invaded and massacred Iranians (sometimes with poison gas), during the 1980s, so these Mujahedin have little resonance among Iranians. Even Washington now considers them a crazy cult.

Change is coming from the struggle between Iranian militants and moderates, not the influence of outside forces. Some of the regime's sharpest critics were leaders of the 1979 revolution, including Grand Ayatollah Hossein Ali Montazeri, one of the most senior figures of Shia Islam, now held in house arrest in the holy city of Qom for denouncing repression and demanding reform. "Either officials change their methods and give freedom to the people, and stop interfering in elections, or the people will rise up with another revolution," he warned. Another voice is that of 2003 Nobel Peace Prize winner Shirin Ebadi, a lawyer and regime opponent who defends Iranians' human rights. She also cites the Koran to show Islam should not discriminate against women, a view shared by many Iranian women. Iran could be the birthplace of Islamic feminism.

The spirit of Iran's Islamic Revolution lives on in this Tehran cemetery memorial to the fallen of the Iran–Iraq war of 1980–1988. Iranian losses were horrifying—possibly a quarter of a million killed, many of them boys. Note the women in chadors in the foreground. (Mehrdad Madresehee)

THE REVOLUTION BURNS OUT

Iran fits Crane Brinton's classic theory of revolution (see box on page 312): The Shah's regime loses its legitimacy. Antiregime groups form, rioting breaks out, and the Shah leaves. Initially moderates take power, but the ruthless Khomeini forces soon dump them and drive the revolution to a frenzied high point. But this burns itself out; eventually a "Thermidor," or calming down, arrives. It was almost as if Iranians had read Brinton—every stage, that is, except the last, and even that seems to have happened without a clear-cut Thermidor. Instead, there may be a low-key, rolling Thermidor that led to Khatami's election in 1997.

No revolution lasts forever. In Iran we see an effort to become stable and normal, opposed by Islamic conservatives. Time is probably on the side of the normalizers. Many mullahs have corrupted themselves; some do not go onto the street in clerical garb. Mullahs run the *bonyads*, foundations originally set up to redistribute the wealth of the Shah and his supporters. These *bonyads* now control billions of dollars and much of Iran's industry. They are supposed to be run for the good of all, a sort of Islamic socialism, but in practice they have made their mullahs rich, powerful, and corrupt while their industries are run poorly. As Lord Acton observed (see page 32), power corrupts.

Aware of this, many Iranians want the mullahs to return to the mosque and get out of government and the economy. Even some mullahs wish it, as now they see that running a country ruins their reputation and their spiritual mission. Chant Iranian demonstrators:

KEY CONCEPTS

BRINTON'S THEORY OF REVOLUTION

The great Harvard historian Crane Brinton in his 1938 *The Anatomy of Revolution* argued that all revolutions pass through similar stages. He compared several revolutions, but his main model was the French. Brinton's stages are as follows:

- The old regime loses its governing effectiveness and legitimacy. It becomes inept and indecisive. Intellectuals especially become **alienated** from it. An improving economy provokes discontent and jealousy.

- The first stage of revolution comes with the growth of antiregime groups. Triggering the revolution is a political problem—such as whether the three estates should meet separately or together—that the old regime cannot solve. Rioting breaks out, but troops sent to crush it desert to the rioters. The antiregime people easily take over power amidst popular rejoicing.

- Moderates initially seize power. They opposed the old regime, but as critics rather than as revolutionaries. They want major reform rather than total revolution. Extremists accuse them of being weak and cowardly, and true enough, they are not ruthless enough to crush the extremists.

- Extremists take over because they are more ruthless, purposeful, and organized than the moderates. In what Brinton likened to a high fever during an illness, the extremists whip up revolution to a frenzy, throwing out everything old, forcing people to be good, and punishing real or imagined enemies in a reign of terror. In France, this stage came with Robespierre; in Iran, with Khomeini.

- A **Thermidor**, or calming-down period, ends the reign of terror. Every revolution has a Thermidor, which Brinton likened to a convalescence after a fever, because human nature cannot take the extremists and their revolutionary purity for too long. Power may then fall into the hands of a dictator who restores order but not liberty—a Napoleon.

Brinton's theory became a classic and has largely stood the test of time. Revolutions do seem to pass through stages, although their timing cannot be predicted with accuracy. Iran has followed the Brinton pattern.

"The mullahs live like kings, while the people are reduced to poverty." Another factor is that now most Iranians were born after the Shah and have no personal commitment to the Islamic revolution. They want jobs and more freedom, and they can vote at age sixteen.

KEY TERMS

alienated   Psychologically distant and hostile.

Thermidor   Month when Robespierre fell, a calming down after a revolutionary high.

GEOGRAPHY

HOW MANY IRANIANS?

Islam traditionally frowns on family planning: The more babies the better. After the revolution, Iran's mullahs urged women to produce a generation of Muslim militants; subsidized food helped feed them. Iran's rate of population growth averaged 3.5 percent a year during the 1980s, one of the world's highest. Despite the murderous war with Iraq, since the 1979 Revolution Iran's population doubled from 34 million to 68 million.

By the early 1990s, though, the government, realizing it could not subsidize or employ the vast numbers of young Iranians—two-thirds were born after the Revolution—reversed the high-births policy. Amid economic decline, families now can afford fewer children. Clinics now offer all manner of contraception free of charge (but not abortions). Women agents go door-to-door to promote family planning. Food and other family aid is decreased after a family has three children. One Muslim cleric even issued a *fatwa* in favor of smaller families. From an average 7 births per woman in 1986, the fertility rate dropped to half, to 3.6 births per woman over her life in 1993, actually much lower than before the revolution. By 2002, the rate of population growth was down to a modest 1.1 percent. The turnaround on births is an indication the revolution is over.

Will there be a point at which we can say the Iranian revolution is finally over? The reestablishment of diplomatic ties between the United States and Iran—something many Iranians want to happen soon—would indicate that point had passed some time earlier. Khatami mentioned "dialogue" with Americans (but not with Washington) but pulled back when conservative forces objected. Other indications would be the mullahs giving up control of the *bonyads* and the *faqih* becoming a figurehead or "dignified" office.

WHAT IRANIANS QUARREL ABOUT

WHICH WAY FOR IRAN'S ECONOMY?

Iran has changed rapidly, partly under the Shah and partly under the Islamic Revolution. The countryside has received schools, electricity, health care, and tractors. Infant mortality, a key measure of health care, fell from 169 per 1,000 births in 1960 to 33 in 1996. Average life expectancy jumped twenty years, from 50 to 70. Literacy has climbed from less than half to three-fourths. More Iranian women than ever are in schools and universities (segregated from males, of course).

The Iranian economy was hurt by revolution, war, isolation, and mismanagement. Although total oil income has increased, per capita GDP has barely recovered to pre-1979 levels. And much of the increase is due to the 2004 runup in world oil prices. If oil prices fall,

COMPARISON

IS SAUDI ARABIA NEXT?

The 9/11 attacks suggested that the Kingdom, as Saudis call their country, is lurching into instability. Fifteen of the nineteen hijackers were Saudis. Al Qaeda terrorists set off bombs in the Kingdom. Islamists like Osama bin Laden, son of a Saudi billionaire, represent the same kind of forces that overthrew the Shah in Iran. The Saudi regime is almost paralyzed by fear of this. It tries to buy off threats and deflect discontent by funding extremist religious schools (many in Pakistan) and minimizing Islamist recruitment.

The House of Saud conquered the country in the 1920s based on the austere Wahhabi creed of strict Islam and is highly vulnerable for the same reasons as the Shah of Iran. Saudi Arabia is less democratic than Iran is now, and the legitimacy of the royal family has eroded amidst charges of abandoning Wahhabism in favor of Western pleasures. Of the five thousand Saudi princes, more than five hundred are eligible to become king, an invitation for a succession struggle.

Oil created some very rich people, including the princes, but left many poor Saudis far behind. Earlier, the oil revenues allowed the regime to buy loyalty with subsidies for thousands of Saudis. But oil prices fluctuate, and the population exploded from 7 million in 1980 to 20 million in 2004, cutting per capita Saudi income in half. Forty percent of the population is under fourteen. Cushy jobs no longer await young Saudis; many are unemployed and discontented. Shia Saudis from the oil-producing Eastern Province carry out bombings (with Iranian backing), including American targets.

News from the Kingdom is rigorously censored—nothing negative is allowed—and until 9/11 Washington never criticized "our good friends," the House of Saud. It was the same way we treated the Shah. After 9/11 some Americans called Saudi Arabia a false friend and supplier of money and personnel for Islamist terrorism. A succession struggle over the new king could destabilize the Kingdom. It

Iran is in trouble. There is some growth, but inflation is still hefty, and unemployment (estimated at 20 percent) and poverty are worse than under the Shah. Iran needs some 1.5 million new jobs a year. Pay is low so people hold two or three jobs to make ends meet. Many jobs and business dealings, as in Russia, are off the books. The oil industry, still the pride and basis of the Iranian economy, needs replacement parts and up-to-date technology. Its productivity is miserable. U.S. pressure has kept most oil companies from cooperating with Iran. The *bonyads* are run badly and corruptly, and increasingly Iranians notice this.

By giving all Iranians a welfare floor (including subsidized food and gasoline) while simultaneously damaging Iran's great source of revenue (its petroleum connection with the West), Tehran could run out of money. Iran has run large annual budget deficits, which translate into persistent inflation. The Shah left a foreign debt of $8.4 billion, which the Khomeini regime, amid great hardship, repaid, swearing Iran would never fall into imperialist clutches again. But by 1996, Iran's foreign debt was a dangerous $33 billion. The high oil prices of 2004 and 2005 allowed Iran to escape its debt problem and may be too late to do anything to prevent a Saudi revolution. Reforms can hasten revolution, as we saw in Iran. Controlled moves to democracy, such as these, might stabilize the Kingdom.

- Allow some opposition parties. Make sure they are moderate, and let them criticize the regime in a constructive way. Make sure there are several parties (some conservative, some liberal, none radical) to divide public discontent.
- Permit a semifree press along the same lines as parties: limited criticism only.
- Crush and suppress Islamists. Do not ease up on them. These people are out to destroy you, and if they take over they will not be moderate or democratic.
- Hold legislative elections but among parties ranging from conservative to moderate. Gradually, you can let other parties participate.
- Have the new legislature redistribute wealth in the form of heavy taxes on the rich, especially on members of the royal family, who must be seen taking a financial hit. This is to defuse mass anger over the royals' great and unfair wealth.
- Do not automatically follow U.S. policy in the region, as that delegitimizes your regime. Limit any American presence; it is a cultural irritant and natural fodder for Islamic extremists. (Saudi leaders did not support our 2003 invasion of Iraq and had U.S. troops leave. They are not stupid.)
- Crack down on corruption, especially among the highest officials and princes. Show that you mean business here, and that the crackdown will be permanent.

Have we learned anything from Iran? Would any of this work to head off a revolution? Maybe, but it would require the willingness of the House of Saud to cut its own wealth and power, and that is something ruling classes rarely do. But if Saudi Arabia cannot transition to some kind of democracy, revolution and then U.S. military involvement is likely. The Persian Gulf and its oil is one place we do not walk away from.

induce a temporary prosperity. The **hezbollahis** still try to supervise much of Iranian society, but they are an increasingly resented minority, the functional equivalent of the old Soviet Communist party. And you recall what happened to them.

The Islamic Revolution did not dismantle the Shah's statist economy. The state still controls 60 percent of Iran's economy (biggest part: the oil industry). The *bonyads* control another 10 to 20 percent. Only about 20 percent of Iran's economy is in private hands. Theoretically, foreigners can invest in Iran, but most are scared off by the many and tangled limits and regulations. Investors must pay numerous bribes. Iran's is not a free-market economy. The big question: Should it become one?

KEY TERM

hezbollahi   "Partisan of God," fanatic supporter of Islamism.

POLITICAL CULTURE

THE UNITED STATES AND IRAN

A culture gap hinders Americans and Iranians from understanding each other. We have not been clever in dealing with the Iranian Revolution. Part religious, part nationalistic, part cultural, and part anti-tyranny, it defied our predictions and efforts to tame it. When we tried to deal with "Iranian moderates" in 1986, we got humiliated. When we tilted toward Iraq in its war against Iran, we supported a fiendish dictator (Saddam Hussein) whom we twice fought ourselves. In 1988 a U.S. destroyer mistook an Iranian jetliner for an attacking fighter, shot it down with a missile, and killed all 290 aboard. Iran, and indeed the whole Persian Gulf, is a tar baby: Once you punch it, you get stuck worse and worse.

But if we are calm and clever, things may work out. Iran's Islamic revolution is over and moderates could eventually take over. Most Iranians want contact and dialogue with the United States. In the long term, Iran needs us. We can provide the petroleum technology and other means to modernize the country. If an aggressive Russia starts rebuilding its Caucasus empire, Iran would need U.S. support. Historically, Russia always had territorial designs on Persia; the United States never did.

Anthropologists point out that when two Iranian *bazaaris* quarrel, by long tradition they simply shun and ignore each other for some years. Gradually, the quarrel fades and they cautiously reestablish relations with each other. After a while, the quarrel is forgotten. It is a civilized way to handle a quarrel. We might take a leaf from Persian folkway in dealing with Iran.

Iranians do not understand American culture. Americans are in many ways the opposite of Iranians; we are direct, unsubtle, and prone to violence: cowboys. Americans like guns and military solutions, even though most see America as good and trying to do good in the world. We are poorly informed about the Gulf region. Few Americans know as much about Iran as the student who has just read this chapter. To win mass support our presidents use simplified rhetoric—"axis of evil"—and notice only later that it sets back quiet efforts to improve U.S.-Iranian relations (desired by two-thirds of Iranians). Loose talk about knocking out Iran's nuclear facilities may make matters worse. U.S. threats lead to Iranian counterthreats

Iranians must watch their rhetoric too. Your mass chanting of *Marg bar Amrika!* ("Death to America!") sounds ominous when Iran is working on nuclear bombs. Do you really want to kill us? Then you'd better stop saying so. After 9/11, we take these things very seriously. The U.S. commitment to making sure the oil of the Persian Gulf flows in a friendly fashion is one point Americans agree on in foreign policy. No amount of bombings can persuade us to abandon this policy. And we can "make your economy scream." Those were Kissinger's words describing what we did to Chile when it came under Marxist rule. (We are probably doing it to you now.)

So stop sponsoring or encouraging terrorism. When a bomb goes off in Beirut, we smell Iranian money funneled through Syria. Do not develop nuclear bombs, which are more likely to provoke than deter the United States. Turn to your own tradition and simply shun America, doing nothing against us. And when you are ready to resume contact and economic growth, let us know in a public way. We understand that you are in a long struggle against an odious theocracy and cannot move prematurely. Eventually, the rule of the mullahs will pass and relations will thaw. We were friends once and can be again. Foolish moves on either side could lead to a war neither wants.

GEOGRAPHY

STRATEGIC WATERWAYS

These are mostly narrow choke points connecting two bodies of water. Hostile control of them causes one or more countries discomfort or fear. Here are the main ones:

Turkish Straits (Dardanelles and Bosporus), connecting the Black and Mediterranean Seas.
Strait of Gibraltar, connecting the Atlantic and the Mediterranean.
Suez Canal, connecting the Mediterranean and Red Seas.
Bab al Mandab, connecting the Red Sea and Indian Ocean.
Strait of Hormuz, connecting the Persian Gulf and Indian Ocean.
English Channel, connecting the Atlantic Ocean and North Sea.
Skagerrak, connecting the Baltic and North Seas.
North Cape, dividing the Atlantic from the Barents Sea.
Cape of Good Hope, where the Atlantic and Indian Oceans meet off the southern tip of Africa.
Strait of Malacca, connecting the Indian Ocean and South China Sea, East Asia's oil lifeline.
Korea (Tsushima) Strait, connecting the East China Sea and Sea of Japan.
Panama Canal, connecting the Atlantic and Pacific Oceans.

You are the captain of a small tanker that has just loaded oil in Kuwait for delivery in Umea, Sweden. Which bodies of water—including seas, oceans, straits, and canals—do you pass through? (Note: Supertankers are too big for Suez; they have to go around Africa. But small tankers still pass through Suez.)

Opposing arguments show up in Majlis debates over economic policy, which have become thinly disguised battles over the future of strict Islamic rule. As we have considered, Islamism is a surrogate socialism; that is, it blends Islamic correctness with collectivist economics. In the minds of many Islamists, socialism is the logical extension of Islam, for Islam preaches equality and leveling of class differences. Thus, they claim, Islam is the true and best path to a just society of equal citizens, where no one is either rich or poor. What the Marxists, Socialists, and Communists talked about, they say, we can deliver.

Most moderates respond that socialism and/or statism is not the way to go, that they just keep Iran poor and backward. The collapse of the Soviet system demonstrates socialism does not work, and the decline of Iran's economy demonstrates statism does not work. Besides, they note, there is no Koranic basis for government control of the economy. It is perfectly feasible to combine free-market capitalism with the alms-giving required of Muslims to achieve social justice. If we keep declining economically, moderates also worry, we

GEOGRAPHY

BOUND ISRAEL

Israel is bounded on the north by Lebanon;
on the east by Syria and Jordan;
on the south by Egypt;
and on the west by the Mediterranean Sea.

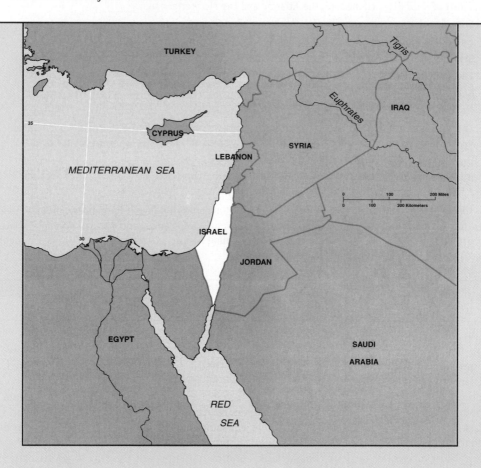

POLITICAL CULTURE

A FATWA ON RUSHDIE

One of the more horrifying examples of the Iranian revolution was the turning of a **fatwa** into an international death warrant. In 1989 Khomeini issued a *fatwa* ordering the execution of British author Salman Rushdie, a lapsed Muslim of Indian origin. Rushdie had just published his *Satanic Verses*, a fantasy on the life of Muhammad that was extremely offensive to devout Muslims. A semiofficial Tehran foundation offered a reward of $1 million (later raised to $2.8 million) for killing Rushdie, who went into hiding for years. Even now, he appears rarely and cautiously; he knows they mean it.

The Western world was aghast at this order to kill someone in a faraway country for writing a book. The entire concept of the *fatwa* underscores the cultural differences between Islamic and Western civilizations. (In 1993, the top Saudi cleric issued a *fatwa* that the earth is flat and anyone claiming it round should be punished as an atheist.) Iran's relations with most of Europe deteriorated. Even many Iranians are embarrassed and apologetic over the *fatwa* and wish it rescinded. Khomeini's successors claim that he is the only one who can rescind it, and he died a few months after issuing it. Even though the Tehran government says it has dissociated itself from the *fatwa* on Rushdie, it harms Iranian relations with other countries.

will never be able to build a first-class army and so will be vulnerable to hostile outside forces. And if our towering unemployment problem is not solved soon, the whole Islamic revolution could be doomed. The best and quickest way to solve these problems is the free market. State ownership of major industries, especially petroleum, is what the Shah tried, and we certainly do not want to follow in his footsteps. Such are the arguments of Iranian moderates. Notice that outright rejection of the Islamic revolution is not one of their points.

THE VEILED DEBATE ON ISLAM

Iran will always be a Muslim country, but what kind of Islam will it have? A moderate kind that keeps out of most direct political involvement or a militant kind that seeks to guide society by political means? Judging by the Khatami landslides in 1997 and 2001, most opt for the first kind. The 2005 election of Ahmadinejad makes one wonder.

Because the Council of Guardians bars openly liberal candidates, public debate on the religion question is muted. No one risks being branded "anti-Islamic." Still, one can infer

KEY TERM

fatwa   Ruling by Islamic jurist.

that such a debate is taking place. One of the stand-ins for a discussion of Islam in public life is the debate on what kind of clothing is admissible, especially for women. Even for men, though, blue jeans were frowned upon, partly because they represent American culture. Liberals say they do not; jeans are simply a comfortable and international garment with no political connotations.

Before the Islamic revolution, urban and educated Iranian women dressed as fashionably as European women. Then suddenly they could not use makeup and had to wear the veil and *chador*, the single-piece head-to-toe garment designed to cover feminine attractiveness. Devout Muslims, including many women, say this attire is better than Western clothing as it eliminates lust, vanity, and distinctions of wealth. (Notice how some U.S. schools are coming to similar conclusions about school uniforms.) Western clothes and makeup are the first steps toward debauchery and prostitution, they argue. But in subtle ways urban Iranian women dress in a manner that pushes to the limit of the permissible in public (and in private dress as they wish). The veil and *chador* are no longer mandatory on the street, so long as a woman is dressed very modestly without makeup and with hair and forehead covered by a kerchief. Women still risk Islamic *komitehs* (morals police) stopping them on the street and sending them home or to jail. Young people suspected of having a good time may be beaten by *basij* (militia). These volunteer squads are some of the most obnoxious features of the Islamic regime and have alienated urban and educated Iranians.

WHAT KIND OF FOREIGN POLICY?

The guiding lights of the Islamic revolution had aspirations beyond Iran. Some still have. They saw themselves as the revitalizers of the entire Islamic world and tried to spread their revolution, especially among Shias but also among Muslims in general. One of their earliest areas of concern were the Shias of southern Iraq, long a suppressed 60 percent of Iraq's population. The Sunni Arabs of the middle of Iraq are only about 20 percent, but they monopolized political power. Many of the main Shia shrines are in southern Iraq, where Khomeini was exiled in 1964. Upon taking power in Tehran, the Khomeini people propagandized Iraqi Shias and urged them to join the Islamic revolution. This was one of the irritants—but hardly a sufficient excuse—for Iraqi dictator Saddam Hussein to invade Iran in 1980.

Wherever there are Shias, Iranian influence turned up: southern Lebanon, Kuwait, Bahrain, and Saudi Arabia. Funds, instructions, and explosive devices flowed through this connection. Iran, along with Iraq, Syria, and Libya, were placed on the U.S. State Department's list of countries sponsoring terrorism. Iran feels it must take a leading role in destroying Israel, which it depicts as a polluter of Islamic holy ground (Jerusalem is also sacred to Muslims) and outpost of Western imperialism. Under the Shah, Tehran had good (but informal) relations with Israel and quietly sold it most of its oil. Suddenly that totally changed, and Iran supports Lebanon's *Hezbollah* (Party of God), which harasses Israel's northern border. (One of the best information sources for critical Iranians is Israeli radio, which broadcasts to Iran in Farsi.)

How many enemies can a country handle at once? On several sides, Iran now faces enemies. By trying to spread its revolution in the 1980s, it made these enemies. And it has no allies that can do it any good. This has put Iran into a tight squeeze, limiting its economic growth and requiring it to maintain armed forces it cannot afford. Many thinking Iranians want to improve relations with the West, even with America. Hostility brings nothing but trouble and no rewards. A few militant mullahs want to keep up the hatred, no matter what it costs the country. Revolutionary Iran has been both the victim and prac- titioner of terrorism. Antiregime forces, particularly the nutty Mujahedin-e Khalk, assas- sinated several Iranian leaders, including one prime minister. In return, Iranian hit squads in Europe took out several regime opponents, including a former prime minister and the leaders of a breakaway Kurdish movement.

DO REVOLUTIONS END BADLY?

Burke (see box on page 34) was right: Revolution brings in its wake tyranny far worse than that of the regime it toppled. Iran is a good example: The Shah was a dictator, but rule of the mullahs is worse. Only in America did revolution lead to the establishment of a just, stable, democracy—and the American revolution was a very special, limited one, aimed more at independence than at revolution. The twentieth century is littered with failed rev- olutions: fascist, communist, and now Islamist. The remaining Communist countries that still celebrate and base their legitimacy on an alleged revolution, Cuba and North Korea, are hungry and isolated. Communist China and Vietnam, by partly integrating their economies with world trade, have so far been spared this fate.

Why do revolutions end badly? Several writers have attempted to answer this question. Burke argued that the destruction of all institutional and political structures leaves people confused and ripe for dictatorial rule. François Furet wrote along similar lines that the French Revolution unleashed such chaotic forces that it had to "skid out of control." Crane Brinton wrote that revolutions fall into the hands of their most ruthless element, who then proceed to wreck everything until they are replaced in a "Thermidor." Hannah Arendt wrote that revolution goes astray when revolutionists try to solve the "Social Question" (how to bring down the rich and help the poor); to do this they must institute a tyranny. It is in- teresting to note all these writers were, to some extent, conservatives. Radicals and leftists often refuse to admit revolutions end badly; if something goes wrong they tend to blame in- dividuals for "betraying" the revolution.

The unhappy revolution is something Iranians ponder. Although few want a return of the Pahlavis, many Iranians know the Islamic revolution has turned out wrong. At least under the Shah there was economic growth, however unfairly distributed, and mod- ernization. Now there is economic decline and unemployment. Most Iranians live more poorly than before. Certain mullahs and their friends, those in charge of the *bonyads*, do well. Given a chance, most Iranians would throw these rascals out. The mullahs and their security and judicial forces try to make sure this never happens. They have some bases of support—more than the Shah had—among the religious and the poor who have benefited from Islamic handouts.

Iran is now caught in a stalemate between reformist and conservative forces. Eventu- ally, the reformists will win because a big majority of Iranians see reforms as an urgent ne- cessity. The longer the conservatives stonewall, the greater the danger of political violence, fueled by millions of angry, unemployed young Iranian males. What can the United States do? U.S. threats just play into the hands of hardliners, but the right combination of firm- ness (over Iran's uranium enrichment efforts) and carrots (trade) could start a dialogue. Time and economic difficulties have calmed the Iranian revolution. I am convinced that Iran will one day be free and we will be friends again.

KEY WEB SITES

Government in general
netiran.com

Presidency
www.president.ir

News Sources (none independent)
Iran Daily
www.iran-daily.com

National news agency
www.irna.com/en

Iran News
www.irannews.freeservers.com

KEY TERMS

alienated (p. 312)

ayatollah (p. 296)

canon law (p. 297)

containment (p. 294)

fatwa (p. 319)

hajj (p. 306)

heretic (p. 307)

hezbollahi (p. 315)

Islam (p. 291)

Islamism (p. 303)

Islamist (p. 297)

jihad (p. 291)

Koran (p. 300)

Majlis (p. 292)

modernizing tyrant (p. 294)

mosque (p. 293)

mullah (p. 296)

OPEC (p. 295)

Ottoman (p. 293)

secular (p. 293)

secularization (p. 302)

shah (p. 292)

Shia (p. 291)

Sunni (p. 291)

theocracy (p. 297)

Thermidor (p. 312)

velayat-e faqih (p. 297)

FURTHER REFERENCE

Abdo, Genieve, and Jonathan Lyons. *Answering Only to God: Faith and Freedom in Twenty-First Century Iran*. New York: Henry Holt, 2003.

Adelkhah, Fariba. *Being Modern in Iran*. New York: Columbia University Press, 2000.

Crone, Patricia. *God's Rule: Government and Islam*. New York: Columbia University Press, 2004.

Diamond, Larry, Marc F. Plattner, and Daniel Brumberg, eds. *Islam and Democracy in the Middle East*. Baltimore, MD: Johns Hopkins University Press, 2003.

Jahanbegloo, Ramin, ed. *Iran: Between Tradition and Modernity*. Lanham, MD: Lexington, 2003.

Keddie, Nikki R. *Modern Iran: Roots and Results of Revolution*. New Haven, CT: Yale University Press, 2003.

Mackey, Sandra. *The Iranians: Persia, Islam, and the Soul of a Nation*. New York: Dutton, 1996.

Menashri, David. *Post-Revolutionary Politics in Iran: Religion, Society, and Power*. Portland, OR: F. Cass, 2001.

Moin, Baqer. *Khomeini: Life of the Ayatollah*. London: I. B. Tauris, 1999.

Schirazi, Asghar. *The Constitution of Iran: Politics and the State in the Islamic Republic*. London: I. B. Tauris, 1998.

Sciolino, Elaine. *Persian Mirrors: The Elusive Face of Iran*. New York: Free Press, 2001.

Watt, William Montgomery. *Islamic Political Thought*. New York: Columbia University Press, 1998.

Yaghmaian, Behzad. *Social Change in Iran: An Eyewitness Account of Dissent, Defiance, and New Movements for Rights*. Albany, NY: SUNY Press, 2002.

Yu, Dal Seung. *The Role of Political Culture in Iranian Political Development*. Brookfield, VT: Ashgate, 2002.

Zahedi, Dariush. *The Iranian Revolution Then and Now: Indicators of Regime Instability*. Boulder, CO: Westview, 2000.

16

Lessons of Six Countries

1. States often precede and create nations. Countries are rather artificial things, the product of governments instilling a common culture over many generations. A working, effective government is the crux of nationhood; those without one are "failed states."

2. The modern state has existed only about half a millennium and is not necessarily the last word in political organization. The emergence of the European Union suggests a new entity beyond the nation-state.

3. Most boundaries are artificial. Where one country ends and another begins is a political decision, often contested. The expansion and contraction of Germany is an example of how fluid some boundaries can be.

4. Most countries have core areas, often where the state began, that are still home to the country's capital. Outside of these core areas, in the periphery, regionalism and resentment at being governed by a distant capital often grow. Thus peripheral areas often vote differently than core areas.

5. The past is alive and well in current politics. The past forms a country's political institutions, attitudes, and quarrels. The past is especially lively in the resentments of aggrieved people, for example among regions and social groups that feel they have been shortchanged.

6. Wars are dangerous to political systems and other living things. War, said Marx, is the midwife of revolution. Several of our countries have undergone total system change as a result of war.

7. Economic growth is destabilizing, especially rapid growth. Economic growth and change bring new people into politics, some of them bitterly discontent. Do not think economic growth solves political problems; it often makes them worse. Democracy must accompany economic growth in order to head off revolution.

8. A system that cannot change to meet new challenges may be doomed. The wisest rulers are those who make gradual and incremental changes in order to avoid sudden and radical changes. Rulers who wait to reform until revolution is nigh may actually fan its flames by offering concessions. All regimes tend to petrify; the good ones stay flexible.

9. Solid, time-tested institutions that people believe in are a bulwark of political stability. No political leader, however clever, has pulled functioning institutions out of a hat. They require time, intelligence, and continual modification.

10. Constitutions rarely work the way they are intended and written. Many factors modify the working of constitutions: popular attitudes, usages that change over time, powerful parties and interest groups, and behind-the-scenes deals.

11. Everywhere, parliaments are in decline. Some have become little more than window dressing; some are under such tight executive and/or party control that they have lost their autonomy, and only a few are fighting to regain it. As governance becomes more complex and technical, power flows to bureaucrats and experts.

12. Everywhere, bureaucracies are in the ascendancy. In some systems, the permanent civil service is already the most powerful institution. Bureaucrats tend to see themselves as indispensable, the saviors of their countries. No country has yet devised a way to control its bureaucracies.

13. Multiparty systems tend to be less stable than two-party systems. Much depends on other factors, such as the rules for forming a cabinet or choosing the executive. Reforms can stabilize multiparty systems so that their behavior is not much different from two-party systems.

14. Electoral system helps determine party system. Single-member districts with a simple plurality required to win tend to produce two-party systems because third parties have difficulty surviving in such systems. Proportional representation tends to produce many parties.

15. There are no longer purely federal or purely unitary systems. Instead, the trend is for federations to grant more and more power to the center, while unitary systems set up regional governments and devolve some powers to them.

16. Most cabinets consist of about twenty ministers. By American standards, other cabinets are large and their portfolios rather specialized. In the United States, there is a reluctance to add new departments. Elsewhere, ministries are added, deleted, combined, or renamed as the prime minister sees fit; the legislature automatically goes along.

17. In some ways, prime ministers in parliamentary systems are more powerful than presidents in presidential systems. If they have an assured and disciplined majority in parliament, prime ministers can get just about whatever they want with no deadlock between executive and legislative. Prime ministers who have to rely on coalitions, of course, are weaker.

18. Most people, most of the time, are not much interested in politics. As you go down the socioeconomic ladder, you usually find less and less interest in political participation. Radicals deny this when they call for "power to the people," but they are usually middle-class intellectuals, sometimes intent on power for themselves. Mass participation in politics tends to be simple and episodic, such as voting every few years.

19. Democracy arouses mixed enthusiasm in most countries. Countries with a history of democratic rule have democratically inclined masses. More typically, masses admire regimes that give them law and order, a feeling of national greatness, and a sense of material progress. More-educated people have more democratic values.

20. Political culture is at least as much a reflection of government performance as it is a determinant of the workings of government. Political culture can be taught—intentionally or inadvertently—by a regime. Countries with a cynical, untrusting political culture have usually earned it with decades of misrule. By the same token, a democratic regime that does a good job over many years firms up democratic attitudes.

21. Social class is only one factor in establishing political orientations. Often other factors, such as religion and region, are more important. Usually these three—class, religion, and region in varying combinations—explain a great deal of party identification and voting behavior.

22. Religion is important in politics. In Iran, the two merge. More typical are political parties based on religion, as in Nigeria, or religiosity (degree of religious feeling), as in Mexico and the United States.

23. Political systems are rarely totally ideological, but neither are they totally pragmatic. Parties and regimes usually talk some ideology—to justify themselves to the masses, if for no other reason—but at the top, rulers tend to pragmatism in making decisions. Ideology as window dressing is a common political device.

24. Every country has its elites, the few with much influence. Depending on the system, party elites, labor elites, business elites, military elites, even religious elites may assume great importance. Elites pay attention to politics, usually battling to preserve and enhance the status of the groups they lead. Elites rather than masses are the true political animals.

25. Elites, especially intellectual elites, create and articulate political ideas (ideologies, reform movements, media commentary), something the masses rarely do. Further, elite attitudes tend to be more democratic than mass attitudes.

26. Education is the usual gateway to elite status. Except in revolutionary regimes, most elites now have university educations. Some elites are selected by virtue of the special colleges they attend. Educational opportunity is never totally equal or fair; the middle class usually benefits most from it.

27. Much of politics consists of competition and bargaining among elites. Occasionally elites, in order to gain leverage on competing elites, refer matters to the masses in elections or referendums and call it democracy. Of all the political interactions discussed in this book, notice how relatively few of them involve mass participation.

28. Mass politics is easier to study than elite politics. With mass politics—elections, voter alignments, public opinion—political scientists can get accurate, quantified data. But since much of elite politics is out of the public eye, we have to resort to fragmentary anecdotal and journalistic data. This means that some of the most crucial political interactions are hard to discern and even harder to document.

29. Democracy grows when elites open their decisions and deals to public scrutiny and approval. Typically, bargains are struck among elites and then presented to parliament and the public. Much legislative and electoral behavior is in ratifying decisions made earlier among elites.

30. Politicians are endlessly opportunistic. Most will do whatever it takes to get, keep, or enhance their power. To this end, they will change their views and policies. This is not necessarily deplorable, however; it lets democracy work because it makes politicians bend to the popular will.

31. Politicians are addicted to money. They need it for election campaigns and sometimes to make themselves rich. Countries with very different institutions and political cultures thus often have similar scandals over money.

32. Parties are balancing acts. Parties are invariably composed of different groups, factions, and wings. Some parties split apart over personal and ideological differences. To hold the party together, politicians dispense favors, jobs, and promises to faction leaders. This holds for both democratic and authoritarian parties.

33. Once the army has taken over a government, there is always the possibility it will do so again. Democracy and reformism are often short-lived phenomena between periods of military rule. Praetorianism can be seen as an incurable, self-reinfecting illness endemic in much of the Third World.

34. Most of humanity lives in the Third World, roughly defined as Asia, Africa, the Middle East, and Latin America. Some are making good progress to prosperity and democracy; others, encumbered by institutional, ideological and cultural rigidity, are not.

35. The Third World is trying to get into the First. One of the big problems of West Europe is the new class of foreign workers—Pakistanis in Britain, Algerians in France, Turks in Germany—that come for jobs and often stay. Likewise, the United States is a magnet for Mexicans. Given the differential rates of birth and economic growth, the trend is increasing and has become a major political issue worldwide.

36. Within Third World countries, people are flocking to the cities. Overpopulation and few jobs in the countryside push people to the cities, where they often live in shantytowns. The Third World already has the globe's biggest cities, most surrounded by shantytowns.

37. Racism can be found nearly everywhere. Most nations deny it, but discrimination based on skin color, religion, or ethnic group is widespread. When asking if there is racism, look to see what a country does, not what it says. Underdog racial and ethnic groups are locked out of economic and political power.

38. Cutting welfare benefits is extremely difficult; recipients take them as a right and protest angrily. Conservatives often come to power with promises to end the welfare state, but they seldom touch the problem. Once a benefit has been extended, it is almost impossible to withdraw it. The most conservatives can do is restrain expansion of the welfare system.

39. Likewise, cutting state sectors of an economy is difficult. Most countries have state ownership, control, or guidance over the economy (the United States relatively little). In countries as diverse as Russia, Mexico, Nigeria, and Iran, getting the government out of the economy meets great opposition from those who have something to lose. Thus many governments talk about privatization but delay doing it.

40. Much of what people and politicians quarrel about is economic. Some economists go so far as to claim that economics is the content of politics. That is going a little too far, since there are important political conflicts that are not directly economic, such as questions of region, religion, and personality. Still, on any given day, people are most likely to be arguing who should get what. Study economics.

41. At almost the same time, countries rediscovered the market economy. Most found that statist control retards growth. Markets are now the intellectual trend, but not everyone likes them.

42. Democracy depends a great deal on economic development. Poor countries rarely sustain democracy. Middle-income and richer countries are mostly democracies. The likely reason: Economic growth generates a large, educated, and moderate middle class that starts insisting on political participation.

43. Inflation is easy to ignite, but it hurts growth, sours attitudes, and can even bring down governments. Several of our countries came under severe political pressure from inflation that destroyed people's means of making a living and their confidence in government.

44. Unemployment is a problem nearly everywhere and one few governments solve. Worldwide, there is a struggle for jobs, ranging from difficult in West Europe to desperate

in the Third World. The Soviet Union was able to provide jobs but only because its industry and agriculture were grossly inefficient.

45. Many political issues are insoluble. They are the surfacing of long-growing economic and social problems that cannot be "fixed" by government policy. Often only time and underlying economic and social change gradually dissolve the problem. Politics has been overrated as a way to cure problems. Often the best politics can do is keep things stable until time can do its work.

46. Things get more political, not less. As government takes on more tasks, what were previously private interactions become political interactions with all the fighting that entails. No country will ever run out of political problems. As soon as one is solved, new ones appear, usually over the administration of the problem-solving mechanism.

47. Things do not always get better. Some political systems are unable to handle massive and multiple stresses; they turn into "weak states," characterized by crime, corruption, and insecurity.

48. Political movements, parties, ideologies, and regimes are hard to judge by a priori criteria. We seldom know how something is going to work until we see it in practice for a while. We learn what is good and bad by studying results.

49. Whenever you look closely at political phenomena, you find they are more complicated than you first thought. You discover exceptions, nuances, and differentiations that you did not notice at first. You can modify and sometimes refute generalizations—including the ones offered here—by digging into them more deeply.

50. Ultimately, in studying other countries we are studying ourselves. One of the lessons that should have emerged from this book is that neither our country nor we as citizens are a great deal different from other countries and peoples. When you compare politics, be sure to include your own system in the comparison.

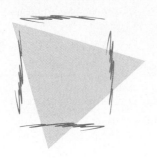

Glossary

Following are some frequently used words or technical terms from the field of comparative politics. Each is defined here in its political sense. The country where the term originated or is most commonly used is given where appropriate, but often the word is now used worldwide.

absolute decline   Growing weaker economically compared to one's own past.

absolute poverty   Extremely low income, defined by World Bank as living on under $1 a day.

absolutism   Royal dictatorship in which king amasses all power.

affluence   Having plenty of money.

agitprop   (Soviet Union) Combination agitation and propaganda; mass-mobilization arm of Soviet Communist party.

alienated   Psychologically distant and hostile.

Allies   World War II anti-Axis military coalition.

alternation in power   Overturn of one party by another in elections.

anachronism   Something from past that does not fit present times.

ancien régime   French for old regime, monarchy that preceded Revolution.

Anglican   Church of England, Episcopalian in America.

anglophile   Someone who loves England and the English.

anticlerical   Favoring getting Roman Catholic church out of politics.

antithetical   Ideas opposed to one another.

apartheid   Literally, "apartness," system of strict racial segregation in South Africa from 1948 to early 1990s.

apolitical   Taking no interest in politics.

apparatchik   "Man of the apparatus," full-time CPSU functionary.

aquifer   Underground water-bearing layer.

arable   Useable for agriculture.

aristocrat   Person of inherited noble rank.

Article 9   No-war clause in Japan's constitution.

aryan   (Iran) Old Persian name for Iran; used by Nazis as alleged superior branch of white race.

asset-stripping   Selling off firm's property and raw materials it controls for short-term profit.

austerity   Cutting government expenditures, belt-tightening.

authoritarian   Nondemocratic or dictatorial politics.

authority   Power of political figure to be obeyed.

autocracy   Absolute rule of one person in centralized state.

autonomy   Partial independence.

ayatollah   (Iran) "Sign of God," top Shia religious leader.

backbencher   (Britain) Ordinary MP with no executive responsibility.

Big Mac Index   Quick estimate of purchasing power parity by comparing world prices of well-known hamburger.

bilateral opposition   Centrist parties or governments being undermined from both sides.

bimodal   Two-peaked distribution.

bloc   Grouping or alliance.

Bolshevik   "Majority" in Russian; early name for Soviet Communist party.

bonyad   (Iran) Islamic foundation that owns and runs parts of Iran's economy.

bound   To name bordering countries.

Bourbon   French dynasty before Revolution.

bourgeois   Middle-class.

Boxer   Major Chinese antiforeigner rebellion in 1900.

Bronze Age   Beginning of metal-working and cities, about 3,500 years ago.

Buddhism   Asian religion that seeks enlightenment through meditation and cessation of desire.

bureaucracy   Civil service; connotes rigid, hierarchical administration.

bureaucratized   Heavily controlled by civil servants.

burghers   Originally, town dwellers; by extension middle class; French *bourgeoisie*.

by-election   Midterm election for vacant seat in Parliament.

cabinet   Group of ministers or secretaries who head executive departments of government; in Europe, synonymous with government.

cadre   French "framework," used by Asian Communists for local Party leader.

caesaropapism   Combining top civil ruler (caesar) with top spiritual ruler (pope), as in Russia's tsars.

caliphate   Islamic dynasty.

canon law   Internal laws of Roman Catholic Church.

capital   Accumulated wealth, either money or goods, that is used to produce more goods.

capital flight   Tendency of businesspersons in countries with shaky economies to send their money out of country.

capital goods   Implements used to make other things.

carpetbagger   In U.S. usage, outsider attempting to run in different constituency.

caste   Hereditary social stratum or group.

catalyst   Element that starts or speeds up an action.

catchall   Parties that welcome all and offer little ideology.

Caucasus   Mountainous region between Black and Caspian Seas.

caudillo   Military chief or strongman, specifically one who takes over government.

causality   Proving that one thing causes another.

Celts   Pre-Roman inhabitants of Europe.

censure   Condemnation of executive by legislative vote.

center   Politically moderate or middle-of-the-road, neither left nor right. In federal systems, powers of nation's capital.

center-peaked   Distribution with most people in middle, a bell-shaped curve.

center-periphery tension   Resentment of outlying areas at rule by nation's capital.

center-seeking   Parties trying to win big vote in center by moderate programs.

Central America   Countries between Mexico and Colombia.

Central Asia   Region between Caspian Sea and China.

Central Committee   Large, next-to-top governing body of most Communist parties.

centralization   Concentration of administrative power in nation's capital, allowing little or no local autonomy.

central office   London headquarters of British political party.

charisma   (pronounced "kar-isma"; Greek for gift) political drawing power.

chief of government   Country's top political executive, either prime minister or president, who engages in day-to-day political affairs; also called head of government.

civility   Keeping reasonably good manners in politics.

civilization   City-based culture with writing, social classes, and complex economic and political organization.

civil society   Humans after becoming civilized. Modern usage: associations between family and government.

class bias   Slanting of jobs, schools, and political power to favor one class at expense of another.

class struggle   Basic tenet of Marxism that social classes, especially the working class and the rich, are of necessity antagonistic toward each other's interests.

class voting   Tendency of a given class to vote for the party that claims to represent its interests.

cleft country   In Huntington's theory, a country split by two civilizations.

clientelism   Government favors to groups for their support.

coalition   Multiparty alliance to form government.

cohabitation   French president forced to name premier of opposing party.

Cold War   Period of armed tension and competition between the United States and the Soviet Union, approximately 1947–1989.

colonialism   Gaining and exploitation of overseas territories, chiefly by Europeans.

Comecon   Trading organization of Communist countries, defunct.

Common Law   System of judge-made law developed in England.

Common Market   Now European Union; grouping of West European nations that eliminated tariffs and trade and labor restrictions between members.

Commons   (Britain) Lower, popularly elected, and more important house of Parliament.

commonwealth   A *republic*.

communism   Economic theories of Marx combined with organization of Lenin.

comprehensive school   Publicly funded British secondary school, equivalent to U.S. high school.

Confederation of British Industry   Leading British business association.

Confucianism   Chinese philosophy of social and political stability based on family, hierarchy, and perfection of manners.

consensus   Agreement among all constituent groups.

conservatism   Ideology aimed at preserving existing institutions and usages.

consociation   Sharing of political power at executive level, giving all major parties cabinet positions.

constituency   District or population that elects legislator.

constitution   Written organization of country's institutions.

constitutionalism   Degree to which government limits its powers.

constitutional monarchy   One whose powers are limited.

consumer goods   Things people use, such as food, clothing, and housing.

consumption   Buying things.

containment   U.S. policy throughout Cold War of blocking expansion of communism.

Continent, the   British term for continent of Europe, implying they are not part of it.

co-opt   To enroll other groups in your organization, rendering them harmless.

core   Region where state originated.

corporatism   Representation by branch of industry, device of Mussolini.

corruption   Use of public office for private gain.

Cortes   Spain's parliament.

coup   Extralegal seizure of power, usually by military officers.

CPSU   Communist Party of Soviet Union.

cross-cutting cleavages   Multiple splits in society that make group loyalties overlap.

Crown   Powers of British government.

cult of personality   Dictator who has himself worshipped.

cumulative   Reinforcing one another.

cynical   Untrusting; belief that political system is wrong and corrupt.

Cyrillic   Greek-based alphabet of Eastern Slavic languages.

deadlock   U.S. tendency for executive and legislature, especially when of opposing parties, to block each other.

decentralization   Diffusion of administrative power from nation's capital to regions, localities, or economic units.

decolonization   Granting of independence to colonies.

de facto   In practice although not officially stated.

default   Not being able to pay back loan.

deferential   Accepting leadership of social superiors.

deflation   Overall decrease in prices, opposite of inflation.

deification   Glorification of leader into artificial god.

deindustrialization   Decline of heavy industry.

demagoguery   Crowd-pleasing promises that cannot be fulfilled.

demobilization   Tranquilizing or even anesthetizing mass interest in politics, often attempted by dictators.

democracy   Political system of mass participation, competitive elections, and human and civil rights.

demography   Study of population growth.

dependency theory   Radical theory that rich countries keep poor countries poor by siphoning off their wealth.

deregulation   Cutting governmental rules on industry.

desiccation   Drying out.

destalinization   (Soviet Union) Criticism and downgrading of Stalin that occurred under Khrushchev.

devaluation   Decreasing worth of your currency in relation to others.

developmentalism   Early 1960s theory that we could develop Third World lands.

devolution   Central government turning some powers over to regions.

dignified   In Bagehot's terms, symbolic or decorative offices.

diplomatic recognition   One state announces it is ready to do business with another.

dissident   Person who openly criticizes his or her political system.

divide and rule   Roman and British imperial ruling method of setting subjects against each other.

division   Vote in House of Commons.

dominant-party system   One in which one party is much stronger than all others and stays in office very long time.

dries   In Thatcher's usage, Tories who shared her *neoliberal* vision.

Duma   Russia's national parliament.

dynastic cycle   (China) Rise, maturity, and fall of imperial family.

eclectic   Drawn from variety of sources.

efficient   In Bagehot's terms, working, political offices.

egalitarian   Policy aiming at making persons more equal in income, political power, or life opportunities; a leftist political viewpoint.

Eire   Republic of Ireland.

ejido   Land owned in common by villages.

electoral alignment   Temporary coalition of parties in order to win elections.

electoral franchise   Right to vote.

electoral system   Laws structuring manner in which persons are elected to office, such as from single- or multimember districts, and by proportional representation or simple plurality.

electorate   That part of population entitled to vote.

elites   The top or most influential people.

emigration   Moving out of your native country.

endemic   Persistent, seemingly permanent problem.

entitlement   Spending programs citizens are automatically entitled to, such as Social Security.

entrepreneurial   Starting your own business.

environmentalism   Political movement stressing industrial, chemical, and nuclear dangers to environment.

Establishment   Half in jest, supposed monopoly of clubby social elite in British politics.

Estado Nôvo   (Brazil) "New State," Vargas's corporatistic welfare state.

ethnicity   Cultural characteristics differentiating one group from another.

euro   (symbol: €) Currency for most of West Europe since 2002; value has fluctuated between $0.85 and $1.35.

European Union (EU)   Federation of most European states; began in 1957 as *Common Market*.

Euroenthusiast   Likes EU and wishes to strengthen it.

Eurosceptic   Does not wish to strengthen EU at expense of national sovereignty.

excess liquidity   Too much money floating around.

Exchequer   Britain's treasury ministry.

exclave   Part of country separated from main territory.

extraterritoriality   Privilege of Europeans in colonial situations to have separate laws and courts.

faction   Party within a party.

factious   Tending to break up into quarreling *factions*.

failed state   One incapable of exercising even minimal governing power.

fatwa   Ruling by Islamic jurist.

federalism   System in which component areas have considerable autonomy.

fertility rate   How many children average woman bears.

feudalism   Political system of power dispersed and balanced between king and nobles.

fiefdom   Land granted by king to noble in exchange for support.

first-order civil division   Main units countries are divided into, such as departments in France.

fiscal   Related to taxes and public spending.

Five-Year Plans   Stalin's forced industrialization of Soviet Union starting in 1928.

flight capital   Money owner sends out of country in fear of losing it.

Four Tigers   South Korea, Taiwan, Hong Kong, and Singapore.

FPTP   "First past the post," short way of saying "single-member districts with plurality win."

fragmented   Marked divergence of views among subgroups and little or no consensus.

franchise   Right to vote.

French Revolution   1789 popular ouster of monarchy.

fusion of powers   Combination of executive and legislative as in parliamentary systems; opposite of U.S. separation of powers.

Gang of Four   Mao's ultraradical helpers, arrested in 1976.

GDP   Gross Domestic Product, sum total of goods and services produced in country in one year.

generalization   Finding of repeated examples and patterns.

gensek   Russian abbreviation for "general secretary," powerful CPSU head.

gentry   Better-off, educated class in traditional societies.

geopolitics   Influence of geography on politics and use of geography for strategic ends.

gerontocracy   Rule by elderly.

gerrymander   Drawing electoral-district boundaries to favor one party.

glasnost   Gorbachev's policy of media openness.

globalization   World becoming one big capitalist market.

Good Friday agreement   1998 pact to share power in Northern Ireland.

Gosplan   Soviet central economic planning agency.

government   A particular cabinet, what Americans call "the administration."

grammar school   Private British nonboarding school, equivalent to U.S. day school.

Great Leap Forward   1958–1960 failed Chinese effort at overnight industrialization.

Great Purge   Stalin's murder of thousands of Communist party members from 1936 to 1938 on faintest suspicion of disloyalty.

gringo   (From the Spanish for "gibberish") Foreigner, specifically *norteamericano*, pejorative.

Gulag   Soviet central prisons administration.

Guomindang   Chinese Nationalist party ousted from mainland in 1949; earlier spelled Kuomintang and abbreviated KMT.

hacienda   (Mexico) Large country estate with Spanish owner (*hacendado*) and Indian serfs.

hajj   Muslim pilgrimage to Mecca.

Han   Original and main people of China.

hard currency   Noninflating, recognized currencies used in international dealings, such as dollars and euros.

head of state   Symbolic national leader, either monarch or president, who normally stands above the political fray.

heckling   Interrupting a speaker.

hegemony   Being the top or commanding power.

Helsinki Final Act   1975 agreement to make Europe's borders permanent.

heretic   Someone who breaks away from a religion.

hezbollahi   "Partisan of God," fanatic supporter of Islamism.

home rule   Giving region some autonomy to govern itself.

Huguenots   French Protestants.

human capital   Education, skills, and enthusiasm of nation's work force.

Hundred Flowers   1956 Chinese campaign to encourage different views; crushed when views grew critical.

hyperinflation   Very rapid inflation, more than 50 percent a month.

hyperurbanization   Overconcentration of populations in cities.

ideal-typical   Distilling social characteristics into one example.

identity   Recognition by people of their nationality, ethnic group, region, or party.

ideology   Belief system to improve society.

IMF   International Monetary Fund, grants loans to promote economic stability.

immigration   Resettling into new country.

imperialism   Powerful, rich countries spreading their influence around globe.

inchoate   Not yet organized, incoherent.

indirect rule   British colonial governance through native hereditary rulers.

industrialization   Shifting country's economy from agriculture to industry.

inequality   Degree of difference in wealth, income, social status, or political power among individuals.

infant mortality rate   Number of live newborns who die in their first year, per thousand; standard measure of nation's health.

inflation   Systematic rise of almost all prices.

informal economy   Under-the-table transactions to avoid taxes and regulations.

infrastructure   Network of highways, railroads, electricity, and other basic prerequisites of economic growth.

input-output table   Spreadsheet for economy of entire nation.

institution   Established rules and relationships of power.

institutionalize   To make a political relationship permanent.

intelligentsia   Russian (from Italian) for "educated class."

intendants   French provincial administrators, answerable only to Paris; early version of *prefects*.

interested member   MP known to represent interest group.

interest group   Association aimed at getting favorable policies.

interior ministry   In Europe, department in charge of local administration and national police.

investiture crisis   Fight between popes and monarchs over who had right to crown latter.

Irish Republican Army   Anti-British terrorists who seek unification of all Ireland.

Islam   Religion founded by Mohammed.

Islamism   Islam turned into political ideology.

Islamist   Someone who uses Islam in political way.

-ism   Suffix indicating ideology.

jihad   Muslim holy war.

junior minister   MP with executive responsibilities below that of cabinet rank.

junta   (Pronounced Spanish-style, "khun-ta") group that pulls military coup.

kickback   Fee paid to government official for a contract.

kleptocracy   Rule by thieves.

knighthood   Lowest rank of nobility, in Britain carries title of "Sir."

kolkhoz   (Soviet Union) Collective farm.

Komsomol   (Soviet Union) Communist youth organization.

Koran   Muslim holy book.

kow-tow   (China) Literally head to ground; to prostrate oneself.

Kremlin   Moscow fortress, center of Russian government.

kulaks   (Soviet Union) Class of better-off peasants Stalin ordered liquidated as part of farm collectivization.

labor-force rigidities   Unwillingness of workers to change jobs or location.

laissez faire   French for "let it be"; doctrine advocating no government interference in free-market economy.

Land   (plural *Länder*) Germany's first-order civil division, equivalent to U.S. state.

landlocked   Country with no seacoast.

Latin America   All countries south of the United States.

Law Lords   Britain's top judges, members of Lords.

left   Politically more radical; aiming at greater equality.

legitimacy   Mass perception that regime's rule is rightful.

Levellers   Radicals during English Civil War who argued for equality and "one man, one vote."

liberal democracy   System that combines tolerance and freedoms (liberalism) with mass participation (democracy).

liberalism   Originally ideology to minimize government supervision of economy and society; current U.S. usage, welfare measures and greater equality.

liberation theology   *Vatican II* view that helping poor through direct political action is Christian duty.

life peers   Distinguished Britons named to House of Lords for their lifetimes only, does not pass on to children.

lingua franca   In multilingual situation, one language used overall.

Lockean   Following thoughts of John Locke, who emphasized natural right to "life, liberty, and property."

Long March   (China; 1934–1935) Exodus of Chinese Communist party from southern to northern China to escape *Guomindang*.

Lords   (Britain) Upper, originally aristocratic house of Parliament; less important than Commons.

machismo   Strutting, exaggerated masculinity.

macroeconomy   Big picture of nation's economy, including GDP and its growth, productivity, interest rates, and inflation.

mafia   Criminal conspiracy.

Magna Carta   1215 agreement to preserve rights of English nobles.

Majlis   Arabic for assembly; Iran's parliament.

majoritarian   Electoral system that encourages dominance of one party in parliament, as in Britain and the United States.

Malthusian   View that population growth outstrips food.

Manchu   Last imperial dynasty of China, also known as *Qing;* ruled from seventeenth century to 1911.

Manchukuo   Japanese puppet state set up in Manchuria.

Manchuria   Northeasternmost area of China.

Mandarin   (China) Traditional administrator, schooled in *Confucian* classics.

man-land ratio   How much *arable* land per person.

Maoism   (China) Mao's redo of Marx, basing revolution on poor peasantry and continuing revolution indefinitely.

marginal   Poor person on edge of society and economy.

Marshall Plan   Massive U.S. financial aid for European recovery.

Marxism-Leninism   Communism, ideology combining Marx's economic and historical theories with Lenin's organizational techniques.

Marxist   Follower of socialist theories of Karl Marx.

mass   Most of citizenry, everyone who is not *elite.*

mass line   Mao's theory of revolution for China.

Menshevik   Russian for "minority"; less-radical faction of Russian Social Democrats, which Lenin repudiated.

mercantilism   Theory that nation's wealth is its gold and silver, to be amassed by government controls on economy.

Mercosur   "Southern market"; free-trade area covering southern part of South America.

meritocracy   Advancement based only on intellectual ability.

Mesoamerica   (Spanish for Middle America) Southern Mexico and northern Central America.

mestizaje   Intermingling of Spanish and Indian.

microeconomy   Closeup picture of individual markets, including product design and pricing, efficiency, and costs.

micro-loan   Small unsecured loan (of a few hundred dollars) to beginning businesses.

middle class   That of professionals or those paid salaries, typically educated beyond secondary school.

Middle Kingdom   China's traditional name for itself.

middle way   Supposed blend of capitalism and socialism; also called "third way."

minister   Head of major department (ministry) of government.

Mitteleuropa   German for Central Europe.

mixed monarchy   King balanced by nobles.

mobilize   To bring new sectors of population into political participation.

modernization   Becoming modern; also theory that this process follows certain known paths.

modernizing tyrant   Dictator who pushes country ahead.

monetarism   Friedman's theory that rate of growth of money supply governs much economic development.

money politics   Lavish use of funds to win elections.

Mongol   Central Asian dynasty, founded by Genghis Khan, that ruled China in thirteenth and fourteenth centuries.

moribund   Near death, stagnant.

mosque   Muslim house of worship.

MP   Member of Parliament.

mullah   Muslim cleric.

multiculturalism   Preservation of diverse languages and traditions within one country.

multinational   Country composed of several peoples with distinct national feelings.

multiparty   Party system of three or more competing parties.

Muslim   Follower of Islam, also adjective of *Islam*.

NAFTA   1994 North American Free Trade Agreement among the United States, Canada, and Mexico.

narcotraficante   Drug trafficker.

Narodniki   From Russian "people," *narod*; radical populist agitators of late nineteenth century.

nation   Cultural element of country; people psychologically bound to one another.

national interest   What is good for country as a whole in international relations.

nationalism   Belief in the greatness and unity of one's country and hatred of rule by foreigners.

Nationalist   Chiang Kai-shek's party that unified China in late 1920s, abbreviated KMT.

nationality   Belonging to nation or, in East Europe and ex-Soviet Union, to ethnic group.

nationalization   Governmental takeover of private industry.

near abroad   Non-Russian republics of old Soviet Union.

neoliberalism   Revival of free-market economics.

Neolithic   New Stone Age, beginning of agriculture, about 10,000 years ago.

NEP   Lenin's New Economic Policy that allowed private activity 1921–1928.

New Class   Djilas's description of new Communist elite of party leaders, bureaucrats, and security officials.

New Labour   Tony Blair's name for his very moderate Labour party.

no-confidence   Parliamentary motion to oust current cabinet.

nomenklatura   Lists of sensitive positions and people eligible to fill them, the Soviet elite.

nonaggression pact   Treaty to not attack each other, specifically 1939 treaty between Hitler and Stalin.

Normans   Vikings who settled in and gave their name to Normandy, France.

norteamericanos   "North Americans"; U.S. citizens.

objective   Judged by observable criteria.

October Revolution   1917 Bolshevik seizure of power in Russia.

old boy   Someone you knew at boarding school.

oligarchy   Rule by a few.

omnipotent   All-powerful.

OPEC   Cartel of oil-rich countries designed to boost petroleum prices.

Open Door   U.S. policy of protecting China.

Opium War   1839–1842 British-Chinese war to enable Britain to sell opium to Chinese.

opportunist   Unprincipled person out for self.

opposition   In parliamentary systems, parties in parliament that are not in cabinet.

Orangemen   After King William of Orange (symbol of Netherlands royal house), Northern Irish Protestants.

Ottoman   Turkish imperial dynasty, fourteenth to twentieth centuries.

Oxbridge   Slang for Oxford and Cambridge universities.

Pahlavi   Iranian monarchy 1925–1979, overthrown by Islamic revolution.

pan-Africanism   Movement to unite all Africa.

paranoia   Unreasonable suspicion of others, not same as fearful.

parliament   National assembly that considers and passes laws. When capitalized, Britain's legislature, specifically its lower chamber, *Commons*.

Parliamentarians   Supporters of Parliament in English Civil War.

parliamentary system   Political system in which cabinet is responsible to, and can be ousted by, parliament; chief executive is prime minister who is not elected directly.

parochial   Focused on local concerns only; ignorant of national politics.

participation   Citizen involvement in politics such as voting, helping party or candidate, or contacting officials.

particularism   Region's sense of its difference.

party identification   Psychological attachment of voter to particular political party.

party image   Way electorate perceives given party.

party list   Party's ranking of its candidates in PR elections; voters pick one list as their ballot.

party system   Number and competitiveness of parties in given country; five general types: no-party, one-party, two-party, dominant-party, and multiparty systems.

passé   Outmoded, receded into past.

patronage   Giving government jobs to political supporters.

peerage   British Lord or Lady, higher than *knighthood*.

per capita   GDP divided by population, giving approximate level of well-being.

periphery   Nation's outlying regions.

perestroika   Russian for "restructuring," Gorbachev's proposals to reform Soviet economy.

permanent secretary   Highest British civil servant who runs ministry, nominally under a minister.

personalismo   Politics by strong, showoff personalities.

personality cult   Adulation and deification of political leaders, such as Stalin and Mao.

petrify   Become rigid, unable to change.

plebiscite   *Referendum*, mass vote for issue rather than for candidate.

pluralism   Autonomous interaction of social groups with each other and on government.

pluralistic stagnation   Thesis of Beer that interest groups out of control produce policy log jam.

plurality   Largest quantity, even if less than majority.

policy   The specific choices governments make.

Politburo   "Political bureau," small, top governing body of most Communist parties.

political culture   Values and attitudes of citizens in regard to politics and society.

political generation   Theory that age groups are marked by great events of their young adulthood.

political geography   Ways territory and politics influence each other.

portfolio   Minister's assigned ministry.

Positivism   Philosophy of applying scientific method to social problems and gradually improving society.

postmaterialism   Theory that modern culture has moved beyond getting and spending.

power   Ability of A to get B to do what A wants.

praetorianism   Tendency for military takeovers.

pragmatic   Without ideological considerations, based on practicality.

precedent   Legal reasoning based on previous cases.

premier   French for prime minister.

president   Elected head of state, not necessarily powerful.

presidential system   Political system in which powerful president is elected directly and separately from parliament and cannot be ousted by parliament.

priísmo   Ideology and methods of PRI.

prime minister   Chief of government in parliamentary systems.

privatization   Selling state-owned industry to private interests.

production   Making things.

productivity   Efficiency with which things are produced.

proletariat   Marx's term for class of industrial workers.

proportional representation   Electoral system that assigns parliamentary seats in proportion to party vote.

protective tariff   Tax on imported goods to prevent them from undercutting domestic products.

Protestant ethic   Theory of Max Weber that hard work and capitalist reinvestment originated in Protestant Christianity.

protest vote   Ballot cast against existing regime.

pseudo-   Prefix for "fake."

public finances   What government takes in, what it spends, and how it makes up the difference.

public school   In Britain, private, boarding school, equivalent to U.S. prep school.

purchasing power parity   Way of comparing cross-nationally how well people live based on how much they can buy rather than on how much currency they earn.

purge   Stalin's "cleansing" of suspicious elements by firing squad.

quarrels   As used here, important, long-term political issues.

quasi-federal   Halfway federal.

Question Hour   Time reserved in British Commons for MPs to question members of cabinet.

quixotic   (From Don Quixote) Romantic, unrealistic efforts to achieve mistaken goals.

reactionary   Seeking to go back to old ways, extremely conservative.

recession   Economy going downward.

Rechtsstaat   Literally, state of laws; state based on written rules and rights.

red-brown   Possible combination of Communists and Fascists, brown standing for Hitler's brownshirts.

Red Guards   (China) Radical youths who, at Mao's behest, attacked traditions and authorities during Cultural Revolution.

redistribution   Taxing better off to help worse off.

referendum   Mass vote on issue rather than on candidates, same as *plebiscite*.

Reform Acts   Series of laws expanding British electoral franchise.

reformism   Political movement aiming at change and improvement in moderate and non-coercive way.

regionalism   Political movement that emphasizes regional autonomy and distinctiveness.

regressive tax   Tax that is lighter on rich than on poor.

reify   From Latin *res*, thing; to take theory as reality.

relative decline   Failing to keep up economically with other nations.

remittance   Money sent home.

renminbi   China's currency, worth about 12 U.S. cents.

republic   Country not headed by monarch. Also civil division of Communist federal systems and now of Russia.

republican   In its original sense, favoring getting rid of monarchy.

revolution   Sudden and complete overthrow of regime.

Rhodes scholarship   Founded by a South African millionaire; enables top English-speaking students to attend Oxford.

right   Politically more conservative, favoring preservation of or return to previous status quo.

romanticism   Hearkening to ideal world or mythical past.

Roman law   Legal system in most of Europe and Latin America based on relatively fixed codes, as opposed to judge-made common law.

Royalists   Supporters of king in English Civil War.

rule of anticipated reactions   Friedrich's theory that politicians plan moves in anticipation of how public will react.

rump state   Leftover portions of country after dismemberment.

runaway system   Influential people use their powers to amass more power.

russification   Making non-Russian nationalities learn Russian.

safe seat   Constituency where voting has long favored given party.

Sahel   Narrow band south of Sahara, arid but not yet desert.

samizdat   (Soviet Union) Russian for "self-published"; manuscripts, often by dissidents, circulated underground.

savanna   Tropical grasslands south of *Sahel*.

seat   Membership in legislature.

Second Vatican Council   1962–1965 meetings that modernized Roman Catholic Church and turned it to problems of poverty; also called Vatican II.

secular   Long-term, irreversible trends; also nonreligious.

secularization   Cutting back role of religion in government and daily life.

select committee   Specialized committee of Commons focusing on a ministry.

semipresidential   System with features of both presidential and parliamentary systems.

sexenio   (from *seis años*) Six-year term of Mexico's presidents.

shah   Persian for king.

sharia   Muslim religious law.

Shia   Minority branch of Islam.

shock therapy   Sudden replacement of socialist economy with free-market one.

Siberia   From Russian for "north"; that part of Russia east of Ural Mountains but not including Central Asia.

single-member district   Sends one representative to parliament.

Slavophiles   Nineteenth-century Russians who wished to develop Russia along native, non-Western lines.

sleaze factor   Public perception of politicians on the take.

social class   Layer or section of population of similar income and status.

social cleavages   Division of society along class, regional, religious, or ethnic lines or over important issues.

social costs   Taxes for medical, unemployment, and retirement benefits that are paid by employers.

socialism   Political movement aiming at greater equality by means of welfare measures and/or nationalization of industry.

socialize   To teach political culture, often informally.

social mobility   Movement of individuals from one class to another, usually upward.

solidarity   Feeling of cohesion within social class.

South America   Continent south of Panama.

sovereignty   Last word on law in given territory; boss on your own turf.

soviet   Russian for "council"; name of 1917 revolutionary bodies and of legislatures in Soviet Union.

sovkhoz   (Soviet Union) State farm where workers were employees.

sphere of influence   Semicolonial area under control of major power.

Stalinist   Brutal central control over Communist party.

state   Institutional or governmental element of country.

State Duma   Lower house of Russia's parliament.

state of nature   Humans before civilization.

statism   Idea that strong government should run things, especially major industries.

statute   Ordinary law, usually for specific problem.

steady-state   System that preserves itself with little change.

strategic   Important to life of nation.

strategic variable   Factor you can change that makes a big difference.

structure   Institutions of government such as constitution, laws, and branches.

structured access   Permanent openness of bureaucracy to interest-group demands.

subject   Originally, subject of the Crown; now another term for British citizen.

subjective   Judged by feeling or intuition.

sub-Saharan   Africa south of the Sahara.

subsidy   Government financial help to private individual or business.

Sunni   Mainstream branch of Islam.

Supreme Soviet   National legislature of Soviet Union, defunct.

swing   Those voters who change party from one election to the next.

symbol   Political artifact used to stir mass emotions.

system change   Displacement of one set of political institutions by another.

Taiping   Major religion-based rebellion in nineteenth-century China.

Tatar   Mongol-origin tribes who ruled Russia for centuries.

technocrat   Official, usually unelected, who governs by virtue of economic and financial skills.

temporal   Of this world, opposite of spiritual.

terrorism   Use of violence and fear thereof for political ends.

Thatcherite   Free-market, anti-welfarist ideology of former British Prime Minister Margaret Thatcher.

theocracy   Rule by priests.

theory   Firm generalizations supported by evidence.

Thermidor   Month when Robespierre fell, calming down after revolutionary high.

Third World   Most of Asia, Africa, and Latin America.

Thirty Years War   1618–1648 Habsburg attempt to conquer and Catholicize Europe.

Tories   Faction of British Parliament that became the Conservative party; "Tories" is now their nickname.

torn country   In Huntington's theory, one with a Westernizing elite but traditional masses.

totalitarian   Political system that attempts total control of society, as under Stalin and Hitler.

Trades Union Congress   TUC, British labor federation equivalent to U.S. AFL-CIO.

trade surplus   Exporting more than you import.

traditional Tory   Moderate or centrist Conservative, not follower of Thatcher.

transparency   Exchanges of money open to public scrutiny.

Treasury   British ministry that supervises economic policy and the funding of other ministries.

treaty ports   Areas of China coast run by European powers.

Trotskyist   Follower of Marxist but anti-Stalin theories of Leon Trotsky.

turnout   Percentage of those eligible who vote in given election.

"two-plus" party system   Two big parties and several small ones.

tyrannical   Coercive rule, usually by one person.

Ukraine   From Slavic for "borderland"; region south of Russia, now independent.

underclass   Permanently disadvantaged people.

unicameral   Parliament with only one chamber.

unification   Process of pulling nation together out of diverse regions.

unimodal   Single-peaked distribution of political attitudes or opinions; a bell-shaped curve.

unilinear   Progressing evenly and always upward.

unimodal   Single-peaked distribution.

unitary   System in which power is centralized in capital and component areas have little or no autonomy.

unit labor costs   What it costs to manufacture same item in different countries.

urbanization   Shift of population from countryside to city.

value-added tax   Large, hidden national sales taxes used throughout Europe.

vary inversely   As one thing goes up, another goes down.

Vatican   Headquarters of Roman Catholic church.

Vatican II   Short name for *Second Vatican Council*.

velayat-e faqih   (Iran) "Guardianship of the religious jurist," theocratic system devised by Khomeini.

volatile   Rises and falls quickly.

voluntarism   Belief that human will can change world.

vote of no confidence   Parliamentary vote to oust cabinet.

wage restraint   Unions holding back on compensation demands.

war communism   Temporary strict socialism in Russia 1918–1921.

warlord   In 1920s China, general who ran province.

Warsaw Pact   Soviet-led alliance of Communist countries, defunct.

weak state   One unable to govern effectively; corrupt and crime-ridden.

welfare   Redistributive measures that provide health care, food, housing, and insurance to poorer classes.

welfare state   Political system that redistributes wealth from rich to poor, standard in West Europe.

Westernizers   Nineteenth-century Russians who wished to copy West.

wets   In Thatcher's usage, Tories too timid to apply her militant *neoliberalism*.

Westminster   British Parliament building.

whig democracy   Democracy with limited participation, typical of democracy's initial phases.

Whigs   Faction of British Parliament that became Liberal party.

whip   Parliamentary party leader who makes sure members obey party in voting.

Whitehall   Main British government offices.

Wirtschaftswunder   German for "economic miracle."

working class   That of those paid hourly wage, typically less affluent and educated.

World Trade Organization   120-plus members open selves to trade and investment; has quasi-judicial powers.

xenophobia   Fear and hatred of foreigners.

Yalta   Town in Soviet Crimea where in 1945 U.S., British, and Soviet leaders decided postwar status of Germany and East Europe.

zemtsvo   Local parliaments in old Russia.

Index